DATE DUE

DEMCO 38-296

CONTEMPORARY MUSICIANS

Explore your options!

Gale databases are offered in a variety of formats

The information in this Gale publication is also available in some or all of the formats described here. Your Gale Representative will be happy to fill you in. Call toll-free 1-800-877-GALE.

GaleNet

A number of Gale databases are now available on GaleNet, our new online information resource accessible through the Internet. GaleNet features an easy-to-use end-user interface, the powerful search capabilities of BRS/SEARCH retrieval software and ease of access through the World Wide Web.

Diskette/Magnetic Tape

Many Gale databases are available on diskette or magnetic tape, allowing systemwide access to your most-used information sources through existing computer systems. Data can be delivered on a variety of mediums (DOS-formatted diskettes, 9-track tape, 8mm data tape) and in industry-standard formats (comma-delimited, tagged, fixed-field).

CD-ROM

A variety of Gale titles are available on CD-ROM, offering maximum flexibility and powerful search software.

Online

For your convenience, many Gale databases are available through popular online services, including DIALOG, NEXIS, DataStar, ORBIT, OCLC, Thomson Financial Network's I/Plus Direct, HRIN, Prodigy, Sandpoint's HOOVER, the Library Corporation's NLightN and Telebase Systems.

ISSN 1044-2197

CONTEMPORARY MUSICIANS

PROFILES OF THE PEOPLE IN MUSIC

SEAN POLLOCK, Editor

VOLUME 18
Includes Cumulative Indexes

GALE

DETROIT · NEW YORK · TORONTO · LONDON

STAFF

Sean Pollock, *Editor*

Stacy A. McConnell, *Associate Editor*

Maria Munoz, *Assistant Editor*

Paul Anderson, Suzanne Bourgoin, Rich Bowen, Carol Brennan, John Cohassey, Ed Decker, Robert Dupuis, Simon Glickman, Joan Goldsworthy, Kevin Hillstrom, Laura Collier Hillstrom, Robert R. Jacobson, Alison Jones, Ondine LeBlanc, Debra Power, James Powers, Joanna Rubiner, Paula Pyzik Scott, Pamela Shelton, Sonya Shelton, Geri J. Speace, Gretchen VanCleave, Link Yaco, *Contributing Editors*

Neil E. Walker, *Managing Editor*

Marlene S. Hurst, *Permissions Manager*
Maria Franklin, *Permissions Specialist*
Edna Hedblad, *Permissions Associate*

Mary Beth Trimper, *Production Director*
Shanna Philpott Heilveil, *Production Assistant*
Cynthia Baldwin, *Product Design Manager*
Barbara J. Yarrow, *Graphic Services Supervisor*
Randy Bassett, *Image Database Supervisor*
Pamela A. Hayes, *Photography Coordinator*
Willie Mathis, *Camera Operator*

Cover illustration by John Kleber

∞™ This book is printed on acid-free paper that meets the minimum
requirements of American National Standard for Information Sciences—
Permanence Paper for Printed Library Materials, ANSI Z39.48-1984.

ISBN 0-7876-0099-7
ISSN 1044-2197

10 9 8 7 6 5 4 3 2 1

Contents

Introduction ix

Cumulative Subject Index 239

Cumulative Musicians Index 263

Introduction

Fills the Information Gap on Today's Musicians

Contemporary Musicians profiles the colorful personalities in the music industry who create or influence the music we hear today. Prior to *Contemporary Musicians,* no quality reference series provided comprehensive information on such a wide range of artists despite keen and ongoing public interest. To find biographical and critical coverage, an information seeker had little choice but to wade through the offerings of the popular press, scan television "infotainment" programs, and search for the occasional published biography or exposé. *Contemporary Musicians* is designed to serve that information seeker, providing in one ongoing source in-depth coverage of the important names on the modern music scene in a format that is both informative and entertaining. Students, researchers, and casual browsers alike can use *Contemporary Musicians* to meet their needs for personal information about music figures; find a selected discography of a musician's recordings; and uncover an insightful essay offering biographical and critical information.

Provides Broad Coverage

Single-volume biographical sources on musicians are limited in scope, often focusing on a handful of performers from a specific musical genre or era. In contrast, *Contemporary Musicians* offers researchers and music devotees a comprehensive, informative, and entertaining alternative. *Contemporary Musicians* is published twice yearly, with each volume providing information on more than 80 musical artists and record-industry luminaries from all the genres that form the broad spectrum of contemporary music—pop, rock, jazz, blues, country, New Age, folk, rhythm and blues, gospel, bluegrass, rap, and reggae, to name a few—as well as selected classical artists who have achieved "crossover" success with the general public. *Contemporary Musicians* will also occasionally include profiles of influential nonperforming members of the music community, including producers, promoters, and record company executives. Additionally, beginning with *Contemporary Musicians 11,* each volume features new profiles of a selection of previous *Contemporary Musicians* listees who remain of interest to today's readers and who have been active enough to require completely revised entries.

Includes Popular Features

In *Contemporary Musicians* you'll find popular features that users value:

- **Easy-to-locate data sections:** Vital personal statistics, chronological career summaries, listings of major awards, and mailing addresses, when available, are prominently displayed in a clearly marked box on the second page of each entry.

- **Biographical/critical essays:** Colorful and informative essays trace each subject's personal and professional life, offer representative examples of critical response to the artist's work, and provide entertaining personal sidelights.

- **Selected discographies:** Each entry provides a comprehensive listing of the artist's major recorded works.

- **Photographs:** Most entries include portraits of the subject profiled.

- **Sources for additional information:** This invaluable feature directs the user to selected books, magazines, and newspapers where more information can be obtained.

Helpful Indexes Make It Easy to Find the Information You Need

Each volume of *Contemporary Musicians* features a cumulative Musicians Index, listing names of individual performers and musical groups, and a cumulative Subject Index, which provides the user with a breakdown by primary musical instruments played and by musical genre.

Available in Electronic Formats

Diskette/Magnetic Tape. *Contemporary Musicians* is available for licensing on magnetic tape or diskette in a fielded format. Either the complete database or a custom selection of entries may be ordered. The database is available for internal data processing and nonpublishing purposes only. For more information, call (800) 877-GALE.

Online. *Contemporary Musicians* is available online through Mead Data Central's NEXIS Service in the NEXIS, PEOPLE and SPORTS Libraries in the GALBIO file.

We Welcome Your Suggestions

The editors welcome your comments and suggestions for enhancing and improving *Contemporary Musicians.* If you would like to suggest subjects for inclusion, please submit these names to the editors. Mail comments or suggestions to:

The Editor
Contemporary Musicians
Gale Research
835 Penobscot Bldg.
Detroit, MI 48226-4094
Phone: (800) 347-4253
Fax: (313) 961-6599

King Sunny Adé

Singer, guitarist

Ordained the "King of Juju Music" in the late 1970s by a group of journalists and music critics, King Sunny Adé has been a major musical force in his native Nigeria since the mid-1960s and an international star since the early 1980s. His style of juju—which is primarily a form of praise music sung in a local Nigerian Yoruba language that merges guitars with percussion in a lively style—is a so-called "synchro" style that utilizes synthesizers and other electronics technology, including computers.

Adé was greatly influenced by the "So wa mbe" style of juju pioneered by Tunde Nightingale and "is one of juju's great innovators," according to Jon Pareles in the *New York Times.* Noting Adé's dynamic stage presence and versatility as a singer, Pareles also stated, "Mr. Adé, whose unruffled tenor is one of rock's kindliest voices, will pick up a melody above the velvety harmonies of the backup singers, or smilingly trade call-and-response dialogues with them, or take his turn in friendly dance competitions...while a drummer encourages him with improvisations."

Adé is noted for opening up juju music to listeners the world over. As Chris Stapleton and Chris May wrote in *African Rock,* "in Europe and North America he has been responsible for taking juju out of its small cult following and nudging it, slowly but surely, toward the mainstream album market." Pareles pointed out that Adé elevated juju "from street music played by a few instruments into a big-band style that can shimmer and crackle."

Defied Parents to Play Music

While growing up, Adé spent much of his time in the arts center of Oshogbo in the Ondo State of Nigeria. He became musically active as a teenager, playing drums with juju bands fronted by Sunday Ariyo and Idowu Owoeye. The son of a Methodist minister, he greatly disappointed his parents by quitting college in 1963 to pursue his musical interests full-time. His family was of royal lineage and frowned upon music as a low-caste pursuit. At first Adé joined a traveling musical comedy troupe, but by 1964 he was playing lead guitar in Moses Olaiya Adejumo's Federal Rhythm Dandies. After also playing briefly with Tunde Nightingale, he decided in 1965 to form his own group, Sunny Adé and His High Society Band. The next year he changed his group's name to the Green Spots, presumably a playful reference to I. K. Dairo's Blue Spots, a legendary juju band from the 1950s. The Green Spots played "a speedy but relaxed style of juju characterized by tight vocal harmonies and deliciously melodic guitar work," according to the *Guinness Encyclopedia of Popular Music.*

For the Record . . .

Born Sunday Adeniyi, on September 1, 1946, in Oshogbo, Nigeria; 12 children.

Part-time percussionist with Sunday Ariyo's and Idowu Owoeye's juju bands, 1958–63; dropped out of school to play full-time with local juju bands, 1963; played guitar with Moses Olaiya Adejumo and Tunde Nightingale, mid-1960s; formed own group, Sunny Adé and His High Society Band, 1965; changed his band's name to the Green Spots, 1966; released first single, "Challenge Cup," 1967; changed name of his group to the African Beats, late 1960s; established his own record label, Sunny Alade Records, 1975; opened up juju nightclub in Lagos, Nigeria, mid-1970s; performed three-month tour in England, 1975; signed contract with Island Records, 1982; formed new band, Golden Mercury, after salary disputes with original band members; has released over 40 albums, plus many singles and EPs.

Addresses: Home—Nigeria. Record company—Mesa/ Blue Moon Records (Distributed in United States by Rhino Records), 209 East Almeda, #101, Burbank, CA 91502.

It didn't take long for Adé to become a mega-star in his country. His first single with the Green Spots, "Challenge Cup," concerned a local soccer team championship and became a major hit in 1967 with sales of over 500,000 copies. His first album, *Alanu Loluwa*, was released the same year on the African Songs label. Renaming his group the African Beats in the late 1960s, Adé began steadily releasing albums that typically sold over 200,000 copies each in Nigeria, with many of the sales coming from bootlegged versions. His group released some 12 albums from 1967 to 1974 and was in constant demand as a live act, often performing with 20 to 30 members on stage.

After contract disputes with African Songs, Adé decided to create his own label in 1975. Called Sunny Alade Records, the company was linked to the Decca label in England. Around that time he also opened the Ariya, his own juju nightclub in Lagos, which became the main performance venue for the African Beats when the group wasn't on tour. He took his group out of the country in 1975 for a three-month tour of England, playing mostly to expatriate Nigerian audiences at small halls and community centers during cultural theme nights.

Throughout the 1970s, Adé built his reputation as an innovator in juju music. In 1976 he added a steel guitar to his instrumental mix, and he frequently experimented with new beats and guitar styles. By the end of the decade he was one of the three top names in juju, along with Ebenezer Obey and Dele Abiodun.

Became Worldwide Phenomenon

Hoping to capitalize on growing interest in African music in the United Kingdom, Adé started his African Series of releases with the *Sound d'Afrique* compilation album in 1981. His plans agreed with those of England's Island Records, which was eager to find a replacement for the tropical music of Bob Marley, who had died in 1980. Island Records signed Adé to a contract in 1982 for releases in Europe and North America. Adé responded with the highly acclaimed *Juju Music,* which made the hit charts in the United States. With his album supported by extensive promotion and media exposure, Adé became a worldwide phenomenon and was in constant demand for performances. "[Adé's] guitar line-up, weaving intricate melodic patterns against a background of thundering percussion, the call-and-response 'conversations' of the talking drums and the infectiously winning, 'African-prince' style of the man himself—all gave off strong commercial signals," noted *World Music.*

Adé confirmed his ability to transcend cultural barriers in a concert at London's Lyceum Ballroom in January of 1983. Stapleton and May's discussion of this concert confirmed Adé's new international star status: "Raved over without exception by the weekly music press, many of whose critics hailed Adé as one of the emergent dance-music stars of the year, Adé and his band played to a hugely enthusiastic multi-ethnic audience, proving that—in a live context at any rate—juju's use of Yoruba rather than English-language lyrics was no barrier to overseas acceptance."

International Appeal Faltered

The popularity of *Juju Music,* as well as Adé's next album, *Synchro System,* was due in large part to French producer Martin Meissonnier. Meissonnier helped to expand Adé's appeal by bringing in synthesizers and Linn drums without negating the music's roots in traditional Yoruba music or making the songs unpalatable to long-time Nigerian fans. However, Island's expectations were high, since the company was looking for someone with the mass appeal of Bob Marley. "Sunny Adé's Yoruba lyrics and complex rhythms were less readily accessible than the English lyrics and regular rhythms of the reggae greats he was supposed to replace," noted *World Music*. When sales trailed off for *Aura*, Adé's third album with Island, the label dropped his contract. Bad news continued from that point for Adé, whose musicians began making demands for salary increases following triumphant tours of the United States and Japan. Adé claimed that he couldn't meet their demands because he had so many musicians and because there were limited audiences for his performances. As a result of these unresolved disputes, Adé was forced to form a new band, which he called Golden Mercury.

Perhaps bitter over his recent troubles, Adé made a thematic shift in his lyrics. Although his songs had often dealt with the myriad of social problems in Nigeria, he now began writing about rumors, jealousy, destiny, and even family planning. Some controversy arose over "Wait for Me," a song he released in 1989 that urged population control and was later discovered to have been underwritten by the U.S. Agency for International Development, Office of Population. The song was particularly ironic coming from Adé, who had 12 children at the time.

Since 1974, Sunny Adé has released more than 40 albums, as well as numerous singles and EPs. After concentrating on his business affairs and not releasing any studio recordings for a decade, he released *E Dide (Get Up)* on the Mesa label in 1995. Reviewer Frank Scheck noted in the *Christian Science Monitor* that the album's "crisp, modern arrangements" were influenced by contemporary American blues and country music and featured pedal steel guitar. This U.S. studio recording followed a 1987 tour in the Americas and a 1992 performance at the Montreal Jazz Festival. Today King Sunny Adé records and performs mainly in Nigeria, where he is still arguably the country's most successful recording artist.

Selected discography

Sunny Adé Live Play, Sunny Alade, 1976.
The Message, Sunny Alade, 1981.
Ju Ju Music, Island, 1982.
Synchro System, Island, 1983.
Aura, Island, 1984.
Live Live Juju, Rykodisk, 1987.
The Return of the JuJu King, Mercury, 1988.
Live at the Hollywood Palace, I.R.S., 1994.
E Dide (Get Up), Mesa, 1995.

Also released videos *Live at Montreaux*, 1983, and *Ju Ju*, 1988.

Sources

Books

Broughton, Simon, Mark Ellingham, David Muddyman, and Richard Trillo, *World Music: The Rough Guide*, Rough Guide, 1994.
The Guinness Encyclopedia of Popular Music, vol. 1, edited by Colin Larkin, Guinness, 1992.
Stapleton, Chris, and Chris May, *African Rock: The Pop Music of a Continent*, E.P. Dutton, 1987.

Periodicals

Christian Science Monitor, January 8, 1996.
Down Beat, October 1992.
New York Times, July 16, 1992.
Progressive, September 1990.

Online

King Sunny Ade home page—http://www.nwlink.com:88/graviton/ksahome.htm.
Hall of Records—http://www.rykodisc.com/3/catalog/artist/5.html.

—Ed Decker

Altan

Traditional Irish music band

Driven by more than a half-dozen critically acclaimed albums and a relentless touring schedule, the band Altan emerged during the 1990s as one of Ireland's premiere traditional musical groups. Armed with both instrumental virtuosity and a healthy respect for the musical traditions upon which it draws, Altan's energetic vision came to be held in high regard by purists as well as those with more eclectic tastes. The band's progress was temporarily derailed in 1994, however, when flutist Frankie Kennedy—co-founder of the group with his wife, lead vocalist Mairead Ni Mhaonaigh—died of cancer. Mhaonaigh and her bandmates struggled with that loss, but eventually recorded the highly regarded 1996 release *Blackwater.* "Nobody spoke about it, but it was understood that Frankie wasn't going to be replaced," said band member Mark Kelly. "He was missed in the studio, and the sound he produced on the flute was missed. But looking back on it, I think it's right that he should be missed, that we weren't just bashing ahead without him."

Beginnings in Dublin

Band founders Kennedy and Ni Mhaonaigh launched their musical careers in Dublin, Ireland, where both worked as elementary school teachers in the early 1980s. The couple married in 1981 and began to play as a duo in local taverns and other venues. Even at that early juncture, Kennedy and Ni Mhaonaigh tapped into the rich and largely undiscovered musical tradition of Ni Mhaonaigh's home region.

Whereas Kennedy hailed from the strife-ridden city of Belfast, Ni Mhaonaigh grew up in northwest Donegal, Ireland, where Gaelic was still commonly spoken. The daughter of well-known fiddler Francie O'Mhaonaigh, Ni Mhaonaigh was exposed to the region's music from an early age. When she and her husband looked about for material to incorporate into their act, they naturally turned to the county of Donegal, home of many learned and private traditional musicians.

As Scott Alarik noted in the *Boston Globe,* "Kennedy and Ni Mhaonaigh spent years trekking the back roads and far places of Donegal, sitting in on sessions in village taverns, asking to be introduced to older players and singers." They were quickly accepted in the region's musical community, for as Ni Mhaonaigh told the *Wall Street Journal's* Earle Hitchner, "they know we're not taking advantage of them, and that we respect and cherish what they give us." With each passing month, the duo immersed themselves further in the region's unique musical tradition, which melds classic Irish music with the rhythms of Scotland.

Critical Accolades

In 1983 Kennedy and Ni Mhaonaigh released their first album, *Ceol Aduaidh.* A collection of Gaelic songs and Ulster jigs and reels highlighted by Ni Mhaonaigh's hauntingly pure soprano voice, the work caused an immediate stir. As Hitchner remarked, "The album's strikingly fresh material and aggressive fiddle and flute playing rippled through an entire generation of traditional performers in Ireland's South, awakening them to the rich musical repertoire and rhythms native to the north." Buoyed by the reaction to *Ceol Aduaidh,* Kennedy and Ni Mhaonaigh began work on a new group of ballads and jibs culled from Northern Ireland's rich musical landscape. The result was 1987's *Altan,* the album that marked the beginning of the band of the same name. Supported by bouzouki player Ciaran Curran, who later became a permanent member of the band, as well as guitarist Mark Kelly, *Altan* further cemented the reputation of Ni Mhaonaigh and Kennedy in Ireland's music community.

The couple subsequently decided to establish a band, Altan, named after a lake near Ni Mhaonaigh's childhood home. As its membership filled out over the ensuing months, the band recognized that they shared a common commitment to traditional Irish music. But as Ni Mhaonaigh recalled, her husband's vision was a key component of the band's early success. "Frankie want-

For the Record . . .

Members include **Frankie Kennedy** (born September 30, 1955, in Belfast, Northern Ireland; married Mairead Ni Mhaonaigh, 1981; died of cancer, September 19, 1994), flutist; and **Mairead Ni Mhaonaigh** (born July 26, 1959, in County Donegal, Ireland, daughter of Francie O'Mhaonaigh, a fiddler; married Frankie Kennedy, 1981), vocals and fiddle; **Ciaran Curran** (born June 14, 1955, in Enniskillen, County Fermanagh, Northern Ireland), bouzouki; **Daithi Sproule** (born May 23, 1950, in County Derry, Northern Ireland), guitar and vocals; **Ciaran Tourish** (born May 27, 1967, in Buncrana, County Donegal, Ireland), fiddle; **Dermot Byrne** (born in Donegal, Ireland), accordion; and **Jimmy Higgins**, bodhran.

Kennedy and Ni Mhaonaigh were elementary school teachers in Dublin before forming band; first incarnation was husband-wife duo of Kennedy and Ni Mhaonaigh in early 1980s; eponymous debut as Altan on Green Linnet Records released in 1987; first U.S. tour, 1988; released *The Red Crow* in 1990, the first of three consecutive NAIRD award-winning albums for band; performed at White House on St. Patrick's Day, 1994; released *Blackwater,* their first album on a major label, in 1996.

Selected awards: National Association of Independent Record Distributors and Manufacturers (NAIRD) Award for best Celtic/British Isles album for *The Red Crow* (1990), *Harvest Storm* (1992), and *Island Angel* (1993); Best Traditional Album of 1993, *Q* and *Hot Press* magazines, for *Island Angel.*

Addresses: *Record company*—Virgin Records, 338 North Foothill Rd., Beverly Hills, CA 90210.

ed the band to bring traditional music to another level without having to compromise; to make it a popular music without having to be a pop or rock band to do it," she told Alarik. "He thought this music was as good as blues or reggae, and that we didn't have to fuse with any other type of music in order to succeed. Why do that when the music itself speaks so well for itself?"

In 1989 Altan released *Horse With a Heart,* a well-received album that featured the extraordinary fiddle playing of Dublin's Paul O'Shaughnessy in addition to Ni Mhaonaigh's own expert fiddle work. A year later the band released *The Red Crow,* the first of three Altan

records to win the prestigious Celtic/British Isles Album of the Year Award from the National Association of Independent Record Distributors and Manufacturers (NAIRD). By this time the band, which was touring around the world to sold-out audiences, was enjoying both critical and commercial success.

In 1992 the band released *Harvest Storm,* another collection of reels, jigs, and ballads that garnered critical praise. Reviewers repeatedly cited Ni Mhaonaigh's beautiful voice, the musicians' expert playing, and the band's impeccable musical instincts.

Cancer Strikes Kennedy

In June 1992 Kennedy learned that he had Ewing's sarcoma, a particularly vicious type of cancer that attacks bone structure. He subsequently endured surgery, radiotherapy, and chemotherapy in an effort to rid his body of the cancer while simultaneously continuing his work with Altan. In 1993 the band released *Island Angel,* an album that Great Britain's *Q* magazine described as a "combination of headspinning drive and pure melancholy." The review went on to remark that these qualities give the band "a one-two punch that is unmatched in contemporary folk circles." Boosted by *Island Angel,* which was cited as the fourth-best-selling album of world music of 1994 by *Billboard,* Altan came to be regarded not only as a great touring act, but also as a headliner for music festivals from Europe to the United States.

Although his health continued to deteriorate, Kennedy took steps to ensure that Altan would continue long after he was gone. "All I wanted to do was be home with Frankie," Ni Mhaonaigh told Alarik, "but he insisted I continue with the band. The way he put it was that I should go so that when he'd be better the band wouldn't have faded away, there would be something for him to come back to.... It was the hardest part for me, but now I know he was very subtly preparing me, so that when he did pass away I would be used to being on the road with the lads."

The Band Moves On

Kennedy died in September 1994. After a period of mourning, the band resumed their touring. "It was a choice for Mairead whether or not she wanted to do it," fiddler Ciaran Tourish told Hitchner, "but she felt the longer she would have left it, the more difficult it would be to get back into it. In retrospect, it was good therapy for all of us in trying to deal with his passing." Indeed, the band—composed at this point of Ni Mhaonaigh,

Tourish, Curran, guitarist Daithi Sproule, and accordionist Dermot Byrne—repeatedly noted that Kennedy would have been disappointed if his death had caused Altan to disband.

In 1995 Altan released a greatest-hits package, and a year later they released *Blackwater,* an album that continued the band's unbroken string of critical and popular successes. *People* reviewer Lyndon Stambler summed up critical reaction to the album when he wrote that "the band's first album on a major label [Virgin] is a heartfelt collection of stirring jigs, reels and hornpipes and of soulful folk ballads. It is sure to strengthen its reputation as one of the finest traditional bands in Ireland and solidify its growing following in the U.S." Hitchner concurred, remarking that the album was "Irish musical tradition at its unadulterated best, spurred by dazzling instrumental playing, memorable singing, and deft arrangements."

Even after switching to a major label iin 1996, the band assured its fans that it had no intention of compromising its adherence to traditional music. As Ni Mhaonaigh told Hitchner, "The reason we would never play another type of music is we don't know it and we don't come from that background. I think bands can quickly lose their way when they veer off from what they do best."

Selected discography

Altan, Green Linnet, 1987.
Horse With a Heart, Green Linnet, 1989.
The Red Crow, Green Linnet, 1990.
Harvest Storm, Green Linnet, 1992.
Island Angel, Green Linnet, 1993.
The First Ten Years (1986-1995), Green Linnet, 1995.
Blackwater, Virgin, 1996.
The Best of Altan, Green Linnet, 1997 (includes Limited Edition CD *Altan Live*).

Frankie Kennedy and Mairead Ni Mhaonaigh released *Ceol Aduaidh* on Green Linnet, 1983.

Sources

Acoustic Guitar, May-June 1994.
Billboard, October 23, 1993.
Boston Globe, May 11, 1995.
Boston Herald, May 10, 1995.
Folk Roots, January-February 1994.
Irish Echo, May 10-16, 1995.
Irish Music, August, 1995.
New York Times, March 15, 1994.
People, July 15, 1996.
Wall Street Journal, February 22, 1996.
Washington Post, May 11, 1995.

Online

http://celtic.stanford.edu/artists/Altan.html
http://www.sonic.net/~jmagers/altan/
http://home.earthlink.net/~cglassey/altan.html

Additional information for this profile was obtain from Green Linnet press materials.

—*Kevin Hillstrom*

Barenaked Ladies

Rock band

Canada's Barenaked Ladies have developed a rabid following despite only limited mainstream success. Though the all-male and usually fully dressed band established themselves on their debut album as a "wacky" pop act, they have found their reputation for rock comedy something of an impediment as they have matured. Yet their well-crafted, harmonious records and energetic live shows converted many skeptics. "Their folk-rock-based style encompasses everything from alternative rock to harmony-laced pop to jazzy swing," wrote John Roos in the *Los Angeles Times*, "and is built on solid musicianship, smart lyricism and the distinctively creamy, colorful vocals of Steven Page." Page, like guitarist and fellow co-founder Ed Robertson, told *Billboard's* Timothy White that the pop form suited his purposes perfectly. "I like to write pop to fool people with the hooks," he noted, "but inside, I hide all the sweetness, darkness, and musicianship found in the grandest themes of a great mythic rock song. For me, pop is a tight, strategic little package that's second to none."

© Denise Sofranko/MICHAEL OCHS ARCHIVES/Venice, CA

For the Record . . .

Members include **Andrew Creegan** (left group 1994), keyboards; **Jim Creegan,** bass; **Kevin Hearn** (joined group 1996), keyboards; **Steven Page** (born June 22, 1970, Scarborough, Ontario, Canada), vocals; **Ed Robertson** (born October 25, 1970, Scarborough, Ontario), guitar and vocals; **Tyler Stewart,** drums.

Group formed in Toronto, Canada, c. 1988; released debut EP *Barenaked Ladies* on own Page Publications label, 1991; signed with Sire/Reprise and released *Gordon,* 1992; contributed to *Coneheads* film soundtrack, 1993; contributed to *Friends* television soundtrack, 1995; released "enhanced" CDs *Born on a Pirate Ship* and *Shoe Box,* 1996.

Awards: Juno Award (Canada) for Band of the Year, 1991; Canadian platinum certification for *Gordon,* 1992.

Addresses: *Record company*—Reprise, 75 Rockefeller Plaza, New York, NY 10019-6979; 3300 Warner Blvd., Burbank, CA 91505-4694. *Management*—Nettwerk Productions, Box 330-1755 Robson St., Vancouver, B.C., Canada V6G 3B7. *Internet*—Official Barenaked Ladies World Wide Web Site: www.repriserec.com/BarenakedLadies. Unofficial BNL site: www.cs.mun.ca/~craig/bnl/.

Barenaked Ladies began as a duo in the Toronto suburb of Scarborough, Ontario. The town was home to Page and Robertson, who met in high school and became an acoustic act in the late 1980s. Influenced by classic melodic pop and the new-wave style of rock that was the precursor to "alternative" music, Page and Robertson began developing their offbeat, folky sound. They came up with their name while bored at a concert by legendary singer-songwriter Bob Dylan; laughing themselves sore, they came up with increasingly outrageous band names. "Barenaked Ladies" was intended to convey "what we called [naked women] when we were eight or nine years old and we were frightened and excited and totally naïve about the whole situation," Page told *Throwrug*.

Soon Page and Robertson found themselves touring college campuses, where the experience of warming up for a comedy troupe sharpened their humorous between-song patter. "People came expecting to see a comedy show," Page told the *Los Angeles Times*, and

as a result Barenaked Ladies "found a lot of adversity in the audience. We started [the funny patter] to make ourselves more comfortable on stage."

Superstars in Canada

Joined by brothers Jim and Andrew Creegan on bass and keyboards, respectively, and drummer Tyler Stewart, Barenaked Ladies coalesced into a tight musical unit. Their comedic ad-libs and tuneful, quirky songs endeared them to the growing legion of alternative rock fans in the Toronto-area scene. As a result, the band's self-released debut EP became the first independent record to achieve gold sales certification in Canada. The EP featured the single "Be My Yoko Ono," a typically playful romantic plea to the wife of Beatle John Lennon. The success of this recording was not lost on the major labels; Sire/Reprise signed the band and in 1992 released their full-length debut, *Gordon*.

In addition to recapping "Yoko Ono," *Gordon* contains additional madcap pop songs stuffed with cultural references—including "Brian Wilson," about the troubled leader of pop icons the Beach Boys, and "Grade 9," a frantic ska number in which the band admits its fondness for 1980s synth-rockers Duran Duran while throwing in quotes from songs by Canadian progressive rockers Rush. A sensation in Canada, *Gordon* hit the platinum mark in that country in a little more than a week, dominated the album charts for two months, and remained a chart presence for most of 1992, ultimately scoring four hit singles. Barenaked Ladies were named Group of the Year at the Juno Awards, Canada's version of the Grammies, and collected a mountain of adoring press clips.

Struggled in U.S.

In America, *Gordon* failed to rise above cult status. Both the band and their label were unpleasantly surprised, but the band toured relentlessly and continued to charm audiences worldwide. Their professionalism was such that Robertson played a show in Vancouver shortly after hearing of his brother's death in a motorcycle accident. "We're a pretty great team," Page told Mike Boehm of the *Los Angeles Times*, adding that the Vancouver show "is one of those things that made us realize that." Despite his grief, Robertson "pulled it off like a total pro," Page added. "I don't think anyone in the audience noticed."

Barenaked Ladies returned with 1994's *Maybe You Should Drive*, a slightly more serious album. Produced by Ben Mink—best known as k.d. lang's producer—

collaborator—*Drive* showcased the band's increasing sophistication and depth, both musically and thematically. Due to the new "Adult Album Alternative" radio format, which helped such artists as Hootie and the Blowfish, Counting Crows, and The Cranberries achieve mainstream status, the album's offbeat, romantic singles "Jane" and "Alternative Girlfriend" earned some rotation. Despite some success, the strain of constant touring led Andy Creegan to leave the band. Initially, Page told *Los Angeles Times* writer Roos, "we thought, 'What are we gonna do now—we're only four-fifths of a band?' But once we realized we could actually be four-fourths of a band, then everyone had a better chance of stretching out. I think we've become more focused, and now that we're a quartet, there's more space to be heard and it's easier for everyone to have some input." The band took further solace in the fact that they appeared as characters in the DC comic book "Anima."

CD-ROMs, Macaroni, and Socks

Fired up by realizations of their growing popularity, Barenaked Ladies headed into the studio and emerged with the ambitious *Born On a Pirate Ship*. In addition to documenting the group's continued maturation—especially their increasingly focused songwriting and intricate close harmonies—the 1996 disc was released in an "enhanced" format for CD-ROM, and contained audio and video samples and a bevy of interactive features. Another enhanced CD, *Shoe Box*, was released the same year. Page told Roos that this format was pushed by the band's management. "Personally, I'm into the whole cyber thing," he added. *Entertainment Weekly* praised the group's "delightful harmonies" as well as the creative design of *Shoe Box*, which it dubbed "a spirited and kooky romp."

While the band may be labored to escape the "kooky" label, their live shows have turned into comedic rituals. Longtime fans, for example, hurl Kraft macaroni at the stage during the song "If I Had $1,000,000," in which the Ladies express their admiration for the dinner of champions. Other audience-participation incidents have become legendary. "We did a show in Ontario, a big arena show, thousands and thousands of people there,"

Robertson recalled in *Art & Performance.* "Late in the set, a sock landed on the stage. I said something like, great, [alternative superstars] Pearl Jam get ladies' underwear and we get a sports sock. So Tyler was playing and he says, 'I want to see all your socks, give me all your socks.' Before I could say anything—Boom," the band was inundated with socks, "and it just f—ing reeked." Yet Barenaked Ladies have generally savored the experience of performing. "Our concerts are a key component of what we do," Robertson ventured in a biography on their Internet website. "We're geared to giving people a good time. We approach it as an ongoing conversation with our audience."

Selected discography

Barenaked Ladies, (includes "Be My Yoko Ono"), Page Publications, 1991.
*Gordon, (*includes "Be My Yoko Ono," "Brian Wilson," "If I Had $1,000,000," and "Grade 9"), Sire/Reprise, 1992.
"Fight the Power," *Coneheads* soundtrack, Warner Bros., 1993.
Maybe You Should Drive, (includes "Jane" and "Alternative Girlfriend"), Sire/Reprise, 1994.
"Shoe Box," *Friends* soundtrack, Reprise, 1995.
Born on a Pirate Ship, (album/enhanced CD), Reprise, 1996.
Shoe Box, (enhanced CD), Reprise Records/Warner Interactive, 1996.
Rock Spectacle, Nettwerk/Reprise, 1996.

Sources

Art & Performance, February 17, 1995.
Billboard, December 7, 1995; August 31, 1996.
Entertainment Weekly, March 8, 1996.
Los Angeles Times, September 8, 1994; March 29, 1996.
Maclean's, March 8, 1993.
Newsday, January 27, 1995.
Throwrug, June, 1995.

Additional information was provided by Reprise publicity materials, 1996, and materials from Barenaked Ladies sites on the World Wide Web.

—*Simon Glickman*

Beck

Singer, guitarist

© Ken Settle

In 1994 Beck rode his fluke hit single "Loser" to stardom. Buoyed by heavy rotation on MTV and all-around raves for the song's odd rap-folk, stream-of-consciousness flavor, "Loser" assumed generational anthem status. This was due in large part to the emerging critical consensus surrounding the song, which held that its mordant lyrics—festooned as they were with pop culture references and downbeat non-sequiters—fit in nicely with popular "Generation X" mythology. "On the strength of 'Loser,'" wrote *Entertainment Weekly*'s Mark Lewman, "[Beck] has, much to his own dazed bemusement, become a pop star without even trying." Over the next two years it became clear that Beck's new-found stardom would have little effect on his musical interests, which often took him into radio-unfriendly territory. Armed with a major-label recording contract that permitted him to continue to record for small independent labels, he released two records before coming out with his second major-label release, *Odelay.* The album was widely praised by critics who assured readers that Beck was no one-hit wonder.

L.A. Roots

Beck Hansen was born and raised in Los Angeles, though he did live with his maternal grandparents in Kansas City for a brief time (his grandfather was a Presbyterian minister). Beck's father was a bluegrass street musician, an occupation that piqued his son's interest in music at an early age. By ninth grade, Beck's disillusionment with school prompted him to drop out and take a succession of entry-level jobs, from stock boy to video store clerk. "I'm sure there's something good about high school, but not any of the ones I went to," he told Jancee Dunn in *Rolling Stone.* But he struggled in the work world as well; he recalled that he was even fired from his stock boy job. "They didn't like the way I dressed," he told Dunn. "Not that I was dressing outrageously or anything. They just didn't like my style. I was just wearing jeans and a shirt from Sears. I don't know. They had high expectations for stock positions."

By the time he was about 16, Beck had purchased a guitar and begun following in his father's street-playing footsteps. "I just carried my guitar everywhere," he reported to Dunn. "I was just kind of ready for any sudden jamboree that might befall me. I used to play down at Lafayette Park, near where I used to live as a kid, and all these Salvadoran guys would be playing soccer, and I'd be practicing a Leadbelly song. The Salvadoran guys would just be shaking their heads." Indeed, Beck was a dedicated student of the works of

For the Record . . .

Born Beck Hansen, July 8, 1970, in Los Angeles, CA; father was a street musician; mother (Bibbe) was a member of underground L.A. punk-drag band Black Fag.

Started playing on streets at age 16; released first single, "Loser," on Bong Load Custom Records, 1993; signed with DGC label, which released his first album, *Mellow Gold*, 1994; member of 1995 Lollapalooza tour; after making two records on independent labels, released *Odelay* in 1996.

Addresses: *Record company*—DGC Records, 9130 Sunset Blvd., Los Angeles, CA 90069.

folk and blues legends such as Woody Guthrie, Fred McDowell, and Mississippi John Hurt. As he grew older, though, he became increasingly interested in grafting those musical genres onto rap and other modern musical styles. This interest intensified after he paid a visit to New York's East Village anti-folk scene in the late 1980s.

By age eighteen Beck was playing at local L.A. clubs and passing out armloads of tapes. He eventually caught the attention of a small record label called Bong Load Custom Records, which released his odd song "Loser" as a single. To the amazement of all, the song became a tremendous hit in the metropolitan area, and recording industry talent scouts were soon courting the artist with abandon. Or as Dunn described it, "when ['Loser'] became an instant hit on local radio, major labels set upon Beck like starving rats in a peach barrel." After receiving assurances from Geffen subsidiary DGC that he would be allowed to release songs on independent labels as well as DGC, Beck signed on.

"Loser" Hits It Big

In 1994 DGC released Beck's first album, *Mellow Gold*, which the artist termed "my idea of the K-Mart Satan record." The nationwide popularity of "Loser" ensured the album good sales, but critics quickly noted that the record had many additional treasures. *Rolling Stone* critic Michael Azerrad commented that "Beck makes ultrasurreal hip-hop-folk that harkens back to 'Subterranean Homesick Blues,'" adding that "Beck's verbal collages get close to the truth of his milieu and our times. Think of it as generational code or stream of uncon-

sciousness. But it's really called poetry." *Knight-Ridder* writer Tom Moon called the album "thought-provoking," commenting that "with little regard for linear thought, Beck shuffles advertising catch-phrases and other artifacts of contemporary life into a recombinant testimonial, an intentionally obscure commentary on things we'd just as soon overlook. It's triumphantly anti-professional, idiot-savant music in which a heartfelt solo can be provided by kazoo as easily as guitar." Even underwhelmed critics such as *Musician's* Dave DiMartino—who wrote that the album's underlying themes of victimization, anger, and "self-absorption are not only unattractive and innocuous, they're wimpy"—admitted that "Beck's lyric gifts are obvious and his musical influences...more or less impeccable."

Beck returned to the world of independent labels for his next two efforts, *Stereopathetic Soulmanure* (on Flipside) and *One Foot in the Grave* (on the K label). The latter album was particularly interesting, for its songs—though warped as always by Beck's distinctive artistic prism—provided telling insight into the artist's traditional folk and blues roots. As David Browne wrote in *Entertainment Weekly*, "*Grave* is a genial throwaway—both a loving tribute to, and a gentle mocking of, various folk musics—that is clearly not meant to be *Mellow Gold*'s big follow-up."

Releases *Odelay*

In 1996 Beck unveiled his major label follow-up, the well-received *Odelay*. The songs on *Odelay*, produced in collaboration with the renowned Dust Brothers (John King and Michael Simpson), continued where *Mellow Gold* left off. Brimming with oddball pop culture references and disconcerting imagery, the record further burnished Beck's reputation as one of the music world's more unique talents. *Newsweek's* David Gates called the album "American eclectic music, a '90s analogue to the genre-smooshing slumgullion of Bob Wills, Elvis Presley or Bob Dylan."

For his part, Beck seemed to remain bemused by his fame and his reputation as a "slacker" icon. "Smart, funny and strange, he floats along in his own time-space continuum," reflected Dunn. "He seems unattached to any particular group or generation despite the slacker albatross around his neck." Nor does he take too seriously an approach to his creative output. As he told Dunn in 1996: "I remember talking to some journalist in Hong Kong, and he read me out lyrics to one of my songs that weren't anything close to the ones I wrote. They were so much better. I've been kicking myself ever since that I didn't write down what he thought they were."

Selected discography

Golden Feelings, Sonic Enemy, 1993 (EP).
A Western Harvest Field by Moonlight, Finger Paint Records, 1994.
Mellow Gold, DGC, 1994.
Stereopathetic Soulmanure, Flipside, 1994.
One Foot in the Grave, K, 1994.
Odelay, DGC, 1996.

Sources

Entertainment Weekly, March 27, 1994; April 8, 1994; August 5, 1994.

Knight-Ridder Tribune News Service, April 1, 1994.
Musician, April 1994.
Newsweek, August 5, 1996.
New York Times, March 27, 1994; June 23, 1996.
New Yorker, April 18, 1994.
Playboy, July 1994.
Rolling Stone, April 7, 1994; July 11, 1996.
Spin, July 1994; December 1994.
Stereo Review, July 1994.
Village Voice, March 29, 1994.

Additional information for this profile was provided by Geffen Records, Inc.

—*Kevin Hillstrom*

Jello Biafra

Singer

In 1986, Dead Kennedys vocalist and Alternative Tentacles label founder Jello Biafra became the target of a First Amendment case when a controversial poster by Academy Award-winning artist H.R. Giger was included with the Dead Kennedys' album *Frankenchrist*. The poster, according to Biafra in *Billboard*, "[depicted] the putrefication [sic] of our consumer culture. If we thought it was harmful or exploitative, we never would have used it to begin with." Although Biafra was acquitted of the charges, he commented about the repercussions of the case in a *Billboard* guest editorial: "Any time artists have to so much as think twice about what they say in their songs out of fear of legal or career consequences, that's censorship in its ugliest form: muzzling of the mind."

Jello Biafra was born Eric Boucher in 1959 in Boulder, Colorado. According to an Alternative Tentacles publicist, his stage name was created during the late 1970s and derived from the Central African Bight of Biafra, which was receiving considerable news coverage at the time. The singer coupled it with the name of the famous gelatinous confection because he thought it "sounded good."

Biafra's early influences included composer Carl Orff and his father's extensive ethnic record collection. In high school, bored with the predominantly country-rock music on the radio, he began purchasing records with sleeves he found interesting, as well as others from the bargain bin at a local used record shop. Biafra reminisced in *Incredibly Strange Music Volume II:* "Looking back, this was the advantage of living in a country-rock town: Stooges for a dime, MC5 for a quarter, 13th Floor Elevators, Nazz, and Les Baxter for free...." Jello was also inspired by a rock-hating music critic from the *Denver Post* who "seemed to have obsessive and detailed knowledge of music he *didn't* like.... When he trashed someone like Black Sabbath he'd ... compare them to other bands he loathed, thus giving me that many more names to look for.... Just imagine my sense of accomplishment when he devoted an entire scathing column to Dead Kennedys' *Fresh Fruit for Rotting Vegetables!*"

Biafra formed the Dead Kennedys in 1978 in San Francisco after seeing a Ramones concert. The band's debut album *Fresh Fruit for Rotting Vegetables* was released on IRS Records, distributed by A & M. Due to A & M's initial reluctance to release the album, it was instead distributed through a label called Faulty Products. Bob Laul, national sales director for IRS and Faulty Products vice president spoke to *Billboard* in favor of the band: "A & M thought the (group's) name was in bad taste, but we think of them as the American

Sex Pistols." The Dead Kennedys' ferocious, guitar-driven sound and politically sarcastic lyrics inspired numerous hardcore punk-rock groups.

Biafra Runs for Mayor of San Francisco

In 1979, the outspoken Biafra was challenged by a friend to run for mayor of San Francisco. His platform included banning automobiles from the city limits, auctioning off high city positions in public, establishing a legal board of bribery to set fair prices for liquor licenses and building code exemptions, legalizing squatting in vacant buildings, and requiring Market Street businessmen to wear clown suits. He attracted much mainstream media coverage and came in fourth out of ten candidates.

Through the Dead Kennedys' albums, Biafra continued to hone the band's musical attack, drawing inspiration from such unlikely sources as surf-guitar instrumentals, bluegrass, exotica and lounge music, and bizarre rock-hybrid records that he had acquired during tours around the world. He explained in *Incredibly Strange Music Volume II*, "Especially for someone who's trying to make their *own* music, roots are not enough—why not explore the *roots* of the roots? There are plenty of garage and surf-instrumental bands who never ask themselves: 'What were the people who created the *original* music listening to?'...When I first came to San Francisco there was an unspoken edict: if you want attention, don't hide behind formulas; every band must be *different*."

Embroiled in First Amendment Trial

Jello Biafra founded the record label Alternative Tentacles during the early eighties to release albums by the Dead Kennedys and its cohorts, thus avoiding the inherent distribution problems associated with major labels reluctant to release controversial material. In 1986, however, inclusion of an H. R. Giger poster with the Dead Kennedys' *Frankenchrist* album prompted Los Angeles City Attorney Michael Guarino to prosecute Biafra and his label for distributing harmful material to minors.

Despite a lack of support from the music industry, Biafra was acquitted. Costs and stress resulting from the case broke up the Dead Kennedys and nearly bankrupted Alternative Tentacles. In a *Billboard* guest editorial, Biafra advised: "A continued lack of backbone plays right into the hands of those who say making love on record or in the movies is more dangerous than cops who kill suspects on TV shows. Any compromise to cultural vigilantes just encourages them to go further. This will ultimately hurt even the major labels right where it stings the most—in the pocketbook."

Biafra Goes on the Lecture Circuit

After the Dead Kennedys disbanded, Biafra collaborated with numerous like-minded musicians and began touring solo with a spoken-word act. His monologues follow a similar vein to Dead Kennedys lyrics, but their pacing and lack of thunderous musical backing enables the words to sink deeper. His diatribes, which concern such subjects as censorship, anti-establishment pranks, and grass-roots politics, attract a dedicated following. One of his most popular pieces, "Grow More Pot" from the *I Blow Minds For A Living* album, is a well-researched argument in favor of the industrial use of hemp, complete with an anti-smoking caveat in which Biafra quotes U.S. Department of Agriculture reports and back issues of *Popular Mechanics*.

Jello Biafra remains as vigilant as ever, providing an alternative to mainstream information outlets. He warns in *Incredibly Strange Music Volume II*, "One of the worst forms of censorship going on today is: depriving people of basic information so they can make informed decisions about what to do with their lives and everybody else's lives."

Selected discography

(With the Dead Kennedys), *Fresh Fruit for Rotting Vegetables*, IRS, 1980, reissued, Alternative Tentacles.
(With the Dead Kennedys), *In God We Trust, Inc.*, Alternative Tentacles, 1981.
(With the Witch Trials), *The Witch Trials EP*, Alternative Tentacles, 1981.
(With the Dead Kennedys), *Plastic Surgery Disasters*, Alternative Tentacles, 1982.

(With the Dead Kennedys), *Frankenchrist*, Alternative Tentacles, 1985.

(With the Dead Kennedys), *Bedtime for Democracy*, Alternative Tentacles, 1986.

(With the Dead Kennedys), *Give Me Convenience or Give Me Death*, Alternative Tentacles, 1987.

No More Cocoons, Alternative Tentacles, 1987.

High Priest of Harmful Matter—Tales from the Trial, Alternative Tentacles, 1989.

"Die For Oil, Sucker," Alternative Tentacles, 1990.

(With D.O.A.), *Last Scream of the Missing Neighbors*, Alternative Tentacles, 1990.

I Blow Minds for a Living, Alternative Tentacles, 1991.

(With Lard), *The Power of Lard*, Alternative Tentacles, 1991.

(With NoMeansNo), *The Sky Is Falling and I Want My Mommy*, Alternative Tentacles, 1992.

Beyond the Valley of the Gift Police, Alternative Tentacles, 1992.

(With Lard), *The Last Temptation of Reid*, Alternative Tentacles, 1992.

(With Tumor Circus), *SelfTitled*, Alternative Tentacles, 1993.

(With Tumor Circus), "Meathook Up My Rectum," Alternative Tentacles, 1994.

(With Mojo Nixon), *Prairie Home Invasion*, Alternative Tentacles, 1994.

Sources

Books

Carducci, Joe, *Rock and the Pop Narcotic*, Redoubt Press, 1990.

Robbins, Ira A., ed. *Trouser Press Record Guide 4th edition*, Collier Books, 1991.

Vale, V. and Andrea Juno, *Incredibly Strange Music Volume II*, RE/Search Publications, 1993.

Periodicals

Billboard, March 14, 1981; May 9, 1981; June 14, 1986; September 5, 1987; September 12, 1987; October 10, 1987.

Nation, October 24, 1987.

Rolling Stone, July 17, 1986; January 29, 1987; October 8, 1987.

Variety, April 1, 1987; August 26, 1987; September 2, 1987.

Village Voice, April 29-May 5, 1981; July 1, 1986.

Additional information for this profile was obtained from Alternative Tentacles publicity materials.

—James Powers

Big Audio Dynamite

Rock band

Archive Photos/Jon Hammer

Although Big Audio Dynamite consists of six band members, the media and public generally focus their attention on *de facto* leader Mick Jones. From 1976 to 1982 Jones was a member of the Clash, an English punk band that was once hailed as "the only band that matters." "In five years," wrote Jon Solomon in *Color Red,* "Jones and the Clash wrote five albums' worth of songs that helped change the shape of the punk to come." *Guitar World*'s Matthew Caws added, "The Clash delivered much more than punk ever promised—five albums worth of exquisitely written pop songs played with unparalleled fire and spirit." In 1983 Jones was "chucked out of" the Clash, as he often puts it, though animosity didn't seem to be the reason. It was more probably due to his yearning for technology. Just a year later Jones formed Big Audio Dynamite because he felt the time was right to try something completely new.

Big Audio Dynamite has gone through a great many changes since they started in 1984. In 1985 the band in its original incarnation released its first work, *This Is Big Audio Dynamite,* which Solomon described as "something of a revolutionary album." *Music Paper* wrote that this release turned Jones's "punk world upside down...[It's] crammed with techno/house beats, reggae, some punk attitude and a whole lot of pop songs." The song "E=MC^{2}," considered the first rock record to use sampling technology, as well as a second track titled "Bed-Rock City," became highly popular in dance clubs and formed the foundation of Big Audio Dynamite's alternative music fan base.

The band went on to record *No. 10 Upping Street* in 1986. Jones recruited former Clash pal Joe Strummer as the album's producer as well as cowriter. In 1988 *Tighten Up Volume '88* was released, followed by 1989's *Megatop Phoenix. Pulse's* Andrew Goodwin called *Megatop Phoenix* Big Audio Dynamite's finest work so far, commending the combination of acid-house beats and reggae baselines.

Big Audio Demise?

No explanation was given for the demise of the band's original line-up, and when Jones' decision to continue under the Big Audio moniker incited a lawsuit from other founding members, Big Audio Dynamite, or B.A.D., started anew as B.A.D. II. Goodwin, who had noted *Megatop Phoenix*'s heavy African-American influences, wrote that the band's 1991 release *The Globe* "shifted its invocations of blackness from dancehall toasting to straight-out rap." The most prominent track on the album, "Rush," became a *Billboard* Number One

Modern Rock single in 1991. Goodwin commented that "the fractured mix on 'Rush' showed that Jones had not forgotten one golden rule of punk, invoked via hip-hop's heart-stopping breakdowns—be unpredictable."

Following *The Globe*, B.A.D. II kept up an extensive touring schedule and also changed their name again, this time to Big Audio. Despite conflicts with their label, the band continued to experiment with their music and in 1993 created a soundtrack for the critically lauded Rob Weiss film *Amongst Friends*. 1993 also saw the release of *Lost Treasures of Big Audio Dynamite I & II*, a collection of 12-inch singles and remixes released in Japan and Australia that became a highly recommended import in the States.

How to Escape a Bad Label

In 1994 Big Audio released *Higher Power*. One song from that album—"Rock with the Caveman"—was included on *The Flintstones* soundtrack. The album was not particularly well-received by either critics or audiences. Apparently however, the album was made simply to finish up a contract with the band's record label so they could break away as soon as possible. Even before the commercial failure of *Higher Power*, however, B.A.D.'s U.S. fan base had become scattered. The 1991 single "Rush" got the most airplay of any of their songs in the U.S., although in Europe the band had continually been a top draw.

"We're still around," Jones remarked to Mark Brown in the *Orange County Register* in 1995, "we're still devel-

oping and progressing. We're still learning to make our thing great. At the moment we're having sort of a rejuvenation period." That rejuvenation was developing out of changes in the music industry. As Jones told the *Music Paper*, "Right after *The Globe* the grunge [music] thing happened, which, as everyone knows, is punk all over again with more fuzz tones. To me, [that] was fine because punk, as The Clash played it, was [a] kind of warmed-over [version of the rock band The] Who, but with more anger."

New Directions in a Neo-Punk Era

After grunge came a new punk movement in the early-to-mid-1990s led by such bands as Green Day, The Offspring, and Rancid. Although Rancid was often perceived to be derivative of the Clash, former Clash members neither objected to the new movement, nor did they jump on the growing bandwagon of old punk bands reforming to take advantage of the resurgence of their music.

The reemergence of Clash-like punk may have inspired yet more changes in Jones's band. First, another new line-up reclaimed the name Big Audio Dynamite, along with a new record label. Secondly, Jones got back to his roots. In *Guitar World* Jones recalled the beginnings of B.A.D.: "I didn't want to do the same thing, because I knew I wouldn't have a chance....So I tried to do something as far away from the Clash as possible....Over a period of time, I sort of forgot what I was good at—guitar chords and melodies."

The result was 1995's *F-Punk*. *Guitar World's* Caws called it the "most cohesive" album since their first, "bridging the gap between rock and underground dance music—this time acid house, ambient and the ultra-fast beats of jungle." *BAM's* Tom Lanham described it as "leaner, meaner, and more ill-tempered than anything this often-forgettable group has done since its sharply inventive '85 debut."

Although *F-Punk* received much critical attention, Rancid's album *And Out Came the Wolves...* ironically "out-clashed the former Clash guitarist," wrote Brown, "with tracks modeled almost note-for-note on classics from The Only Band That Matters." What this says about the future of Big Audio Dynamite is unclear. Big Audio Dynamite has lasted longer than the Clash, and Jones is still matter-of-fact about simply continuing to make music regardless of how "big" the band's popularity becomes. Although Jones and his buddies from the Clash don't seem to have an interest in reuniting, their adolescent children are currently playing in a new band: The Clash Kids.

Selected discography

As Big Audio Dynamite

This Is Big Audio Dynamite (includes "E=MC2" and "Bed-Rock City"), Columbia, 1985.
No. 10 Upping Street, Columbia, 1986.
Tighten Up Volume '88, Columbia, 1988.
Megatop Phoenix, Columbia, 1989.
Kool-Aid (released in U.K. only), 1990.
F-Punk, Radioactive Records, 1995.
Planet Bad: Big Audio Dynamite's Greatest Hits, Columbia, 1995.

As B.A.D. II

The Globe (includes "Rush"), Columbia, 1991.
On The Road '92, 1992.
Amongst Friends (soundtrack recording,) 1993.
Lost Treasures of Big Audio Dynamite I & II (released in Japan and Australia only), Sony, 1993.

As Big Audio

Higher Power (includes "Rock with the Caveman"), Columbia, 1994.
(Contributor) *The Flintstones* (soundtrack recording), 1994.

Sources

BAM, May 19, 1995; July 28, 1995.
Boston Phoenix, July 7, 1995.
CMJ, June 26, 1995.
Color Red, November 1995.
Guitar World, December 1995.
Hits, October 9, 1995.
Music Paper, August 1995.
Orange County Register, October 28, 1995; November 10, 1995.
Pulse!, August 1995.
San Francisco Bay Guardian, July 5, 1995.
San Jose Mercury News, June 23, 1995.

Additional information for this profile was obtained from Radioactive Records press materials, 1995.

—*Joanna Rubiner*

Rory Block

Guitarist, singer

MICHAEL OCHS ARCHIVES/Venice, CA

Aurora, nicknamed "Rory" Block, is one of the most successful blues guitarists recording today—a significant feat in a field that has usually relegated female talent to vocals. Block initially had an uphill battle against the general lack of popularity of blues—especially blues performed by women—and the path to her musical freedom first led through a maze of different genres: folk, country, pop, R&B, and even disco. Ultimately, the experience brought her a versatility that reviewers declaimed once whe had established a secure blues reputation via Rounder Records. The author of a a 1996 *Relix* review, for example, dubbed Block "not only one of the finest contemporary exponents of country-blues guitar playing, but...a well-rounded artist with depth, vision and feeling."

Born around 1950 in rural New Jersey, Block spent her formative years in Greenwich Village in New York City. Her large family, headed by Allan Block and Rory's stepmother, made music a mainstay of life. "My whole family was an orchestra," Rory told Jas Obrecht in a 1983 *Guitar Player* interview. "Cellos, violins, pianos—everybody played a different instrument. We used to get together with other families on Sunday afternoons and have classical jam sessions." Rory's contributions to these jams included classical recorder, which she had mastered by the age of eight, and classical guitar, which she began learning at age 11.

Immersed in Blues

The family's musical leanings were reinforced in Block's father's Greenwich Village Sandal Shop—he worked primarily as a leathersmith—which served as a gathering place for many of the leading folk and blues musicians of the era. John Sebastian, one of the regulars on the Village folk scene, recalled the Sandal Shop in the liner notes for Block's 1981 recording, *High Heeled Blues:* "As the singing faded in [Washington] Square, the hard core would gather at this comfy workplace to hear Mr. Block and his friends play some music. These friends were the cream of the touring traditional musicians—Doc Watson, Mississippi John Hurt, Clarence Ashley—a musical feast, with a menu that changed every week. Every time I managed to get in, I learned something. And every time I went in, I saw a pretty brown-haired girl sitting on the edge of the crowd. It took me several visits to figure out that this was Allan's daughter. It didn't take me long to figure out that she was a hell of a guitar player. These old guys with their guitars were taking a shine to Rory Block, showing her stuff the rest of us couldn't possibly figure out from records or one afternoon of observation." A fiddler himself, Mr. Block trained his daughter to accompany him on guitar

For the Record . . .

Born Aurora Block, c. 1950, in New Jersey; daughter of Allan Block, a leathersmith and folk musician. Grew up in Greenwich Village, New York City. Children: Thiele (born c. 1967) and Jordan (born c. 1974).

Began performing as a teenager at folk festivals with father. Cut first album with Stefan Grossman, c. 1966. Retired from performance for eight years, resurfacing with RCA contract in 1975 and released self-titled debut album. Experimented with several different labels—Chrysalis, 1977-1978, and Blue Goose, 1976—before signing with Rounder Records, 1981. Proceeded to release almost annual recordings with Rounder, from *High Heeled Blues*, 1981, to *Tornado*, 1996.

Awards: W.C. Handy Acoustic Blues Album of the Year Award for *When a Woman Gets the Blues*, 1995.

Addresses: *Record company*—Rounder, One Camp Street, Cambridge, MA, 02140.

in the style of country flatpicking. She earned her first performance credits backing her father at folk festivals and on two tracks of an Elektra/Asylum album called *Elektra String Band Project.*

Rory determined early that her own passion was for blues. She concentrated first—around the age of 14—on mastering the standards and styles of 1930s blues, which she learned to mimic perfectly from recordings. "I wanted nothing more than to religiously transcribe all the old recordings note-for-note," she told Osbrecht. "I wanted to get the tunings right and to reproduce the songs historically, accurately....I was so intensely into that form of music that for two years I dedicated most of my time to listening. I played all the time, night and day. The guitar was like a second skin." At 15 Rory left home, heading for California with Stefan Grossman, one of the guitarists who had introduced her to blues. Together they recorded an instructional album called *How to Play Blues Guitar* that "introduced countless guitarists in the '60s to some of the refined subtleties of acoustic blues," according to Osbrecht. When the album was originally released on the Elektra label, Block appeared under the pseudonym "Sunshine Kate."

When her son Theile was born around 1967, Block put aside her musical career until the mid-1970s. "During all that time," she told Osbrecht, "I didn't think about

being a professional. Then about eight years after I went underground, I had a terrible ache, an empty feeling: My music—where is it?" So Block began playing again, and touring with her young family, which now included her second son, Jordan. She also found that her approach to the music had changed—that she was less the student and more the musician. She told *Guitar* in 1996 that "In the beginning there was this tremendous reverence for the exact item. I didn't feel like I could sing it—I wanted to worship it." Things changed so that her music "now started sounding like a Rory Block song." Her resurgent enthusiasm ran into trouble, however, in the search for a recording company. She was an anomaly at the time, a white woman with a guitar playing not folk but blues, a blues musician with the finesse and complexity of classical training. To make herself more marketable, she wrote R&B songs and advertised herself with a touring road band.

Major Label Identity Crisis

The strategy apparently paid off in 1975 when Block landed her first contract with a record company, RCA, for a self-titled debut. Right away, however, the identity crisis began; as Block told Osbrecht, "The producers didn't feel that R&B was appropriate for me or that people would accept it. They felt I sounded a little too black, so they wanted to whitewash it a little bit. As a result, the album sounded a little bit country-ish, a little bit folky." Nonetheless, the album was accepted by reviewers and radio stations, and Block found a new label—Blue Goose—for her 1976 release *I'm in Love.* Although she was allowed to devote one side of the album to acoustic blues, the album displayed even more of a split personality, touting discofied R&B on its first side. Again, Block's work met with warm reviews and an even wider radio audience than had its predecessor.

Chrysalis Records picked Block up for her next few releases, including *Intoxication* in 1977 and *You're the One* in 1978. While the first album presented an R&B sound that Block was comfortable with, the producers worried that R&B was too outmoded and demanded disco for *You're the One.* Following that effort, Block decided she needed a return to basics and made one of the most important moves of her career: she turned away from major labels in favor of the small, folk-oriented, Massachusetts-based Rounder Records. "When you first enter the music business," she told Marc D. Allan of the *Indianapolis Star* in 1996, "everybody knows you try to do your absolute best and shoot for the best. So, after getting discouraged with the 'best,' I thought I'd go to a sweet label, a nice, friendly label and see if they want to do something more natural."

Block's debut release with Rounder, *High Heeled Blues* in 1981, finally allowed her to express her first musical love and acoustic skill in recorded form. The album's success was followed the next year with *Blue Horizon*, in which Block expanded her role to producer. "*High Heeled Blues* and *Blue Horizon*," Osbrecht noted, "became unexpected successes, the first LP outselling all of Rory's previous releases combined. The albums revitalized the guitarist's stage career, allowing her to comfortably face an audience alone for the first time." Block confirmed Osbrecht's assessment, telling him that "After *High Heeled Blues*, the gigs just started rolling in. The phone started ringing, and it hasn't stopped. Playing blues simplifies everything, and at the same time it has increased my audience tremendously....The acoustic approach has given me my roots identity all over again."

According to *Sing Out's* reviewer in 1994, Block's work for Rounder "highlights her contemporary country blues vocals and guitar work" and showcases "her true strengths more fully." The accolades have continued unabated since those initial Rounder recordings, even as Block has experimented with different formats, sometimes committing blues standards faithfully to tape, sometimes presenting her listener with more of her original compositions. *Angel of Mercy* and *Tornado* have recently demonstrated Block's skill as a composer, eliciting consistent respect from critics and fans.

Committed to Blues History

One reviewer of *Angel of Mercy* in a 1994 *Sing Out* article applauded the album's format of all original compositions and broader musical experiments: "On this recording, with an all-star group of supporting players, Block maintains those blues roots, but adds healthy doses of folk, pop, and gospel to produce a sound that will appeal to fans of Bonnie Raitt." 1996's *Tornado* again emphasizes the original, featuring nine of Block's own compositions. *Guitar* magazine approved the effort, claiming that Block "emerges as a performer with a river-deep respect for blues traditions but also the ability to transcend the idiom, crossing over into a more pop-oriented milieu."

Exemplifying Block's commitment to blues history were *Mama's Blues* and *When a Woman Gets the Blues*, released in 1991 and 1995 respectively. The reviewer

for *Sing Out* hailed the first as a "[return] to the Mississippi blues that have been, since her teenage days, her musical cornerstone." According to *Los Angeles Times* reviewer James E. Fowler, *When a Woman Gets the Blues* "represented a return to her acoustic blues roots." The 1995 project happened at the request of Rounder, which wanted an all acoustic album to follow the more anomalous sound of *Angel of Mercy*. Block voiced her appreciation for that request, noting how different it was from her early career. As she told Kerry Dexter in *Acoustic Musician*: "To get to the point where your record company is actually asking you to make a blues record...this is a beautiful day. I feel very uplifted."

Selected discography

How to Play Blues Guitar, Elektra, c. 1966.
Rory Block, RCA, 1975.
I'm In Love, Blue Goose, 1976.
Intoxication, Chrysalis, 1977.
You're the One, Chrysalis, 1978.
High Heeled Blues, Rounder, 1981.
Blue Horizon, Rounder, 1982.
Mama's Blues, Rounder, 1991.
Angel of Mercy, Rounder, 1994.
When a Woman Gets the Blues, Rounder, 1995.
Tornado, Rounder, 1996.

Also released instuctional video *The Power of Delta Blues Guitar*, Homespun Video, 1990.

Sources

Acoustic Musician, May 1996.
Billboard, June 1, 1996.
Folk Roots, December 1989.
Guitar, September 1996.
Guitar Player, November 1983; April 1990; December 1991.
Indianapolis Star, July 6, 1996.
Los Angeles Times, May 16, 1996.
Relix, June 1996.
Sing Out, August-October 1991; August-October 1994.
Stereo Review, May 1996.
USA Today, March 26, 1996.

Additional information for this profile was obtained from Rounder Records.

—Ondine Le Blanc

Blue Rodeo

Rock/country/folk/pop band

The essence of Blue Rodeo's music was born out of influences by Elvis Costello, the Beatles, and the Rolling Stones. The band's synthesis of rock, country, folk, and pop has remained steady throughout Blue Rodeo's career, as they have refused to be categorized in one simple genre. While the roster of band members has changed over the years, co-songwriters and singers Greg Keelor and Jim Cuddy—sometimes likened to the Beatles' duo John Lennon and Paul McCartney—have passionately led the band from anonymity to stardom in Canada and significant recognition in America.

The Canadian band Blue Rodeo officially took root in 1984. Greg Keelor and Jim Cuddy had known each other in high school, but didn't begin playing together until five years after graduation. After coming up with the band's name—which hinted at their twinge of country sound—Keelor and Cuddy invited original drummer Cleave Anderson to take part. Anderson recruited bass player Bazil Donovan, who had coincidentally answered the band's renowned ad in *NOW Magazine,* which read; "If you've dropped acid 20 times, lost three or four years to booze and can still manage to keep time, call Jim or Greg." Keyboard player Bobby Wiseman hooked up with the band through his older brother's friendship with Keelor, and Blue Rodeo was complete.

Blue Rodeo began by playing the Toronto clubs and wherever else they could get a gig. The band credits this willingness to play anywhere with their eventual success. Cuddy was quoted in *Rolling Stone* as saying, "We've played between 175 and 200 shows every year since we started. That's the way we spread the word in Canada: If somebody would have us, we'd play there."

Blue Rodeo's first two albums, *Outskirts* in 1987 and *Diamond Mine* in 1989, both received critical acclaim and won double-platinum awards. These initial recording efforts fostered a growing throng of devoted fans and attracted the attention of musicians Kris Kristofferson and Elvis Costello.

Awarded Blue Ribbons

1989 was a busy year for Blue Rodeo. Mark French replaced Anderson on drums. The band toured Germany that year, opening for Edie Brickell and New Bohemians, and also appeared at the Montreux Jazz Festival. Blue Rodeo received their first of three consecutive Juno Awards—Canada's equivalent to the Grammys—for Canadian Band of the Year, and performed at the ceremony with Robbie Robertson and The Band. The band appeared as Meryl Streep's backup band in the movie *Postcards From The Edge* when the actress heard their music in her chauffered limosine as she rode back and forth to the movie's set.

Blue Rodeo's third album, *Casino,* featuring newcomer Mark French on drums, was released in 1990 after being written, rehearsed, and recorded in just four months. Once the album was completed, the band's manager, John Caton, left the music business due to a serious heart condition. When Blue Rodeo's original record company, Risque Disque—which was owned by Caton—suspended operations due to financial difficulties, the band switched to Atlantic Records for the release of *Casino.*

Casino's appealing mix of pop, country, and blues provided the band's breakthrough to the American music scene. Nicholas Jennings stated in *Maclean's,* "[*Casino*] is already getting airplay on radio stations ranging from rock to easy listening, a rare feat that proves that the band can bridge a variety of styles with its country-tinged pop sound." Keelor didn't feel a great pressure or urgency to succeed in the United States. He was quoted in *Rolling Stone* as saying: "The question always arises if we're worried about not being popular in the States. We have to keep reminding people that we've got an awfully good thing going in Canada—we constantly do cross-country tours and sell a lot of records up here. As far as I'm concerned, anything else that happens would be like winning the lottery." The

For the Record . . .

Members include **Cleave Anderson,** drums; **Jim Cuddy,** guitars and vocals; **Bazil Donovan** (born in Halifax, Nova Scotia), bass; **Greg Keelor,** guitars and vocals; and **Bobby Wiseman,** piano and acetone. Later members include **Kim Deschamps** (born in Kirkland Lake, Ontario; joined group, 1992), pedal steel and lap steel guitars; **Mark French** (joined group, 1989; left group, 1993), drums; **James Gray** (joined group, 1993), keyboards, and **Glenn Milchem** (born in 1963; joined group, 1992), drums.

Group formed in 1984 in Canada; signed with Risque Disque and released first album, *Outskirts,* 1987; signed with Atlantic Records, 1990; signed with Discovery Records, 1993.

Awards: Toronto Music Award for Best Group, 1988, 1989; Casby Award for Best Group, 1988, 1989; Juno Award for Best Single, 1989; Juno Award for Canadian Band of the Year, 1989, 1990, 1991, 1996.

Addresses: *Record company*—Discovery Records, 2034 Broadway, Santa Monica, CA 90404. *E-mail*—info@bluerodeo.com. *Fan club*—P.O. Box 185, Station C, Toronto, Ontario, Canada M6J 3M9.

band began a national Canadian tour in January of 1991, covering all ten provinces and Labrador to promote the album. They also appeared on NBC's *The Tonight Show* in August of that year.

Rode for the Cause

Between recording and touring, Blue Rodeo remained true to its belief in quietly supporting various causes. They have played benefits for anti-nuclear and disarmament groups, and they have also spoken out in favor of native rights. They also performed at the Stein Valley Festival in British Columbia in 1990 to voice their concern for the endangered West Coast rainforest.

Blue Rodeo's 1992 release, *Lost Together,* reinforced the band's foothold in both the Canadian and American music scenes. The album showcased the talent of band newcomers Kim Deschamps—formerly of the Cowboy Junkies—on pedal & lap steel, mandolin, and banjo, as well as Glenn Milchem—formerly of Andrew Cash's band, and still with Groovy Religion—on drums. Blue Rodeo's sound took on a new edge in *Lost Together,*

and their efforts toward musical growth were broadly recognized. Parke Puterbaugh stated in *Stereo Review:* "*Lost Together* is a cornucopia of solid tunes and strong arrangements from a Canadian band that just keeps getting better and better." The band's country tendencies are not abandoned on *Lost Together.* Nicholas Jennings stated in *Rolling Stone* that "with their latest album, Cuddy and Keelor have steered the group in a decidedly more urban direction: although *Lost Together* still features some of their old familiar twang, the most exciting tracks are those with a grittier, downtown feel."

Rodeo on the Range

Blue Rodeo's fifth album, *Five Days in July,* introduced James Gray on keyboards and accordion. Guest musicians included singer and pianist Sarah McLachlan, cellist Anne Bourne, and guitarist Colin Linden. Although originally intended to be a demo, the work became an album as the group's music ignited at the unusual recording location at Keelor's farmhouse in Ontario. Keelor stated in the album's promotional literature: "We set up in the living room...people hung out and we played music. It was great to make music in this atmosphere, people always walking around and the sun coming in the windows." Any concern of losing the Blue Rodeo sound by recording in such an unconventional place was dismissed. Larry LeBlanc wrote in *Billboard:* "One worry was that by recording together quickly and being outside a conventional studio, the performances might be too ragged. To their relief, what the band members heard on tape exceeded their expectations." Sales of the acoustic album topped triple-platinum.

Blue Rodeo's sixth album, *Nowhere to Here,* was released in 1995 and revealed a darker side to the band's sound. While continuing to combine country, rock, and folk in their unique genre, the band explored new depths in songs infused with emotional lyrics that spoke of suicide, relationship woes, and desperation. This new direction and the band's extensive touring led to a greater international audience, and Blue Rodeo was awarded another Juno Award for Canadian Band of the Year in 1996. Vic Garbarini stated in *Playboy:* "Blue Rodeo hail from Canada. *Nowhere to Here* is another of their pristine country-rock albums that outclass their American cousins. They do rebel on some mesmerizing jams that capture the spirit of their live shows."

Selected discography

Nowhere to Here, Discovery Records, 1995.
Five Days in July, Discovery Records, 1993.
Lost Together, Atlantic Records, 1992.

Casino, Atlantic Records, 1990.
Diamond Mine, Risque Disque, 1989.
Outskirts, Risque Disque, 1987.

Sources

Periodicals

Billboard, December 11, 1993.
Maclean's, February 18, 1991; August 26, 1991; July 13, 1992.
Playboy, January 1996.
Rolling Stone, May 2, 1991.
Stereo Review, November 1992.

Online

Blue Rodeo's Official Internet Site, www.bluerodeo.com, 1997.

—*Alison Jones*

Bone Thugs-N-Harmony

Rap group

Rappers Bone Thugs-N-Harmony offer a preview of their music in their name: hardcore rap and rhythm—the "thug" element—combined with the smooth harmonies of contemporary R&B. With that sound the group has crossed genres, logging hit releases on rap, pop, and R&B charts. Hip hop fans nationwide have embraced the group with such passion that, according to Heidi Sigmund Cuda of the *Los Angeles Times,* they "put Cleveland on the rap map." The five young men who make up the band keep their birth names and dates secret, instead presenting themselves to the world with the common surname Bone, which they adopted in 1992 to express their fraternity. Layzie Bone and Flesh-N-Bone—the crew's one part-time member—are birth brothers, while Wish Bone is their cousin, Bizzy Bone a stepbrother, and Krayzie a friend from early childhood. In the Bone standard of family, however, they are all brothers. Journalists speculate that they are now in their mid-twenties.

The five grew up together in the St. Clair-East 99th Street block of Cleveland's Northeast Side, one of the city's poorest neighborhoods. All five experienced poverty first-hand in their own homes and, in their teen years, set about making a living through the most lucrative route available to them: selling crack cocaine. In an interview with *USA Today*'s Edna Gundersen, Layzie explained the necessity driving that choice: "We sold dope to get us through the young years. We didn't have clothes to go to school. We had to hustle. The dope game is easy to get into." Even Wish's mother concurred, telling Sacha Jenkins in a 1996 *Vibe* interview that they "weren't out there stickin' nobody up, but they was doin' what they had to do." Even in this early incarnation, the five already functioned as a tight-knit group, referring to themselves collectively as the Band-Aid Boys. They lived together, sharing all of their resources, as early as their mid-teens.

On Quest for Eazy-E

The group's move from drug sales to music was motivated, according to Layzie, by his and Flesh's encounter with the primary hazard of the drug trade—violence. "I was shot in the head," he told Peter Castro in an article for *People.* After that, he concluded: "I realized I had to do something with my life, and that's when I pursued rap. It's a miracle that I'm alive." The group already had some experience rapping together, as Wish told Jenkins: "We'd be sellin' drugs under the streetlights and doin' our little raps." But now they decided to turn the hobby into a vocation, which meant finding a producer. Like so many aspiring rappers around the country, they put in calls to executives at record companies, hoping to find someone who would listen. They focused most of their energy, however, on Eric "Eazy-E" Wright, veteran of the legendary rap group N.W.A. and founder of Ruthless Records. N.W.A.'s landmark 1989 release *Straight Outta Compton* had left its mark on the young men, impressing them with the "truth" of its songs. "We knew he was the man," Wish told Cuda. "The music of N.W.A. was the first time we heard anybody rapping about how we were living. He was telling our stories, and we trusted him."

Determined to reach Eazy-E, the quintet scrounged together the money for one-way bus tickets to Los Angeles. They left on November 23, 1993 for a three-day Greyhound trek and spent four months on the city streets, putting in frequent calls to Ruthless Records. When finally they had Eazy-E himself on the phone, the group pulled together an impromptu "audition," each Bone rapping his piece and passing the phone to the next. Nothing came of the call except the news that Eazy-E was, in fact, on his way to Cleveland for a show. So the group rustled up the money for the return ticket and found their way backstage at the theater. The audition in a dressing room convinced Eazy-E, who quickly signed the group to Ruthless. Wholly taken up with the new act, Eazy-E put aside his own projects long enough to serve as executive producer for their first recordings.

Having finally landed their mentor, Bone Thugs-N-Harmony arrived on the rap scene. For over a year, Eazy-

E nurtured their career, continuing to serve as their executive producer and teaching them the business skills he had taught himself over the years. The growing relationship was cut short, however, when Eazy-E died on March 26, 1995, from complications from AIDS. Briefly, the young rappers thought they had lost everything with the loss of their friend. "When we found him," Wish told Cuda, "we found our way out. Then he died right before [our success] happened, and it seemed like we were gonna be left in the streets right back where we came from." However, the group's potential was already apparent, and Ruthless Records continued to support them.

Took the Top of the Charts

A year after they bought the bus ticket to Los Angeles, the Bone Thugs were riding a luxury tour bus around the country to promote their first album. The EP *Creepin on ah Come Up,* released in June 1994, reached the top of the charts in pop, R&B, and rap. It remained on the *Billboard* R&B chart for over two years, by which time it had become a triple-platinum album. The EP's debut single, "Thuggish Ruggish Bone," sold over 500,000 copies on its own. Music industry honors followed in the shape of nominations, including three for the Grammies, one for the American Music Awards, and one for the *Soul Train* Awards. The city of Cleveland declared October 30 Bone Thugs-N-Harmony Day.

The chart-topping precedent of Bone Thugs' releases continued unabated through their second album, *E. 1999 Eternal,* released in the spring of 1995. Sales of 307,000 in the first week debuted the album in the No. 1 position on the *Billboard* pop chart. Within a year, sales had reached two million copies. One single from the album, "Tha Crossroads," moved so quickly up the charts after its release in May 1996 that it ranked with the legendary success of the Beatles's "Can't Buy Me Love" and Whitney Houston's "I Will Always Love You."

Rap with Rhythm Was Recipe for Success

The sound responsible for that success blended R&B harmony with the lyrics and rhythm of hardcore rap, bringing together two of the most current trends in popular music. "Basically," wrote a reviewer for the *Source* in March, 1995, "they kick more smooth rhymes, in their complex flow, while delivering hard 'reality' lyrics that hit with force." Although other groups were doing similar things, many commentators credited Bone Thugs-N-Harmony with a skill that set them apart. Jenkins, for example, asserted that "When the Bones' quick-tongued, Pig Latin-ish rhymes merge with their crooning patterns and the slow, keyboard-heavy beats that crawl along underneath, the result is a hybrid that seems to have fallen to Earth like an asteroid—or Skylab. And because of their uniqueness, there's no middle ground fanwise: You either think Bone Thugs-N-Harmony are space junk, or you think they shine brighter than the sun."

One detractor was David Bennun, writing for *Melody Maker.* Finding *E. 1999 Eternal* "tedious beyond description," Bennun nonetheless described his reaction at length. "*E. 1999* represents the fullest flowering yet of mainstream rap's trend towards ever smoother music and bloodier content. . . . Bone Thugs offer the worst of both worlds—R'n'B vapidity with witless shoot-em-up lyrics. They've reached the formulaic, play-dead depths of heavy metal's dweebiest hours." Few reviewers agreed with Bennun, however, tending instead to heap the group with praise. Russell Simmons, the rap mogul who created Def Jam records, declared to Jenkins that "They're the most original thing that has come to hip hop in a long time." J-Mill, interviewing the rappers for the *Source* in 1994, similarly contended: "Their style bristles with originality: each beat is enhanced with a syncopated flow. In addition, they bring harmony into their rhymes, with certain portions stated in unison, resulting in an elaborate, complicated style that will be hard to duplicate."

Like most rappers, Bone Thugs-N-Harmony use their lyrics to describe the mainstays of their day-to-day lives: community, loss, violence, marijuana, and the Ouija. This last is less common in the world of rap music and has, consequently, invited the assumption that the group's members must be devil worshippers. While they acknowledge the role the Ouija played in their past—they claim that it predicted the date of their first album release—they insist on their present distance from it. Wish told Jenkins that "Ouija is a devil's game," and Krayzie added that it will "have you addicted. You're supposed to play it with two people, but it'll have you to where you want to play by yourself. And that's where you slip." Explaining their new direction, Layzie told Jenkins "We been growin' up, and gettin' into the Bible. We want to go to heaven, and we knew that shit wasn't right."

Central to their music are the images from their Cleveland neighborhood, which they feel a certain responsibility to capture in words. Less confrontational than some hardcore rappers, as Cuda noted, their music "is designed not to push hot buttons but simply to reflect their upbringing." Layzie explained that distinction as the difference between "gangsta" and "thug" in the interview with Gundersen. "Gangsta rap is a killin' way," he told her. "We talk about the struggle. We don't say we gonna flat out kill you. Our music is education on where we come from."

The rappers haven't relaxed since the release of *E. 1999 Eternal* but have instead been busy consolidating that success. "The media try to say they're all about smokin' weed," D.J. U-Neek, who has mixed for the rappers, told Jenkins, "but Bone's making business moves. They got groups signed, they got films comin'. The shit is amazing to see." The film is underway with Russell Simmons, and their label—Mo Thugs—is cutting records with several new talents. They also devote energy and money to an array of charities, including Urban AID, which raises money for AIDS foundations. Much of their charity work is designed to bring money back into the neighborhood they come from, such as Cleveland's Midnight Basketball League, and the many "donations" they make to help people out in their community. As Jenkins noted, "they take care of their people—when one of their extended crew is trying to get on his feet, the Bones are right there with money, shelter, or whatever's needed."

Selected discography

Creepin on ah Come Up (includes "Thuggish Ruggish Bone"), Ruthless, 1994.
E. 1999 Eternal (includes "Tha Crossroads"), Ruthless, 1995.
Faces Of Death, Ruthless, 1996.

Sources

Los Angeles Times, June 15, 1996.
Melody Maker, October 21, 1993.
People Weekly, July 8, 1996.
Source, December 1994; March 1995.
USA Today, August 15, 1995.
Vibe, February 1995; May 1996.

Additional information for this profile was obtained from Relativity Records.

—*Ondine Le Blanc*

Dee Dee Bridgewater

Singer

Archive Photos, Inc.

D ee Dee Bridgewater's lives, personal and professional, have taken a lot of unexpected turns since she first emerged as a top jazz diva in the early 1970s. Her quest to create a life satisfying on both levels has included stops on both coasts of the U.S., a return to her childhood hometown in Flint, Michigan, and finally a flight across the ocean to Paris, where she has lived for the last several years. Along the way, Bridgewater has established herself as one of the best and most versatile vocalists of her generation, as well as a skilled actress. Her career entered as new phase in the 1990s, as she took over creative and financial control of her own work. The result has been a couple of Grammy Award nominations and a degree of international recognition that had eluded her in the past.

Bridgewater was born Denise Garrett on May 27, 1950, in Memphis, Tennessee. Her father, Matthew Garrett, was a prominent trumpet player in the Memphis jazz scene, and had worked as a sideman with the likes of Nat (King) Cole. When Dee Dee—Denise's nickname since infancy—was three years old, the family moved to Flint, Michigan, where Matthew opted for the security of a teaching job. The Bridgewaters remained in Flint for the rest of Dee Dee's childhood.

While her friends listened to the pop hits of the day, Garrett immersed herself in jazz at home. Among the many vocalists she admired, Garrett's favorite was Nancy Wilson. She plastered her room with photographs of Wilson and taught herself to mimic Wilson's style. Garrett formed a vocal trio called the Irridescents while she was still in high school, but that group was shortlived. After her graduation in 1968, she enrolled at Michigan State University. It was there that Garrett began to bloom as a performer, working college clubs and jazz festivals with a quintet led by saxophonist Andy Goodrich.

Hit Big Apple with Husband Cecil

In 1969 the Goodrich group performed at a festival at the University of Illinois in Champaign, where Garrett caught the eye and ears of John Garvey, director of the U. of I. jazz band. A few months later, Garvey invited Garrett to join his ensemble for a six-week tour of the Soviet Union. The band included trumpet player Cecil Bridgewater. Garrett and Bridgewater married in 1970, and shortly thereafter moved to New York, together in search of a successful career in jazz.

Cecil caught on first in New York, working initially with noted pianist Horace Silver and then landing a steady job with the Thad Jones-Mel Lewis Orchestra, the de

Born Denise Garrett, May 27, 1950, in Memphis, TN; daughter of Matthew Garrett (a musician and teacher) and Marion Hudspeth; married Cecil Bridgewater, 1970; daughter: Tulani; married Gilbert Moses, c. 1975. *Education:* Attended Michigan State University, 1968, and University of Illinois, 1969; studied with pianist Roland Hanna.

Began professional singing career with saxophonist Andy Goodrich, 1968; performed with Thad Jones-Mel Lewis Orchestra, 1972-74; recorded with many top jazz artists during this period; performed in Broadway musical *The Wiz,* 1974-76; performed in a variety of pop and jazz venues, with occasional television and film appearances, 1976-1985; resumed singing career in Paris, 1985; starred in stage musical *Lady Day* (tribute to Billy Holiday), 1986-1987; resumed recording career on Verve label, 1990—.

Awards: Tony Award for best supporting actress in a musical for *The Wiz,* 1975; Grammy Award nominations for *Keeping Tradition* (Verve, 1993), and *Love and Peace: A Tribute to Horace Silver* (Verve, 1995).

Addresses: *Home—* Paris, France. *Record company—* Verve Records (Polygram), 825 8th Ave., New York, NY 10019.

facto house band at the legendary Village Vanguard jazz club. When Jones and Lewis discovered that Dee Dee could sing, she joined the group as well, and remained its featured vocalist from 1972 through 1974. During this period, she returned to the U.S.S.R., this time with the Jones-Lewis orchestra, and also performed in Japan. Her steady gig at the Village Vanguard put Bridgewater at the center of the New York jazz scene, and she became much sought after for session work by some of jazz's biggest names, including Dizzy Gillespie, Max Roach, and Roland Kirk. In 1974 she was named best new vocalist in *Down Beat* magazine's annual poll.

Eased on Down to Broadway

In 1974 Bridgewater decided to audition for the Broadway musical *The Wiz,* an updated African-American version of the classic *The Wizard of Oz.* She landed the part of Glenda, the good witch of the South. The part was relatively small, but included several featured songs.

Bridgewater's performance earned her the 1975 Tony Award for best supporting actress in a musical. Having divorced Cecil Bridgewater by this time, she also landed her second husband, *Wiz* director Gilbert Moses.

Bridgewater grew tired of Broadway by 1976. She quit *The Wiz* that year and moved to Los Angeles, with an eye toward trying her hand at film acting and pop singing. Although she remained primarily a jazz singer, Bridgewater sought to stretch her talents in more commercially viable directions. The next several years were frustrating ones. Caught between the worlds of jazz and pop, Bridgewater was unable to find a comfortable spot in the hearts of either audience. She was especially bothered by the mediocre "Black muzak" that record producers tried to make her sing. By the mid-1980s, Bridgewater was ready to abandon her musical career entirely. In 1985 she moved back to Flint to live with her mother, who was in poor health.

Tribute to Holiday Revitalized Career

The following year, Bridgewater moved to Paris, where, like so many jazz artists before her, she found a public far more appreciative of her talents than American listeners had ever been. In 1986 and 1987 she starred in the one-woman show *Lady Day,* a musical about the life of Billie Holiday. She performed in other musicals as well, including a revival of *Cabaret.* Meanwhile, Bridgewater resumed her singing career. She toured the Far East with a band that included such notable players as Clark Terry, James Moody, and Jimmy McGriff. By the end of the 1980s, Bridgewater had established herself as one of the top jazz vocalists in Europe.

In 1990 Bridgewater released *In Montreaux,* her first album on the Verve label. By this time she had managed to regain creative and financial control over her projects, a fact reflected in her choice of material for the album, notably a medley of Horace Silver compositions. *In Montreaux* served notice to the jazz world that Bridgewater was once again a force to be reckoned with. Her next recording, *Keeping Tradition,* was nominated for a 1993 Grammy award. The Bridgewater-Silver connection became even more concrete in 1994, when Bridgewater got the idea for her next album while performing the Silver tune "Love Vibrations." The resulting recording, *Love and Peace: A Tribute to Horace Silver,* was released the following year. It earned Bridgewater another Grammy nomination, and brisk crossover sales in Europe landed the album on the pop charts on that continent.

Bridgewater performed to an enthusiastic audience at the Village Vanguard in 1996, more than 20 years after her earlier brush with fame at that venue. Although she has remained based in Paris, her successful return to the U.S. was music to the ears of audiences on the side of the Atlantic where jazz was born.

Selected discography

(With Thad Jones-Mel Lewis Orchestra) *Suite for Pops,* 1972.
Live in Paris '87, Affinity, 1987.
In Montreaux, Verve, 1990.
Keeping Tradition, Verve, 1993.
Love and Peace: A Tribute to Horace Silver, Verve, 1995.
(With Heiner Stadler) *Ecstasy,* Labor, 1996.

Sources

Down Beat, October 21, 1976; December 1995.
Emerge, April 1996.
New York Times, April 21, 1975.

—*Robert R. Jacobson*

David Bromberg

Singer, instrumentalist

Often considered "a musician's musician throughout his career"—according to Richard Skelly on the *All Music Guide* website—David Bromberg has logged up many impressive credits both as a backing musician and solo act. Over the years he has played everything from the guitar and banjo to the violin for a wide range of well-known artists, ranging from Bob Dylan and Jerry Jeff Walker to John Denver and Blood, Sweat, and Tears. His work as a sideman can be heard on over 100 albums that clearly demonstrate the incredible range of his artistry. However, his varied musical interests during his career may have limited his fame. As Skelly wrote, "[Bromberg's] musical eclecticism over the years may have cost him some fans, but a typical Bromberg concert can be a musical education."

Bromberg has often been cited for his mastery of numerous musical styles on stringed instruments. "Proficient on guitar (primarily acoustic), violin, mandolin and banjo, Bromberg's music took in elements of folk, blues, bluegrass, rock, comedy and lengthy narrative stories often stuck in between choruses," noted the *Guinness Encyclopedia of Popular Music.* His flair as an entertainer has been duly noted by many reviewers. Bromberg's "delivery, a combination of deadpan seriousness and weird, twisted humor, kept the crowd entertained and off balance as he changed pace and direction with his songs and stories," wrote Jerry Vovcsko in the *Worcester Evening Gazette* about the performer's rendition of "I Was Framed" at the West Main Street Cafe in Northboro, Massachusetts, in 1988.

Entered New York Folk Scene

David Bromberg took up guitar while ill with the measles at age 13, according to Irwin Stambler in the *Encyclopedia of Folk, Country & Western Music.* He soon developed an interest in blues and folk music, becoming a big fan of recordings by Pete Seeger, the Weavers, Josh White, Django Reinhardt, and Big Bill Broonzy. Stambler claimed that White's *Josh White Comes Visiting* album, which also featured Broonzy, was a major inspiration for Bromberg. While in high school, Bromberg developed skills with other instruments, then began majoring in musicology after entering Columbia University. School proved no match for the lure of performing in the fertile folk music scene of New York City's Greenwich Village, however, and Bromberg dropped out of college to devote himself to gigs in small clubs and coffeehouses.

Key to Bromberg's musical development was meeting Jerry Jeff Walker in the mid-1960s, whom he backed as a musician for four years. Bromberg's guitar work can

For the Record . . .

Born September 19, 1945, in Philadelphia, PA. *Education:* Columbia University; Kenneth Warren School of Violin Making.

Studied to become a musicologist in college, 1960s; played backing guitar for Phoenix Singers, early 1960s; performed as session artist for numerous artists in New York City, 1960s; worked frequently with Jerry Jeff Walker, 1960s; contributed session work on over 80 albums, 1960s–70s; performed at Isle of Wight Festival, 1970; signed recording contract with Columbia Records, 1971; released first album, *David Bromberg,* 1971; signed contract with Fantasy Records, 1976; formed own backing group, 1970s; contributed to *Hillbilly Jazz,* 1977; stopped performing and dedicated himself to repairing violins and other instruments, 1980; formed David Bromberg Big Band, 1980s.

Addresses: Record company—Rounder Records, One Camp Street, Cambridge MA 02140. *Residence*—Hyde Park, NY.

be heard on Walker's famed recording of "Mr. Bojangles." Recommendations by Walker and folk singer Tom Paxton helped Bromberg break into session work. "The first time I was in the studios was either with Screamin' Tony McKay or Rusty Evans," he told *Guitar Player* in March of 1973. "I didn't get paid for it as it was just going in for the thrill of being able to record. And that's where I found out that studio situations are tricky and that recording is not always the same thing as playing."

Developing a reputation as a multifaceted musician, Bromberg became one of the most sought after studio musicians in New York City. His eclectic mix of frontmen during the late 1960s and early 1970s included Jay and the Americans, Rick Derringer, Chubby Checker, Carly Simon, Mississippi John Hurt, Ringo Starr, John Prine, and Richie Havens. He performed on Bob Dylan's *Self Portrait* and *New Morning* albums in 1970 and 1971, respectively, and by the middle of the decade had logged up credits on over 80 albums.

Bromberg landed a recording contract with Columbia Records after a highly regarded performance at the Isle of Wight Festival in 1970. His first release, the self-titled *David Bromberg,* came out the following year. Bromberg was never able to attract a wide audience, but earned steady critical acclaim for his recordings and performances as a frontman. He was also able to enlist many noteworthy performers as contributors to his works. His *Demons in Disguise* and *Wanted Dead or Alive* albums featured appearances by members of the Grateful Dead, and his *Midnight on the Water's* stellar list of credits included Emmylou Harris, Linda Ronstadt, Dr. John, Jesse Ed Davis, Bonnie Raitt, and Ricky Skaggs.

In 1976 Bromberg switched labels to the San Francisco-based Fantasy Records. The next year he contributed to a highly acclaimed album called *Hillbilly Jazz,* which featured other acoustic musicians such as Vassar Clements and D.J. Fontana. Eventually he formed his own regular backing group that he called "The World's First Folk Orchestra," according to Stambler. "The band just crept on me," said Bromberg about the group, according to Stambler. "I started out with just a bass player. Wherever we played, musicians I'd met on the road would come and sit in."

Formed Large Band

Following the release of his *You Should See the Rest of the Band* in 1980, Bromberg broke up his group and announced that he would no longer perform live. That same year he moved to Chicago to study at the Kenneth Warren School of Violin Making, and began devoting himself to the repair of instruments. Later in the 1980s, Bromberg rematerialized onstage with his David Bromberg Big Band, which offered a mix of country, blues, rock, New Orleans- style brass, and bluegrass, as well as other musical styles. "Bromberg works hard and pulls it all off with his string playing, offbeat charisma and a very effective support of a tight, resourceful band," wrote Fernando Gonzalez in the *Boston Globe* in his review of the band's 1987 reunion tour performance at Nightstage in Cambridge, Massachusetts.

Following a moratorium on recording that lasted nearly a decade, Bromberg resurfaced with his *Sideman Serenade* on Rounder Records in 1990. Confirming his varied musical tastes, the album was split between a side of city songs and one of country songs. "The city songs run the gamut from blues to a surprisingly effective instrumental samba, while the country tunes stay closer to home but offer surprises in personnel," said reviewer Michael Point in the *Austin American-Statesman.*

Throughout the 1990s Bromberg has continued to retain a loyal following, and he performs at regular intervals in selected clubs. Every year he makes a highly anticipated appearance at the famed New York City club, the Bottom Line. Despite being heralded over the years for his skill as a musician, Bromberg has always maintained his modesty on the subject. "Anything I do, I have to really work on," he was quoted as saying by Stambler. "Some people are just disturbingly brilliant on the guitar without much work, but with me, I have to practice and practice, just sitting down and getting locked into it."

Selected discography

David Bromberg, Columbia, 1971.
Midnight on the Water, Columbia, 1975.
How Late'll Ya Play 'Til?, Fantasy, 1976.
Reckless Abandon, Fantasy, 1977.
Sideman Serenade, Rounder, 1990.

Sources

Books

Clarke, Donald, editor, *The Penguin Encyclopedia of Popular Music,* Viking, 1989, p. 159.
Larkin, Colin, editor, *The Guinness Encyclopedia of Popular Music, Volume 1,* Guinness Publishing, 1992, p. 558.
Stambler, Irwin, and Grelun Landon, *The Encyclopedia of Folk, Country & Western Music,* St. Martin's Press, 1983, pp. 72–73.

Periodicals

Austin-American Statesman, November 3, 1989.
Boston Globe, February 24, 1987; July 12, 1990, section CAL, p. 8.
Chicago Tribune, October 12, 1989, section 5, p. 3.
Guitar Player, March 1973.
New York Times, February 16, 1992, section WC, p. 16.
Sweet Potato, March 18, 1988.
Worcester Evening Gazette, July 15, 1988.

Additional information for this profile was obtained from Rounder Records publicity materials, as well as the *All Music Guide* website on the Internet (http://www.cduniverse.com).

—*Ed Decker*

Buffalo Tom

Rock band

The Massachusetts-based trio Buffalo Tom "crafts rootsy garage-rock pop songs that tap the essence of 'real life' with infectious melodies and knife-edged lyricism," Scott Carlson wrote in *A&E*. Jon Steltenpohl added in *Consumable:* "Their sound mixes the power three-piece sound of Sugar or Hüsker Dü with the pure pop of a band like the Smithereens. The result is a pure, no-frills style of bare bones music which you can still sing along with." In their nine years of existence, Buffalo Tom has gone from Boston cult favorite to alternative-radio mainstay, but they have yet to live up to *Rolling Stone*'s prediction that they would become "the next R.E.M."

Buffalo Tom formed in 1988, when three college friends from Amherst, Massachusetts—Bill Janovitz, Chris Colbourn, and Tom Maginnis—began playing parties and local clubs together. All three were originally guitar players, but Colbourn switched to bass and Maginnis learned to play drums to accompany Janovitz's guitar and vocals. Maginnis explained the origin of the band's name to Steltenpohl in an interview for *Consumable:* "A friend of ours was just kind of playing around with the name 'Buffalo Bill,' perhaps since there was Buffalo Springfield. Bill's the lead singer, and I'm just more of the shy guy in the back playing drums, and they thought it was pretty funny to have 'Buffalo Tom.' We didn't think too seriously about it at the time because we were just playing parties and shows at school, and it just kind of stuck."

The members of Buffalo Tom began to have bigger ambitions when they saw the success of bands like the Replacements and Hüsker Dü—"bands that to us were normal people," as Colbourn told Rob Galgano of *You Could Do Worse.* "We thought we could do that, too." The band attracted a cult following on the Boston music scene with their live shows and made a demo tape of three songs that they sent to a number of record companies. "The only real response was from a guy in Holland who had a label," Maginnis explained to Steltenpohl. "He just slowly sent us some more money and wanted to hear some more demos, and those eventually became our first album."

Stampeded onto the Scene

When recording the songs for their self-titled debut album, the group looked to a friend from western Massachusetts, J Mascis—founder of the band Dinosaur Jr. "He had put out a couple of records, so we asked him to come in and help out because we didn't know what the heck we were doing," Maginnis admitted to Steltenpohl. Mascis was eventually credited as producer on both *Buffalo Tom* and its follow-up, *Birdbrain,* and his early influence was so apparent that some critics called Buffalo Tom "Dinosaur Jr., junior." Mascis also brought Buffalo Tom to the attention of the independent record label SST, which released *Buffalo Tom* in the United States. "At that time, you know, they were a pretty hip indie label and all our favorite bands were on SST, so we were amazed that we actually had a record on SST," Maginnis recalled to Steltenpohl. Buffalo Tom's early releases garnered significant airplay on college radio stations, while their frequent concerts at small venues earned them strong grass-roots support.

Albums Attracted Herd of Fans

The band signed with Beggars Banquet in 1990. The label released their next four albums and helped them break into commercial alternative radio. Their 1992 release, *Let Me Come Over,* shows Buffalo Tom "finding a magical middle point between furious distortion and calm grandeur," reported a reviewer for *The War against Silence.* While several songs received airplay, including the moody "Taillights Fade," the album did not find a wide audience. By contrast, 1993's *Big Red Letter Day*—which was recorded in Los Angeles and produced by the legendary Robb Brothers—tripled the band's sales to over 85,000 units. It also marked a bit of a departure for Buffalo Tom, as the group left their punk-rock and grunge reputation behind and went for a cleaner sound. The album features the song "Treehouse," which Steve Gullick of *Melody Maker* called "a

For the Record . . .

Members include **Chris Colbourn,** bass, vocals; **Bill Janovitz,** guitar, vocals; **Tom Maginnis,** drums.

Group formed in Amherst, MA, in 1988; released self-titled debut album on independent label SST, 1989; signed with Beggars Banquet and released *Birdbrain,* 1990; contributed to Velvet Underground tribute album *Heaven and Hell,* 1990, and to benefit album *Sweet Relief,* 1993; appeared in television series *My So-Called Life,* ABC, 1994; performed "Lolly Lolly Lolly Get Your Adverbs Here" for the *Schoolhouse Rock* tribute album, 1996.

Addresses: *Office*—Buffalo Tom, P.O. Box 88 Back Bay Annex, Boston, MA 02117. *E-mail*—thbuffalos@aol.com. *Record company*—Beggars Banquet Records, Ltd., 274 Madison Avenue, Suite 804, New York, NY 10016.

rumbustious, rock 'n' soul shouter...unlike anything Buffalo Tom have done before." This work also includes the singles "I'm Allowed" and "Sodajerk." The success of *Big Red Letter Day* earned the band a spot on one of the hottest concert tours of that summer, along with Live, PJ Harvey, and Veruca Salt.

Buffalo Tom's eagerly awaited 1995 album, *Sleepy Eyed,* was recorded at Dreamland Studios in Woodstock, New York, inside a converted nineteenth-century church. "It's got nice, big stained glass windows," Colbourn told Carlson in *A&E.* "The sun comes in during the day and we would record rock songs, and at night we'd light the candles along the wall and record songs like 'Twenty-Points' at two o'clock in the morning. It's nice. It really is haunting." Many of the songs on the album deal with relationships and the pain of everyday life. For example, "Souvenir" describes a dysfunctional family, and "Twenty-Points" explores how couples tend to keep score. Janovitz wrote 11 of the songs on the album, while Colbourn contributed three.

Carlson described the music on *Sleepy Eyed* as "a return to a gritty sound and a straightforward approach that sharply contrasts the pristine production" of *Big Red Letter Day,* adding that "the guitar is a blunt instrument and Janovitz's honest, raspy and sometimes straining voice is reminiscent of Rod Stewart imitating Paul Westerberg." Steltenpohl commented that "*Sleepy Eyed* works because the guitars are raw,

the lyrics are real, and whether it's a loud, raucous song or a melancholy ballad, the songs latch onto you." Some other reviewers were less complimentary, including *Audio*'s Mike Bieber, who characterized the songs on *Sleepy Eyed* as uneven in quality and remarked that "such peaks and valleys give the album an untethered feel, hastening its arrival on my shelf, where it'll gather dust for a few years."

Roamed toward Crossover Success

Prior to the release of *Sleepy Eyed, Billboard* noted that Buffalo Tom had long been "poised at the brink of crossover status" and was in some ways approaching "a make-or-break stage in its career." Though the band had attracted numerous fans and by many accounts was continuing to grow musically, they still had not emerged as a major mainstream success. "I'd be lying if I said we were totally satisfied," Janovitz admitted to David Sprague of *Billboard.* "But we've long ago exceeded our day-one expectations. We've never gone backwards, always moved forward in small increments. My heroes have all done that—people like Tom Waits, Van Morrison—all have a small, dedicated audience, which I'd rather have."

The band planned to continue refining their sound and using their experience to bring greater depth to their music. "A lot of my big heroes wrote beautiful albums in their forties," Colbourn told Carlson. "There is something to be said for the confidence and the things you learn in life as you get older. If you can keep it together enough to integrate that into your music, then there is no limit." Unlike many other groups, the members of Buffalo Tom remained close friends despite the pressures of recording and touring. "I couldn't go through this kind of a journey with anyone that isn't a friend," Colbourn admitted to Gullick. "We've got to know each other so well. Way beyond brothers. I always say, if you're gonna start a band, start with a bunch of friends and teach them how to play. That's how we did it."

Selected discography

Singles

"Sunflower Suit," Megadisc, 1989.
"Enemy," Caff, 1990.
"Crawl," Megadisc, 1990.
"Birdbrain," Situation Two, 1990.
"Fortune Teller," RCA/Situation Two, 1991.
"Velvet Roof," RCA/Situation Two, 1992.
"Taillights Fade," RCA/Situation Two, 1992.
"Mineral," Beggars Banquet, 1993.

"Sodajerk," EastWest/Beggars Banquet, 1993.
"Summer," EastWest/Beggars Banquet, 1995.

Albums

Buffalo Tom, SST, 1989.
Birdbrain, Beggars Banquet, 1990.
Let Me Come Over, Beggars Banquet, 1992.
Big Red Letter Day, Beggars Banquet, 1993.
I'm Allowed (EP), Beggars Banquet, 1993.
Sleepy Eyed, Beggars Banquet, 1995.

Sources

A&E, October 12, 1995.
Audio, November 1995.
Billboard, June 3, 1995.
Euphony, October 20, 1995.
Melody Maker, October 2, 1993; July 1, 1995; July 8, 1995.
Rolling Stone, February 21, 1991.
The War against Silence, August 24, 1995.

Additional information for this profile was obtained from the on-line versions of *Consumable* and *You Could Do Worse* 'zines.

—Laurie Collier Hillstrom

Bush

Rock band

Archive Photos/Scott Harrison

Bush frontman Gavin Rossdale quipped in *Details*: "I understand why people are suspicious of us. *I'd* be suspicious of us." The British rock band rose to fame in the mid-1990s with a thrashing alternative sound more reminiscent of Seattle grunge than London Britpop; the suspicion to which Rossdale alluded had to do with their lack of "indie" credentials and his own matinee-idol looks. Despite being labeled "Nirvanawannabes" by detractors, Bush rocketed up the U.S. charts with their multi-platinum debut album, *Sixteen Stone,* and also seemed poised to achieve huge sales with their 1996 follow-up, *Razorblade Suitcase.* Whether Rossdale and his bandmates would be "taken seriously," as one very ironic magazine cover wondered, remained to be seen.

Singer-songwriter and rhythm guitarist Rossdale was born and raised in North London. His parents divorced when he was 11, and he grew up under the care of his physician father. He already tended toward adolescent rebellion when his older sister introduced him to punk rock. In school, he told *Details*, "I was intimidated a lot and I would just sit in the back." He dropped out by age 17, and a few years later began to play with various rock bands. Eventually, his pop-oriented group Midnight got a record deal. "We got signed way too young in the mid-'80s, when everyone was throwing all this money around," the singer recollected in *Rolling Stone.* "So as far as the A&R community in London, was concerned, I was soiled."

Nirvana Influenced Heavy Sound

Rossdale went to Los Angeles for half a year, hoping to find a new project and scraping by as an assistant on music video shoots. Though things didn't fare particularly well for him there, he did see a performance by Nirvana at the Roxy nightclub that had a pronounced impact on his musical direction. He returned to England and hooked up with guitarist Nigel Pulsford, formerly of the indie band King Blank. Though the two bonded over their love for such influential alternative bands as the Pixies—who also strongly influenced Nirvana—their band Future Primitive was a far cry from the sonic barrage they would later craft into Bush. The two later enlisted bassist Dave Parsons, formerly of the notorious glam-pop band Transvision Vamp, and continued to play around London.

Eventually, the band came to the attention of drummer Robin Goodridge, an engineer and former member of dance-rock experimentalists Beautiful People. "I thought Gavin was a rock star but the drummer was shite," he told *Details*. He took over percussive duties and the band—renamed Bush after the Shepherd's Bush neigh-

For the Record . . .

Members include **Gavin Rossdale** (born October 30, 1967, in London, England), guitar, vocals; **Robin Goodridge** (born 1967), drums; **Dave Parsons** (born c. 1964), bass; **Nigel Pulsford** (born c. 1963), guitar.

Band formed c. 1993 in London, England. Signed with Hollywood Records, c. 1994; left Hollywood and signed with Trauma/Interscope Records, which released debut album *Sixteen Stone,* 1994.

Awards: Platinum certification for *Sixteen Stone,* 1996; received Viewer's Choice Award and MTV Video Music awards, 1996.

Addresses: *Record company*—Trauma/Interscope, 10900 Wilshire Blvd., Suite 1000, Los Angeles, CA 90024. *Internet*—www.bushonline.com.

borhood in London that had spawned them—began entertaining offers. In 1993, A&R executive Rob Kahane signed Bush to his own label, which was affiliated with Hollywood Records, a subsidiary of the Walt Disney Company. When Kahane lost influence at Hollywood, however, the band found themselves with a completed record that they were unable to release. Fortunately, Interscope/Trauma published their debut, *Sixteen Stone,* in 1994.

Overnight Teen Idols

The album scored immediately on modern rock radio stations, thanks to the heavy rotation given its first single, "Everything Zen." With its grunge-influenced bombast, the single appealed to the audience that was still mourning the suicide of Nirvana's Kurt Cobain. The accompanying video capitalized on Rossdale's lovely visage and turned the band into teen idols in the U.S. virtually overnight. Ironically, their success in England was far more gradual and limited. "Here it's been more of a natural growth," Pulsford noted of their homeland in a 1996 *huH* magazine interview. "In the States we were thrust into the big arena rather quickly."

More hits followed, notably the ballad "Glycerine" and the thundering anthem "Machine Head." Poor reviews and sniping from the hipper stratum of the rock world didn't seem to slow the album's momentum over the ensuing two years, and Bush won the Viewer's Choice

Award at the 1996 Video Music Awards. "I think that's kinda the award for us to win," Gavin said pointedly in his acceptance speech, "you know, we've always been the most favorite with the people out there, the real people, as opposed to the non-real people."

Though accusations abounded charging that Bush had exploited the hard-won inroads made by Nirvana and other alternative rock innovators, much of the criticism leveled at Bush in the wake of their phenomenal success had to do with their audience. Because many of their admirers were teenage girls who worshipped Gavin, Bush were derided as a pinup band. Goodridge even joked in *Details* about the band's importance in young girls' lives. "We're their first band," he declared, "so we'll take them hand in hand, write about their first boyfriend, their first heartbreak, the whole gamut of events." Later, he added, Bush would provide "a graduation record. After that, we'll have a rather directionless first-year-out-of-school album—that'll be an ambient, underwater thing. [Avant-garde musician and producer] Brian Eno can produce it."

Pinup Blues, Sophomore Album

Rossdale was somewhat more defensive about the issue of his looks. "You know," he mused in *Details,* some people might like the band because of things that have less to do with the music, and that doesn't flatter me. I was a musician for years, so if my appearance is all there is, then why wasn't I successful with my other bands? Because they weren't good enough." He was particularly angered by a *Rolling Stone* cover photo that showed him shirtless on a bed; next to this cheesecake pose, the magazine asked archly why Rossdale wasn't taken seriously. "They really sucker-punched me," he complained in an MTV profile, claiming that the magazine had promised not to use the shirtless shot on the cover. "They didn't need to f— me up like that," he groused.

Rossdale's public friendship with other celebrities also kept him in the news. Of special note, because of the Nirvana connection, was his appearance at various places with Courtney Love, Cobain's widow. Yet both have denied that they were romantically involved. Love—famous for eviscerating other celebs in interviews—confirmed what most people have observed in Rossdale: his decency. "He asked me not to say he's nice," she averred in *Spin.* "But I'm *me* and even I can't say anything mean about him." Rossdale also spent a great deal of time with Gwen Stefani, singer for the popular band No Doubt, and despite much press speculation, neither would declare that they were in a romantic relationship. "I have a somewhat ambiguous love life,"

Rossdale confirmed in *Details,* and seemed content to keep it that way for the time being.

Bush tempted further comparisons to Nirvana by hiring producer Steve Albini—the man who recorded Nirvana's second major-label effort—to work behind the boards on their sophomore album, *Razorblade Suitcase.* Released amid much advance hype in late 1996, the album got off to an auspicious start with the single "Swallowed." The *Los Angeles Times* indicated that the album was not a huge step forward for the band. Most of the songs, argued reviewer Sara Scribner, "are well-crafted diversions, never quite hooky or even memorable. Radio programmers will be pleased, but Bush isn't any closer to earning its hefty paycheck." It seemed that reviews would have, if anything, even less impact on *Razorblade's* success. Bush had cultivated a devoted fan base with the "real people," and was determined to hold onto it.

Selected discography

Sixteen Stone (includes "Everything Zen," "Glycerine," and "Machine Head"), Trauma/Interscope, 1994.
Razorblade Suitcase (includes "Swallowed"), Trauma/Interscope, 1996.

Sources

Details, July 1996.
huH, April 1996.
Los Angeles Times, November 17, 1996.
Rolling Stone, April 18, 1996.
Spin, December 1996.

Additional information was provided by materials from MTV Online, Bushnet and other Internet sites.

—*Simon Glickman*

Busta Rhymes

Rap singer

Without undue humility, said Busta Rhymes in the *Los Angeles Times*, "There's no bounds to rap music, and there's no limits to what Busta Rhymes can express." The unpredictable rapper—who first achieved fame as a teenager in the group Leaders of the New School—leapt into the first rank of hip-hop with his 1996 solo debut, *The Coming,* and its lead single, "Woo hah!! Got You All in Check." Busta's frantic delivery, explosive energy and outrageous attire cut through hip-hop's cool demeanor like a hot knife through butter. And unlike the gangsta-leaning MCs who dominated the first half of the 90s, he expressed impatience with street credibility. "I don't want to hear about this issue of keeping it real no more," he asserted in a record company biography. "It's all hype. It's time we all saw through it." He later commented, "I don't just represent a 20-block radius known as my 'hood," to *Los Angeles Times* writer Cheo Hodari Coker. "I represent the universe."

Busta—born Trevor Smith to a Jamaican mother and U.S.-born father in Brooklyn, New York—moved with his family to the suburbs of Long Island during his adolescence. While his deep, booming voice comes from his father, the rapper reported to Coker, "when it came down to discipline in my family, the true barker was Moms. That's where my real energetic side comes from." Only after he arrived in "Strong Island," as fellow natives and rap revolutionaries Public Enemy called the borough, did Busta began to dream of rhyming. "I was mad small," he recollected in Elektra Records press materials, "but I would start entering rap contests, lip synch contests, anything to show my skills." Fortunately, he claimed, hailing from Brooklyn stood him in good stead, since "Bronx, Brooklyn and Queens was where all the good hip hop was coming from at that time."

"C.L.A.M.P."

Busta was still in junior high school when he hooked up with another rapper, Charlie Brown. The pair eventually caught the attention of Public Enemy leader Chuck D. as well as the group's producers, Eric Sadler and Hank Shocklee. Sadler and Shocklee—known in the rap world as The Bomb Squad—helped the young Busta and his friends to refine their approach. As Busta noted in his bio, "Eric used to repeat this phrase to remind us what to concentrate on: C.L.A.M.P., which stood for Concept-Lyrics-Attitude-Music and Performance. He used to say when you get that down to a science, then you'll be there."

Refining this blend took some time, but Busta, Charlie, and their friend Dinco D. worked hard on their unison raps and choreography. After adding Busta's cousin

Custmaster Milo as a DJ, they found their identity as Leaders of the New School. With the assistance of Chuck D., the quartet landed a deal with Elektra in 1989. The group's debut album, *A Future Without a Past...*, appeared in 1991 and was hailed by *Spin* as "high-energy hip hop" that "recaptures some of the giddy joys of rap." Their 1993 follow-up, *T.I.M.E.,* also enjoyed critical raves. *The Source* deemed it "a rarity in hip-hop: a sophomore album that's better than the debut," and singled out Busta's work for special praise. "Busta get[s] buttnaked and wild," the magazine proclaimed; "he growls, grunts, chants and basically continues to break all musical rules." According to *Los Angeles Times* writer Coker, "the group brought a lively energy to its shows and recordings by performing singsong routines in unison rather than the normal rap pattern of just one or two main voices. The music was accompanied by lively choreographed stomps." The group also appeared as guests on an album by "Godfather of Soul" James Brown.

Cartoonish Persona

Busta has cited as influences not only old-school funk master George Clinton and rock guitar icon Jimi Hendrix but some other figures that are, if anything, even more animated. "Secret Squirrel, Tom and Jerry, Courageous Cat," he enumerated in *Spin,* adding some other cartoon favorites: "A lot of the old s--t, too—Popeye, Mighty Mouse. That s--t just stays on at my crib 24 hours [a day]." He was able to demonstrate the range of his own cartoonish funkateer persona after Leaders took a

hiatus in 1993. He put in guest appearances with R&B hitmakers Boyz II Men, hip hop explorers A Tribe Called Quest, and many others. "The rapper has proved virtual nitroglycerin as a guest star," noted *Spin* writer Chris Norris. Busta also lent his presence to several films, including John Singleton's university drama *Higher Learning* and the rap comedy *Who's the Man.*

Shortly after LONS took a break, Busta—a member of the Five Percent sect of Islam—saw the birth of his son, T'ziah. He dedicated his album to the memory of another, now deceased, son, Tahiem Jr., but has not discussed this loss in the press. He spent the next few years in Brooklyn experiencing what he described to *Spin's* Norris as "normal, middle-class, standard-living s—t like how I came up." By the time he'd completed his solo album, *The Coming,* T'ziah was three years old and—according to his proud papa—a delight. "That's the coolest age to be around kids," he told Norris. "They don't bicker, they're not looking for their moms, they just want to chill." It was the arrival of T'ziah, he insisted to Coker, that made the solo effort a necessity. "I would never have done a solo record voluntarily," he claimed. "I love the group, and we're still gonna record albums. But now that I've had the chance to flourish and to blossom, I'm gonna capitalize on the best of both worlds."

Blew Up with *The Coming*

Working with a variety of producers, Busta was able to expand his range on *The Coming.* "Usually when I'm rhyming," reads a quote from his Elektra biography, "I only get to rhyme 16 bars. Here I get to show other things. The record is energized on many different levels, including the Busta wild shit." In addition to the masssive "Woo hah!!," which was complemented by a frenetic, stylized video that earned heavy rotation on MTV, the album also features "It's a Party," a duet with female soul divas Zhané. Reviews of the album were mixed from a musical standpoint, but tended to celebrate Busta's vocal skills. *Rolling Stone* complained that "the mixes are simple, droopy and slow," but added that the rapper's "quavering rips and verbal acrobatics liven up the joint. He hurdles beats and measures in a single bound." Reviewer Eric Berman concluded, "Despite his musical shortcomings, Busta Rhymes is a master MC and one of hip-hop's most jovial and vivid personalities, whose creativity on the mike may give rap a much needed shot in the arm." Coker, reviewing the disc for the *Los Angeles Times,* found it "short on deep themes but long on dazzling displays of rhyme skill." He cited the recording as proof "that there are still compelling hip-hop records to be made without dramatic narratives or weighty social politics."

Busta toured behind *The Coming* in an omnibus rap show that also boasted the Fugees, Cypress Hill, and A Tribe Called Quest. He promised a reunion with his LONS mates before long, but in the short time expressed nothing but gratitude. "Every time my voice is recorded," he told Coker, "I'm extremely happy. Hiphop is paying my bills and feeding my family." Rather than cop an "arrogant attitude and mad face," he added, he wanted to emphasize his accessibility: "I want the whole world to feel like they can approach and embrace me."

Selected discography

With Leaders of the New School

A Future Without a Past..., Elektra, 1991.
James Brown, *Universal James* (appears on "Can't Get Any Harder"), Scotti Brothers, 1992.
T.I.M.E., Elektra, 1993.

Solo albums

The Coming (includes "Woo hah!! Got You All in Check" and "It's a Party"), Elektra, 1996.

Has also made guest appearances on recordings by Boyz II Men, A Tribe Called Quest, Craig Mack, Bounty Killer, and others.

Sources

Los Angeles Times, April 21, 1996; May 26, 1996; July 25, 1996.
Rolling Stone, May 2, 1996.
Source, November 1993.
Spin, July 1991; August 1996.
Vice, September 1996.

Additional information was provided by Elektra Records publicity materials, 1996.

—*Simon Glickman*

Cabaret Voltaire

Alternative rock band

An influence on many subsequent alternative bands, Cabaret Voltaire primarily used electronics and musical collage to create their high-tech sound. Originally, the group started as a trio of guitarist and synthesist Richard H. Kirk, singer and bassist Stephen Mallinder, and keyboardist and sampler Christopher Watkins. They got together in Sheffield, England in 1972, and named their band after a popular Dada hangout.

The Dada artists of the 1920s had invented the technique of collage as a form of chaotic artistic expression. Cabaret Voltaire infused their music with this influence by combining recorded samples of sounds, voices, and tape manipulations. Stephen Mallinder told Robert Payes in *Musician* that the band began with a desire "to annoy as many people as possible," and they have attempted to maintain that theme throughout their career. Jim Aikin and Kyle Kevorkian wrote in *Keyboard* magazine that Mallinder's vocals "vividly depict an age in which people are controlled by politicians, the media, and the military."

Cabaret Voltaire released its first recording in 1978, the EP *Extended Play*, on Rough Trade records. As the label's third single ever, *Extended Play* made both the band and the record company a popular success. The EP, which included a cover version of Lou Reed's song "Here She Comes Now," was described by a writer for *The Trouser Press Record Guide* as "unpredictable sounds and eerie, disembodied vocals manipulated over a very physical beat."

Expanded into Middle Eastern Influence

The following year, Cabaret Voltaire released two singles on Rough Trade, "Mix-Up" and "Nag, Nag, Nag." In 1980, the group put out a live record called *Live at the YMCA 27-10-79*, as well as three LPs: *Three Mantras*, *The Voice of America*, and *1974-1976*.

The first full-length recording, *Three Mantras*, includes influences from Arabic and other non-Western music, while *The Voice of America* combines new and old material. The title track of the latter, "The Voice of America/Damage Is Done," incorporates taped samples and sparse electronic sounds to artistically depict both the repressive and libertarian aspects of American life. The LP *1974-1976*, released on Industrial Records, includes a series of experiments and other material from Cabaret Voltaire's earliest days.

In 1980, Industrial released Richard H. Kirk's first solo LP, *Disposable Half-Truths*, beginning a series of side

For the Record . . .

Members include **Richard H. Kirk**, guitar, synthesizer, horns, clarinet; **Stephen Mallinder**, bass, vocals; and **Christopher Watkins** (left band without replacement, 1981), organ, tapes.

Band formed in 1972; signed with Rough Trade Records, 1978; released debut *Extended Play* EP, 1978; Watkins left band, 1981; released *Live in Sheffield* under the name Pressure Company, 1982; signed with Some Bizarre/Virgin Records, 1983; signed with Caroline Records, 1985; signed with EMI Manhattan Records, 1987; signed with Instinct Records, 1992; released trilogy: *Plasticity, International Language, The Conversation*, 1992-1994.

Addresses: *Record company*—Instinct/Caroline, 9838 Glenoaks Blvd., Sun Valley, CA 91352.

projects from the members of the band. Cabaret Voltaire continued their speedy recording schedule with three more LPs in 1981—*3 Crépuscule Tracks, Live at the Lyceum,* and *Red Mecca.* The two new recordings set a different trend in the group's sound, directed less toward art noise and more toward dance music. *Red Mecca* included a version of Henry Mancini's score for Orson Welles' *Touch of Evil.* Each of the other tracks featured a film title and played on the film noir theme.

One reviewer wrote in the *New Statesman,* "Cabaret Voltaire's *Red Mecca* is the first masterpiece of British electronic pop....It's the pulse of *Red Mecca* that can't be taken for granted: the beat shifts from sound to sound and so changes the implication—now crisp, now lethargic. The band's tricks are in the background—snatches of conversation, radio talk, meanings to be reached through the agitation."

New Decade Resulted in Duo

By the end of 1981, Chris Watkins decided to leave the band to work on English television. From that time on, Cabaret Voltaire became a duo featuring Kirk and Mallinder. On the 1982 recording *2x45* featuring two 12-inch EPs, Kirk and Mallinder took the band's direction toward a more naturalistic sound with an emphasis on acoustic instruments like the clarinet and saxophone (played by Richard H. Kirk). The duo also produced *Hai! Live in Japan* on Rough Trade that same year.

Continuing with side projects, Stephen Mallinder put out his first solo LP, *Pow-Wow,* on Fetish Records in 1982. Cabaret Voltaire also played a show to raise money for the Polish Solidarity union. Due to contractual obligations, however, they released *Live in Sheffield* under the name Pressure Company. The following year, Cabaret Voltaire left Rough Trade for a new record contract with Some Bizarre, a division of Virgin Records known for its eccentric music groups.

Kirk and Mallinder came out with *The Crackdown* in 1983 on Some Bizarre/Virgin. It included the singles "Sensoria" and "James Brown." The same year, Cabaret Voltaire created its own label called Doublevision. They released the soundtrack for Peter Care's film *Johnny Yes/No* (recorded prior to Watkins' departure) and Kirk's solo album *Time High Fiction* on the new label.

Launched U.S. Success

The mid-1980s brought Cabaret Voltaire some popularity in the United States. After the release of 1984's *Micro-Phonies,* the group played their first East Coast show at the Ritz in New York in May of 1985. They went on to release *Drinking Gasoline* and *The Arm of the Lord* on Caroline Records the same year. *The Arm of the Lord* was reissued on compact disc as *The Covenant, The Sword, and The Arm of the Lord,* and includes the songs "I Want You" and "Motion Rotation." Mallinder also released his second solo album, *Pow-Wow Plus* on Doublevision.

Cabaret Voltaire's prolific output slowed after 1985, following the release of the EP *The Drain Train.* Richard Kirk began to spend more time on his side projects that year with two solo albums, *Black Jesus Voice* and *Ugly Spirit.* Kirk and former Box singer Peter Hope joined together to record *Hoodoo Talk* on Native/Wax Trax!, which didn't hit the stores until 1988.

In 1987, Cabaret Voltaire signed their first deal with a major U.S. label, EMI Manhattan records. The LP *Code* included the guitar contribution of Bill Nelson and a co-producer, Adrian Sherwood. Sherwood contributed some foundation and structure to Cabaret Voltaire's usually chaotic style. One reviewer for *Musician* wrote: "This is anything but machine music... cybernetic as the Cab's sound may be, their sensibility is surprisingly pop, pulling appealing hooks from the microchip throb of 'Here to Go' or 'Sex, Money, Freaks.'"

During the same year, Rough Trade released a compilation of earlier material called *The Golden Moments of*

Cabaret Voltaire. This album heralded the band's first extended vacation. They had become frustrated with the corporate creative stranglehold they felt at EMI and left the label. Giant Records released another compilation in 1988 called *Eight Crépuscule Tracks,* consisting of three tracks from original versions, a few new singles, and a previously unreleased version of "The Theme from *Shaft.*" In 1990, Mute-Restless reissued Cabaret Voltaire's back catalog all the way back to the Rough Trade days, along with a double album of rarities and unreleased material called *Listen Up with Cabaret Voltaire* and *The Living Legends,* which contained early singles from their history as a trio.

Cabaret Voltaire returned in 1990 with their first original release in three years, *Groovy Laidback and Nasty* on Parlophone. By this time, some fans had thought the band had called it quits. The LP included several back-up singers along with a variety of collaborative co-producers. By 1992, the duo had signed a new deal with Instinct Records and released the first album of a trio titled *Plasticity.* Two discs in the collection, *International Language* and *The Conversation,* appeared in succeeding years. The latter returned Cabaret Voltaire to its earlier style by focusing more on pieces and textures than actual songs.

Always evolving and changing, the duo expressed their desire to remain innovative in *Keyboard* magazine. "As far as I'm concerned, once things become mainstream, it's time to move on," Kirk told Greg Rule. "It's time to change what you do. That's basically what Cabaret Voltaire has been about. It's always nice to try and stay a little bit ahead of the game. It probably means you'll never be rich, but it's an interesting position to be in, just the same."

Selected discography

Extended Play, Rough Trade, 1978.
Live at the YMCA 27-10-79, Rough Trade, 1980; reissued, Mute-Restless, 1990.
Three Mantras, Rough Trade, 1980; reissued Mute-Restless, 1990.
The Voice of America, Rough Trade, 1980; reissued Mute-Restless, 1990.
1974-1976, Industrial, 1980.
3 Crépuscule Tracks, Rough Trade, 1981.
Live at the Lyceum, Rough Trade, 1981; reissued, Mute-Restless, 1990.
Red Mecca, Rough Trade, 1981; reissued, Mute-Restless, 1990.
2 X 45, Rough Trade, 1982; reissued, Mute-Restless, 1990.
Hai! Live in Japan, Rough Trade, 1982; reissued, Mute-Restless, 1990.
The Crackdown, Some Bizarre/Virgin, 1983.
Johnny Yes/No, Doublevision, 1983; reissued, Mute-Restless, 1990.
Micro-Phonies, Some Bizarre/Virgin, 1984.
Drinking Gasoline, Caroline, 1985.
The Arm of the Lord, Caroline, 1985.
The Drain Train, Caroline, 1986; reissued, Mute-Restless, 1990.
Code, EMI-Manhattan, 1987.
The Golden Moments of Cabaret Voltaire, Rough Trade, 1987.
Eight Crépuscule Tracks, Giant, 1988.
Listen Up with Cabaret Voltaire, Mute-Restless, 1990.
The Living Legends, Mute-Restless, 1990.
Groovy, Laidback and Nasty, Parlophone, 1990.
Plasticity, Instinct, 1992.
International Language, Instinct, 1993.
The Conversation, Instinct, 1994.

Sources

Books

The Trouser Press Record Guide, Ira A. Robbins, editor, Collier Books, 1992.

Periodicals

Keyboard, February 1986, February 1988, April 1994.
Musician, September 1985, January 1988.
New Statesman, December 18, 1981.
Stereo Review, February 1988.

—Sonya Shelton

James Carter

Saxophonist

Many up-and-coming jazz players in the nineties fall into one of two major movements: the "conservative" neo-traditionalists or the "innovative" avant-gardists. Saxophone player James Carter has been claimed by spokesmen from both camps. Art Ensemble of Chicago member Lester Bowie, speaking for the avant-garde, told *Down Beat*, "He's the tenor player of the future. I haven't heard anyone who can touch him.... He can do just about anything he wants to do. He goes all the way back to the old swing, so he's very well versed." In the same *Down Beat* article, neo-traditionalist Wynton Marsalis enthused, "I think that James is a tremendous musician.... I'd have to say that in terms of talent, he's one of the top three or four kids that I've run across."

James Carter was born on January 3, 1969, in Detroit, Michigan. Music surrounded the Carter household; his mother played piano and violin, his brother Kevin was a guitarist with Parliament-Funkadelic, his oldest brother Robert was the lead vocalist for the soul band Nature's Divine, and his father listened to a wide variety of music. Carter told *Option*, "My father was a very stern critic on what was being played in the house radio-wise. B. B. King was his main cat, but I could wake up on any given day and hear all facets of music—Barry Manilow, Sly Stone, or Parliament-Funkadelic."

Childhood Beginnings

The first saxophone young Carter played was one owned by a boarder his family took in, Charles Green, who played with the group War. James's mother bought him an antique model, and his brother introduced him to Donald Washington, a private tutor whom Carter refers to as his "musical father." In addition to teaching James to play the saxophone, Washington exposed him to artists spanning the history of jazz, as well as other genres of music.

As a teenager, Carter honed his craft at the Blue Lake Fine Arts Camp and the Interlachen classical music camp. He toured Scandinavia in 1985 as a member of the Blue Lake Jazz Ensemble student band, then returned to Europe with the faculty band the Blue Lake Monster. That year, he met Wynton Marsalis and impressed him with the ability to recognize complex chords by ear with his back turned.

Carter met Lester Bowie in 1988 at a Detroit Institute of Arts event. A lack of musical opportunity in Detroit prompted Carter to move to New York, where Bowie was his first employer. In New York, James was noticed by bandleader Julius Hemphill, who was organizing a sextet of saxophonists. In addition to playing on Hemp-

For the Record . . .

Born James Carter, January 3, 1969, in Detroit, MI; married Tevis Williams, August 31, 1996.

Began playing saxophone c. 1980; recorded and toured with Lester Bowie Organ Ensemble, Julius Hemphill Sextet, and Mingus Big Band, c. 1990-1992; toured and recorded with his quartet, c. 1993-1996; appeared in film *Kansas City* with other jazz musicians, c. 1996.

Addresses: *Record company*—Atlantic Records, 75 Rockefeller Plaza, New York, NY 10019.

hill's 1990 work *Long Tongues: A Saxophone Opera*, Carter played on two sextet albums, *Fat Man and the Hard Blues* and *Five Chord Stud*. Reviewing the former, *Down Beat* commented: "The group plays the tar out of Hemphill's thick compositions, uniquely arranged with middle-rich (but never muddy) songs."

In 1993, following a year with Lester Bowie's Organ Ensemble, James Carter recorded his debut as a leader *J.C. On the Set*. This album featured bassist Jaribu Shahid and drummer Tani Tabbal, with whom Carter had played in high school. On the basis of that disc, *The Penguin Guide To Jazz* characterized Carter as "an accomplished multi-instrumentalist.... What's striking, on the strength of the three deployed here, is how much he sounds like himself on all of them, even when he's explicitly paying homage to saxophonists of the past."

A Virtuoso with Spirit

Carter's mastery of several reed instruments, as well as his ability to filter numerous influences through an individual voice, earned him a comparison to multi-reed player Roland Kirk. Columnist Gary Giddins wrote in the *Village Voice*: "In James Carter, we have at long last something of an heir to Kirk's scholastic understanding of the instrument's history, as well as virtuoso exuberance and capricious spirit. Carter is neither afraid to play to the gallery nor confound its assumptions. He can apparently play anything, projecting himself in timbres that range from plummy to guttural, from arch ripeness to unholy shrieking."

The 1995 ballad album *The Real Quietstorm* was followed by *Conversin' With the Elders*, on which Carter's quartet is joined by diverse guests. Among the contrib-utors were traditionalist Count Basie Orchestra veterans Harry "Sweets" Edison and Buddy Tate, as well as avant-gardists Lester Bowie, Hamiet Bluiett, and Detroit-based Larry Smith. The musicians reinterpret standards from the history of jazz, from big band classics "Moten Swing" and "Lester Leaps In" to Charlie Parker and John Coltrane standards, as well as a piece by composer Anthony Braxton. Buddy Tate commented about the recording sessions in *The Washington Post*: "Years ago, everybody wanted to be identified as himself.... [That's] what James has got—his own style, his own thing. He doesn't copy off anybody. He's going to go a long, long way."

Appeared in *Kansas City*

Carter's latest projects include his screen debut in Robert Altman's film *Kansas City* alongside many leading jazz players of the nineties. The film is set in 1934 during the swing era in Kansas City's jazz clubs, and the characters are modeled after musicians of that era. Carter's was inspired by Duke Ellington's tenor player Ben Webster. He commented on the sense of history in the film in *The Washington Post*: "The whole vibe was still there.... It's like everything came full circle, being involved with a project that's about Kansas City at a particular time that fostered the music that I have grown up listening to—from Jay McShann and Count Basie to Bird ad infinitum—and being part of something that will basically last forever—this gathering of musicians."

Carter is living up to the mountain of hype associated with his work. He summed up his philosophy to *Option*: "You can play all the right notes but you have to cultivate the spirit so the music grooves with some kind of nobility....If you're not going to take the music anywhere new you might as well stay home and listen to old records."

Selected discography

(With others), *Tough Young Tenors*, Antilles, 1991.
(With Julius Hemphill Sextet), *Fat Man and the Hard Blues*, Black Saint, 1991.
(With Lester Bowie), *The Organizer*, DIW, 1991.
(With Lester Bowie), *Funky T, Cool T*, DIW, 1992.
(With Julius Hemphill Sextet), *Five Chord Stud*, Black Saint, 1994.
J.C. On the Set, DIW, 1994.
Jurassic Classics, DIW, 1995.
The Real Quietstorm, Atlantic, 1995.
Conversin' With The Elders, Atlantic, 1996.

(With others), *Kansas City Original Motion Picture Soundtrack*,
   Verve, 1996.
(With Saxemble), *Saxemble*, Qwest, 1996.

Sources

Books

The Penguin Guide to Jazz on CD, LP, and Cassette, edited
   by Richard Cook and Brian Morton, Penguin, 1994.

Periodicals

Billboard, June 1, 1996.
Buffalo News, June 28, 1996.
Chicago Sun-Times, April 7, 1996; April 15, 1996.
Down Beat, December, 1992; November, 1994; April, 1995;
   September, 1995.
Entertainment, June 14, 1996.
Jazz Notes, Summer, 1996.
Minneapolis Star Tribune, April 11, 1996.
Option, May/June, 1996.
Rolling Stone, December 1, 1994; August 24, 1995.
St. Paul Pioneer Press, April 10, 1996.
Spin, April, 1996.
Village Voice, January 25, 1994; May 16, 1995; July 18, 1995.
Washington Post, June 30, 1996; July 3, 1996.

—James Powers

Catherine Wheel

Rock band

Commented Catherine Wheel's lead singer Rob Dickinson in a Web site interview with David S. Faris: "Believe it or not, we're not dour-faced young men." While it is true that this English band has been considered one of those "mope rock" or "shoe gazer bands"—full of angst and painful introspection—the band has moved away from those earlier descriptions as their music has developed. Dickinson added, "We spend most of our time having a reasonable amount of fun in this band. Musically, it's still quite difficult for us to be *chipper,* but that kind of English sense of humour which is somewhat sarcastic has kind of appeared now, maybe for the first time. I'm glad, because I think it's definitely part of what we are."

For several years Dickinson and Catherine Wheel mate Brian Futter played in different local bands together around the seaside town of Great Yarmouth, England. While playing with the short-lived Ten Angry Men, the pair met drummer Neil Sims. Dickinson then left his drumming behind and started to learn guitar. He and Futter began writing songs that they recorded on an 8 track machine in Futter's bedroom. Around June of 1990 the guys put an add in the paper looking for a bassist whose influences included bands like Stone Roses, My Bloody Valentine, and Ride. Dave Hawes answered the ad, they bonded, and Catherine Wheel was formed.

Signed after Their First Gig

Right away the band found a gig at the Arts Center in Norwich, England. The band frantically began to practice and tried to think of a name. They don't remember exactly what prompted Dickinson to suggest Catherine Wheel—the gruesome torture device that dates back to the fourth century—but they all liked the name.

It didn't take long for Catherine Wheel to get noticed. Their first gig was in September of 1990. The promoter for the venue, who also ran an indie label named Wilde Club Records, signed the band and helped them put out their first EP, *She's My Friend.* The album was released in January of 1991 and got rave reviews in various weekly music magazines. After one more EP on Wilde Club, the band was picked up by major label Fontana/Mercury.

In 1992 Catherine Wheel made their American debut with the album *Ferment. Rolling Stone's* Ted Drozdowski wrote: "Over that album's iron-fisted back beat, guitarists Rob Dickinson and Brian Futter spray-painted a 3-D day-glo rainbow through songs like the android sex fantasy 'Black Metallic,' the cut that raised their band

For the Record . . .

Members include **Rob Dickinson**, vocals and guitar; **Brian Futter**, guitar; **Dave Hawes**, bass; and **Neil Sims**, drums.

Band formed in 1990 in Great Yarmouth, England; released first EP, *She's My Friend*, on Wilde Club Records, 1991; signed with Fontana/Mercury Records and released major label debut, *Ferment,* 1992.

Addresses: *Record company*—Mercury Records, 825 Eighth Ave., New York, NY 10019. *Official web page*—http:\\www.catherinewheel.com.

from cultdom." *Chrome* followed in 1993. Drozdowski commented that on this album Catherine Wheel "threw dirt on the palette to create bitter sugar like 'Crank,' a spray of tuneful noise with lyrics about isolation." These first two releases generally led critics to place Catherine Wheel in the category of mope rock. In the *Boston Phoenix*, Drozdwoski called *Ferment* and *Chrome* "the best examples since Pink Floyd's heyday of what a great band with a broad palette can do within the rock genre."

Style Change

It wasn't until 1995 and the release of *Happy Days* that Catherine Wheel showed the world that they could not be easily categorized. Faris said that "*Happy Days* presents the group in a new state, one of unrestrained emotional expression, through their cranked-up, sped-up songs that pound out tight riffs rather than fueling their effects pedals into a distorted haze." *USA Today*'s Edna Gundersen, who gave the album three and a half stars, explained: "The upbeat title doesn't mean the brilliant British guitar band...abandoned its signature moodiness on this third and best album." If anything, the music just got harder.

Dickinson told Drozdowski in the *Phoenix*, "We didn't decide, 'The time is right—it's fashionable to make a hard-hitting heavy record.' I think it's much more than that. We toured an incredible amount over the last few years. And the energy of the band live became this very tangible, powerful thing." To Faris, Dickinson elaborated: "That's how our music changes, and that's how we change, through this touring process...we became radically different at the end of six months....I think that's why there is a quantum leap between these records."

The difference on *Happy Days* was immediately apparent. On the two albums before *Happy Days*, wrote the *New York Times*'s Jon Pareles, "many of Catherine Wheel's songs floated into a dazed introspection and solipsism. But now the band gets angry as well as depressed." *Entertainment Weekly* commented that "epic melodies merge with spiky punk and swelling pop, and the result is absolutely pummeling." Regarding the single "Waydown" and its video, *People*'s Jeremy Helligar wrote, "It sounds like a tense nervous headache, but it's catchy enough to send Catherine Wheel rolling right up the charts."

Found a Sense of Place

In 1996 Catherine Wheel released *Like Cats & Dogs,* an album consisting of previously unreleased tracks and outtakes from the band's relentless recording schedule. This interim release while the quartet began work on a new album was culled from a small portion of Catherine Wheel's accumulation of extra tracks on their UK EPs. *Like Cats & Dogs* effectively highlighted the other side of the group previously known only to the most ardent fans and import collectors. In his Mercury Records press materials, Dickinson recalled, "we were getting tons of inquiries from people in America who were frustrated about not being able to get hold of our singles from [England].... These more subconscious tracks are just as important as anything on our three albums and just as much the heart of the band."

In the *Phoenix*, Dickinson told Drozdowski, "For a rock band to have any sense of worth or substance, they have to have their own sense of place.... Now I feel very strongly that we have.... We've developed our own sort of entity, which is what any band is about." With each new development in their sound, the media and the public have taken more and more notice of these hard-to-classify English rockers. Far from the frightening images of a plane crash in the video for "Waydown," this band is just reaching cruising altitude.

Selected discography

She's My Friend (EP), Wilde Club Records, 1991.
Ferment (includes "Black Metallic"), Ferment/Mercury, 1992.
Chrome (includes "Crank"), Ferment/Mercury, 1993.
Happy Days (includes "Waydown"), Ferment/Mercury, 1995.

Sources

Boston Phoenix, May 26, 1995.
Entertainment Weekly, June 22, 1995.

Musician, September 1995.
New York Times, August 25, 1995; October 12, 1995.
People, June 12, 1995.
Rolling Stone, June 15, 1995.
USA Today, June 6, 1995.

Additional information for this profile was obtained from Mercury Records press materials, 1996, and from the World Wide Web.

—*Joanna Rubiner*

Paul Chambers

Bassist

Upon winning *Down Beat* magazine's 1956 "New Star Award," jazz bassist Paul Chambers entered the national spotlight as one of the finest young talents of the hard bop jazz scene. Best known for his eight-year tenure with Miles Davis, Chambers appeared as a guest recording artist with numerous musicians, including the debut albums of John Coltrane, Kenny Burrell, and Cannonball Adderly. His bass bow style was largely responsible for carrying forth the bowing approach pioneered by Jimmy Blanton, an early bassist with the Duke Ellington Orchestra, and reintroducing the arco or bowed style as a featured technique in the modern jazz idiom.

Paul Laurence Dunbar Chambers, Jr. was born on April 22, 1935, in Pittsburgh, Pennsylvania. While attending the Pittsburgh school system, Chambers took up music after one of his instructors selected him to play baritone horn. Following the death of his mother in 1948, Chambers went to live with his father in Detroit, where he switched to tuba and eventually pursued the study of the double bass. By 1952 he was receiving private lessons from a bassist in the Detroit Symphony Orchestra and, while attending Cass Technical High School, played in the school's symphony orchestra. During this time, Chambers's formal symphonic training coincided with a strong interest in bebop jazz. "I started to listen to Charlie Parker and Bud Powell at age fifteen," recalled Chambers in *Down Beat*. "At first I played along with

records and I used to try to pick out some of the things Parker...would do." As jazz critic Leonard Feather pointed out in the liner notes to the album *Whims of Chambers*, "Oscar Pettiford and Ray Brown, the first bassists [Chambers] admired, were followed in his book by Percy Heath, Milt Hinton and Wendell Marshall for their rhythm section work, Charles Mingus and George Duvivier for their technical powers and their efforts in broadening the scope of jazz bass. [Jimmy] Blanton, of course, is his all-time favorite."

Chambers's musical aspirations, however, were not shared by his father, who insisted he become a professional baseball player. When Chambers attempted to practice his instrument at the family home, his father expressed his disapproval by throwing his school-practice bass down the stairs. Determined to become a bassist, Chambers pursued his musical studies at the homes of pianists Hugh Lawson and Barry Harris. Chambers then embarked on a musical apprenticeship in Detroit's flourishing jazz club scene, performing with such artists as Thad Jones and Kenny Burrell at Klein's Show Bar, the Rouge Lounge, and the Bluebird Inn.

New York and Miles Davis Quintet

In 1955 Chambers went on tour with saxophonist Paul "Vice Pres" Quinchette. After his stint with Quinchette, he moved to New York and joined a group led by trombonists J.J. Johnson and Kai Winding. He then worked with pianist Benny Green's combo and George Wallington's group at Greenwich Village's Cafe Bohemia—a unit comprised of saxophonist Jackie McLean, trumpeter Donald Byrd, and drummer Art Taylor. Soon after, McLean brought Chambers to the attention of Miles Davis, who was seeking a bassist for his quintet. "Everybody was raving about Paul," recalled Davis in his memoir *Miles*.

After hearing Chambers, Davis immediately hired the young bassist for his quintet, which featured saxophonist Sonny Rollins, pianist Red Garland, and drummer Philly Joe Jones. As Jack Chambers noted in *Milestones I*, "Davis must have known from the beginning that he had put together a rhythm section of great potential. Chambers fitted in immediately with Garland and Jones." Following a few rehearsals, Davis's quintet opened at Café Bohemia. "Paul Chambers was the baby of the group," commented Davis in *Miles*, "being only twenty, but he was playing like he had been around forever."

By September of 1955 Rollins left Davis's quintet and was replaced by Philadelphia-born saxophonist John

Coltrane. In October of the same year, the newly formed quintet made their first recordings for Columbia while Miles was still under contract with Prestige. The group's first issued album, recorded in November of 1955, emerged as a set of fine ballads entitled *Miles*. In his original review of the album, Nat Hentoff, as quoted in the book *Milestones I*, stated that Chambers "lays down a rhythm that could carry an army band." The quintet subsequently recorded two 1956 sessions for Prestige which produced the albums *Cookin'* and *Relaxin'*. In describing the former album in *Hard Bop*, David Rosenthal wrote:"Garland, Chambers, and Jones comprised one of the most cohesive rhythm sections in the history of jazz, a trio closely attuned to each other and to Davis and Coltrane."

Material from the sessions also yielded two more albums, *Workin'* and *Steamin'*. With these early sessions, wrote Bill Cole in *Miles: The Early Years*, "Paul Chambers was setting the standard of double bass playing that would not be easily matched." Cole also noted the close working relationship between Chambers and his bandleader: "If Miles was going up the register, Chambers would be moving right along with him, suddenly stepping to a lower octave, giving the solo a funky street feeling."

Solo Recording Artist

With the periodic absence of Coltrane in March 1956, Davis brought in Sonny Rollins to record *Miles Davis Allstars*, a session backed by Chambers, pianist Tommy Flanagan, and drummer Art Taylor. As observed in *Modern Jazz*, "The Flanagan-Chambers-Taylor rhythm section was probably the lightest, most distinct rhythm section modern jazz had enjoyed up to that time. Paul Chambers brought a large, dark, buoyant, sound to the group." During his stint with Davis's quintet, Chambers also recorded several solo albums. In 1955 he cut *In Transition* with guest artists Pepper Adams and John Coltrane, who also appeared on his 1956 solo efforts *Paul Chambers* and *Whims of Chambers*, an effort which brought together the talents of Donald Byrd, John Coltrane, Kenny Burrell, Horace Silver, and Philly Joe Jones. His 1957 release, *Bass on Top*, featured Burrell and pianist Hank Jones.

In 1956 Chambers, Garland, Philly Joe Jones, and John Coltrane made a guest appearance on Sonny Rollins's Prestige album *Tenor Madness*. In September of 1957 Coltrane assembled the musicians for his only Blue Note album, *Blue Train*. Free to select his sidemen for the recording, Coltrane called upon Chambers and another former Detroiter, trombonist Curtis Fuller. "The rhythm section comprised of [pianist] Kenny Drew, Paul Chambers, and Philly Joe Jones is superb," wrote Robert Levin in the album's liner notes. "Drew is a blues rooted pianist with a swinging cohesive technique. Chambers and Jones are known primarily for their sparkling work with Miles Davis." Fuller, who often rehearsed with Coltrane, recalled in *Thinking Jazz* his creative association with Chambers: "Paul Chambers lived all the way in Brooklyn, and he would get in the subway and, gig or no gig, he would come over and practice. He got this thing from Koussevitsky—Poloniase in D Minor—and he'd say, 'Hey Curtis, let's play this one.' It wasn't written as a duet, but he would run that down together for three of four hours. A couple of days later, we'd come back and play it again. The whole thing was just so beautiful, the camaraderie."

During May of 1957, Chambers played bass on Davis's album *Miles Ahead*, a session for a large ensemble arranged by Gil Evans. In *Miles Davis: The Early Years*, Bill Cole discussed the role of the bass on Davis's and Evans's jazz orchestral effort: "[Chambers] plays many sequences with the tuba which are moving in opposite directions, handling them flawlessly in excellent intonation." In the summer of 1957, Chambers toured with Davis's group, which featured Sonny Rollins, Red Garland, and drummer Art Taylor. With the departure of Rollins and Taylor, Davis rehired Philly Joe Jones and eventually assembled a sextet fronted by the saxophones of Coltrane and Cannonball Adderly. Davis credited Chambers with, as stated in his memoir *Miles*, the pivotal role of "anchoring all [the] creative tension between the horns." Backed by the Garland-Chambers-Jones rhythm section, the sextet recorded Davis's

1958 album *Milestones*. In the album's liner notes, Charles Edward Smith wrote that Chambers's "rare beauty of tone is combined, in his playing, with an extraordinary technical gift and, underlying it, such a strong sense of swing that he could carry the rhythm all by himself."

In March of 1958 Chambers and drummer Jimmy Cobb, along with pianist Tommy Flanagan, made up the rhythm section for the album *Kenny Burrell and John Coltrane*. Included on the album is Flanagan's number "Big Paul" dedicated to Chambers. "Paul Chambers' walking introduction to the tune," observed Joe Goldberg in the album's liner notes, "brings back an entire era. Flanagan and Cobb slip easily under him, as if they have all the time in the world." After Philly Joe Jones left Davis's band in May 1958, Cobb joined Davis's quintet. In July and August of 1958, Davis and arranger Gil Evans brought in Chambers and tubaist Bill Barber to provide the low-end accompaniment for his orchestral jazz album *Porgy and Bess*. On the numbers "The Buzzard Song" and "Bess, You Is My Woman Now," observed Barry Kernfield in *The Blackwell Guide to Recorded Jazz*, Chambers and Barber "are paired together, but not as bass instruments; instead they play a jumpy low-pitched melody" intended to blend with Evans's score for the brass and woodwinds sections.

Further Explorations with Davis and Coltrane

During February 1959, the Kelly-Chambers-Cobb section backed Cannonball Adderly for his album *Cannonball Adderly Quintet in Chicago*. In March and April of the same year, Chambers and Cobb served as the core rhythm section for Davis's album *Kind of Blue*. One of the most influential recordings of the decade, *Kind of Blue* produced two standards, "So What" and "All Blues," both of which contain brilliant introductory statements by Chambers and pianist Bill Evans. Chambers's bass work on "So What" and "All Blues" became jazz classics that have found their way into the repertoire of nearly every modern jazz ensemble.

A month following the *Kind of Blue* session in 1959, Kelly and Chambers rejoined drummer Art Taylor for John Coltrane's groundbreaking album *Giant Steps*. On "Naima" Chambers provides the accompaniment on a composition that echoed Coltrane's later harmonic explorations. On *Giant Steps* Coltrane paid tribute to his friend Paul Chambers by including the minor blues entitled "Mr. P.C." In the album's liner notes Nat Hentoff wrote: "Paul Chambers ... provides excellent support ... [and] for insight into the bass' function, it might be valuable to go through the record once, paying attention primarily to Paul."

In 1960 Chambers continued his path as a studio musician. Within a ten-piece band setting, which included drummer Roy Haynes, he appeared on Oliver Nelson's acclaimed MCA album *Blues and the Abstract Truth*. He also appeared on Art Pepper's *Gettin' It Together* and Hank Mobley's *Roll Call* and *Work Out*, which found Chambers in the company of Wynton Kelly, Philly Joe Jones, and guitarist Grant Green.

Left Davis's Band

For Miles Davis's recording of the 1959 album *Someday My Prince Will Come*, Chambers and drummer Jimmy Cobb joined Jamaican-born pianist Wynton Kelly. The Kelly-Chambers-Cobb rhythm section also backed Davis for his historic 1961 live recordings at San Francisco's Blackhawk. That same year, the section's contributions were honored in the 1961 *Down Beat* poll that awarded Davis's unit Best Combo. While on the west coast in June 1962, the Kelly-Chambers-Cobb rhythm section—joined by saxophonist Johnny Griffin—backed Wes Montgomery for a live performance which appeared as Montgomery's Riverside album *Full House*.

In 1963 Chambers and Kelly left Davis's band. Davis later related, in *Miles*, the cause for Chambers's and Kelly's departure: "I was having trouble with them because they wanted more money and wanted to play their own music...and by this time they were in great demand." Soon afterward, Cobb also left Davis and joined Chambers and Kelly in the formation of a critically acclaimed trio.

In 1965 Chambers and drummer Art Blakey backed Hank Mobley for his album *The Turnaround*. In *The Guide to Classic Recorded Jazz*, Tom Piazza described the recording as "a strongly swinging set in which Mobley's toughest edge is brought out." Two years later, Chambers recorded several albums with saxophonist Sonny Criss and worked with pianist Barry Harris at New York's West Boondock Club. After years of heavy substance abuse, Chambers died from tuberculosis on January 4, 1969.

In the liner notes to *Giant Steps*, John Coltrane proclaimed Chambers "one of the greatest bass players in jazz." Indebted to earlier stylists such as Oscar Pettiford, Percy Heath, and Charles Mingus, Chambers pursued an individual style that accompanied hundreds of the finest jazz men of the hard bop school. Chambers's use of micro-tones, pitch inflection, and inventive chromatic figures exemplified an approach that scholars have termed a lyrical bass style. "He was the master of tempo," observed Bill Cole in *John Col-*

trane, "playing in any combination of changes and syncopated lines, and when he applied his revolutionary technique to medium tempo blues he was an unbeatable accompanist." With numerous and exceptional recordings to his credit, Chambers's musicianship continues to serve as a model for those who continue to pursue the art of jazz double bass.

Selected discography

High Step, Blue Note, 1955.
In Transition, Transition, 1955.
A Delegation from the East: Chambers' Music, Jazz West, 1956.
Just For Love, 1956.
Whims Of Chambers, Blue Note, 1956.
Bass on Top, Blue Note, 1957.
Chambers' Music, Blue Note, 1957.
The East/West Controversy, Xanadu, 1957.
Paul Chambers Quintet, Blue Note, 1957.
Ease It, Affinity, 1959.
Go, Vee Jay, 1959.
1st Bassman, Chameleon, 1960.

With Miles Davis

Miles, Prestige, 1956.
Relaxin', Prestige, 1956.
Cookin', Prestige, 1956.
Workin', Prestige, 1956.
Steamin', Prestige, 1956.
Round About Midnight, Columbia, 1956.
Collector's Items, recorded 1956.
Miles Ahead, Columbia, 1957.
Milestones, Columbia, 1958.
Porgy and Bess, Columbia, 1958.
Sketches of Spain, Columbia, 1960.
Someday My Prince Will Come, Columbia, 1961.
Miles Davis at Carnegie Hall, Columbia, 1961.

With John Coltrane

John Coltrane, Prestige.
Coltrane Plays For Lovers, Prestige, 1956.
John Coltrane With Hank Mobley—Two Tenors, Prestige, 1956.
John Coltrane—The First Trane, Prestige, 1957.
Traneing In, Prestige, 1957.
Blue Train, Blue Note, 1957.
Lush Life, Prestige, 1958.
The Believer, Prestige, 1958.
Stardust, Prestige, 1958.
The Master, Prestige, 1958.
Bahia, Prestige, 1958.
Soul Trane, Prestige.
Kenny Burrell and John Coltrane, 1958, reissued on Original Jazz Classics, 1987.
Bags and Trane, Atlantic, 1959.
Giant Steps, Atlantic, 1960.

With others

Presenting Cannonball Adderly, Savoy, 1955.
Sonny Rollins, *Tenor Madness*, Prestige, 1956.
Sonny Clark, *Sonny's Crib*, 1957.
Lee Morgan, *The Cooker*, Blue Note, 1957.
Wynton Kelly, *Kelly Blue*, Original Jazz Classics.
Wynton Kelly, *Smokin' at the Half Note*, Verve.
Hank Mobley, *Soul Station*, Blue Note.
Hank Mobley, *Roll Call*, Blue Note.
Johnny Griffin, *A Blowin' Session*, Blue Note, 1957.
Johnny Griffin, *Interplay For Two Tenors*, Prestige, 1957.
Cannonball Adderly Quintet in Chicago, Mercury 1958, reissued as *Cannonball & Coltrane*, 1961.
Oliver Nelson, *Blues and the Abstract Truth*, MCA, 1960.
Dexter Gordon, *Dexter Calling*, 1960.
Kenny Durham, *Whistle Stop*, Blue Note, 1961.
Art Pepper Gettin' It Together, Contemporary, 1961.
Wes Montgomery, *Full House*, Riverside, 1962.
Wes Montgomery: The Small Group Recordings.
Kenny Burrell, *Jazzmen From Detroit*, Savoy.

Sources

Books

Berliner, Paul F, *Thinking Jazz: The Infinitive Art of Improvisation*, University of Chicago Press, 1994.
Chambers, Jack, *Milestones I*, Beech Tree Books, 1985.
Cole, Bill, *John Coltrane*, Da Capo, 1993.
Cole, Bill, *Miles Davis: The Early Years*, Da Capo.
Davis, Miles and Quincy Troupe. *Miles, The Autobiography*, Simon & Schuster, 1989.
Kernfield, Barry, *The Blackwell Guide*, Oxford University Press, 1991.
Piazza, Tom, *The Guide to Classic Recorded Jazz*, University of Iowa Press, 1995.
Rosenthal, David H., *Hard Bop: Jazz and Black Music 1955-1965*, Oxford University Press, 1992.

Periodicals

Down Beat, January 11, 1956; March 7, 1956.

Additional information for this profile taken from liner notes by Leonard Feather, *Whims of Chambers*; Robert Levin, *Blue Train*; Charles Edward Smith, *Milestones*; Nat Hentoff, *Giant Steps*; and Joe Goldberg, *Kenny Burrell and John Coltrane*.

Personal interview with Carl Hill, Detroit, Michigan, September, 1996.

—John Cohassey

Vassar Clements

Singer, songwriter, violinist

MICHAEL OCHS ARCHIVES/Venice, CA

Since beginning his career as a session musician in Nashville, Tennessee during the 1960s, Vassar Clements has gone on to become perhaps the best-known fiddler in the United States, or perhaps the world. Renowned for his willingness to play music reflecting a wide range of genres—from traditional bluegrass and country, to pop, rock, swing, and even jazz—Clements has won numerous awards over the years since he first transcended his original status as a sideman and moved to center stage. With five Grammy nominations and more than 3,000 recorded performances to his credit, critics have—in reference to another world-class violinist—dubbed him the "Isaac Stern" of the fiddle. With a multi-dimensional, riveting, jazzy style that is characterized by a spontaneous, moody feel and a lighting-fast delivery, Clements does more than just perform a piece of music when he draws a bow across the strings of his eighteenth-century fiddle; he recreates it, reshapes it, gives it new life. In addition to his mastery of several musical instruments—including violin and viola, cello, string bass, guitar, mandolin, and banjo—he is also a prolific composer of instrumental music. Clements has accomplished all this despite the fact that he does not read a lick of music.

Born April 25, 1928, near Kinard, South Carolina, Clements was raised in Kissimmee, Florida. Although not considered traditional bluegrass country, Kissimmee provided the young Clements with a fertile musical background, thanks to Saturday-night radio shows like *Grand Ole Opry* and programs featuring some of the popular swing bands of the thirties and forties. As Clements recalled in a Vassillie Productions press release, "bands like Glenn Miller, Les Brown, Tommy Dorsey, Harry James, and Artie Shaw were very popular when I was a kid. I always loved rhythm so I guess in the back of my mind the swing and jazz subconsciously comes out when I play, because when I was learning I was always trying to emulate the big band sounds I heard on my fiddle."

Master of Country Violin

Although Clements began as a guitar player, he shifted his attention to the violin when a local band he was playing with needed a different sound. Unfamiliar with the instrument, he attempted to teach himself and eventually received some much needed assistance from famed bluegrass fiddler Chubby Wise, who had visited the Clements home to call on a friend. By the time he was 14 Clements had mastered the instrument. Determined to make music his life's work, he traveled to Nashville to audition for a seat in Bill Monroe's crack band, the Blue Grass Boys. Although he didn't have

For the Record . . .

Born April 25, 1928, near Kinard, SC; married; wife's name, Millie.

Began performing with Bill Monroe and the Blue Grass Boys, 1949-58; debuted on stage of Grand Ole Opry, 1949; toured with Jim and Jesse McReynolds, 1958-61; worked variously as a real estate salesman, mechanic, and potato chip franchise owner, 1962-67; performed as studio musician, Nashville, beginning 1967, appearing on more than 3,000 recordings; toured with Faron Young, 1968; toured with John Hartford and the Earl Scruggs Revue, 1968-72; performed on legendary *Will the Circle Be Unbroken* album, 1972; signed with Mercury Records, 1973; cameo appearance in film *Nashville*, 1975; performed with Jerry Garcia as part of group Old and In the Way, 1973; has toured or recorded with numerous musicians, including David Grisman, the Allman Brothers, the Byrds, the Grateful Dead, Paul McCartney, Linda Ronstadt, Doc Watson, and Bob Wills.

Awards: MRL Living Legend Award, 1991; RCA Honors Award for lifetime achievement in the recording arts; British Fiddlers award; five Grammy nominations, including 1987, for *Together at Last*.

Addresses: *Management*—Vassillie Productions, P.O. Box 567, Hermitage, TN 37076. *E-mail*—vassarmu@ ix.netcom.com.

any luck the first time he tried out for the taciturn Monroe, Clements found that persistence does indeed pay off. He finally got a gig with the late "Father of Bluegrass Music" when a telephone operator-friend told Clements that Monroe had been overheard saying that he was looking for a fiddle player. Joining the Blue Grass Boys in 1949, Clements remained with the bluegrass pioneer until 1958, when he left to perform with bluegrassers Jim and Jesse McReynolds, who toured the country demonstrating their famous cross-picking mandolin style in addition to being regulars on the stage of Nashville's Grand Ole Opry. By 1962, however, Clements was forced to leave the McReynolds brothers and sideline his musical career due to a battle with alcohol. With the help of family and friends, he was able to get his personal life back under control, and Clements moved to Nashville five years later with a renewed commitment to his music.

In Nashville, Clements worked as a session musician for various Music City recording studios. He also got a

steady gig playing tenor banjo at Nashville's Dixieland Landing Club. By 1969 he was on the road again, this time participating in singer Faron Young's touring band, while still performing solo dates when the opportunity arose. In 1971 Clements joined up with singer/songwriter John Hartford and his band, the Dobrolic Plectorial Society, to record *Aereo Plane*. While the group's innovative quasi-bluegrass stylings—which were popular with audiences at the historic first annual "Bean Blossom" bluegrass festival, organized in 1971 by Bill Monroe himself—foreshadowed "newgrass" music yet to come, Clements found himself out of a job by the end of the year when the group disbanded. Coincidentally, banjo wizard Earl Scruggs was in need of a fiddle player for his stage show, the Earl Scruggs Revue, and teamed up with Scruggs.

Will the Circle Be Unbroken

The 1960s and early 1970s saw a resurgence of interest in old-time American music, sparked in part by the Newport Folk Festivals of the late 1950s, the civil rights movement, and the work of musical traditionalists like Pete Seeger, Burl Ives, Odetta, and a host of other folk groups. The new generation of acoustic-based musicians inspired by earlier musical forms and instrumentation included singers like Bob Dylan, Joan Baez, and Joni Mitchell. One of the most important recordings to come out of this era was 1972's *Will the Circle Be Unbroken,* an album that featured the Nitty Gritty Dirt Band alongside such stellar country, bluegrass, and folk artists as Roy Acuff, Mother Maybelle Carter, Merle Travis, Jimmy Martin, Doc Watson, and Earl Scruggs. Attesting to his stature as a musician, Clements was asked to perform on fiddle. He agreed, and his stylings in such tunes as "Orange Blossom Special" and the Clements-penned "Lonesome Fiddle Blues"— later echoed on Charlie Daniels's smash crossover hit "The Devil Went Down to Georgia"—became classics. *Circle* went on to become a phenomenal country-pop crossover success.

Clements' work on *Circle* introduced his style to a younger, non-bluegrass audience and jump-started his own solo career as a progressive fiddler of "new acoustic" music. The fiddle virtuoso soon found himself on stage or in the studio with such diverse performers as the Allman Brothers, the Byrds, the Boston Pops, the Grateful Dead, Linda Ronstadt, Paul McCartney, and Jerry Jeff Walker. In 1973 he joined forces with newgrass mandolinist David Grisman, guitarist Peter Rowan, bassist John Kahn, and the Grateful Dead's Jerry Garcia—who cut his teeth on bluegrass banjo long before fronting the Dead—to record a live album, *Old and In the Way.* This popular recording further fueled

Clements's move towards a career as a soloist, and further spread the word about bluegrass music to younger audiences.

Solos into "New Acoustic" Music

In 1973 Clements signed with Mercury/Polygram records and released his first solo LP, 1975's *Vassar Clements.* In this recording he is joined by John McEuen, Charlie Daniels, and Hartford. Since then, Clements has recorded over 25 albums that span musical genres from bluegrass to jazz. In addition to promoting his own brand of what he terms "hillbilly jazz," he has continued to remain active in numerous projects, and was featured in a cameo performance in the Robert Altman film *Nashville,* released in 1975.

Moving increasingly to the edges of "country" in his creative projects, the jazz and swing influences that Clements absorbed during his youth allowed him to sideline as a jazz musician. *Once In a While* was recorded during a jam session with Dave Holland, John Abercrombie and Jimmy Cobb, all ex-band members of jazz master Miles Davis. 1987's *Together At Last,* with Italian jazz violin virtuoso Stéphane Grappelli, provided Clements with one of his five Grammy award nominations. Throughout the 1970s and 1980s Clements worked to broaden his musical experience beyond the traditional limits of his pre-*Circle* studio work. Clements first album of pure, traditional bluegrass music was *Grass Routes,* released on Rounder Records in 1992.

Clements's "hillbilly jazz" performances, even more than his work in country and bluegrass, continue to provide audiences with a true expression of his exceptional technical and creative abilities. Impossible to pigeonhole into one or even two musical genres, a complete list of Clements's extensive musical accomplishments reads like a musical melting pot. To say that Vassar Clements is a musicians' musician is an understatement. His modesty and professionalism have won him the admiration of critics, and the respect of his musical peers.

Selected discography

(With John Hartford and others) *Aereo Plane,* Warner, 1971.

(With the Nitty Gritty Dirt Band and others) *Will the Circle Be Unbroken,* United Artists, Vol. 1, 1972, Vol. 2, 1989.
Crossing the Catskills, Rounder, 1973.
(With Old and In the Way) *Old and In the Way,* BMG, 1973.
Vassar Clements, Mercury, 1975.
Superbow, Mercury, 1975.
Southern Hillbilly Waltzes, Rhythm, 1975.
(With David Bromberg) *Hillbilly Jazz,* Flying Fish, 1976.
Bluegrass Session, Flying Fish, 1977.
(With Jesse McReynolds and Buddy Spicher) *Nashville Jam,* Flying Fish, 1979.
Vassar, Mercury, 1980.
More Hillbilly Jazz, Flying Fish, 1980.
Westport Drive, Mind Dust, 1984.
Hillbilly Jazz Rides Again, Flying Fish, 1987.
(With Stéphane Grappelli) *Together at Last,* Flying Fish, 1987.
New Hillbilly Jazz, Shikata, 1988.
(With John Hartford and Dave Holland) *Clements, Hartford and Holland,* Rounder, 1988.
Grass Routes, Rounder, 1992.
(With others; and producer) *Saturday Night Shuffle: A Celebration of Merle Travis,* Shanachie, 1993.
(With John Abercrombie, Jimmy Cobb, and Dave Holland) *Once in a While,* Flying Fish.

Sources

Books

Editors of *Country Music* magazine, *Comprehensive Country Music Encyclopedia,* Random House, 1994.
Rosenberg, Neil V., *Bluegrass: A History,* University of Chicago Press, 1985.
Smith, Richard D., *Bluegrass: An Informal Guide,* a cappella books, 1995.

Periodicals

Bluegrass Unlimited, December 1990.
Nashville Tennessean, August 15, 1971.

Additional information for this profile was provided by Vassillie Productions.

—Pamela Shelton

Holly Cole

Singer

While Holly Cole's rebelliousness and eclectic taste may irritate some jazz purists, they have made her a cult figure in other circles. She can turn a piano bar standard like "I'll Be Seeing You" by Fain/Kahal—which normally evokes nostalgia for the "old familiar places" lovers have been—into a slow dirge about love's futility. When her ballad "Calling You" hit the airwaves in Japan in 1992, it quickly became the most requested song on Japanese radio. Cole attributes these different reactions to the anti-authoritarian subtext in her work, especially with regard to sexual politics. As she explained to *Maclean's* writer Nicholas Jennings, "I love it [in Japan]....The fans perceive me as a strong, independent woman who's in control of her career. That's not too shabby." Still, her attitude would not carry her far without the artistic gift of her voice. She complements her eccentric interpretations with a fluid vocal spectrum from low growls to a soaring upper register. In this way, her style is reminiscent of Ella Fitzgerald, one of her idols. For a jazz artist, Cole has always sold a lot of records—a fact that may also annoy aficionados of a more esoteric jazz style.

Wild Child

Holly Cole was born in Halifax, Nova Scotia in 1963. She is the only daughter of parents who were both business managers and enthusiastic amateur musicians. Her father Leon was a child prodigy on the piano and now hosts a radio show, *RSVP*, featuring classical music. He formerly worked as a radio executive for Canadian Broadcasting. Holly's mother Carolyn is a classically trained pianist and the director of the National Exhibition Centre, an arts center in Fredericton, New Brunswick, where Holly and her family lived during her youth. In Cole's family, music was as much a part of the daily routine as dinner or brushing your teeth. Other relatives shared the musical bug. Her grandfather, Bill "Bompie" Underwood, entertained the Canadian troops during World War II, and one of Cole's first memories was of Uncle Bompie playing "The Tennessee Waltz" on the accordion. She recorded that song later on the album *Don't Smoke in Bed.* This tapping of personal childhood memories is characteristic of Cole.

Holly was a wild child, the kind who did cartwheels in the house to shock the grownups. "I used to think it was great to see the reaction I could get," she told *Maclean's* in 1993; "Singing jazz got a similar response from my parents at first. I think I maybe did it partly out of rebelliousness." Her father tried to teach her the piano, but when she refused to practice, he eventually gave up trying to teach her the instrument. In school, she made teacher-parent conferences an ordeal for her parents. Holly's childhood friend Grace Bauer recalled her as loud and funny, a born troublemaker. Once Holly tried to get Bauer to drink unreconstituted lime juice to see how she would react. Her childhood friend also remembered an incident at a McDonald's restaurant when Holly asked to taste the milkshake of the man ahead of them in line. When the man hesitated to give it to her, Holly grabbed it and took a swig. The horrified patron got himself another drink.

In the Woods

During her childhood Cole found solace with the horses at a local stable. She got up at 6:00 in the morning to visit a horse that her parents boarded there, and after school, Holly would return to the stable and stay until nine o'clock. She loved the stable's equestrian events, and would sometimes camp out in the stalls overnight. As she said to Michael Posner of *Chatelaine,* "I was really in my own little world...as obsessed with riding as I am with music now." She had hoped to become a veterinarian.

These circumstances were disrupted when Cole's parents divorced in 1977. Consequently, the 14-year-old Holly was left without the refuge of her parents' musical home. Her initial response was to pay more attention to her horses and to deny the reality of the breakup. After a year, she moved to her maternal grandparents' home in New Brunswick. Perpetually dissatisfied, Holly took

For the Record . . .

Born in 1963, in Halifax, Nova Scotia; daughter of Leon (a Canadian Broadcasting Company executive) and Carolyn (an arts administrator) Cole; *Education:* attended Halifax West High School; briefly studied voice at Humber College, 1981.

Began singing in Toronto clubs, 1981; formed the Holly Cole Trio with pianist Aaron Davis and bassist David Piltch, 1985; premiered at Toronto's Stage Door Cafe and developed a cult following; first album, *Girl Talk,* went gold, selling 50,000 copies, 1990; signed with Manhattan Records and EMI Music; second album, *Blame It on My Youth,* also went gold, 1991; toured in Canada; released third album, *Don't Smoke in Bed;* won Japan's Grand Prix Gold Discs awards for Best Jazz Album and Best New Artist for *Don't Smoke in Bed,* 1993.

Addresses: Home—Toronto, Canada. *Record company*—Alert/EMI Records and Metro Blue/Capitol Records.

off to live with her 26-year-old boyfriend, a nonconformist who had built his own house in the woods. Once, she hitchhiked to Halifax West High School, but the distance and her lack of enthusiasm soon caused her to drop out.

Cole's continuing relationship with her brother Allen steered her back to music. On a trip to visit him at Boston's Berklee College of Music, where he was studying jazz piano, Holly first heard Sarah Vaughan and other female jazz singers. Now 17, Holly was infatuated. "I couldn't believe it," she recalled, according to *Chatelaine.* "I don't know what it was. Part of it was I needed a female role model, especially at that age." She listened to German cabaret music and began to envision herself as a performer. When Allen moved to Toronto, Canada in 1981, Holly moved there to stay with him. Although she originally intended to study voice at Humber College, she instead began to sing at local clubs.

Found Her Niche in Bar Scene

Holly was a hit on the bar scene in Toronto. She had finally found an outlet for her image-breaking spirit. Her interpretations were imaginative and impressed the musically knowledgeable Toronto crowd. Pianist Aaron

Davis heard her sing in 1985 and was so taken with her that he obtained her number and planned a meeting. Holly beat him to it by calling him the next day and setting up a gig. Holly was great in duets with the piano, scatting in and over the chords. Davis called his friend David Piltch, a bass player, and together they formed a group called the Holly Cole Trio. They began at the Stage Door Cafe in Toronto and soon had a devoted following. Holly's brassy and sassy onstage presence cemented the group's inventive jazz appeal.

The singer's social awareness is evident in her unsentimental treatment of classic love songs. The group's first album, *Girl Talk* (1990) features a cover of Lerner and Loewe's "On the Street Where You Live" that uses mechanical sound effects to give the song an ironic twist. Some were annoyed by the iconoclastic pose. *Down Beat* delivered a scathing review to the group's second album, *Blame It on My Youth* (1992), in which Cole's eccentric intonations struck the reviewer as amateurish. However, such criticism did not stop the album from finding an audience on three continents. In particular, Japanese listeners embraced the Holly Cole Trio; Japanese sales of *Blame It on My Youth* exceeded 100,000 copies. The group won the Best Jazz Album and Best New Artist awards at Japan's 1993 Grand Prix Gold Disc awards, the country's equivalent of the Grammys. Cole was even hired to do a jingle on Japanese television for an automobile manufacturer.

Onstage, dressed in a black evening gown, Holly Cole comes across as a sultry lounge singer with a wry attitude. She has found an audience that otherwise listens to pop acts. "I try to find the middle ground between the Judy Garland pool of tears and the completely controlled, robotic performance, " she told *Maclean's;* "And I think that the subtext that Aaron, David and I bring to the songs is often a lot more interesting than the in-your-face text." In 1995, the group released the album *Temptation* for Capitol Records, which continued her exploration of a surprisingly fertile commercial niche for off-beat jazz.

Selected discography

Girl Talk, Alert/EMI, 1990.
Blame It on My Youth, Manhattan/Capitol, 1992.
Don't Smoke in Bed, Manhattan/Capitol, 1993.
Temptation, Metro Blue/Capitol, 1995.
It Happened One Night, Metro Blue/Capitol, 1996.

Sources

Chatelaine, October 1993.
Down Beat, October 1992.

Entertainment Weekly, September 17, 1993; August 18, 1995.

Maclean's, July 19, 1993.

Stereo Review, March 1995.

—*Paula Scott*

Counting Crows

Rock band

Counting Crows made their debut in 1993 with *August and Everything After,* an album recorded in a cavernous Los Angeles mansion. The sound of the band—and the vocals of its burly frontman, the dreadlocked Adam Duritz—instantly drew comparisons to such earlier rock giants as Van Morrison and The Band. Some critics subsequently dismissed the band as derivative, but other reviewers contended that the group was a creative, talented addition to the rock music universe. As *Melody Maker* remarked, "Counting Crows are unashamedly steeped in a classic rock tradition, but there's nothing stale or hoary about this music. It's vibrant and alive, bright and brilliant in the here and now." While critics bickered about the merits of the album, music fans came down solidly in favor of the band, making *August and Everything After* one of the best-selling albums of 1994. In 1996 the band released a second album, *Recovering the Satellites,* that received a predominantly warm reception from critics and fans.

A New San Francisco Band

As the group's lead singer, chief songwriter, and cofounder (along with guitarist David Bryson), Duritz was easily the most visible and recognized member of Counting Crows. He was born in Baltimore, Maryland, but his doctor father relocated the family several times during his childhood. Duritz's family eventually wound up in the San Francisco area, where he met Bryson. The two quickly discovered that they shared a long-held passion for music. "It's been my life since fifth grade," Bryson said in *Guitar Player.* "I can't even imagine wanting to do anything else."

By 1991 Bryson and Duritz were playing San Francisco-area clubs as an acoustic, folk-oriented duo, but both wanted to start a full band. They soon recruited keyboard player Charlie Gillingham, drummer Steve Bowman, and bassist Matt Malley. Subsequent jam sessions encouraged the quintet to continue working together. Soon Counting Crows, as the band called itself, was playing to packed clubs throughout San Francisco. The steadily building buzz around the band attracted talent scouts from a number of major record labels, and the group eventually signed with Geffen.

After securing noted producer T-Bone Burnett to help guide them in the creation of their debut album, the band sequestered itself away in an empty, crumbling Los Angeles mansion. "We got in there and stripped the songs and each other down to the bone," Duritz told *Musician*'s Bill Flanagan. "It was a real painful process, but we needed to learn how to be a band. We needed to learn what it would really take to make this level of an album, what you have to demand of yourself. I had no idea. We knew what we wanted, but we didn't know what it was going to take." Two months later, the band had completed *August and Everything After.*

Debut Album Flies High

Released in September 1993, *August and Everything After* had an immediate impact, despite the fact that Duritz and the band had placed a number of restrictions on the marketing of the album (they successfully restrained Geffen from releasing a single from the album and quashed efforts to place advertisements in rock magazines). Instead, Counting Crows made certain that the band stood or fell on its own merits. "It's real natural that way," Duritz told Mark Brown of the *Knight Ridder/Tribune News Service.* "If you buy the record that way, you know you want to hear it. They have a lot of money invested with us. They're taking a risk. But it's working." Indeed, the album rose steadily up the charts, buoyed by the band's touring, a *Saturday Night Live* appearance, and the pervasive presence of their video for the song "Mr. Jones" on MTV and VH-1.

Another factor in the album's popularity (it eventually sold six million copies) was its largely favorable critical reaction. *Melody Maker* called *August and Everything After* "often awesomely assured, [an] exhilarating mix of soul, R&B, folk, country, and rock 'n' roll." *Time* reviewer Christopher John Farley concurred, commenting that

Band members include **Adam Duritz**, vocals, piano, harmonica (born August 1, 1964, in Baltimore, MD); **David Bryson**, guitar (born November 5, 1961); **Dan Vickrey**, guitar (born August 26, 1966, in Walnut Creek, CA); **Matt Malley**, bass (born July 4, 1963); **Charles Gillingham**, keyboards (born January 12, 1960, in Torrance, CA); **Ben Mize**, drums (born February 2, 1971). Vickrey joined band just before release of debut album, while Mize replaced **Steve Bowman** (born January 14, 1967), who played on *August and Everything After,* after its release.

Band formed by Duritz and Bryson in August 1991 in San Francisco, California; signed with Geffen records, 1992; performed Van Morrison song at Rock and Roll Hall of Fame induction ceremony, 1993; released *August and Everything After,* 1993; Duritz contributed vocals to "Going Back to Georgia" for Nanci Griffith's *The Flyer,* 1995; released *Recovering the Satellites,* 1996.

Addresses: *Fan club*—Counting Crows, P.O. Box 5008, Berkeley, CA 94705; *e-mail address:* http://countingcrows.com. *Record company*—Geffen Records, 9130 Sunset Blvd., Los Angeles, CA 90069-6197.

"the Crows' debut CD . . . shows that this Bay Area band is capable of creating credible, sometimes beautiful, rock 'n' roll." There were dissenting voices, however. One of the most venomous reviews of *August and Everything After* was submitted by *Entertainment Weekly*'s David Browne, who wrote that "it's bad enough that such blatant calculation has gone into the band's look. Even worse is the album itself. Sluggish and meandering, with tastefully correct organs and mandolins, the songs are mostly the sort of plodding, earnest 'rock music' usually made by men twice their age." He went on to call Duritz's lyrics "laughable attempts at rock lyrics-as-poetry."

A number of reviewers also commented on the similarity of Duritz's emotional singing style to that of Van Morrison, a comparison that greatly annoyed the Crows' lead man. "I really hate [the comparisons]," he told Brown. "I've gotten a lot of this flack. I threw one 'sha la la' in as a joke on the record. The next thing I know I'm the second coming of the Belfast Cowboy [a Morrison nickname]. I don't get it. I can see where I learned from his singing. [But] all these other writers jump on it as an

easy reference point....Where did I borrow from Van Morrison? Just singing emotionally? That seems an obvious given." Writing in *Musician,* Bill Flanagan called the Duritz-as-Morrison-imitator accusation "a dubious rap. Anyone who sings emotional soul-inflected vocals over acoustic guitar is going to sound a bit like Van....When the roll of Morrison imitators is called up yonder, Adam will be down in the middle of the list with Rickie Lee Jones, Joan Armatrading, and Bono—behind Seger, Springsteen, Costello, and the other twenty or thirty disciples we could all name if we had nothing else to do, or if it mattered."

Band Grapples with Newfound Fame

By mid-1994 Counting Crows was one of the best-known bands in America. However, the band—and especially Duritz—found that their new fame had a sometimes disconcerting flavor. "It's really wonderful to be able to do this art, this thing that I am so moved to do and support myself by doing it," Duritz remarked to Flanagan. "That's a real gift, a blessing not to be scoffed at. But at the same time, there's all these really crappy parts to it. You bare your soul to these people and you don't think about it when you do it, because it's what you do as a writer. But you're making millions of people your confidant. And then they expect to come talk to you and be your friend. That's hard." Unnerved by all the attention—and the suffocating coverage of his personal life (he has dated actresses Mary Louise Parker, Courteney Cox, and Jennifer Aniston during the past few years)—Duritz came down with a case of writer's block that lasted for the better part of two years.

For much of 1994 and 1995 Counting Crows stayed out of the studio, stymied by Duritz's struggles and a band-wide recognition that the stakes had become very large for them. "It's hard," Duritz admitted to Flanagan, "because if we make a misstep right now we'll carry it forever. You can become a great, great songwriter and never get that 'Cougar' out of your name."

Eventually, the Crows returned to recording, bolstered by a new batch of confessional, relationship-oriented songs from Duritz, who eventually worked through his writing difficulties. The result was *Recovering the Satellites,* released in the fall of 1996. Many critics echoed the thoughts of *Mojo* magazine, which characterized it as the "work of a considerably improved band." Anthony DeCurtis added in *Rolling Stone:* "In song after song, [Duritz] searches for what can last in a world that too often generates hopes and aspirations that only end in disappointment. . . . The past few years haven't been easy for this band, but there's much more to come. Counting Crows are here to stay."

Selected discography

August and Everything After, Geffen, 1993.
Recovering the Satellites, Geffen, 1996.

Sources

Audio, January 1994.
Entertainment Weekly, February 10, 1994.
Guitar Player, June 1994.
Knight-Ridder/Tribune News Service, December 20, 1993.
Melody Maker, March 5, 1994.
Mojo, November 1996.
Musician, May 1994.
New York Times, April 3, 1994.
People, October 21, 1996.
Pollstar, January 17, 1994.
Q, November 1996.
Rolling Stone, October 20, 1993; December 3, 1993; June 30,
    1994; November 28, 1996.
San Francisco Chronicle, April 10, 1994.
Spin, May 1994.
Time, February 14, 1994; October 21, 1996.

—Kevin Hillstrom

Sheryl Crow

Singer, songwriter

AP/Wide World Photos

After several years of back-up singing for established artists—and one aborted bid at launching a solo career—Sheryl Crow burst onto the pop music scene with 1993's *Tuesday Night Music Club,* a strong album that included two hit singles, "Leaving Las Vegas" and "All I Wanna Do." Blessed with a voice well suited to her rock and roll material and what *Rolling Stone*'s Elysa Gardner termed "naughty-cheerleader good looks," Crow became a ubiquitous presence on MTV and VH-1. In the fall of 1996, two years after her debut, Crow released a second album, *Sheryl Crow.* Well-received by both critics and the record-buying public, *Sheryl Crow* seemed to confirm that the singer had every intention of establishing herself as more than a one-album wonder.

Crow was born in 1962 in Kennett, Missouri, a sturdy Midwestern community that served as the backdrop for an outwardly normal childhood. "Sheryl was a cheerleader and a twirler," her sister Kathy recalled in an interview with *Rolling Stone*'s Fred Schruers. "She wasn't shy about getting out and doing something, even if it meant that she had to be out by herself doing it." But while Crow was a popular, athletic student who posted good grades, she endured many nights of what she would later call "sleep paralysis," a condition she shared with her mother. "There would be nights where I would be so afraid to go to sleep," she told Schruers. "In sleep paralysis, sometimes you get to the point where you are sure you're going to die in the dream, and your breathing stops and all that. It's a bizarre and twisted feeling where you feel completely paralyzed."

Headed to L.A.

After graduating from Kennett High School, Crow moved on to the University of Missouri and took music and education classes. After graduation, she relocated to St. Louis, where she spent her days working as a music teacher at an elementary school. Her nights, meanwhile, were spent singing lead vocals in a variety of local rock bands. In 1986 she abruptly left St. Louis for the West Coast, a move that stunned her family and friends. "I'd just broken up with a boy and I was really bummed out," Crow recalled in a conversation with *Newsweek*'s Karen Schoemer. "I got in my car with a box of tapes and I drove from Missouri out to L.A., 28 hours by myself, nonstop. I didn't know a soul in L.A. I pulled in on the 405 at 4:30 in the afternoon, and sat in traffic and just cried my eyes out. Like 'Oh my God, what have I done?'"

Crow's break came after only six months, however, when she crashed a closed audition and landed a job singing back-up for Michael Jackson's 1987 interna-

For the Record . . .

Born February 11, 1962, in Kennett, MO; daughter of Wendell (a lawyer and trumpeter) and Bernice (a piano teacher) Crow. *Education:* Received degree in piano and voice from University of Missouri at Columbia, c. 1984.

Played in Kennett-area bands in late 1970s, early 1980s; played in a Columbia, Missouri-based band called Cashmere; worked as elementary-school music teacher in St. Louis for two years; also sang and played keyboards in St. Louis-area bands; moved to Los Angeles, c. 1986; joined Michael Jackson's *Bad* tour as back-up singer, 1987-89; sang back-up for Don Henley, Rod Stewart, 1989; signed with A&M Records, 1991; released debut A&M album, *Tuesday Night Music Club,* 1994; performed on the 1995 USO tour for American troops stationed in Bosnia; released *Sheryl Crow,* September 1996.

Awards: Three Grammy Awards, including best new artist, for *Tuesday Night Music Club,* 1995.

Addresses: *Record company*—A&M Records, 1416 N. La Brea Ave., Hollywood, CA 90028.

tional concert tour. "Being a background singer—putting on a tight black dress and doing choreography—has very little to do with being a musician," she told Robert Seidenberg in *Entertainment Weekly.* "But I'd much rather have been doing that than slinging hamburgers somewhere." Yet at the conclusion of the tour—during which the tabloid press identified her as Jackson's lover—the exhausting pace of the tour caught up with her. Tired and wracked once again with depression, Crow endured several difficult months. "When I went through a really bad bout of depression, my mom would call, and my mom and I are very close," she told Schruers, "but she would call, and she would say, `You're a cute girl, you're smart, you've got everything in the world going for you,' and that would just make it worse. Because then it makes you even loathe yourself more for being sick."

Signed with Major Label

Late in 1989, Crow secured a job singing back-up for Don Henley, a gig that eventually led to work with Rod Stewart and several other big-name acts. Her studio session work soon caught the attention of A&M Records,

which signed her to a recording contract in 1991. Company executive Al Cafaro told Schruers that Crow was "a very, very strong person, with an ultimate, overriding confidence in herself, but constantly assessing where she's at and what's going on." The record company soon arranged to record a solo album for the young singer, but the final product was a mess. *Entertainment Weekly's* David Browne wrote that the album's "songs lumber from ersatz gospel to forced psychedelia; the production has the sterile glaze of `80s pop." Todd Gold, writing in *People,* similarly characterized it as a "slick, soulless album." Fortunately for Crow, the decidedly overproduced album was never released. "Had we put out the first bunch of tracks," Crow later told Schoemer, "I would never have been heard of again."

Crow eventually became friends with a group of L.A. musicians who informally jammed together under the name "Tuesday Night Music Club." Their sessions formed the basis—once A&M execs got wind of the sound—of what would become an album much more suited to everyone's liking. The record that became her 1993 debut, *Tuesday Night Music Club,* put together with the help of a stellar group of musicians and studio wizards that included David Baerwald, David Ricketts, Kevin Gilbert (Crow's boyfriend for a time), and Bill Bottrell. Over the course of just a few sessions the group constructed the outline for *Tuesday Night Music Club,* and Bottrell and Crow fleshed out the album over the next few months.

However, in the months following the album's release, Crow and a number of musicians who performed on the album clashed bitterly over a number of issues, from the nature of Crow's tour in support of the album (she recruited lesser-known musicians for the touring band to save money) to her false assertion on David Letterman's show that "Leaving Las Vegas" was autobiographical (Baerwald, a friend of soon-to-be-deceased *Leaving Las Vegas* novelist John O'Brien, had come up with the song's basic underpinnings).

Driven to establish herself as a legitimate talent, Crow toured tirelessly in the months following the album's release. "Sheryl toured her ass off," Cafaro told Schoemer. "Without that, none of your efforts at radio or video airplay have lasting impact." Indeed, Crow's touring helped give the second single, "All I Wanna Do," the fertile ground it needed to become a monster hit in the summer of 1994. After seven months of struggling to spur album sales, "All I Wanna Do" gave *Tuesday Night Music Club* the push it needed. Within a matter of weeks, the debut was a hit (eight million copies were eventually sold) and Crow had become a fixture on cable television's video-music channels. Critics noted that the attention was well-deserved. "Her melodic, quirky songs of sexual tension, fulfillment and harassment on *Tuesday Night Music Club* are both thoughtful and plain fun," wrote *Playboy*'s Vic Garbarini. David Hiltbrand, reviewing the album for *People,* compared Crow's singer/songwriter abilities to those of Rickie Lee Jones.

A subsequent appearance at Woodstock in 1994 further added to Crow's reputation, as did the three Grammy Awards she received in 1995, including one for Best New Artist of 1994. But after awhile she began to retreat somewhat from the public spotlight. "I was really, by the end of it, very overexposed," she told Schoemer in a 1996 interview with *Newsweek.* "I've said that it's really great for other female artists to look at me and know what not to do. Part of it was my own fault. I'm an accessible person. I'm willing to do whatever. Not for the fame, but I just kind of went along with it."

Silenced Critics with Follow-Up

In 1995 Crow began to lay the groundwork for her second album, mindful of persistent rumors that she would not have hit it big were it not for the talents of the other *Tuesday Night Music Club* musicians. The final result was 1996's *Sheryl Crow,* an album that established her as a talented artist in her own right. "While still working with collaborators," wrote *Rolling Stone*'s Gardner, "[Crow] operates more like a leader than a club member this time, writing a few songs independently and imbuing all of them with a greater sense of who she is and where she comes from. The lyrics seem grittier and more intimate...and the craftsmanship is strong and self-assured." *Entertainment Weekly*'s Browne lauded *Sheryl Crow* as "a loose, freewheeling yet remarkably robust album that tugs at your heart and feet—sometimes within the same tune."

The album was also controversial; one song, "Love Is a Good Thing," contained lyrics suggesting that guns sold at Wal-Mart stores sometimes find their way into the hands of children. Wal-Mart responded by banning the album from its shelves—a move that industry observers expect will cost Crow hundreds of thousands of dollars in sales, but Crow remained defiant. Indeed, in the weeks following *Sheryl Crow*'s release, the singer seemed more certain than ever of her musical direction and vision. "At the end of the day, I can play a Bob Dylan song and it will be a great song," she told Schoemer. "I hope that 25 years from now some young artist might play one of my songs and it might be a revelation in some way."

Selected discography

Tuesday Night Music Club, A&M, 1993.
Sheryl Crow, A&M, 1996.

Sources

Entertainment Weekly, October 14, 1994; February 24, 1995; September 27, 1996.
Knight-Ridder Tribune News Service, April 7, 1994.
Newsweek, October 24, 1994; September 16, 1996.
New York Times, March 12, 1995.
People, November 29, 1993; September 23, 1996.
Playboy, February 1995.
Rolling Stone, December 15, 1994; October 3, 1996; November 14, 1996.
Stereo Review, November 1993.
Time, March 13, 1995.
Wall Street Journal, September 11, 1996.

—Carol Brennan

Dave Matthews Band

Rock band

Recalling the first time he played with the musicians who would eventually fill out his band, Dave Matthews remarked in *Guitar World*, "We all got together just to jam and I was blown away.... I had never experienced anything like it before. What immediately appealed to me was the spontaneity of their playing. Everything just flows for them." The other musicians—violinist Boyd Tinsley, saxophonist LeRoi Moore, bass player Stefan Lessard, and drummer Carter Beauford—were excited by the results of that April 1991 gig as well, and within a matter of weeks the players coalesced under the banner of the Dave Matthews Band. The group quickly embarked on a wave of furious touring that sparked a devoted cult following and, a few years later, a contract with recording giant RCA. Since then, two well-received albums—1994's *Under the Table and Dreaming* and 1996's *Crash*—have firmly established the Dave Matthews Band as one of rock and roll's most talented and versatile musical groups.

Native of South Africa

Matthews was born in 1967 in Johannesburg, South Africa. The son of a physicist, he grew up in comfortable surroundings but was appalled by the country's political system of apartheid. By the time he graduated from high school, he had participated in a number of marches and other activities designed to end apartheid. "There would be people singing the most incredible music in the face of police with tear gas and bats," he recalled in an interview with the *Boston Globe*'s Steve Morse. "The singing gives a sense of being completely invincible, which is not true, but it *is* in a way. It keeps the spirit of the people up. A lot of that hope and spirit is going to save that country, and has enabled the guilty people there to be forgiven."

After graduating from high school, Matthews left for the United States, eventually settling in Charlottesville, Virginia, with his mother. "I got an inscription letter from the South African army and said, 'I'm out of here,'" he told *Guitar World*. "This, of course, was when apartheid still ruled, and I wasn't going to serve in that army." Over the next several years he worked on his songwriting and guitar playing, supporting himself as a bartender. After a while he became acquainted with LeRoi Moore and Carter Beauford, two highly regarded local jazz musicians. "I served both LeRoi and Carter a lot of drinks," Matthews recalled in *Guitar World*, "and somewhere along the way I told them about this tape I was making and asked if they'd be interested in doing some recording, maybe playing out a little. I didn't ask for any commitment—I wouldn't have dared. They were both

Band members include **Dave Matthews** (acoustic guitar and lead vocals), **Boyd Tinsley** (violin), **LeRoi Moore** (saxophone), **Stefan Lessard** (bass guitar), and **Carter Beauford** (drums).

Group formed in Charlottesville, Virginia, 1989; made first appearance as band in Charlottesville on Earth Day, April 1991; toured throughout early 1990s, including with H.O.R.D.E. festival; released *Remember Two Things* and EP *Recently* on own Bama Rags label; after signing with RCA, released *Under the Table and Dreaming,* 1994, which went triple platinum; participated in 1996 H.O.R.D.E. tour; released *Crash,* 1996.

Awards: Two Grammy Award nominations, 1994, for single "What Would You Say."

Addresses: *Agent*—Red Light Management, P.O. Box 1911, Charlottesville, VA 22903. *Record company*—RCA Records, 1540 Broadway, New York, NY 10036.

older than me, and much better musicians. And when I met Stefan [Lessard], he was some kind of bass prodigy. He was still in high school and was playing upright bass with both Carter and LeRoi, cats twice his age."

Birth of Dave Matthews Band

Once the musicians got together, they quickly realized that Matthews' pop-folk-African music sensibilities and the other players' jazz background made for a tantalizing mix. "We gelled in a really profound way," said Matthews in *Guitar World,* "and it was obvious to all of us that we should stick with it, keep exploring and see what we could come up with." A short time later, the musicians added violinist Boyd Tinsley to the stew, and the fledgling band began making plans to play live.

Over the next few years, the Dave Matthews Band became a fixture on the college concert circuit in the Southeastern United States. Dazzled by the band's high-energy stage presence and unquestioned musical chops, a devoted grassroots following soon emerged. As the band's visibility increased, much was made of Matthews' South African background, since three other members of the band—Moore, Beauford, and Tinsley—are black. However, Matthews expressed little patience with suggestions that the fact of his birthplace

somehow made their collaboration illegitimate. "It's such an absurd idea that by virtue of living in a place that I'm guilty of the sins," he told *huH* magazine, pointing out that the United States has had more than its share of problems with race relations. "My feelings are that South Africa is a raging example to the rest of the world—and most poignantly to America—on a way to deal with the issues of race. In a small period of time, they've done the most thorough and the most relentless purging; it's phenomenal. It's something that America has done the opposite of over the years: we're patching and hiding and shoving under the carpet....If you show the wounds, they have time to heal, but if you hide them, they just fester."

Major Label Debut

The band's blistering live shows, which were on full display during a couple of H.O.R.D.E. tours, where they shared the stage with such bands as Blues Traveler and Phish, soon gained the attention of major record labels. RCA eventually signed the band, and in 1994 the Dave Matthews Band unveiled their first major label effort, *Under the Table and Dreaming.* The album garnered largely favorable reviews from critics impressed with the band's instrumental facility and its unique blend of jazz, rock, and folk. *People* reviewer Geoffrey Welchman remarked that the album "has a beguiling sound all its own, a sound that mixes jazzy acoustic guitar riffs with spiraling sax solos." Buoyed by their live reputation and "What Would You Say," a catchy single that eventually garnered two Grammy nominations, *Under the Table and Dreaming* sold more than three million copies.

Two years later the Dave Matthews Band released their follow-up effort, *Crash.* In contrast to the band's first effort, *Crash* featured a heavier emphasis on electric guitar, courtesy of Matthew's friend, guitarist Tim Reynolds. As with its predecessor, however, the album was hailed as a funky hybrid of roots rock and freewheeling jazz fusion. *Los Angeles Times* reviewer Sara Scribner wrote that "Matthews mostly fuels *Crash* with the same sultry, loose-limbed offering of polyrhythmic, jazzy fusion" that marked the earlier album, and Andrew Abrahams commented in *People* that "as alternative music threatens to become just another bland pop category, the Dave Matthews Band successfully redefines it on its own eclectic terms." *Entertainment Weekly* agreed, noting that "to rock fans burned out on the hordes of Nirvana knockoffs and Hootie hopefuls, the Virginia-based quintet's ear-catching jazz-folk fusion must seem like an entirely new genre."

For his part, Matthews indicated that the band enjoyed putting together *Crash* more than their first RCA album.

"For [*Under the Table and Dreaming*], we did it by the book," he told Morse. "[*Crash*] is more by *our* book. We just got in a circle—reminiscent of our early rehearsals—and played to each other. There was a lot of creating as we went, a lot of jamming, and hours and hours of tape used up. And it really lent itself to an energy. There are very different songs from one to the next, but I feel there was a sensibility that stayed the same."

Armed with two lively, popular records and a devoted grassroots following, the members of the Dave Matthews Band are enjoying their stardom. But Matthews seemed to recognize that fame can be a fleeting thing. "This will pass," he told *huH* magazine. "It may be twenty-five years, it may be two years, who knows? I might go over the edge in a *week*. My time is temporary, so I'm going to make the most of it."

Selected discography

Remember Two Things, Bama Rag, 1993.

Under the Table and Dreaming, RCA, 1994.
Crash, RCA, 1996.

Sources

Baltimore Sun, April 25, 1996.
Boston Globe, April 26, 1996.
Detroit News and Free Press, April 28, 1996.
Entertainment Weekly, November 11, 1994; May 3, 1996.
Guitar Player, August 1996.
Los Angeles Times, April 28, 1996.
New York Post, April 30, 1996; June 11, 1996.
New York Times, May 26, 1996; June 11, 1996.
People, November 7, 1994; May 6, 1996.
Philadelphia Inquirer, June 8, 1996.
Rolling Stone, May 16, 1996; June 27, 1996.
Stereo Review, February 1995.

Additional information was gathered from RCA Records publicity materials, *Spin* magazine, *Guitar World* magazine, and *huH* magazine.

—*Laurie Collier Hillstrom*

Reverend Gary Davis

Singer, guitarist

MICHAEL OCHS ARCHIVES/Venice CA

Gary Davis's finger-picking guitar style influenced many other musicians, including Jerry Garcia, Ry Cooder, Dave Van Ronk, and Bob Dylan. These musicians in turn delivered his bluesy gospel message to a world-wide audience. Songs like "Baby, Can I Follow You Down," "Candy Man," and "Samson and Delilah" define the common perception of American folk blues. According to guitarist and author Stefan Grossman, Davis said he was three weeks old when he became blind from chemicals put in his eyes. Despite this affliction, he showed musical talent immediately, making his first guitar from a pie pan and a stick before he was ten.

One of eight children, Gary was raised by his grandmother on a farm near Greenville, South Carolina after his father decided that his mother could not care for him properly. In the South of the early 1900s street bands provided entertainment, often traveling through the small towns on wagons. The music the young Davis picked up on was a lively combination of spirituals sung in black churches, square dance music, and marches by popular figures such as John Phillips Sousa. Davis's distinctive style can be seen as an attempt to translate these types of music to the guitar. In an interview with Sam Charters, Davis said of his chosen instrument: "The first time I ever heard a guitar, I thought it was a brass band coming through. I was a small kid and I asked my mother what it was and she said that was a guitar."

Invented Showy Guitar Riffs

As a youth, Davis sang at the Center Raven Baptist Church in Gray Court, South Carolina. Later, he played in a string band in Greenville and learned to read Braille at the Cedar Springs School for Blind People in Spartanburg. After slipping on ice and breaking his wrist, the bones were set badly, and he was forced to play with an oddly cocked left hand. This may have become an advantage as it allowed him to finger the chords in a unique way. In 1931 Davis moved to Durham, North Carolina, where he met Blind Boy Fuller, another of many blind street musicians of the time. Music was often the only occupation available to these men and their ranks boasted such legendary figures as Blind Lemon Jefferson from Texas, Blind Eubie Blake, Georgia's Blind Willie McTell and Louisiana's Blind Willie Johnson. From the necessity of playing on the street came a style that was forceful and clear, with crowd-pleasing melodies around which the singer invented showy guitar riffs.

While in Durham, Davis met and married his first wife, but left her after discovering she had been unfaithful.

For the Record . . .

Born April 30, 1896 in Laurens County, SC; died May 5, 1972 in Hammenton, NJ; son of John and Evelina Davis; married Annie Bell Wright, 1937.

Started playing guitar at age six; became a street singer, playing ragtime, spirituals and dance music; moved to Durham, North Carolina, 1927; became an ordained Baptist minister, 1933; made first recordings with the American Record Company, 1935; moved to Mamaroneck, New York, then New York City, 1940; sang on the streets of Harlem and preached at the Missionary Baptist Connection Church; recorded on Stinson Records, Riverside, Prestige and Folkways; recorded *Harlem Street Spirituals*, Riverside Records, 1956; taught guitar to many aspiring musicians, such as Dave Van Ronk and the Grateful Dead's Bob Weir; toured Great Britain, 1964; appeared at Newport Folk Festival, 1968; appeared in movie *Black Roots*, 1970.

He then moved to Washington, North Carolina and became an ordained minister of the Free Baptist Connection Church in 1933. Davis and Blind Boy Fuller journeyed to New York City in 1935 to record for the American Record Company. Although Fuller and another blues singer, Bull City Red, were the more famous participants in these sessions, Davis was able to lay down 15 tracks, among them "I Saw the Light," "I Am the Light of the World," and "You Got to Go Down." Other musicians who recorded this brand of music, which came to be known as the "Piedmont style," included guitarist Brownie McGhee and his partner, harmonica player Sonny Terry.

In 1937 Davis married his second wife, Annie Wright, and together they moved to Mamaroneck, New York, where she found work as a housekeeper. The city's location on the Long Island Sound was close enough to New York City to put Davis in touch with the thriving music business there. He began to record again, making records for producer Moses Asch, and then for the record labels Folkways and Prestige. In 1940 Davis and his wife moved to Harlem to a house on 169th Street where they stayed for the next 18 years. There, Davis became a minister at New York's Missionary Baptist Connection Church and also taught guitar.

In 1974, Davis described his teaching style for *Blues Guitar:* "Your forefinger and your thumb—that's the striking hand, and your left hand is your leading hand. Your left hand tells your right hand what strings to touch,

what changes to make. That's the greatest help! You see, one hand can't do without the other." This finger-picking style was capable of maintaining a melodic line while inserting complex harmonies. "Soldiers Drill," for example, was an instrumental reworking of some Sousa marches. Davis used a large six-string guitar, which he affectionately called "Miss Gibson" after the guitar's manufacturer. Reverend Gary usually tuned the guitar to a relatively difficult E-B-G-D-A-E configuration rather than the "open" tuning favored by most of his fellow street musicians (who could make chords by simply barring across a fret). This provided him with a more complex set of chord possibilities. He alternated major chords and sevenths to give his music the dissonance characteristic of the blues, while picking a melody and variations of the melody. In the liner notes to Davis' album *Say No to the Devil*, critic Larry Cohn compared his instrumental virtuosity in this regard to that of classical guitarist Andres Segovia and banjo player Earl Scruggs.

Source of Genuine Down-Home Blues

Folk music experienced a popular revival in the late 1950s and early 1960s with a growing audience on college campuses and among hipsters in places like lower Manhattan's Greenwich Village. Peter, Paul and Mary recorded a successful version of Davis's "Samson and Delilah," also known as "If I Had My Own Way," originally a song by Blind Willie Johnson. Other young musicians eager to hear the genuine down-home blues flocked to Davis as well. David Bromberg, Taj Mahal, and Dave Van Ronk are among the many guitar players to absorb the Reverend Gary's phrases and intonations first-hand. Davis's guitar lessons at his house were often accompanied by food and drink; invariably, they contained pungent advice on many different subjects, especially religion. Davis was in his late fifties by this time, and played mostly gospel and traditional folk songs, having given up the lascivious saloon ditties of his youth.

The resurgence of American roots music and its practitioners found Davis performing at folk festivals around the country, including the Newport Folk Festival and the Philadelphia Folk Festival. His fame ultimately increased to the point that he was asked to tour Europe. Hearing him in 1962, English music critic Robert Tilling of *Jazz Journal* called him "one of the finest gospel, blues, ragtime guitarists and singers." In 1968 Davis bought a house in the New York City borough of Jamaica, Queens, and continued to teach and perform in the area, always accessible to scholars and the new generation of country blues guitarists. On May 5, 1972, he suffered a heart attack while on the way to a performance in Newtonville, New Jersey. He died at William Kessler Memorial Hospital and is buried in Rockville Cemetery in Lynbrook, New York.

More than two decades after his death, the influence of Reverend Gary Davis can still be felt. As each new generation is introduced to blues, folk, and other forms of traditional American music, Davis's signature guitar stylings and heartfelt vocals continue to move, entertain, and educate.

Selected discography

Harlem Street Spirituals, Riverside, 1956.
Reverend Gary Davis, Folkways, 1958.
Children of Zion, Kicking Mule, 1962.
Pure Religion and Bad Company, Smithsonian Folkways, 1962.
Pure Religion!, Prestige, 1962.
At Allegeny College, Document, 1964.
At Newport, Vanguard, 1965.
New Blues and Gospel, Biograph, 1971.
Say No to the Devil, Prestige/Bluesville, 1990.

Selected films

Blind Gary Davis (short),1964.
Black Roots, 1970.
Reverend Gary Davis, 1971.

Sources

Books

Cusic, Don, *The Sound of Light: A History of Gospel Music*, 1993.
Grossman, Stefan, *Rev. Gary Davis: Blues Guitar*, Oak Publications, 1974.
Grossman, Stefan, *Legends of Country Blues Guitar*, Mel Bay, 1995.
Tilling, Robert, *Oh, What a Beautiful City: A Tribute to Rev. Gary Davis*, 1993.

Periodicals

Acoustic Guitar, Nov./Dec., 1994
Blues Guitar, February 1974.
Cadence, May 1992.
Down Beat, August, 1991; August, 1992.
Folk Roots, June 1991, October 1991, March 1992.
Guitar Extra! 1971 (interview with Dave Van Ronk).
Jazz International, October, 1993.
Living Blues, July/Aug. 1991; July/Aug. 1992; Sept./Oct. 1992; Jan./Feb. 1993.
Musician, Feb, 1993.
New York Times, Dec. 11, 1994.
Rolling Stone, Aug. 8, 1991.
Sing Out!, No. 2, 1991; No. 2, 1992.

—*Paul Andersen*

dc Talk

Christian rock band

The Christian rock group dc Talk has led the recent surge in gospel music's popularity. The heartfelt lyrics and rap beat, as delivered by three young Christian men, put a positive and progressive spin on the previously stereotyped genre. Their spiritual leadership has led to incredible commercial success, both in religious sectors and the mainstream, and established them as a dominant act in the gospel industry.

Toby McKeehan, Kevin Smith, and Michael Tait became friends while attending Jerry Falwell's Liberty University in the mid-eighties in Lynchburg, Virginia. The moniker dc Talk was originally chosen as a reference to Washington, D.C., their stomping grounds while in school. Their record label, ForeFront, nonetheless promoted the initials as standing for "decent Christian," as a marketing effort to appeal to new listeners. In 1989 the group signed with ForeFront Records, moved to Tennessee, and released their self-titled debut album.

Nu Thang, the group's next album, was released in 1990. Distribution of both records was achieved mainly through Christian channels; dc Talk had sold over

AP/Wide World Photos

100,000 copies, and *Nu Thang* surpassed that, but the band was just beginning to tap into a wider market. In 1991 dc Talk toured with Michael W. Smith—one of Christian music's bestselling artists—as his opening act. Following the release of their "Rap, Rock, n' Soul" video, the group began to gain a larger audience.

Is "Christian Rap" an Oxymoron?

dc Talk's Christian rap sound surprised their audiences as the vulgarity and violence usually associated with the rap genre was nowhere to be found in the band's upbeat, optimistic lyrics proclaiming their love of God. The band has defended their use of a formerly stereotyped lewd form of music. McKeehan was quoted in *Christianity Today* as saying, "Rap music did not start out that bad....It's always been explicit, but it hasn't always been explicitly vulgar. This is something I love, and they're ruining it. So I said, hey, if they can make it explicitly vulgar, I can make it explicitly positive and Christian!"

dc Talk's musical focus has been toward reaffirming their Christian faith and sharing their beliefs with their audience. Their songs have been about family values, salvation through Christ, and racism. "Walls" was a gritty number that addressed racial disharmony often traditionally experienced even in churches. Smith, incidentally the only black member of the group, was quoted in *Christianity Today:*"We were singing at a high-school assembly in Jackson, Mississippi. The audience was split down the middle—whites on one side and blacks on the other. But at the end of the song, a white football player walked over and stood right next to a black football player, and they put their arms around each other. The crowd started cheering. It was incredible!"

The success of the band's third album, *Free At Last*, reflected the surge in popularity of dc Talk's sound. An appearance on the *Arsenio Hall Show* helped prompt high sales of the 1992 release, and the album went platinum. *Free At Last* dominated the *Billboard* CCM sales chart in 1993, holding at #1 for 34 weeks. The 1994 Grammy Award for Best Rock Gospel Album was awarded to dc Talk for *Free At Last*, securing their place in Christian music history.

Freak Wannabees

Jesus Freak, dc Talk's fourth album, was released in 1995. Their focus on the album was toward deeper, personal lyrics and a darker, more alternative sound. Tait was quoted in *Billboard*: "I feel that the core fan will continue to support us, and because of the material on this album, I think we'll gain new fans." He couldn't have been more right. The album *Jesus Freak* was preceded in release by the single with the same title. The great success of the single suggested the album's commercial possibilities, but ForeFront launched a mighty marketing campaign to assure high sales. This promotional boost, along with the group's 65-city tour, rewarded dc Talk with a their biggest hit yet. The album sold 85,000 copies in its first week on the market, breaking the record for Christian album sales. *Jesus Freak* soon went platinum and was nominated for the Grammy Award for Best Rock Gospel Album in 1997.

The album's title refers to the band's admiration of Jesus. While a "freak" in the seventies may have been frowned upon, dc Talk checked the dictionary and found that the word didn't dictate such a negative connotation. McKeehan was quoted in *USA Today* as saying, "The third definition and the one I cling to said: 'Freak: Noun. An ardent enthusiast.' So call me an ardent enthusiast of Jesus."

International fame soon followed. dc Talk toured Europe in 1996, discovering a devout following in Germany, Sweden, Ireland, and England. They also played on MTV Europe that year, and gained more worldwide exposure through their appearance on the internationally-televised *Billy Graham Crusade*. While dc Talk's fan base continued to grow, the music industry recognized the need for better promotion of their less commercial type of music. The growing success rate of gospel music astounded distributors who scrambled to cash in. Adam Sandler wrote in *Variety:* "Mainstream music execs took notice, recognizing that audiences for gospel/Christian music are increasing and the genre is showing gains in an otherwise stagnant industry."

In November of 1996, dc Talk signed a deal allowing Virgin Records to handle the secular releases of their recordings. Their Christian distribution remained with ForeFront Records. The split was a result of dc Talk's popularity with the mainstream audience, and Virgin Records' ability to reach that sector through both retail and radio channels. Virgin was also retained to release any solo projects by the individual members of the band. McKeehan was quoted as responding to the deal in *Billboard:* "Our main hope in the Virgin situation is that they can be that promotion and marketing arm into the mainstream that we've never had. We've always wanted our art to be out there for the world to hear, and this is a dream come true for us."

Selected discography

dc Talk, ForeFront Records, 1989.
Nu Thang, ForeFront Records, 1990.
Free At Last, ForeFront Records, 1992.
Jesus Freak, ForeFront Records, 1995.

Sources

Billboard, April 30, 1994; October 21, 1995; November 23, 1996.
Campus Life, January 1995.
Christianity Today, June 24, 1991.
USA Today, December 4, 1995.
Variety, April 1, 1996.

Additional information for this profile was obtained from ForeFront Records promotional materials.

—*Alison Jones*

Deep Forest

Ambient/techno duo

According to *Netbeat*, an Internet e-zine, Deep Forest's Michel Sanchez creates "patient reappropriations of distant sounds and moods that he makes his own before blending them with his roots, producing at the end a cheerful and sparkling 'ethno-introspective-ambient-world-music.'" In their 1993 debut album, Sanchez and musical partner Eric Mouquet melded the dance music popular in France's clubs—a distinctly modern internationalist beat—with the ancient rhythms and tones of the Pygmy tribes of Africa. In their second release, they integrated rhythms taken from European and Asian folk music again with a distinctly modern twist.

Michel Sanchez had grown up immersed in music. He played the accordion from the age of five years and became an organ virtuoso, studying classical music at the Conservatory. Later, his skills as a keyboardist made him a valuable studio session player, and he also found work in advertising. He was known as a Hammond organ specialist. The Hammond has been used extensively in jazz and pop for years to give a lush feel to compositions. It resonates with echoes from both the church and the carnival, a juxtaposition that seemed right to the young Frenchman. Herbie Hancock, whom Sanchez revered, utilized the organ to create a very appealing pop-inflected jazz. Nevertheless, Sanchez remained well grounded in a more classical repertoire, favoring the intellectual yet sensual approach in Ravel, Dutilleux, and Messiaen.

Eric Mouquet, by contrast, was self-taught. He hung out at a local music shop, playing the instruments on display; he also imitated the records his parents kept at home, experimenting with styles from Deep Purple to Bach. As a result, his taste was eclectic and wide-ranging. He liked progressive rock such as Yes and Genesis, as well as jazz players Chick Corea, Dizzy Gillespie, and John Coltrane. He eventually acquired enough skill to obtain work as a studio musician, and it was in this milieu that Mouquet met Sanchez. The two became friends and in 1991 worked together on a rhythm and blues project with Herbert Léonard. Sanchez played the organ, and Mouquet arranged as well as played and wrote the music.

Deep Forest came into being as a result of a trip Michel Sanchez took to Africa in 1991. His studies at the Paris Conservatory had kindled an interest in ethnic instrumentation and percussion, and he began to collect different examples on tape. He returned from Africa full of enthusiasm for tribal music he had been exposed to, especially Pygmy. Sanchez exposed fellow studio musician Mouquet to samples taken from UNESCO recordings. Mouquet was equally enamored and the two decided to integrate the music into a commercial project.

Mouquet was a fan of house music and the harsh metallic sounds of techno-pop. In the clubs, however, a new trend toward a more "world beat" sound was gaining in popularity, one that drew upon the gentler rhythms of reggae and ska. Mouquet and Sanchez set out to create a audio world based in traditional story telling and ritual dancing but also contemporary—a world like a rain forest, enigmatic but attentive, maternal, melodic. As a result of their excellent reputations as studio musicians, they were able to interest Columbia Records in their project. After signing with producers Dan Lacksman and Guilain Joncheray, they headed to the thirty-two track Synsound studio in Brussels, Belgium. Lacksman was a founding member of the techno-pop group Telex, whose "Moscow Disco" became an international underground hit during the 1970s. Other production credits to Lacksman's credit included records by new-wave cult favorites Sparks and Yellow Magic Orchestra.

In the studio, Mouquet and Sanchez wove voices from Burundi, Cameroon, Zaire, and Chad into an elaborate melodic structure lush with synthesizer harmonies and syncopation. The warm refrains and haunting choruses of the Pygmies are complemented by technological special effects on songs like "Hunting," "The First Twilight," "Savana Dance," and "White Whisper."

"Sweet Lullaby," however, became the best-known track on *Deep Forest*. With harmonized vocals set to a vaguely New Age rhythm, Sanchez and Mouquet used a synthesizer to give it a mysterious but catchy feel. "Sweet Lullaby" tells the story of a girl who attempts to quiet her little brother's crying by telling him his parents would not return if he cried. The song creates the atmosphere of an exotic world, escapist but strangely real. The song became an immediate hit in the underground music scene, then gradually gained a wider audience. Differing from most "ambient" tracks—a musical genre revived in the early Nineties to soothe ravers who have "danced themselves out"—"Sweet Lullaby" revealed Deep Forest's ability to retain a spiritual, melodic core inside music heavily dependent on studio technology.

Helped by the popularity of "Sweet Lullaby," *Deep Forest* soon reached the contemporary music charts. The album went double platinum in Australia and also sold well in Japan, Canada and Europe. In the United States, the album rose to number one in the *Billboard* Heatseekers Charts and earned a Grammy Award nomination—a rarity for a French production. Sales eventually reached more than a million-and-a-half copies worldwide, and from the profits Sanchez and Mouquet made a contribution to the Pygmy Fund, a charity to aid the embattled African tribes.

In 1995 Deep Forest released an equally well received follow-up, *Boheme.* Repeating their success with taking unusual musical forms and integrating them with modern technology, Sanchez and Mouquet sampled rhythms from Eastern Europe and Asia and blended them with studio wizardry. A Mongolian choral group sings on "Gathering," for instance, but much of the vocals were performed by a Hungarian chanteuse named Marta Sebasteyenne. One track, "Marta's Song," was described as a "misty mountain chant" by *People* reviewer David Hiltbrand. The track was later included on the soundtrack to the 1995 Robert Altman film *Ready-to-Wear (Pret-a-Porter).* "The juxtaposition of the music's mild-mannered throb and the pinched, nasal throat-singing style makes for quirky ear candy," asserted David Browne in an *Entertainment Weekly* review of *Boheme.*

Though some may question Deep Forest's appreciation of tribal music beyond its commercial potential, Sanchez and Mouquet seem to approach and give their sources the proper respect. In the final analysis, they never presumed their work to be a serious scientific, anthropological expedition, but rather an artistic one.

Selected discography

Deep Forest, Columbia, 1993.
Boheme, Columbia, 1995.

Sources

Audio, December 1991.
Billboard, February 12, 1993; March 27, 1993; June 5, 1993; February 19, 1994.
Entertainment Weekly, December 16, 1994, p. 64; June 2, 1995, p. 54.
Melody Maker, June 30, 1993; February 12, 1994.
New York Times, February 20, 1994.
People, January 16, 1995, p. 23; June 26, 1995, p. 28.
Rolling Stone, April 21, 1994, p. 26.

Additional information for this profile was obtained from the *Deep Forest Home Page* (http://pages.prodigy.com/vista_designs/df_1.htm), Vista Designs, 1996, and a 1996 article in *Netbeat* (http://www.netbeat.com/), 1996.

—Paul Anderson

Del Amitri

Pop band

The blend of acoustic and electric instrumentation, rustic touches, and clever lyrics that characterize Del Amitri's music has made the Scottish pop ensemble difficult to categorize. Despite several successful singles and consistently positive critical notices, the band's sound had seemingly failed to capture the ear of the mainstream listening audience. Since their start in Glasgow in 1983, Del Amitri's music has changed subtly over time, becoming rougher and harder, but this has been a long-term artistic goal rather than an attempt to achieve a prescribed sound. In 1990 Justin Currie, the band's lead singer, told the *Chicago Sun-Times* that the band members felt that the key to success would be "to either have the arrogance or the stupidity not to listen to what other people say....If you allow people to manipulate you into doing things you don't want to do, then I think you're cheating yourselves and the people who buy your records."

Currie writes the majority of Del Amitri's material and almost always serves as the band's spokesperson. He comes across as clever, cynical, and bluntly modest. In

an A&M press release, Currie mused: "Obviously a lot of our songs are quite poppy. But we always set out to make something that sounds like a cross between Neil Young, the Beatles, and the Undertones. It never ends up sounding like that—it always ends up sounding like a pop album, and quite bland." In another instance, the singer-songwriter compared his craft to dishwashing and juggling. The harder, more cynical side of Currie is revealed in his lyrics, as in the line from the album *Waking Hours,* "Whole generations thinking of themselves as infidels and pop stars/While the bomb loses patience we line up and just lean against the bar." Often his songwriting leans toward the dark and melancholy, whether he's reflecting on social problems or heartbreak.

"From the Womb"

As a teenager, Currie, with guitarist Iain Harvie, formed the band in Glasgow in 1983. They adopted the name Del Amitri ("from the womb" in Greek) and recruited Bryan Tolland on guitar and Paul Tyagi as a drummer. The fledgling band recorded "Sense Sickness" with the No Strings independent label, toured with groups such as the Fall and the Smiths, and recorded sessions with

famed British DJ John Peel. By the time Del Amitri signed with Chrysalis Records to record their first album, a new line-up was in evidence, with Tolland joined by second guitarist David Cummings and drummer Brian McDermott replacing Tyagi.

Expectations for Del Amitri were high. Prior to recording their 1985 self-titled release, the band appeared on the cover of *Melody Maker.* The magazine labeled Del Amitri as the next British group expected to achieve international stardom. However, conflict subsequently arose between the band and Chrysalis, and the band's prospects skidded to a halt. In an attempt to revive their fortunes, an independent Del Amitri went on the road with the help of a large fan base, who booked and promoted Del Amitri shows themselves. In 1986 the band toured the United States playing borrowed instruments; the success of this tour resulted in a contract with A&M Records the following year.

Two Happy Songs, One Regular Party Album

In 1990 Del Amitri released its second album, *Waking Hours,* which Michael Rubiner described in *Rolling Stone* as an "exercise in melodic, midtempo guitar rock, leavened with folk and country," adding that "the record is more heartland fare than nouvelle cuisine: unhip, maybe an honest meal." After bemoaning the long lapse between Del Amitri's recordings, *Stereo Review* writer Parke Puterbaugh assessed the album as "honest, wise, and charming" and the band "as winsomely enthusiastic as ever." In the attempt to describe Del Amitri's music, other reviewers have drawn comparisons to Jackson Browne, Steely Dan, and the Beatles; in articles written during the early 1990s, they were often yoked stylistically to their labelmates, the Gin Blossoms. Yet Del Amitri's lyrics have always drawn especial praise from critics; *People's* Jeremy Helligar asserted that the "band's take on heartache has always sounded authentic and impressively clever." Michael Lipton noted in *Request* that Currie and Harvie "appear to draw from a bottomless well of inspiration."

Further proof that the band's fortunes were on the rebound came with their next recording. In 1992 the band produced *Change Everything,* an album that went platinum and included the Billboard Top 40 hit "Always the Last to Know." Writing for Los Angeles's *Daily News,* Bruce Britt called the recording "a refreshing collection of unabashed pop tunes." On this album, Currie, Harvey, Cummings, and McDermott were joined by keyboard player Andy Alston. When Del Amitri recorded their next album, *Twisted,* the band's roster included Currie, Harvie, and Alston, as well as newcomers Jon McLoughlin on guitar and Ashley Soan on drums. This album was touted as a solid follow-up to *Change Everything* as well as an artistic high point for the band. In a *Billboard* interview, Currie proudly noted the stylistic changes evident on this album: "If you're a melodic band, as we are, it's very easy to sound twee....This is the first time we've been able to make a record as raucous as we wanted to." Guitarist Iain Harvie pointed out the thematic shift in *Twisted* in an A&M press release: "On the previous album, Justin just sort of hid in his bedroom and wrote miserable songs....[*Twisted*]'s got two happy songs on it....For us, that's a regular party album."

"A Band, a Guy, or an Italian Dish?'"

With *Twisted,* A&M prepared to give Del Amitri the extra push needed to increase recognition. Product manager Brad Pollack described the band's identity problem in *Billboard:* "It's like, `Is Del Amitri a band, a guy, an Italian dish?'" The record label planned to mount an extensive in-store promotion to lure record shoppers. Despite these problems, Del Amitri appears to have at long last found its audience. David Sprague noted in *Billboard* that the band has benefited from a growing "mature-yet-adventurous" group of adult listeners who support fringe bands such as Del Amitri; Sprague suggested, "Now that `adult' and `hip' can be used in the same description without a trace of irony, Glasgow's Del Amitri may finally attain its long-predicted American breakthrough." Del Amitri responded by pursuing business as usual. In 1996, after finishing yet another tour, the band returned to the recording studio.

Selected discography

Del Amitri, Chrysalis, 1985.
Waking Hours, A&M, 1990.
Change Everything, A&M, 1992.
Twisted, A&M, 1995.

Sources

Books

The Guinness Encyclopedia of Popular Music, edited by Colin Larkin, Guinness Publishing, 1995.

Periodicals

Billboard, January 21, 1995, p. 15.
Chicago Sun-Times, May 25, 1990.
Daily News (Los Angeles), October 14, 1992.
People, March 20, 1995, p. 22.
Press-Enterprise (Riverside, CA), April 24, 1996.
Request, April 1995.
Rolling Stone, October 29, 1992, pp. 65-67.
Stereo Review, July 1990, pp. 80-81.

Additional information for this profile was obtained from A&M Records publicity materials, 1995.

—*Paula Pyzik Scott*

Herb Ellis

Guitarist

John Reeves Photography

He's played with them all—bar groups, college bands, big bands at the end of their exciting era, great jazz trios, popular vocalists, studio bands and top-rated television shows. Since 1941, guitarist Herb Ellis has demonstrated a level of playing that is remarkable both for its consistency of swinging rhythm and inventive solo work. Largely self-taught, the guitarist developed commanding technique and sensitivity. Thus armed, the versatile player could help drive the Oscar Peterson Trio through some of its most up-tempo tunes, accompany Ella Fitzgerald on the most tender ballad or contribute to a demanding recording or television studio scene.

Ellis began playing harmonica and banjo at an early age, but switched when he was eight or nine years old to guitar, spending much of his free time practicing. By the time he entered North Texas State College in 1939, long before that school became the mecca for jazz students, Ellis came under the spell of Charlie Christian, the great guitar innovator whose solos and compositions contributed so much to the Benny Goodman band in 1939-41. Christian's single-string amplified solos changed jazz guitar for all time; his strong rhythm guitar was often overlooked, but not by Ellis. Also enrolled at North Texas State were such upcoming jazz luminaries as reedman Jimmy Giuffre, composer/trumpeter Gene Roland, and bassist Harry Babasin.

Traveling and Recording Extensively

Leaving college in 1941, Ellis joined a band of players from the University of Kansas, stayed with them for about six months, then moved to Kansas City, Missouri, for a period of seasoning during which he developed his style. There he played in the various clubs that remained intact from the seminal days of KC jazz. His session mates there included an emerging Charlie Parker, in his pre-bop mode. The big dance bands were still in vogue when Ellis joined Glen Gray and the Casa Lorna Orchestra, an established band with jazz overtones, in 1944. Here he met pianist Lou Carter, with whom he switched to the more popular band of Jimmy Dorsey. Soon bassist/violinist Johnny Frigo joined this band.

Ellis remained with Dorsey through 1947, traveling and recording extensively, and playing in dance halls and movie palaces. Then came a dramatic turnabout that changed Ellis's career forever. As pianist Lou Carter told this writer in a 1996 interview, "The Dorsey band had a six-week hole in the schedule. The three of us had played together some with the big band. John Frigol, who had already left the band, knew the owner of the Peter Stuyvesant Hotel in Buffalo. We went in there and stayed six months. And that's how the Soft Winds were born."

The Soft Winds Flow

The Soft Winds were an elegant musical trio of kindred souls. Ellis, Carter and Frigo, who then played violin only occasionally, but who has laid aside his bass in recent years to become perhaps the premier jazz violinist, developed an enduring vocal and jazz trio style. The band's sound is sometimes compared to the more popular Page Cavanaugh Trio, a commercially successful group that hesitantly played opposite the Winds in one concert setting. The Soft Winds remained together until 1953, never quite achieving a level of success that their musicality deserved. Their records for Majestic stressed the unison vocal arrangements in their repertoire, often ignoring the swinging, tasteful jazz offerings heard in live performances. "We played six nights a week and practiced five days a week," averred both Ellis and Carter, in developing their fugal, contrapuntal head arrangements.

One frequent sitter-in on the Buffalo stint was pianist Oscar Peterson, who usually joined in on Sunday nights, when his trio's Toronto gigs were precluded by the existing "blue laws." When the Soft Winds began to

dissolve with Frigo's leaving, and the Peterson Trio needed a top guitarist to replace Barney Kessel, Peterson approached Ellis. From 1953-58 the Oscar Peterson Trio wrote chapters of jazz history that still resound through concert halls, night clubs and recording studios. With leader Peterson and Ellis, plus all-world bassist Ray Brown, the trio became perhaps the most-sought-after, most-recorded, and for most critically praised unit of its era. As Scott Yanow wrote in the *All-Music Guide to Jazz,* the group "was one of the great piano trios of all time. It was never so much a matter of Peterson having two other musicians accompany him as it was that they could meet the pianist as near-equals and consistently inspire him. And unlike most trios, O.P.'s had many arranged sections that constantly needed rehearsals and were often quite dazzling."

Canadian musician/disc jockey Don Warner has often related stories of these three great musicians pushing one another during live gigs in a way that kept their music constantly fresh and swinging. As Ellis recalled of this period: "It was probably the highlight of my career to play with those guys—they're the best on their respective instruments. We had a lot of really difficult arrangements. Oscar wrote really hard for us. We'd have to memorize everything. Oscar's a mental giant, you know, and he never forgot anything. He'd give me stuff to play and I'd say, 'I can't play this, Oscar.' He'd say, 'Yes, you can; I know how much you can play.' I'd go practice and, sure enough, he'd be right every time."

In addition to their great live and recorded work as the Oscar Peterson Trio, this unit served as the virtual "house rhythm section" for Norman Grant's Verve records, supporting the likes of tenormen Ben Webster and Stan Getz, as well as trumpeters Dizzy Gillespie, Roy Eldridge, and Sweets Edison and other jazz stalwarts. They were also the mainstays of Grant's Jazz at the Philharmonic concerts as they swept the jazz world, constantly touring the United States and Europe. Ellis left the Peterson Trio in November 1958, to be replaced not by a guitarist, but by drummer Ed Thigpen, perhaps an admission that his shoes could not be filled.

In 1959 and 1960 Ellis toured with the incomparable Ella Fitzgerald and briefly with Julie London, the actress/ singer who hit the charts with "Cry Me A River." Tired of touring, Ellis settled in the Los Angeles area to begin a longcareer working in the movie, recording, and television studios. Among the television shows on which Ellis was a major player were those headlined by Steve Allen, Regis Philbin, Danny Kaye, Red Skelton, Joey Bishop, Della Reese, and Merv Griffin. Of this period, *Down Beat* writer Leonard Feather wrote: "Philbin had the most jazz-oriented house group..., Terry Gibbs'. In fact it was composed entirely of jazz musicians, [including] guitarist Ellis, the only holdover from the Allen show and still one of the great swingers of any decade." Ellis also played on countless film scores during his decade in Los Angeles. Near the end of the 1960s Ellis longed for some additional opportunities to exercise his jazz skills more fully.

Later Ventures

In the 1970s Ellis embarked on a venture that only the most secure artists would dare attempt. He teamed up with other prominent jazz guitarists in a series of duo performances, first individually with Joe Pass and Barney Kessel, then later in a guitar trio format. Ellis, Kessel and Charlie Byrd became The Great Guitars, and in these various configurations Ellis concertized and recorded widely. Ellis performed on the first three recordings of Concord, the prestigious jazz label. Later he teamed up with guitarists Freddie Green, the mainstay of the Count Basie rhythm section, and Laurindo Almeida, the Stan Kenton import, who bridges the jazz and symphonic worlds as well. In addition, Ellis has recorded albums with bassist Ray Brown, reedman Jimmy Giuffre, violinist Stuff Smith, tenor legend Coleman Hawkins, plus a tribute to his mentor, "Hello, Charlie Christian." He has also recorded video instructional tapes.

Ellis continues to perform in handpicked settings, mostly at jazz parties and festivals. After a 37-year affair with one Gibson guitar, he now plays the custom Gibson Herb Ellis model, the ES 165. "I love to play," states Ellis, and often he will freelance, picking up a good group of fellow-swingers for special occasions. One very special event developed in November, 1995, on a jazz cruise. Here the Soft Winds were re-united, with Frigo now playing violin exclusively and Keter Betts sitting in on bass. "None of us had played together for forty years," related Carter. "We got up on the bandstand of the Norway without any rehearsal and swung our butts off!" When originally together, the three musicians had collaborated on at least two songs that enjoyed moderate popularity and are still played today: "I Told Ya I Love Ya, Now Get Out!" and "Detour Ahead."

In his book The Jazz Guitarists, Stan Britt sums up Ellis's contributions in this way: "Throughout all his musical ventures—on-record or otherwise—Ellis evidences the kind of strong consistency and lasting commitment that has made him something of a legend amongst guitarists." And in a 1992 Down Beat "Blindfold Test," guitar icon Les Paul reacted to an Ellis/Pass record in this way: "You get Joe Pass all by himself and he can pretty well stun ya....And the same thing with Herb Ellis. If you're not swinging, he's gonna make you swing. Of that whole bunch of guys who play hollow-body guitar on the front pickup, I think Herb Ellis has got the most drive."

Selected discography

At Zardis', Pablo, 1955.
Oscar Peterson Plays Count Basie, Clef, 1955.
At the Stratford Shakespearean Festival, Verve, 1956.
Nothing But the Blues, Verve, 1958.
Jazz at Concord, Concord, 1973.
Seven Come Eleven, Concord, 1973.
The Legendary Oscar Peterson Trio: Saturday Night at the Blue Note, Telarc, 1990.
Roll Call, Justice, 1991.
Texas Swings, Justice, 1992.

Sources

Books

Berendt, Joachim E., The Jazz Book: From Ragtime to Fusion and Beyond, Lawrence Hill and Company, 1982.
Britt, Stan, The Jazz Guitarists, Blandford Press Ltd., 1984.
Erlewine, Michael, et al, eds., All Music Guide to Jazz, Miller Freeman Books, 1996.
Feather, Leonard, The New Edition of the Encyclopedia of Jazz, Bonanza Books, 1965.

Periodicals

Coda, April 1, 1980.
Down Beat, May 6, 1965; August 1991; April 1992.

Additional information for this profile was obtained from interviews with Lou Carter, December 2, 1996, and Herb Ellis, December 17, 1996.

—Robert Dupuis

Alejandro Escovedo

Singer, songwriter, guitarist

From his origins in the arts community of San Francisco in the 1970s, where he was influenced by such grungy art rockers as Iggy Pop and the Velvet Underground, Alejandro Escovedo has forged a "cowpunk" style that is part earthy hard rock and part country and western. Currently, in his artistic maturity, he has taken his moody and powerful music in a new and artful direction by working with a string quartet and creating folk chamber music. Although he has been recording since 1978 and has six albums to his credit, commercial success largely eluded Escovedo until the release of *With These Hands* (1996). This recent work has sold well and garnered positive critical response from such leading publications as *Rolling Stone, Billboard,* and the *New York Times.* As his career approaches the 20-year mark, Escovedo's style has ranged from crude punk rock, pioneering cowpunk, and hard-edged searing guitar rocker to an experimental fusion of chamber orchestra, rock ballad, and Latin styles. His later work is edgy without being juvenile and mature without being sentimental. In an era of world music, he stands on the edge of commercial success with a musical style that crosses the boundary between art and pop, with clear cross-cultural appeal.

Alejandro Escovedo was born in 1946 (although he has claimed to be up to five years younger) in San Antonio, Texas. He was the seventh of 12 children. His father Pedro, who had come to Texas at the age of 12 years from the northern Mexican town of Saltillo, was an amateur mariachi performer in the 1940s and 1950s. When Alejandro was in his teens, his family moved to Huntington Beach, California. His older brothers Pete and Coke became successful percussionists who played with Santana in the 1960s. Alejandro thereby gained an interest in making music; he hung around Hollywood's glam-rock scene and listened to music such as The Velvet Underground and The Stooges, although he didn't start playing until he was 24 years old.

Joined San Francisco Punk Scene

Escovedo moved to San Francisco in the early 1970s, when he was briefly married. As a college film student, he began making a film about a punk band that couldn't play, and wound up forming his first band with school-mate Jeff Olener, vocalist Jennifer Miro, and Richie Dietrich. The film was never completed, but the group became the Nuns, a punk rock band that developed a large cult following in the area and performed as the opening act for the Sex Pistols' final gig at Winterland. The Nuns released one single, *Savage,* in 1978. By then, however, the musician had grown dissatisfied with the group and decided to leave The Nuns, moving with his new wife, Bobbie Levie, to New York City. Critical of the band's subsequent work, Escovedo later described it as "trying to beat a very dead horse" to Jason Ferguson in *Magnet* magazine.

Escovedo soon teamed up with Los Angeles-based punk rockers Chip and Tony Kinman to form the influential cowpunk group Rank and File. The band released the album *Sundown* in 1982. He and Bobbie had their first child, Maya, in that same year. In 1986 Escovedo again sought a new direction in music and formed the True Believers with his younger brother Javier. The band was more of a pure rock act, geared toward live performance, and featured a three-guitar climax. They put out one critically well received album, *True Believers* (1986) and recorded another that was not released. The group was dropped by EMI and subsequently dissolved.

Professional and Family Crises

Disenchanted with the music business and concerned that the rock musician's lifestyle was hard on his wife, Escovedo took a job as a record clerk at Austin's Waterloo Records. He soon had a reputation for being the hippest record store clerk in the city. When one of his older brothers died in 1987, Escovedo cautiously returned to music with solo performances and, in late 1988, began performing with an informal improvisational group, the Alejandro Escovedo Orchestra. Hardcore

Born in 1946 (some sources say 1951), in San Antonio, TX; son of Pedro (an amateur mariachi player and plumber) Escovedo; brief marriage in early 1970s; married Bobbie Levie, 1978 (committed suicide, 1991); married Dana Smith (a musician with the three-woman garage rock group, Pork), 1994; children: (With Levie) Maya, (with Smith) Paloma, Paris.

Formed punk rock group The Nuns with Jeff Olener, Jennifer Miro, and Richie Dietrich, 1987; formed country-punk band Rank and File with Chip and Tony Kinman, 1982; with brother Javier, created the True Believers, 1986-87; began solo career in 1988, performing with the Alejandro Escovedo Orchestra; also performed in rock quartet Buick MacKane and with Walter Salas-Humara and Michael Hall as The Setters.

Addresses: *Home*—Austin, Texas. *Record company*—Rykodisc, Shetland Park, 27 Congress Street, Salem, MA 01970.

fans who relished Alejandro's earlier hard-driving guitar work were surprised to hear that he was working with a string section. Nevertheless, the musician's utilization of a chamber music quartet was utterly in keeping with the avant-garde background of his youth.

Escovedo's second daughter, Paloma, was born in 1991—a time when his 13-year marriage to his wife, Bobbie, was already troubled. Following a six-month separation, Bobbie committed suicide. Escovedo directed his mourning into songs that would make up his first solo album, *Gravity*, in 1992. His next album, *Thirteen Years*, was released in 1993. The title song was about his marriage to Bobbie; full of grief and guilt, it also voiced themes of survival and recovery. Escovedo toured to support the release of *Thirteen Years* and made several critics' best-of-the-year lists for 1993 and 1994. In 1994 Escovedo won several Austin Music Awards as well.

Solos Spawned New Collaborations

Escovedo's professional and personal catharsis was followed by a series of collaborations with new musical colleagues and old. He entered into a musical collective with Walter Salas-Humara (The Silos) and Michael Hall (The Wild Seeds), releasing an album as the Setters. And, in a counterpoint to his orchestra, Escovedo also performed as part of Buick MacKane, a noisy, beer-

rock, tongue-in-cheek ensemble. At the Waterloo Record shop, Escovedo developed a relationship with Jim Bradt, who worked in Rykodisc's marketing department. This led to the 1994 Rykodisc issue of *Hard Road*, which contains the original *True Believers* LP plus the unreleased second album. Escovedo's personal life also featured a new "collaboration" in 1994, when Escovedo married long-time friend and fellow rocker, Dana Lee Smith. The couple had a son, Paris, the same year.

Escovedo's third solo album, *With These Hands*, was released in 1996. Although still brooding and thoughtful, it emphasized a cautious optimism and family themes. While working on the album, Escovedo discovered that his brother Peter was in the same building, working on another record. As a result, Peter played on Alejandro's album, as did Peter's wife, Juanita, his son Peter Michael, and daughter Sheila E—the spirited percussionist who had previously worked with pop star Prince. Alejandro's brother, Javier, also joined in, as well as daughters Maya and Paloma. Alejandro's father, Pedro, then 89 years-old, served as the inspiration for the title song, "With These Hands." Willie Nelson also performs on the album; although they had never previously met, Nelson was a fan of an old Rank and File video. Escovedo explained to Tim Stegall of the *The Austin Chronicle*, "It was this Village People western.... I'd heard that Willie and his boys would get out there to his country club, smoke beaucoups amounts of ganja...They'd have it on auto-rewind, just so they could watch it over and over and over again, and laugh and laugh."

With These Hands synthesizes a diverse range of influences, including Latin percussion, country and western, hard rock, and the avant-garde. The avant-garde element is most obvious in the song "Tugboat," a tribute to Escovedo's friend, the late English professor Sterling Morrison, who played guitar for the Velvet Underground. In *Request*, Tristram Lozaw described Escovedo's work on the album as balancing "delicate melody with rock 'n' roll animalism, the harrowing with the uplifting." Lozaw concluded, "While Escovedo's increasingly sanguine outlook may signal that the dull ache of his emotional baggage has lifted in favor of loving contentment, his piercing insights into heartache remain."

Selected discography

(With the Nuns) "Savage" (single), 415, 1978.
(With Rank And File) *Sundown*, Slash, 1982.
(With True Believers) *True Believers*, Rounder/EMI, 1986.
Gravity, Watermelon, 1992.
Thirteen Years, Watermelon, 1993.
The End (EP), Watermelon, 1994.

Hard Road (contains an unreleased second album record-
    ed in 1987 for EMI), Rykodisc, 1994.
(With Walter Salas-Humara and Michael Hall) The Setters,
    The Setters, Watermelon, 1994.
Broadcast Vol. 2 (compilation album), KGSR, 1995.
With These Hands, Rykodisc, 1996.

Sources

Austin Chronicle, April 12, 1996.
Billboard, February 10, 1996.
Huh, March 1996.
Los Angeles Times, March 30, 1996.
Magnet, April/May 1996; February/March 1996.
New York Times, April 9, 1996.
Request, April 1996.
Rolling Stone, April 18, 1996; May 2, 1996.

Additional information for this profile was obtained from
Rykodisc press materials, 1996.

—Link Yaco

Everclear

Rock band

Everclear's Art Alexakis was quoted in *Spin* as saying, "When I try to get complex in my songs, I sound stupid. When I write about things that are simple, they come out fine. There's nothing wrong with anthems." The singer-guitarist's rough-edged, melodic anthems, particularly the modern rock hit "Santa Monica," have propelled the Portland, Oregon-based trio to platinum sales. Alexakis's own travails have led him to a stance of wary hope that contrasts sharply with the apathy and cynicism that some feel dominate alternative rock.

Alexakis grew up in the housing projects of Culver City, a West Los Angeles neighborhood. He was the youngest of five children, and after his parents divorced, he and his siblings were raised by their mother. Though he adored music and "never wanted to do anything else," as he said to Richard Cromelin of the *Los Angeles Times,* it was some time before he was able to pursue it unhindered. Influenced by his hard-living brother, George, Art was using hard drugs by age 13. "After my parents split, my dad was never around," he recalled in *Details,* "so George was the man I looked up to." George died of a heroin and cocaine overdose when Art was still an adolescent, and shortly thereafter, Art's girlfriend also died of an overdose. These experiences only made the teen more self-destructive himself. "Heroin wasn't really my thing," he maintained in *Spin,* adding that he preferred stimulants like cocaine and amphetamines. He did inject cocaine, however, and experienced the roller-coaster ride of addiction for many years. "I kicked about four or five times, jonesed badly, and quit finally after I almost killed myself shooting up cocaine," he confessed. "I've been clean for 12 years."

Though Alexakis lived with his father in Houston and his sister in Oregon for short times, he largely grew up in Los Angeles. He attended Santa Monica College and UCLA, worked at various jobs, and got married. During the 1980s he played in several L.A. bands but in 1987 decided to move to San Francisco to start fresh. He worked for a graphic arts company, and played with a couple of acts, but didn't really get his career off the ground until he co-founded the band Colorfinger. Influenced by country and punk rock, the band was impressive enough to get set up its own independent label, Shindig, and to release its own album.

After the group's distribution fell through, the label went bankrupt and Alexakis's marriage dissolved. Through this trying period in his life, Alexakis received some encouragement from Gary Gersh, then an A&R (artists & repertory) executive at Geffen Records. "He sent me a letter saying I think this stuff sounds kind of dated but I think your voice is cool and I think you write really great songs. Please keep sending me stuff," Alexakis recollected to *Addicted to Noise* writer Michael Goldberg. "He wrote by hand, 'Gary.' I sent it to him 'cause he was the guy who signed [avant-rockers] Sonic Youth, which I thought was pretty cool."

Wanting to start anew again, Alexakis decided to move with his new girlfriend, Jenny, to her hometown of Portland. "I moved to Portland because my life was falling apart, because my record label went under, my girlfriend's pregnant, my band's falling apart," he told Goldberg. There he held various jobs, saw the birth of his daughter, Annabella, and decided to put together a new band. He placed an ad for a rhythm section in a local paper, *The Rocket,* listing as desired influences punk and alternative heroes such as X, the Pixies and Sonic Youth, as well as classic rock mainstays Led Zeppelin and Neil Young. The ad elicited a call from bassist Craig Montoya.

"I was kind of overwhelmed by Art at first," Montoya told *Spin.* "I answered his ad and I had to hold the receiver away from my ear, he was so excited." Alexakis dazzled him with plans to make records, hit the road, play at pivotal industry seminars. Montoya noted, "I was like, 'Wow, I've never been outside of the Pacific Northwest.' He became my father figure at about the same time he became Annabella's." Indeed, Alexakis's little girl was only a few days old when her father, Montoya, and drummer Scott Cuthbert gathered in the Alexakis's basement to play. They recorded a demo there that

For the Record . . .

Members include **Art Alexakis** (born c. 1963 in Los Angeles, CA), guitar, vocals; **Scott Cuthbert** (left band c. 1994), drums; **Greg Eklund** (born c. 1970; joined band c. 1994), drums; **Craig Montoya** (born c. 1971), bass.

Group formed in 1991 in Portland, OR. Released EP on Tim/Kerr label and released debut album, *World of Noise*, 1993; signed with Capitol Records, 1994; appeared on *The Late Show with David Letterman*, 1995.

Awards: Platinum certification for album *Sparkle and Fade*, 1996; voted Band of the Year by *Addicted to Noise* magazine, 1995; "Heroin Girl" voted Song of the Year by *CMJ* readers, 1995.

Addresses: *Home*—Portland, OR. *Record company*—Capitol Records, 1750 Vine St., Los Angeles, CA 90028. *Internet*—Nehalem, the Officially Endorsed Everclear Site: www.geocities.com/Paris/2068/.

landed them a spot at the influential South by Southwest music festival in Austin, Texas. Their performance facilitated a deal with the Portland-based indie label Tim/Kerr. After an EP, Everclear put out their debut album, *World of Noise*, which they recorded for $400.

The band's rapid success engendered a great deal of dislike from some veterans on the Portland music scene who saw Alexakis as an opportunistic interloper at best and a wife-batterer at worst. The latter charge was based on one horrible incident, according to Alexakis, of which he's deeply ashamed. "Annabella was only 18 months at the time," he recounted to *Spin*, "and she may not remember any of it, but that was the single lowest moment of my entire life."

Everclear eventually inked a deal with former Geffen Records executive Gersh, who had in the interim become the head of Capitol Records. Drummer Cuthbert departed shortly thereafter and was replaced by Greg Eklund, and the band's first effort recorded for Capitol

catapulted them to fame. Released in 1995, *Sparkle and Fade* chronicled Alexakis's many travails—as evidenced by tracks such as "Heroin Girl"—but also retained a spark of optimism. "This record," Alexakis noted in *Time*, "is about getting out of bad situations." Radio's embrace of the upbeat "Santa Monica," however, ultimately led to the album's platinum sales.

Yet Everclear could hardly be regarded as an overnight sensation. Touring 11 months out of the year, they built a solid nationwide following with raw, energetic performances. "I'm surprised, only because usually good records don't do well," Alexakis told *Ozone*. "I think it's a deep record; I didn't really think it had a smash hit on it. That's the only thing that surprises me—that `Santa Monica' has been as big as it is. But what doesn't surprise me is...we're a good live band. We play a lot, we've worked our ass off to this point. It's not just the one hit that did it; we built up to it." Eklund suggested in an interview for Gannett News Service that Alexakis's songs simply connected with young listeners. "People can identify with what he has to say," he said. "Talking to people who like our music, I find they are dissatisfied with what there is for them, what they've achieved. His songs reflect that. But they are also hopeful."

Selected discography

Nervous and Weird, (EP), Tim/Kerr, 1993.
World of Noise, Tim/Kerr, 1993; Capitol, 1994.
Sparkle and Fade, (includes "Heroin Girl" and "Santa Monica"), Capitol, 1995.

Sources

Addicted to Noise, August 1, 1995.
Details, July 1996.
Los Angeles Times, March 16, 1996.
MusicWorld, August 12, 1996.
Spin, September 1996.
Time, May 27, 1996.

Additional information was provided by a Gannett News Service article, March 1, 1996, and by the online magazine *Ozone*.

—Simon Glickman

Lisa Germano

Violinist

Although Lisa Germano once attracted attention as the violinist for John Mellencamp on his *Lonesome Jubilee* and *Big Daddy* albums, she has since carved out her own place in the music world as the creator of a series of harrowing albums of a stunningly personal nature. Talking online about the strongly autobiographical character of her songs with interviewer Patrick Brennan, Germano observed that "some people who don't get my music or don't like it just say 'It's just so personal. What am I supposed to do? Feel sorry for her?' But, no, that's not it at all. I think that when you write really, really personal things—not always—but your hope is that it reaches a certain thing that everybody feels, becomes a universal thing."

Growing up in a large Italian family in Mishawaka, Indiana, Germano was surrounded by music. Both her parents were musicians as well as music teachers, and an eclectic range of music could often be heard through the rooms and hallways of the Germano home. When Germano was still a youngster, her parents took her to a room filled with instruments and told her to pick one. But choose carefully, they said, for they expected her to study the instrument that she chose until she was 18 years old. Germano later explained that her parents saw musical study not only as a way to give their children an appreciation for music, but also as a path to self-discipline and being comfortable with being alone.

Germano chose the violin, and while she studied and learned to play many classical compositions over the next several years, popular music of the day had a big impact on her as well. "In high school I was still in the beauty-mushy stage," she told *Muse* magazine. "I loved James Taylor and Dan Fogelberg. I liked the Beatles. My brother would bring stuff like Janis Joplin or Steppenwolf home and we thought that was really cool but I would never go play that by myself." By age sixteen, Germano was playing the fiddle in local bluegrass and rock and roll bands.

Around age 20, Germano was struck by a debilitating bout with depression and quit performing. She spent much of the next few years grappling with the condition, which was based in large measure on "a pretty good self-hatred," she told Brennan. According to Germano, subsequent therapy sessions helped her enormously. Shortly after returning to performing at local bars, she received a call that dramatically changed her life. "I was just very lucky," she told *Muse.* "I was playing violin at a country bar and I knew John [Mellencamp]'s drummer, Kenny [Aronoff]. John wanted to put some violin on a song, and I was the only violin player that Kenny knew, so they called me to come and do it. John really liked what I did, I guess, so the next week he asked me to go on tour with him. It was pretty amazing."

Germano's experiences as a member of Mellencamp's band gave her much greater confidence in her musical abilities, but not until she heard the 1985 Kate Bush album *Hounds of Love* did she decide to take the plunge and embark on a solo recording career. "*Hounds of Love* I thought was an amazing record," she told Brennan. "It totally inspired me to make my own records. I always had these songs but I never finished them 'cause I thought they were too emotional." But after being bowled over by Bush's passionate album, Germano decided that she had to make a greater effort to present her own material to the world.

Germano's first album, *On the Way Down from the Moon Palace* (1991) was a self-produced, self-financed album of spectral country-folk that garnered a number of positive reviews. However, it was not until the release of *Happiness* in 1993 that the music world really began to take notice of Germano's talent. (Displeased with the final version of *Happiness* that Capitol released, Germano left the label and re-recorded portions of it for 4AD, which released its own version of the album a number of months later.)

Many critics commented on the breathtakingly honest—if darkly mordant—quality of her lyrics. *Melody Maker*'s Dave Simpson, for instance, called *Happiness* "a voyage into Lisa Germano's psyche, a bleak domain where psychological traumas hang heavy and the artist slowly pulls herself apart."

For the Record . . .

Born in Mishawaka, IN; both parents were music teachers.

Began playing violin at age seven, and performing in bands by mid-teens; joined John Mellencamp's touring band and played on his *Big Daddy* and *Lonesome Jubilee* albums; released first album, *On the Way Down from the Moon Palace*, 1991; left Capitol Records for 4AD label, 1993; released *Excerpts from a Love Circus*—her third 4AD album—in September of 1996.

Addresses: *Artist*—P.O. Box 93595, Los Angeles, CA 90093. *Record company*—4AD, 8533 Melrose Ave., Suite B., Los Angeles, CA 90069.

In 1994 4AD released Germano's third solo album, the harrowing *Geek the Girl*. The critical consensus was that once again Germano had compiled a string of songs of sometimes unnerving honesty and darkness. Citing such grim songs of human frailty and vulnerability as the title track, "Cancer of Everything," and the chilling "Psychopath," *Rolling Stone* reviewer Paul Evans called it a "beautiful, wrenching album," and compared Germano's lyrical insights to those of Kurt Cobain and P. J. Harvey. Sarra Manning commented in *Melody Maker* that "*Geek the Girl* is a difficult album that pushes the listener away with its truculent tone just as it pulls them closer with whispered secrets. You may think it says nothing about the clear glass of your life but beware! Geek the girl lives in us all."

In the fall of 1996 Germano released *Excerpts from a Love Circus*. Like its predecessors, this album featured a plethora of songs of self-doubt and hurt, all gliding languidly through a surreal mix of guitar, violin, percussion, and odd sound effects. Some reviewers expressed a desire to see Germano explore new territory in the future, but most felt that *Love Circus* was a strong work. Writing in *Rolling Stone*, critic Lorraine Ali said that "Germano makes music so beautifully tragic and depressing that it seems nearly fatal," while the *New York Times*'s Jon Pareles observed that the songs "seem to come from some drafty, echoey place, a sickroom or a haunted attic."

Germano makes her home in Bloomington, Indiana, where she has recorded much of her music of the last few years. Two of her closest companions are her cats, Dorothy and Miamo-Tutti, both of whom contribute the odd snarl and purr to *Excerpts from a Love Circus*.

Selected discography

On the Way Down from the Moon Palace, independently released, 1991.
Happiness, Capitol, 1993 (different version of the album later released on 4AD).
Geek the Girl, 4AD, 1994.
Excerpts from a Love Circus, 4AD, 1996.

Sources

Advocate, May 17, 1994, p. 78.
Audio, April 1995, p. 76.
Entertainment Weekly, August 6, 1993, p. 58; October 28, 1994, p. 88; September 20, 1996, p. 83.
Guitar Player, July 1994, p. 121.
Melody Maker, May 21, 1994; October 29, 1994.
New York Times, October 1, 1996, p. C16.
Playboy, July 1993, p. 21.
Rolling Stone, November 3, 1994, p. 98; September 5, 1996, p.64.
Stereo Review, August 1993, p. 83; May 1994, p. 91.

Additional information for this profile was obtained from a 1995 *Muse* magazine interview and Patrick Brennan's "No Straitjacket Required" interview (both available online via the Lisa Germano Home Page), as well as 4AD promotional materials.

—Kevin Hillstrom

Gin Blossoms

Pop/rock band

Arizona's Gin Blossoms were unlikely candidates for fame in the early 1990s, plying well-crafted, melodic pop-rock in an era of loud and anxious alternative music. However, the band's formula of bright, guitar-driven hooks, sweet vocals, and melancholy undertow made them radio staples. "It's just pop music," singer Robin Wilson told the *Los Angeles Times.* "I want to touch people on some fundamental level, in the same way that I've been touched when I hear a pop song that I really love." The Blossoms' dedication to melody has stood them in good stead in the face of various crises, including the firing and subsequent suicide of one of their songwriter-members. Yet the band emerged in 1996 with a sophomore album, the lead single of which was soon in heavy radio rotation. As Wilson noted in a record company bio, "Everything that's happened in the last four years has helped to make us a stronger band and stronger individuals."

The band began in Tempe, Arizona. Bassist Bill Leen and guitarist-songwriter Doug Hopkins had known one another since childhood and previously played in a

AP/Wide World Photos

For the Record . . .

Members include **Doug Hopkins** (bandmember 1987-92; died, 1993), guitar; **Scott Johnson** (joined band, 1992), guitar; **Bill Leen**, bass; **Philip Rhodes**, drums; **Jesse Valenzuela**, guitar; **Robin Wilson** (joined band, 1988), vocals.

Group formed c. 1987 in Tempe, AZ; released debut album, *Dusted,* on San Jacinto label, 1989; signed with A&M Records and released EP *Up and Crumbling,* 1990; released debut album *New Miserable Experience,* 1992; toured with numerous acts, including Toad the Wet Sprocket, Cracker, Goo Goo Dolls, and Neil Young, 1992—; contributed song "Til I Hear It from You" to soundtrack of film *Empire Records,* 1995.

Awards: Gold Records for *New Miserable Experience,* 1994, and *Congratulations I'm Sorry,* 1996.

Addresses: *Record company*—A&M Records, 1416 North La Brea Ave., Los Angeles, CA 90028. *Internet Websites*—A&M Records Gin Blossoms site: amrecords.com/current/ginblossoms/. Unofficial Gin Blossoms Home Page: www.prarienet.org/~eharty/gin_blossoms.html.

number of local bands, including the Psalms. They added guitarist and erstwhile lead singer Jesse Valenzuela and in 1987 made their debut as the Gin Blossoms. The name was inspired by a picture of film comedian W.C. Fields, the colloquial term "gin blossoms" referring to the burst blood vessels visible in his alcohol-ravaged red nose.

A "Bar Band" in Demand

Valenzuela described the group's earliest incarnation as "a bar band" in an interview with *Musician.* Wilson joined the following year as rhythm guitarist and background singer, but soon he and Valenzuela switched vocal duties. Drummer Philip Rhodes signed on shortly thereafter. After gathering a sizable following—comprised largely of college students—the band went into the studio to record an album. Released independently, *Dusted,* with the help of Tom DeSavia, a representative of the music-publishing association ASCAP, received major-label attention. In 1989 the band performed at the South By Southwest music festival in Austin, as well as New York's New Music Awards Ceremony and College Music Journal (CMJ) Music Marathon.

Polygram Records was one of the early industry suitors of the band. Wilson recalled a spree at the company's product closet—where promotional copies of its recordings are kept—in *Phoenix Monthly.* "We reamed 'em," he recalled. "We're totally poor broke and I left with, oh lord, probably thirty CDs and a bunch of tapes. And the stuff that we didn't like we took to a store and sold." Despite such goodies and seafood dinners in upscale restaurants that the company paid for, the band didn't sign with Polygram, electing instead to go with A&M Records. Yet the Blossoms' first attempt at recording an album with A&M was disastrous; ditching what they'd done, the band instead released an EP and hit the road. The regionally successful disc paved the way for a more productive foray in the studio, and the band completed *New Miserable Experience,* its full-length debut, in the summer of 1992.

Tragedy

Hopkins had by this time become a liability. Although he'd written half the material on the album, his drinking was so excessive—according to his ex-bandmates—that he represented an obstacle. Before the album was even finished, the band let him go, replacing him with guitarist Scott Johnson. The circumstances surrounding Hopkins' departure are murky; after he left, the guitarist and songwriter formed another band, the Chimeras, and continued to earn royalties from the songs he'd written with the Blossoms. Yet he claimed to have been given a raw deal in the aftermath of his expulsion from the group. "I understand why they fired me," he declared in an interview quoted by *Rolling Stone,* "but did they have to get so f—ing cold and ruthless about it?" Hopkins received a copy of the Gold Record that *New Miserable Experience* eventually earned, but destroyed it during a binge. In late 1993, he left the hospital where he'd been receiving treatment for his alcoholism, purchased a gun, and used it to end his life.

The success that followed *Experience* after its initial poor sales was bittersweet for Hopkins' ex-bandmates. "I can't explain any personal feelings," Valenzuela told the *Albuquerque Times.* "It's a pretty devastating thing." Yet the band soldiered on, touring relentlessly and scoring several hits, including Hopkins' "Hey Jealousy" and "Found Out About You." The album also scored with critics, who admired the band's musicality and emotional directness.

After the departure of Hopkins, some doubted the Gin Blossoms would be able to write songs of the same caliber. "It's not our responsibility," Wilson insisted tersely in the *Los Angeles Times,* "to live up to Doug's songwriting." The band delivered commercially again with "Til I Hear It from You," co-written by Wilson, Valenzuela, and pop-rock whiz Marshall Crenshaw, a band favorite. The single first appeared on the successful soundtrack to the unsuccessful film *Empire Records*. With this hit and more touring, the band returned to the studio to record a follow-up album.

In the wake of the success of their debut and of Hopkins' death, members of the band were greeted with both plaudits and sympathy, and the second album's title, *Congratulations I'm Sorry*, reflected this double-edged response. Released in 1996, the recording didn't earn the effusive notices of *Experience*. "It's clear that Hopkins brought a level of specificity and skill otherwise lacking" in the band's songs, lamented *Spin*. Citing a lyric about being "like a broken record," reviewer Jeff Salamon opined, "The Gin Blossoms *are* like a broken record, repeating everything they wanna say—and have already said, elsewhere, better." *Rolling Stone* was only slightly more charitable. "Like mashed potatoes and meatloaf, there's not much variety to Gin Blossoms' guileless guitar pop," ventured the magazine's Kara Manning, "but then again, sometime's there's nothing quite so comforting as a guilty pleasure."

"A Bit of a War"

Nonetheless, the second album scored a hit out of the box with "Follow You Down," a typically driving, emotive tune. "You want to know the secret?" Valenzuela asked to the *Albuquerque Tribune*, referring to the band's signature sound. "You get a really crunchy guitar and then a clean acoustic next to it...compress it and stick it over to the side." Wilson asserted in the band's A&M biography that "people like that sort of bittersweet quality that our songwriting has. It's like our name; it sounds pretty but it represents something a bit darker."

The Gin Blossoms went on tour with the Goo Goo Dolls and rock icon Neil Young, and Wilson also devoted his free time to his cover band, The Best Dave Swaffords

in the World. At the end of the band's tour, they received their second gold record. Of the rigors of fame and life on the road, Valenzuela waxed philosophical. "You know, it's a bit of a war, really—a war inside you," he told the *Music Paper*. "On the one hand you want to make as much money and grab all the security you can 'cause you never known when this gravy train will pass by again, right? But you didn't really get into this for the money. You got into it for the music and love of playing. And that love actually carries you through the rough times. But you begin to wonder when you can get back to the creativity of doing what you love most. So it's a bit of a problem, really."

Selected discography

Dusted, San Jacinto, 1989.
Up and Crumbling (EP), A&M, 1990.
New Miserable Experience (includes "Hey Jealousy" and "Found Out About You") A&M, 1992.
"Til I Hear It from You," *Empire Records* soundtrack, A&M, 1995.
Congratulations I'm Sorry (includes "Follow You Down"), A&M, 1996.

Sources

Albuquerque Tribune, February 22, 1996.
Los Angeles Times, March 31, 1996.
Music Paper, April 1994.
Musician, April 1996.
Phoenix Monthly, May 1993.
Review Monthly, April 1994.
Rolling Stone, February 10, 1994; March 21, 1996.
Spin, April 1996.

Additional information was provided by A&M Records publicity materials, 1996.

—Simon Glickman

John Gorka

Singer, songwriter, guitarist

AP/Wide World Photos

John Gorka has no problem with being labeled a folk singer, a title that was once synonymous with "obscure" and "unfashionable." The guitar-playing baritone is proud of his musical heritage and while he has found himself in the media spotlight with increasing frequency, he remains committed to his long-time fans and his established way of working. "My approach has always been low-key, song-driven, touring-based, slow, steady growth," the singer/songwriter said in a press release. Gorka is not interested in trading this formula for a spot on the pop or country charts; he is more interested in building a long career, rather than sparking a brief period of stardom. Because Gorka feels that his sustained success as a musician is dependent on his live performances, he spends over 150 nights on the road each year and continues to play in the small folk clubs where he made his name. Gorka told *Billboard*: "Quite honestly, I will sing for anyone who has an interest in my music. But I don't think a little interest from one part of the world will make me reposition my musical direction. Any changes or growth has to happen naturally, otherwise it won't work."

In 1991 *Rolling Stone*'s Eliza Wing called Gorka "the preeminent male singer-songwriter of what's been dubbed the New Folk Movement." The artist later responded to this compliment in a cynical fashion in *The Performing Songwriter:* "I thought it was a double oxymoron....New/Folk and Folk/Movement. As far as I know, folk music has always been here, never gone away." While folk recordings may now be selling in increased numbers, including Gorka's own, he knows that he and many of his colleagues have been faithful to the genre all along. Gorka began his career during the late 1970s and early 1980s, when only a handful of small labels were making folk records. He started performing while he was in college at the Bethlehem, Pennsylvania folk club, Godfrey Daniels. At first, the young man tended bar and sang on open-mike nights; later he lead the Razzy Dazzy Spasm Band. Moreover, Gorka listened to and carefully studied the performers who headlined there. Eventually he came to know these musicians when he became an opening act.

Compromise and Success

Singer Nanci Griffith first suggested that Gorka enter a contest to play at the 1984 Kerrville Folk Festival in Texas, where he not only performed, but won the show's New Folk Award. His first big break, the award gave a boost to Gorka's visibility and confidence. Gorka's first album came three years later, when the small Minnesota label Red House Records released *I Know*. The success of this album and the praise of fellow artists

For the Record . . .

Born c. 1958 in New Jersey. *Education:* Moravian College (Bethlehem, PA), B.A. in philosophy and history.

First performed at open-mike nights and with the Razzy Dazzy Spasm Band at the Bethlehem folk club Godfrey Daniels; went on the road as a solo act, playing throughout the northeastern United States; released first album, *I Know,* in 1987 with Red House Records; signed with High Street/Windham Hill Records and subsequently released *Land of the Bottom Line* in 1990; tours extensively.

Awards: Won Kerrville Folk Festival's New Folk Award in 1984; awarded Best Folk Songwriter and Best Contemporary Folk Album for *I Know* by the Philadelphia Music Foundation in 1989; video for "When She Kisses Me" voted Best Independent Video by the CMT (Country Music Television) cable channel.

Addresses: *Agent*—Fleming, Tamulevich & Associates, 733-735 N. Main Street, Ann Arbor, MI 48104. *Record company*—High Street/Windham Hill, P.O. Box 5501, Beverly Hills, CA 90211-2713.

soon led to a multi-album deal with a "major league" company, Windham Hill, as well as its subsidiary High Street Records. Gorka had to convince the company that they shouldn't re-record *I Know,* as was prescribed by company founder William Ackerman. Gorka remembered in *The Performing Songwriter,* "I was ready to turn the deal down, because I felt like I couldn't do this to the people who bought the first album. It may not be the biggest audience in the world, but it's the only one I have. I didn't want to betray them in order to get some mysterious larger audience they told me was out there." Both parties compromised, resulting in *Land of the Bottom Line,* which included two "bonus tracks" from the earlier album.

New Label Drummed Up More Attention

With the increased promotion and distribution power of Windham Hill, Gorka's singing and songwriting abilities reached new ears and attracted increased critical attention. Robert Gluck remarked in the *New York Times* that the album "made its way...past the small public radio station and cult audiences familiar with [Gorka's] earlier music to commercial airwaves and larger audi-

ences." Steven Rea praised *Land of the Bottom Line* in the *Philadelphia Inquirer:* "What strikes you first about Gorka's music is his voice: a warm, resonant baritone that both demands your attention and rewards it. It is unforced, plaintive, clear....the songs keen along on catchy, straightforward melodies, and while a good many are tales of broken hearts or broken men, they are laced with irony." Gorka's next two albums, *Jack's Crows* and *Temporary Road,* reflected a happier, less introspective man (he explained in interviews that he had fallen in love). *Jack's Crows* was notable for the attention it received by country radio and video programs; *Temporary Road* showed Gorka's capacity for political commentary in songs such as "The Gypsy Life" and "Brown Shirt," which reflected his thoughts, respectively, on the Gulf War and fascism.

Professional Friendships

Temporary Road, as well as Gorka's subsequent albums *Out of the Valley* and *Between Five and Seven,* are also remarkable for their supporting cast of big-name recording artists. The roster includes Cliff Eberhardt, Nanci Griffith, Kathy Mattea, Mary Chapin-Carpenter, Leo Kottke, and Peter Ostroushko, among a sea of others. Gorka has toured and recorded with an impressive number of folk-country-pop stars that are not only colleagues, but friends. These relationships are part of a nurturing network that helped him start his career and has greatly influenced his on-going work. Gorka notes that this approach is a throwback to less competitive times; he told *The Press* of Atlantic City, New Jersey that "there was not really a whole lot of commercial potential for the music...We all wanted to make a living....There was a lot of camaraderie." In addition to these links to the folk scene, Gorka has also been an important source of songs for singers Maura O'Connell and and Mary Black, who are among some 20 artists who perform covers of his compositions.

A veteran of many live performances, and an outspoken songwriter, Gorka is ironically a shy, quiet man in person. Gorka has explained that he communicates best through his music, and that he began songwriting to overcome the difficulties he had with the spoken word. He told *Rolling Stone:* "I can organize my thoughts better and present what I really want to say....I get my best ideas waking in the morning or going to sleep. The lines that seem to ring true come then. Whenever I learn something I put it into a song." Gorka has also carefully studied his favorite performers, searching for the secret of a good "stage presence." He has concluded that it boils down to being honest, being yourself. And so, John Gorka has developed a quietly confident, very funny onstage presence. Robert P. Gluck described his impact thus: "Whether it's playing without amplification before a small group, or before a crowd at the country's largest gathering of folk artists, the Philadelphia Folk Festival, Mr. Gorka mesmerizes. His brand of humor makes listeners laugh from the gut, taking the bitter edge off his biting, poignant song-poems." With this approach, Gorka hopes to keep entertaining audiences for a long time.

Selected discography

I Know, Red House Records, 1987.
Land of the Bottom Line, Windham Hill, 1990.
Jack's Crows, High Street, 1992.
Temporary Road, High Street, 1993.
Out of the Valley, High Street, 1994.
Between Five and Seven, High Street, 1996.

Sources

Billboard, October 17, 1992, pp. 17-20; November 11, 1995, pp. 5-13.
New York Times, January 20, 1991.
The Performing Songwriter, July/August 1993, pp. 37-40.
Philadelphia Inquirer, June 11, 1990, p. 1E.
The Press (Atlantic City, NJ), October 29, 1995.
Rolling Stone, August 8, 1991, p. 17.

Additional information for this profile was obtained from Fleming, Tamulevich & Associates.

—*Paula Pyzik Scott*

Guided By Voices

Rock band

The Ohio-based band Guided By Voices toiled in obscurity for years, their penchant for melodic-yet-noisy pop ditties appreciated by only a tiny cult following. Eventually, the band gained the attention of the rock press and signed with a major label, but refused to abandon the do-it-yourself ethic they'd followed all along. Their devotees compared the group's prodigious output to the songwriting of such rock giants as Beatles John Lennon and Paul McCartney and the Who's Pete Townshend.

PDXS writer Michael Velez proclaimed that on first hearing their music, "Even the most jaded can be reminded why they began to listen to rock in the first place: the GBV listening experience is a reminder of that eerie and thrilling sense of one's life as rendered by bass, guitar and drums. True to their name, the collected oeuvre of Guided By Voices is akin to a capsule summary of the best rock/pop of the last thirty years." Lead songwriter and vocalist Robert Pollard, discussing the band's name in *Magnet*, seemed to affirm Velez's contention: "the voices of rock are in my head," he declared, "guiding me to make music."

Pollard grew up in the Dayton-area neighborhood of Northridge, where he excelled at sports from a young age. Though his father pushed him toward athletics and discouraged his burgeoning interest in rock music, it was through his father that Pollard first discovered many of the bands who become huge influences. "In the 70s, I started getting into album rock because my dad joined the Columbia Record Club," he told *CMJ*. "You know, where you get 12 records for a penny? He let me choose the albums. I really knew nothing about albums, I was into bubblegum-single rock. So all I went by was the titles and the names of the bands and stuff. I started choosing [progressive-rockers] King Crimson and [Sixties psychedelic blues-rock band] Moby Grape, stuff like that. That was good stuff! So I was into psychedelic music, and then prog, and later punk and postpunk." Such influences helped shaped Pollard's own fledgling attempts at songwriting.

"I Thought It Was Cool"

After high school, Pollard attended Wright State University in Dayton. His interest in sports waned, and he began singing in a slew of rock bands. After graduating, he took work as a schoolteacher; this occupation afforded him the opportunity to devote his free summers to music. With high school pal and guitarist Mitch Mitchell, Pollard played in a metal band in the 1970s, but their tenure ended when they became fascinated with such new-wave experimenters as fellow Ohio band Devo. They then recruited their friend Kevin Fennell as drummer and formed the loose collective that would eventually become GBV. Initially, the band went through a variety of other names first, notably Instant Lovelies and Beethoven and the American Flag. "Guided By Voices was a name I had written in a notebook, and I thought it was cool," Pollard recalled in *Puncture*. "I pictured a record store bin and the names: `Genesis...Gentle Giant...Grateful Dead...Guided By Voices...'"

The band was merely a recreational enterprise, gathering only to learn Pollard's prodigious catalog of twisted pop songs and record them with whatever equipment was available. "We weren't really good enough to play out anywhere," Pollard insisted in *Puncture*. He noted that the group began "playing our weird pop at these seedy redneck bars" and mainly confusing whatever audiences happened to see them. They did at last release a recording, 1986's *Forever Since Breakfast* EP—which Pollard has since described as a reflection of his mid-80s obsession with modern-rock pioneers R.E.M.—but the record didn't make it into many stores. "At first, recording was just a hobby for us," Pollard declared in *CMJ*, adding, "the local feedback we got was really negative. That probably contributed a lot to our lack of confidence." The group reverted to the basement again.

The GBV aesthetic, forged during these lean years, involved home-recorded and often under-rehearsed tunes drenched in tape hiss, song fragments, noise,

For the Record . . .

Members include **Robert Pollard Jr.** (born October 31, 1957, in Dayton, OH), guitar, vocals; **Kevin Fennell**, drums; **Mitch Mitchell**, guitar; **Tobin Sprout** (joined band c. 1990), guitar, vocals; **Greg Demos**, bass; **Jim Pollard**, bass; **Jim Greer** (band-member c. 1995), bass; **Dan Toohey**, bass.

Formed c. 1981, in Dayton, OH; released debut EP *Forever Since Breakfast* on own I Wanna label, 1986; signed with Scat label and released EP *The Grand Hour*, 1993; signed with Matador Records and released *Alien Lanes*, 1995; appeared on Lollapalooza tour, 1995; appeared on *The Jon Stewart Show*, 1995; Pollard and Sprout released solo albums, 1996.

Addresses: *Record company*—Matador Records, 676 Broadway, 4th Floor, New York, NY 10012. *Internet website*—www.gbv.com.

and odd titles such as "Ergo Space Pig." Pollard sang with an affected English accent because British rock had so strongly shaped his style. *Now* magazine described his compositions as "timeless twisted power-pop classics destined to confound historians for generations to come."

After several more releases—most of which piled up in boxes at Pollard's house—the group was no closer to fame and fortune. By the release of 1992's *Propeller*, he was prepared to call it quits. "We were still having fun," he told *Puncture*'s John Chandler, "but people kept asking when I would quit...[messing] around with this band [stuff], if we weren't actually going to play anywhere." After the band was dissolved, however, their work was discovered by Robert Griffin, head of the Cleveland-based independent label Scat. Griffin signed GBV and in 1993 re-released *Propeller*. He also released an EP as well as the album-length *Vampire on Titus*.

Gained Buzz with *Bee*

With the following year's album-length Scat release, *Bee Thousand*, GBV became a hot item in the rock underground. The album, which *CMJ*'s Chris Molanphy declared "a work of offhand genius, a sampler of great tunes that fused all of Pollard's 60s and 70s influences into a fuzzy, dreamy whole," led to a showcase gig at New York's New Music Seminar. The band was then snapped up by Matador Records, a prominent independent label. Soon, their alcohol-fueled live performances were almost as legendary as their mysterious recordings. Schoolteacher Pollard was soon a legend in his own classroom. "The kids think it's an opportunity to take advantage of me," he told *Rolling Stone*. "`Hey, Mr. Rocker'; all that stuff. I'm kind of a nice guy. Discipline isn't my strong point." He admitted, however, that teaching fourth grade had greatly influenced his songwriting, which is rife with werewolves, witches, and robots.

At this point, Guided By Voices—which included guitarist Tobin Sprout, who wrote and sang his own songs with the band, Pollard's brother Jim on bass, Mitchell, Fennell, and a rotating crew of friends—faced the dilemma of a high-profile debut after nearly a decade of toiling in obscurity. Their "lo-fi" recordings had become fashionable in the new alternative rock world, yet GBV never thought of their recording methods as anything but expedient. Their first album for Matador, *Alien Lanes*, preserved the home-recorded feel, however. In conjunction with Scat, Matador also released a box set of early GBV recordings on vinyl.

After being joined by *Spin* writer and GBV fan Jim Greer on bass, the group traveled with the alternative rockfest Lollapalooza, made a television appearance on *The Jon Stewart Show*, and briefly served as the opening act for power-pop superstars Urge Overkill. The latter expedition was disastrous. Pushed offstage by UO's roadies after short sets—even when their fans begged for more—Pollard finally snapped and ended up in a tussle with the crew. Eventually, he told the *Chicago Sun-Times*, "the bouncer, whom I'd been spilling beer on all night, came up and punched me."

Full-Time Job

Pollard was nonetheless afforded the opportunity by his newfound success to quit his teaching job. Married and the father of two, he was at last able to support his family with his band. "My wife cries every time I leave" to go on tour, he confided in *Magnet*. "I tell her, 'I'll be back.' She worries about me. My kids don't mind, but kids are weird." Pollard's children have been the subject of the songs "My Son Cool" and "Your Name is Wild." The latter appeared on 1996's effort *Under the Bushes, Under the Stars*, which Pollard described to *CMJ* as "more anthemic, a little bit more spiritual, and to me, a bit more serious" than previous recordings. Initially recorded in sessions with Breeders frontwoman and GBV fanatic Kim Deal—wife of Greer, who eventually left the band and returned to full-time journalism—and famed indie-rock producer Steve Albini, the album was mostly re-done in Dayton. "The thing about the stuff we did with Steve is, I think we gave him inferior songs," Pollard told *CMJ*. After returning from the road, he claimed, he wrote a superior batch. These were recorded quickly at the Dayton studio.

Critics largely praised *Under the Bushes,* as they did the simultaneously released solo discs by Pollard and Sprout that Matador put out the same year. Of Pollard's *Not in My Air Force*—recorded with current and former GBV members—*Billboard* claimed, "the songs are off the cuff and sometimes underdone, yet they still boast his inimitable, irresistible melodic genius." *Air Force* was "the best GBV-related project since *Bee Thousand,*" according to *CMJ*, which noted in the same issue that Sprout's solo debut *Carnival Boy* was "not to be ignored."

Pollard's sense of mission as a songwriter has continued unabated, fueled by ideas that clash strongly with often apathetic views of the alternative age. "Music today lacks love," he lamented in *Magnet.* "Music from the '60s talked about love—not personal love, but this universal sort of love. I really miss that. People are afraid to express themselves and express love. In the `60s, rock was about people getting together and having fun. That needs to come back." Whether or not Guided By Voices can help bring about such a return remains to be seen, but their prodigious output and devotion to melodic, energetic music has certainly set more than a few hearts racing.

Selected discography

Forever Since Breakfast (EP), I Wanna, 1986.
Devil Between My Toes, Schwa, 1987.
Sandbox, Halo, 1988.
Self-Inflicted Aerial Nostalgia, Halo, 1989.
Same Place the Fly Got Smashed, Rocket #9, 1990.
Propeller (includes "Ergo Space Pig"), Rockathon, 1992.
The Grand Hour (EP), Scat, 1993.

An Earful O' Wax (EP), Get Happy (Germany), 1993.
Vampire on Titus, Scat, 1993.
Static Airplane Jive (EP), City Slang (Germany), 1993.
Clown Prince of the Menthol Trailer (EP), Domino (UK), 1994.
Fast Japanese Spin Cycle (EP), Engine, 1994.
Get Out of My Stations (EP), Siltbreeze, 1994.
Bee Thousand, Scat, 1994.
I Am a Scientist (EP), Scat/Matador, 1994.
Box, Scat/Matador, 1995.
Alien Lanes (includes "My Son Cool"), Matador, 1995.
Tigerbomb (EP), 1995.
The Official Ironmen Rally Song (EP), Matador, 1996.
Under the Bushes, Under the Stars, Matador, 1996.
Robert Pollard, *Not in My Airforce* (includes "Your Name Is Wild"), Matador, 1996.
Tobin Sprout, *Carnival Boy,* Matador, 1996.

Sources

Alternative Press, September 1996.
Billboard, February 24, 1996; September 7, 1996.
Chicago Tribune, February 23, 1996.
College Music Journal (CMJ), May 1995; February 1996; October 1996.
Magnet, April 1996.
Melody Maker, February 4, 1995.
Musician, November 1994.
Now, October 19, 1995.
PDXS, April 26, 1996.
Puncture, Fall 1993; Summer 1995.
Rolling Stone, July 14, 1994; April 4, 1996.
Spin, July 1994.
Washington Post, November 3, 1995.

Additional information was provided by an interview by "Miss Mo" on the America Online internet service, February 24, 1996, and by Matador Records publicity materials, 1996.

—*Simon Glickman*

Tim Hardin

Singer, songwriter, guitarist

MICHAEL OCHS ARCHIVES/Venice, CA

Highly regarded for his plaintive songs whose lyrics searched for elusive answers, Tim Hardin was a tragic figure in the world of folk music who showed great promise with his early albums but then became side-tracked by drug problems and disappointment over his career. Although "Tim Hardin was one of the more memorable singer-songwriters of his day," according to Richie Unterberger in the *Rough Guide* website, his songs, including "Reason to Believe" and "I Were a Carpenter," were more known from their cover versions by Bobby Darin, the Four Tops, Rod Stewart, Wilson Phillips, Colin Blunstone, Scott Walker, and other artists than from Hardin's original recordings. "But Hardin's own versions are graced by one inestimable virtue: his voice—a matchless instrument that sounds world-weary and pained at one moment, hopeful and open-hearted the next," wrote Anthony DeCurtis in the liner notes for *Tim Hardin: Reason to Believe (The Best Of)* in 1994. David Bourne added in the *New York Times* that his "tensely hushed voice, with its hint of sandpaper, took the lyrics far beyond cliché."

Hardin loved the blues, and many of his songs merged blues and folk styles. He also had a jazz musician's sense of improvisation. As Bourne stated that Hardin's "arrangements were those of a jazz musician's, and his phrasing lies somewhere between folk and blues." *The Guinness Encyclopedia of Popular Music* called his music "a unique blend of poetic/folk blues." Hardin's songs were tender and often confessional in tone, filled with longing and a sense of desperation. In his lyrics he lamented dreams that had gone unfulfilled and love that proved highly vulnerable to disappointment. As he sang in "It'll Never Happen Again," "Why can't you be/ The way I want you to be?" Musically, his pieces got right to the core of an emotion with melodies that seemed simple but were deceptively complex. Hardin's songs "were terse and economical, rarely more than three minutes long, and the arrangements forsook traditional folk-rock touches for unconventional instrumentation like vibes and brush drums," wrote Bourne.

Came from Musical Family

"How can we hang on to a dream/How can it really be the way it seems," Hardin wrote in "How Can We Hang On to a Dream," a sentiment that summed up many of his songs. Even Hardin's performing style illustrated his lack of certainty, as he improvised often and rarely sang a lyric the same way twice, according to DeCurtis. Many of his songs were confessional, almost resembling therapy sessions for the artist. "As Bourne said, "An egotist and something of an exhibitionist, Mr. Hardin didn't hesitate to use his songs to chronicle his marriage, the birth of his son, divorce and the inner turmoil brought on by success and its temptations."

Both of Hardin's parents had musical training, and his mother, Molly Small Hardin, was one of the most highly regarded violinists in the country, having served as concertmaster of the Portland Symphony Orchestra when her son was a boy. His father had played in jazz bands while in the army and in college before embarking on a career in real estate. Many famous classical performers visited the Hardin home, but none swayed Hardin toward an interest in their type of music or in any formal music education. "I started fooling around with the guitar in high school and I sang in the Eugene high school choir," said Hardin, according to *The Encyclopedia of Folk, Country & Western Music*. "I never thought of going to college, really, in my life. If you've any kind of talent, man, it just restricts you."

Seeking an identity for himself, Hardin enlisted in the Marine Corps after dropping out of high school. During tours of duty in Cambodia and Laos he further honed his guitar playing and built up a repertoire of folk songs. Upon release from the Corps, he headed east for New York City and briefly studied acting before moving on to Cambridge, Massachusetts, where he became a key member of the growing folk music scene. Before long, Hardin was one of the favorite performers at coffeehouses and small clubs in Cambridge. By 1964 he had developed a following in the folk clubs of New York City's Greenwich Village as well. "His stunning voice and easy way of blending folk, blues and jazz influenc-

es steadily earned him a reputation on the folk scene around Boston and, after he returned in 1963, New York," said DeCurtis. Hardin composed many of his songs in Woodstock, New York, where he lived around the same time that Bob Dylan and The Band were living there.

Festival Performance Sparked Career

One of Hardin's early fans was Erik Jacobsen, a record producer who had worked with the Lovin' Spoonful. Jacobsen helped Hardin record some demos for Columbia that were mostly blues numbers. Hardin was also interested in rhythm and blues at this time, but before long he began to shape the folk voice that established his reputation. After he delivered an impressive performance at the Newport Folk Festival in 1966, Verve signed him to a recording contract that resulted in the release of his first album, *Tim Hardin 1*, that same year. Contributing to the album were noted artists John Sebastian, on harmonica, and jazz instrumentalist Gary Burton, on vibes. Many of Hardin's most critically acclaimed and enduring songs appeared on this LP, including "Misty Roses," "How Can We Hang On to a Dream," and the much-covered "Reason to Believe." Despite the largely positive response to *Tim Hardin 1*, Hardin was deeply disappointed by some of the musical elements added in the studio without his permission, especially overdubbing of strings. Various accounts claim that he actually cried when he first heard the final version.

Critical acclaim for Hardin's first album led to the release of his earlier recordings on an LP entitled *This Is Tim Hardin*. His star continued to rise with *Tim Hardin 2* in 1967, which featured his famous "If I Were a Carpenter," a song that Bobby Darin made a Top Ten hit. The song was also a hit for the Four Tops, and Johnny Cash and June Carter. Now in demand on the folk circuit, Hardin toured steadily throughout the U.S. and Europe during the next several years. However, the quality of his work began to decline due to his own combativeness in the studio, addiction to heroin, drinking problems, and frustration over his lack of commercial success. He often performed poorly or missed shows due to health problems, and at one point actually fell asleep on stage at London's Royal Albert Hall in 1968. That year he released *Tim Hardin 3*, which featured some jazz-tinged numbers.

Substance Abuse Stalled Career

In 1971 Hardin moved to England, where he remained for seven years while performing there and throughout Europe. His albums recorded in the early 1970s paled in comparison to his first albums, by most accounts. A dirth of creativity was made clear by his 1973 album *Painted Head,* which contained no original songs. His last original album, *Tim Hardin 9,* was produced that same year. After moving back to the United States, he based himself in California and set out to find an audience for his work. He continued to perform intermittently in England and on the west coast of the United States as he grappled with health and psychological problems. After reconnecting with Don Rubin, his former executive producer and music publisher during his association with Verve, he began work on a new album for Polygram in late 1980. When he died from an overdose of heroin and morphine in December of that year, he was largely unknown by the listening public.

Selected discography

Tim Hardin 1, Verve/Forecast, 1966.
Tim Hardin 2, Verve/Forecast, 1967.
Suite for Susan Moore and Damion, Columbia, 1969.
Bird on a Wire, Columbia, 1981.
Tim Hardin: Reason to Believe (The Best Of), Polydor, 1987.
Hang On to a Dream—The Verve Recordings, Polydor, 1994.

Sources

Books

Clarke, Donald, editor, *The Penguin Encyclopedia of Popular Music,* Viking, 1989, pp. 513–514.
Clifford, Mike, consultant, *The Harmony Illustrated Encyclopedia of Rock,* Harmony Books, 1988, p.73.
Larkin, Colin, editor, *The Guinness Encyclopedia of Popular Music, Volume 1,* Guinness Publishing, 1992.
Stambler, Irwin, and Grelun Landon, *The Encyclopedia of Folk, Country & Western Music,* St. Martin's Press, 1983, pp. 297–299.

Periodicals

Los Angeles Times, August 26, 1995, Section 6, p. 4.
Melody Maker, April 22, 1989, p. 34.
New York Times, February 20, 1994, Section 2, p. 30.
San Francisco Chronicle, April 3, 1994, p. 35.

Additional information for this profile was obtained from the liner notes to *Reason to Believe (The Best Of)* and *The Rough Guide to Rock* Internet website, Penguin, 1996.

—*Ed Decker*

Joe Henry

Singer, songwriter

Singer-songwriter Joe Henry is a widely respected musical artist whose moody vignettes about life's dark, sorrowful, and uncertain moments have remained powerful over the course of half a dozen albums. "He's about as far from big-picture, collective-experience guys like Jackson Browne, Bruce Springsteen, Bob Seger, and Bruce Cockburn as you can get," mused Thom Jurek in the *Metro Times,* who went on to note that Henry does not fit in with the rock world's canon of "wordsmiths" or confessionalists, either: "Henry's more like a filmmaker using jump cuts and disruptive devices to communicate a musical message that even he doesn't understand fully." Henry concurred, waving off those who would term his tales autobiographical. "I don't really write about myself, and think that it's conceited for songwriters to think that any small revelation they have is worth everybody else hearing about," he told Jurek. "I'm trying for things I can't even understand fully. I just want to set these things in front of people and let them make up their own minds about what's there."

Henry was born in Charlotte, North Carolina, but his father's work with Chevrolet soon took the family to Michigan. He grew up in the Detroit area where he met Melanie Ciccone, whom he eventually married. By the mid-1980s Melanie's sister Madonna was entrenched as one of American music's most well-known stars; Henry, meanwhile, was just beginning his career. In 1985 he and Melanie moved to Brooklyn, New York, where he played at small clubs and began shaping the songs that appeared on his debut album, 1986's *Talk of Heaven.*

Impressed with his first album, A&M Records subsequently signed Henry to their label. Over the next few years he released two albums for A&M, 1989's *Murder of Crows* and 1990's *Shuffletown,* that cemented his reputation as a literate songwriter with a penchant for keeping the odd loose end or unexplained detail in his songs. Shunning the tidy endings and shopworn themes that mark the work of so many other artists, Henry instead opted for a style that was notable as much for what was missing as for what was included. As Jurek later observed, "he asks more questions than he answers, and tells stories that don't add up to a punchline. He's a rhythmic singer who looks for spaces in between the words."

The release of *Shuffletown* also established Henry as a member of the swelling country-tinged "roots-rock" movement, in part because of his studio recording style—employing largely acoustic accompaniment, he recorded the songs live onto two-track master tapes. The result on *Shuffletown,* said *Rolling Stone* critic Bud Scoppa, was "a testament to the effectiveness of unvarnished recording in accurately capturing mood and vitality, as well as sheer, seductive *sound.*"

In 1990 Henry and his wife moved to Los Angeles, where Melanie took a job with Opal Records (she now manages artist/producer Daniel Lanois). In the meantime, Henry's relationship with A&M deteriorated to the point where he would later term his stay on the label as "disastrous." In 1992 Henry left A&M to join the independent label Mammoth, located in North Carolina. His first effort on Mammoth was *Short Man's Room,* another album that received a fair amount of critical praise but only modest sales. A year later Henry released *Kindness of the World,* on which country-rock band the Jayhawks provided much of the instrumental backing. *Guitar Player* reviewer James Rotondi called the album "downright heartbreaking," while Deborah Frost observed in *Entertainment Weekly* that Henry's "plain-sung, pedal-steel-pierced vignettes (in which firemen marry beneath paper bells and hope always squeaks past irony) plumb America's psyche with a classicist's, not a provocateur's, perspective."

In the mid-1990s, Henry made some fundamental changes in his approach to his music. "I was getting a bit bored finding myself in this country-rock thing," he told *Rolling Stone*'s Matt Hendrickson. "I really wanted to do something decidedly more electric because I didn't want to just make the same record again with different songs." Abandoning the live recording process that he had often used in his earlier albums, Henry enlisted the aid of producer Patrick McCarthy, who was well known for his mixing and programming capabilities, in making his next album, 1996's *Trampoline.*

"Seventy-five percent of the record was the two of us in this little studio near my house, with the guitars set up in a circle," Henry explained to Hendrickson. "We just started putting pieces [of music] together. It was like gluing Ernest Borgnine's head on Jayne Mansfield's body. It was a completely eye-opening experience for me, and now I can't imagine doing it any other way."

The resulting album—which also featured Helmet guitarist Page Hamilton on five songs—garnered Henry new levels of critical acclaim as well as his most significant radio airplay with the title track. Blessed with such stand-out tracks as "Ohio Air Show Plane Crash," "Flower Girl," and "Parade," the album seemed to mark a turning point for the artist. *Entertainment Weekly* reviewer Steven Mirkin called *Trampoline* "a searingly honest and compelling album" that "comes at you in oblique, disjointed snatches; woozy and haunted, with slow-motion replays and muffled violence." *Rolling Stone* critic Roni Sarig agreed, writing that "the stylistic shifts make *Trampoline* Henry's most diverse and adventurous work. But if Henry is widening his horizons, he is also focusing his vision. No longer the folk poet spinning archetypal psalms, Henry pares lyrics down to their rawest bits and draws vivid scenes." For his part, Henry admitted to Jurek that "I'm really proud of the way [the album] turned out."

Henry also collaborated with his famous sister-in-law for the first time in 1996. Asked to contribute a song to a benefit album for singer Vic Chesnutt, Henry enlisted the aid of Madonna on a cover of Chesnutt's "Guilty by Association." "I've been answering questions about her for so long, but I find it kind of a relief now, because now there's a reason to talk about her," he told Hendrickson, before wryly adding that "I'm sure she's tired of answering questions about *me,* too."

Selected discography

Talk of Heaven, 1986.
Murder of Crows, A&M, 1989.
Shuffletown, A&M, 1990.
Short Man's Room, Mammoth, 1992.
Kindness of the World, Mammoth, 1993.
Trampoline, Mammoth, 1996.
(With Madonna), "Guilty by Association," *Sweet Relief II: Gravity of the Situation, The Songs of Vic Chestnutt,* Chaos, 1996.

Sources

Acoustic Guitar, July-August 1994.
Entertainment Weekly, November 19, 1993; March 29, 1996.
Guitar Player, March 1994; July 1996.
Metro Times (Detroit), May 1-7, 1996.
New York Times, May 4, 1996.
People, May 6, 1996.
Rolling Stone, March 9, 1989; November 29, 1990; August 20, 1992; April 18, 1996; June 27, 1996.
Spin, February 1994.

—Kevin Hillstrom

Faith Hill

Singer

Since the advent of the "Young Country" movement in the early 1990s, several performers of exceptional talent have appeared on the country music horizon. At the forefront of this new wave out of Nashville has been Faith Hill. With an engaging confidence and a strong, soaring soprano that has been compared to that of Tammy Wynette, the beautiful blonde vocalist has come to embody the future of country music to a new generation of listeners. Bravely addressing social issues like domestic violence, women's rights, and the need for personal independence within her traditional country sound, Hill is esteemed as a role model for her young country music fans, while helping this traditional American musical genre navigate the modern world.

Born Audrey Faith Hill on September 21, 1967, Hill was adopted by two loving parents and raised in Star, Mississippi. Music was always an integral part of her life; she recalls enthusiastically raising her voice in song in church when she was scarcely three years old—and before she even knew many of the words. "Spirituality, religion...they've been the backbone of my life ever since I was a little girl," Hill explained to Bob Paxman in *Country Song Roundup;* "They were a regular part of my upbringing....The music in church was the first music I ever heard." During her teen years, Hill became a fan of strong female vocalists like the late Patsy Cline, Emmylou Harris—and Reba McEntire, who would serve as the young woman's role model in later years. By the time she was 16, Hill had formed her first country band. One of the group's first performances was at a Tobacco Spit competition in nearby Raleigh; from there they moved up the gig ladder, eventually graduating to rodeos and county fairs. Even while performing at these local venues, Hill knew that she would one day head for Nashville and a career in country music. Three years later, with the ink on her high school diploma still fresh and the prayers of her supportive parents encouraging her to follow her dream, 19-year-old Hill found herself Music City-bound.

Made Way in Music City

While Nashville was brimming with people who shared Hill's love of country music, it was also full of aspiring singers. In a strange town, with no friends and no job, Hill's first few months of independence were a scary time. Finally, she got a week-long job selling T-shirts at the city's annual Fan Fair celebration. Finding the encouragement to stay and stick it out, the increasingly streetwise Hill decided to pursue a common-sense strategy: she kept her dreams to herself and got a job as a receptionist at a publishing company owned by singer-songwriter Gary Morris. It would be a year

For the Record . . .

Born September 21, 1967, in Jackson, MS; married (divorced); married Tim McGraw (a country singer), October 1996.

Formed country band in high school; moved to Nashville, 1987; signed with Warner Brothers, 1993; released debut album *Take Me As I Am*, 1994; toured with Reba McEntire, Brooks & Dunn, Alan Jackson, and George Strait, 1994-95; launched Faith Hill Literacy Project, 1996; has appeared on numerous television programs, including *The Today Show, E! Goes Country, Music City Tonight*, and *A Capitol Fourth;* invited to perform at closing ceremonies of 1996 Summer Olympic Games.

Awards: Academy of Country Music, top new female performer award; CMT Europe, rising video star award; and *Billboard* top female country artist award, all 1994; *TNN/Music City News* Star of Tomorrow award, 1995.

Addresses: *Record company*—Warner/Reprise, 20 Music Square East, Nashville, TN 37203-4326.

before her intention to become a singer was fulfilled, and during that year Hill made a point of learning the business side of country music. "Boy, I immediately became right in the center of it all happening," she told *Country Music*'s Bob Millard, describing her work behind the scenes; "I got to see sides of the business that I never even thought existed. I was very, very young and naive. I was very green, but I was thrust into learning real quick."

From Morris's company, Hill moved to an office position at Starstruck Entertainment, a talent management company owned by McEntire. "Reba has shown that you can be in control of your business and still have your creative side," Hill explained to Paxman; "Dolly [Parton]'s done the same thing, and they're both great examples for us." Despite the growing understanding of business gained through working for McEntire, as well as several opportunities to work as a demo singer around town, Hill's big break didn't come until she sang harmony with performer Gary Burr at the Bluebird Cafe, a famous Music City watering hole. Sitting in the audience that night was a talent scout from Warner/Reprise, who instantly spotted Hill's potential and offered the newcomer a recording contract.

Signing with Warner/Reprise in 1993, Hill's debut album *Take Me as I Am* was produced by Scott Hen-

dricks and released the following fall. The first album single slated for national airplay was "Wild One"; it quickly climbed to the number-one slot on *Billboard* magazine's country charts, where it remained for over a month. This would be the first time a debut singer had managed such a feat since Connie Smith in 1964. Hill's second single, an upbeat, two-step county cover of Janis Joplin's blues-based "Piece of My Heart," also headed up the charts. "I got crucified," Hill explained to Jeffrey Zaslow of *USA Weekend,* in recalling the weeks before her second single's release. "Critics, radio stations, Woodstock-era fans—they were like: `Oh, great. Here's this country crap singer trying to do this legendary song.'" But Hill's strong vocals and spirited delivery carried this fresh country interpretation of the rock classic to number one. With other singles, including the title track, gaining popularity, *Take Me As I Am* moved from gold to double-platinum.

The success of Hill's first album fueled a busy 1994 tour schedule that included 150 performances, some as the opening act for performers like McEntire, Brooks & Dunn, and Alan Jackson. In addition to being on the road for months at a time, the hectic schedule put a strain on the young singer's voice. By late 1994 she was in the hospital recovering from vocal surgery. Doctor's orders included three weeks of complete silence. "For a big talker like me," Hill would later tell *People*'s Peter Castro, "that was a huge problem."

Personalized Song Selections

Hill's *It Matters to Me* was released in the summer of 1995 to critical praise. The pop-driven "Let's Go to Vegas," the first single to be released off the singer's sophomore effort, "sounds as if it could happily skip all the way to Nevada," said Mark Lasswell of *People.* Another side of Hill can be heard on singles like "Someone Else's Dream" and the Alan Jackson-penned "I Can't Do That Any More," both of which showcase a straight-talking, independent female voice framed within traditional country stylings. Vocalist Shelby Lynne joined Hill on "Keep Walkin' On," a gospel tune that the duo would also perform during the 1995 Country Music Association (CMA) award presentations. The intense and highly praised single "A Man's Home Is His Castle" movingly confronts domestic violence. Choosing such mature material proved to critics and fans that Hill was no empty-headed chanteuse, but a serious, intelligent woman who took the craft of singing seriously. "I choose the [songs] that hit me the hardest, make me feel the most," the singer told Susanna Scott in *Country Song Roundup.* Hill went on to explain that the process by which she selects material for her albums is very much a reflection of her personal feelings and concerns.

In addition to sharing the benefit of her growing popularity with charitable causes—in 1996 she launched the Faith Hill Literacy Project, aimed at combating family illiteracy—Hill has continued to tour, opening for both Alan Jackson and George Strait in 1995. The following year she began what started as a year-long tour with fellow Young Country talent Tim McGraw. The tour was extended until "when death us do part," after McGraw and Hill tied the knot in October of 1996.

Looking ahead to the future, Hill plans to follow in the footsteps of her role model, McEntire, and combine a successful career with raising a family: "I've always been very independent and wanting to know what's going on in my life and to be in control of things," the vocalist admitted to Millard. But she is driven by more than just an independent spirit and healthy ambition. "As crazy as [things] are now, I always fall back on my upbringing to get through the tough times," Hill revealed to Paxman. "My ultimate goal is to always have God as my pilot, whether it's in my career or my personal life." With two million-selling albums under her belt, Faith Hill seems to be following a clear course toward even greater success.

Selected discography

Take Me as I Am (includes "Wild One," "Piece of My Heart," and "Take Me As I Am"), Warner, 1993.
It Matters to Me, Warner, 1995.

Sources

Books

Comprehensive Country Music Encyclopedia, Random House, 1994.

Periodicals

Country Music, July/August 1994.
Country Song Roundup, December 1995; December 1996; August 1996.
People, September 11, 1995.
USA Weekend, August 27, 1995.

Additional information for this profile was provided by Warner/Reprise press materials.

—*Pamela Shelton*

Hootie and the Blowfish

Pop band

Hootie and the Blowfish made a spectacular debut on the pop music scene in 1994, releasing an album, *Cracked Rear View*, that took the entertainment world by storm. By early 1996 the album had racked up 13 million sales, making it the second best-selling debut album of all time (behind *Boston*'s eponymous 1976 release). Bristling with listener-friendly hooks, hummable melodies, and a "regular-guy" sensibility, the album and its songs weathered a slew of negative reviews to become radio and VH-1 fixtures.

"[*Cracked Rear View*] came across as something fresh and different, in large part because it didn't try to come across as anything fresh or different," explained critic Christopher John Farley in *Time*. "Hootie was embraced as an alternative to alternative, a straight-ahead zig to the posturing zag of the rest of contemporary rock." In 1996 the band released a follow-up album, *Fairweather Johnson*, that garnered somewhat more favorable reviews but also—perhaps inevitably—smaller sales.

Archive Photos/Fotos International

109

Hootie and the Blowfish came together in 1986 on the Columbia campus of the University of South Carolina, where the band members—vocalist Darius Rucker, bass player Dean Felber, guitarist Mark Bryan, and drummer Jim Sonefeld—all attended undergraduate school. The three white members of the band had arrived in Columbia after enjoying comfortable middle-class childhoods—Sonefeld in Naperville, Illinois, Felber and Bryan in Gaithersburg, Maryland—while Rucker had grown up in the poorer black neighborhoods of Charleston, South Carolina.

Frat-House Band

"I had a typical Southern African-American upbringing," Rucker told *Rolling Stone* writer Parke Puterbaugh. "Went to church every Sunday for three hours. We weren't rich by anyone's standards. There was one point where we had my mom and her two sisters, my grandmother and fourteen kids living in a three-bedroom place. We had a lot of hard times, but I loved it. I look at my childhood with very fond memories." Family members recalled that Rucker loved music from an early age. As one of his sisters told Puterbaugh, "he was always singing around the house, using a broomstick as a guitar. Mom played Al Green and Betty Wright, stuff like that, but Darius had his own tunes—a lot of what he heard on the radio and at school. Being a singer was always his dream."

As Rucker grew older, he contributed his rich baritone voice to church, high school, and college choirs, but it was not until 1986, when he hooked up with Felber and Bryan, that he joined a band (Sonefeld left a rival band to join them in 1989). After a brief period in which Rucker and Bryan performed at Columbia-area bars under the moniker of the Wolf Brothers, the pair convinced Felber to join them. The trio called themselves Hootie and the Blowfish, an odd tribute to two South Carolina classmates—one had thick, owl-like glasses, while the other was known for his jowly appearance. "We weren't thinking it was a name we would have forever," Felber admitted to *People*'s Kevin Gray. "We thought we could always think of something better."

Rucker, Felber, and Bryan then lured Sonefeld into the fold. Sonefeld had originally come to the university to play soccer, but he spent much of his free time in Columbia behind a drum kit. Upon joining Hootie, Sonefeld's approach to songwriting quickly made an impact on the other band members. After the lanky drummer put together "Hold My Hand," a song that would be a monster hit for the band a few years later, the other members of the band devoted much greater time and effort to the task of songwriting. "We'd been writing some stuff, but it had a different feel," Bryan told Puterbaugh. "Soni slowed down the groove a little, laid it back the perfect amount. It fit Darius' voice and my guitar style better in the long run."

The band members recalled their early years of bar and frat house gigs fondly, although they also noted that the South's uneasy race relations made for some tense moments. Writer Christopher John Farley noted in *Time* that "Hootie and the Blowfish's very first gig was held at an off-campus fraternity with a reputation for racism—and the interracial band was understandably wary. 'We were a little concerned about going out there and playing,' says Bryan. 'So we brought our Marine buddies along.'"

After college the foursome embarked on full-time touring, swinging through Southern bars, taverns, and fraternity house parties in exchange for modest payments, free beer, and the opportunity to meet young women. People familiar with the band at that time, however, also note that its members showed an early interest in developing their careers beyond the next gig. In 1991 the band produced a self-financed EP called *Kootchypop*. Even though it was only available at their shows, the EP eventually sold a remarkable 50,000 copies. These sales, combined with their knack for selling concert T-shirts, piqued the interest of Atlantic Records talent scout Tim Sommer. "Did I think they'd make a million dollars? No. But I did know they'd sell records," he told Farley. "Before I signed them, they'd already sold half a million dollars worth of Ts. If you can sell a T-shirt, you can sell a record."

Hootie and the Blowfish recorded *Cracked Rear View* in Los Angeles in early 1994. The album was released several months later and immediately became a phenomenon. Buoyed by heavy play on VH-1 and radio and well-received appearances on such shows as *David Letterman,* copies disappeared from record stores with amazing speed. As Farley noted, the music itself was the biggest factor in Hootie's rise: "*Cracked Rear View* featured 11 strong, tuneful songs, with brawny guitar work, commanding percussion, and Rucker's gruff, charismatic voice, which made it all come together." A succession of radio-friendly singles—"Hold My Hand," "Only Wanna Be with You," and several others—kept the album selling well, and as the media rushed to cover the fast-rising band, it became clear that the members' regular-guy personas were a big factor in their success.

Right Band at the Right Time

"We are the most unassuming band in the country," Rucker told Puterbaugh. "We are so no bulls—t. You can look at so many bands out there, and they're writing good songs, but they're mad at this or aloof or whatever. If you look at the four of us sitting in a restaurant, you wouldn't say, 'Oh, that's a band.' I think people really connect with the fact that we could be the guys you're sitting next to in your calculus class." As Puterbaugh himself remarked after watching a Hootie show, "they are not capering around the stage like shirtless punks ... nor are they inciting to riot, a la some of the choicer gangsta-rap acts. There's no hair show, no flash pots, no video screen, no Bee Girl. They're simply standing up there singing their well-liked songs.... Without smoke or mirrors, Hootie's solid, unpretentious pop tunes evoke a surprisingly visceral reaction." Added *Entertainment Weekly* reviewer David Browne, "these average guys from South Carolina were the right band at the right time: a tonic for listeners weary of cynical, anguished alternarockers, music for those who wanted something a little more comforting and unthreatening."

After awhile, the members' passion for golf and other sports became a big topic of discussion. Some people in the music world seemed to regard their love for YMCA pick-up basketball games or a quick nine holes of golf as unbecoming and decidedly uncool, but the band remained unapologetic. "We're sportsbillies," Rucker told Puterbaugh. He added, "it sounds like such bulls—t, but we just love to be together. You've seen it: all we do is laugh. Call each other names and laugh. We never leave each other alone. That's how we've stayed together for ten years, and that's why we don't change."

Despite their success, however, a large element of rock's critical community gnashed their teeth at Hootie's stardom, dismissing *Cracked Rear View* as a lightweight effort. Stoked by the music press, a modest backlash against the band developed. As Mark Jacobson wryly observed in *Esquire:* "Hootie is magic, pure and simple. How else to account for the fact that the Blowfish's *Cracked Rear View* is one of the biggest sellers ever, yet you can't find a single person who admits to liking the group?" Some took the momentum to ugly extremes, seizing on the interracial make-up of the group as a target. "A writer for the *Village Voice* compared the band to a minstrel show," wrote Farley, "and *Saturday Night Live* did a sketch where Rucker leads beer-swilling white frat boys in a countermarch to Louis Farrakhan's Million Man March (apparently, to the mostly white staff at *SNL,* successful blacks must be sellouts)." Such suggestions infuriate Rucker, who told *Entertainment Weekly*'s Chris Willman that "I guess Tupac [Shakur] or those guys are probably more accepted black figures because to white America they are more threatening. White America wants to see the one side of black. They'd love to just show us as thugs and gangsters."

On occasion, the band members expressed irritation with the critical backlash. "[Felber] showed me this article the other day in [*Bass Player*] magazine where this guy does this whole Toad the Wet Sprocket review," Rucker told Farley, "and at the end he says the only drawback with Toad is that they toured with the worst band in the world—Hootie & the Blowfish. I mean, why do you have to go out of your way to bush us? I honestly believe that if we had sold 100,000 records, people would have nice things to say about us. At the beginning of the record there were nice reviews...and all of a sudden—BOOM!—we're the worst band in the world."

Unruffled by Criticism

For the most part, the members of Hootie and the Blowfish seemed unruffled by either their newfound fame or the criticism that descended on them in late 1994 and 1995. As Bryan told Willman, "We're lucky in that we've been successful and all we've had to do is be ourselves. And if the perception of that is 'the revenge of the normal,' then that's fine." Rucker was even more succinct: "Success doesn't suck. Sure, you can't go out as easy as you used to. So?"

In 1996, while *Cracked Rear View* was still selling well, Hootie and the Blowfish released their highly anticipated follow-up, *Fairweather Johnson.* Although it did not enjoy the same phenomenal sales as those of its predecessor, the bandmates expressed satisfaction with the final product. "If we sell 8 million records [of

Fairweather Johnson], someone's gonna say it flopped," Rucker told Willman. "It's not gonna do what *Cracked Rear View* did; we're not that stupid to think it will. It's probably not gonna do half that. So it really doesn't matter when we put it out."

A number of critics gave positive reviews to the new album. "All the qualities that won the group such a huge following are still here: melodies that seem immediately familiar, an infectiously feisty spirit, and a flair for paying simple homage to love, peace, and yes, athletic pursuits," wrote *Rolling Stone* reviewer Elysa Gardner. "But the songs on *Johnson* are palpably more sophisticated than they were in Hootie's breakthrough effort, offering less bombast and more of the texture and emotion that make the best pop intriguing as well as ingratiating." *People* reviewer Peter Castro agreed, writing that "*Fairweather Johnson* plays like a live record, brimming with trademark Hootie harmonies, hooks, feel-good melodies and a wall of sound bound to raise goose bumps." Other critics, though, were less impressed. *Newsweek*'s Karen Schoemer spoke for some when she wrote in a review of *Fairweather Johnson* that "Hootie and the Blowfish peddle cozy, bland escapism. They're mediocre. It may not be a moral offense, but artistically they're guilty in the first degree."

Even though *Fairweather Johnson* proved unable to match the stunning commercial success of *Cracked Rear View*, the critical slings and arrows that have been aimed at the band have not eroded their substantial fan base. As Gardner observed, "what's ultimately most endearing about Hootie and the Blowfish is that they give the impression that, above all, they really appreciate their fans—not a universally embraced practice these days, particularly among the anti-social alternative artists."

Selected discography

Kootchypop, 1991 (EP).
Cracked Rear View, Atlantic, 1994.
Fairweather Johnson, Atlantic, 1996.

Sources

Entertainment Weekly, April 26, 1996; May 3, 1996.
Esquire, August 1996.
Essence, November 1995.
Newsweek, April 22, 1996.
New York Times, March 19, 1995; November 5, 1995; January 5, 1996.
People, April 10, 1995; April 29, 1996.
Rolling Stone, June 15, 1995; August 10, 1995; May 16, 1996.
Time, November 7, 1994; April 29, 1996.

—Kevin Hillstrom

Ian and Sylvia

Folk duo

MICHAEL OCHS ARCHIVES/Venice, CA

Well known to a generation of U.S. folk music lovers as a result of their involvement in the urban folk music revival of the 1960s, the Canadian duo of Ian and Sylvia ranked among their own country's most popular musical sensations during that same decade. From their roots in the coffeehouse folk music culture that came to fruition in large cities like New York's Greenwich Village and Toronto, Ontario, during the late 1950s, Ian Tyson and Sylvia Fricker's musical repertoire soon grew to encompass American and British folk tunes, blues influences, and original compositions; they would even embrace aspects of contemporary country music during the period that produced what was later branded the "Nashville Sound." Many of the duo's most popular songs—which included "Someday Soon," "Four Strong Winds," and "You Were on My Mind"—have not only become folk classics, but have also successfully transcended the musical culture from which they sprang and have gone on to become hits for both rock and country artists. Despite their decision to part company in the mid-1970s, both Tyson and Fricker continue to be important voices within the Canadian music community.

At the time of their first meeting in 1959 at the Village Corner, a Toronto folk music club, Tyson and Fricker were both seeking a change in their life's direction. Tyson, born in 1933 in the far-western Canadian province of British Columbia, had been raised on a small farm. As a teen he had dropped out of school to work as a farmhand and lumberjack, and then had taken to the saddle and ridden the Canadian rodeo circuit. It was the rodeo that indirectly prompted him to pick up a guitar for the first time; Tyson was looking for a way to pass the time while recuperating from a broken leg, the result of a rodeo mishap. "Back in the '50s, not many people played the guitar," he later explained to *Country Song Roundup*'s Jennifer Fusco-Giacobbe. "It was really a folk process," Tyson added. "Everybody just taught themselves." Although he made an attempt to escape his rural roots by enrolling in the Vancouver School of Art and embarking on a career as a commercial artist, Tyson soon found himself drifting back to the rodeo ring after graduation. And his creative instincts were drifting away from art and toward music. During his constant travels across Canada, he began to earn extra money by playing his guitar and singing at small folk clubs.

Fricker, meanwhile, was searching for a way to escape her humdrum life as a jewelry store clerk in her hometown of Chatham, Ontario. The daughter of a department store manager and a music teacher, she sang in the church choir that her mother led until the blues-based rhythms drifting into her small farming community from a Detroit, Michigan, radio station inspired an interest in folk harmonies. By the time she was 15,

Fricker was determined to make something more of her life; inspired by the success of musicians like Pete Seeger, the Weavers, and Jean Richie, she wanted to become a folk singer. Teaching herself guitar, the young vocalist built a repertoire of British and American folk songs by memorizing tunes from folk song anthologies obtained from the Chatham Public Library. Quitting her clerking position soon after graduating from high school in 1958, Fricker moved to the city of Toronto, found a day-job at a local clothing store, and became singing partners with Tyson. While Fricker performed as a solo act at a small club called the Bohemian Embassy, she and Tyson also began working on arrangements of traditional ballads: Tyson, on guitar, sang lead while Fricker performed background harmonies. The pair took their work seriously, rehearsing at least three times a week.

Crossing over to the U.S. Folk Music Scene

By early 1959 Tyson and Fricker were performing part-time at the Village Corner under the name Ian and Sylvia. The pair became a full-time musical act in 1961 and married four years later. Although their raw, mountain-style sound quickly became popular with Toronto audiences, a trip to Columbia, South Carolina, to perform at a cotillion ball convinced the pair that they had what it took to move beyond "local talent" status. Ian and Sylvia traveled to New York City in the early 1960s, where they became involved in the very active Greenwich Village folk scene. Meeting up with Albert Grossman, manager of such popular acts of the era as Bob Dylan, Peter, Paul and Mary, and fellow-Canadian Gordon Lightfoot, proved to be the couples' first real break into the U.S. market. Grossman agreed to manage the duo and scheduled a concert tour that quickly found Ian and Sylvia performing before folk fans at leading clubs from Chicago to Los Angeles. As the urban folk revival grew, fueled by the civil rights movement, so did the Canadian duo's popularity, particularly among college students.

In 1962 Tyson and Fricker recorded their first album, *Ian and Sylvia*, under contract with Vanguard, the only large-scale record label then specializing in folk acts. Although the album did not produce large-scale sales, it did spread the tradition-flavored work of the duo to even more listeners, broadening their loyal (if still relatively small) following among American folk music aficionados.

At this point Ian and Sylvia began to develop their unique character within the folk music genre. U.S. folk music was growing in stature and scope due to the work of artists such as Bob Dylan and Arlo Guthrie, who wrote many of their own songs. Both Tyson and Fricker started to follow suite and began composing original material. Sylvia's inspiration was the blues, while Ian wrote of the rural life he had left behind in the Canadian west. Their next two albums, *Four Strong Winds* and *Northern Journey*, reflected this more contemporary direction. The albums also brought the duo to an international audience when they were released in 1964, sparking a performance schedule that would include major folk festivals both around the United States and overseas.

Songwriting Efforts Hold Timeless Appeal

During the mid- to late-1960s the couple wrote and recorded several memorable tunes, including Tyson's "Four Strong Winds" and "Someday Soon," as well as Fricker's "You Were on My Mind," which in 1965 would be a top five pop hit for the folk group We Five. "Four Strong Winds" became a number three country hit for singer Bobby Bare in 1964 and survived the passage of time to become a pop single for rock singer Neil Young more than 15 years later. "Someday Soon," a favorite of country star Lynn Anderson—as well as of folksinger Judy Collins, who recorded the Tyson-penned tune in the 1970s—was transformed into a hit on the country charts for the second time by Suzy Bogguss almost three decades after Ian and Sylvia first recorded it. Remarking on the universality and continuing popularity of certain types of songs, Bill C. Malone notes in his scholarly *Singing Cowboys and Musical Mountaineers* that the rambler theme "assume[s] a bittersweet poignancy in such rodeo songs as Ian Tyson's `Someday Soon,'... which document[s] the strains in human relationships often wrought by nomadic occupations or lifestyles."

In listening to the recordings that followed Ian and Sylvia's debut LP, one was immediately aware of the eclectic mixture of styles that were represented: from bluegrass, French Canadian tunes, and pop to cowboy ballads and folk melodies. By writing their own material the duo also effectively showcased the differences in their individual musical personalities. Fricker, with a soprano voice that ranged in tone from a demure lilt to a nasal, confrontative wail, wrote material that sometimes broke with songwriting convention. Her overall style was idiosyncratic compared with that of Tyson, whose warm, mellow tenor found its truest footing in songs inspired by his love of the West and traditional themes of love, loss, and loneliness. In addition to such richly creative and diverse music, *Four Strong Winds* also marked Ian and Sylvia's decision to begin using session musicians on their recordings, thereby supplementing Tyson's acoustic guitar with electric bass and guitar and a variety of other instruments. In the albums that followed *Northern Journey*, the couple searched for a single "sound" that would unite them; they would finally find it in Nashville, Tennessee.

Influenced by New-Style Country Sound

Ian and Sylvia originally traveled to Nashville in 1968 with the intention of recording with some of the best session musicians that could be found in one place. Whether acoustic or electrified, Music City has always been notable for the quantity of talented musicians that make Greater Nashville their home. Not surprisingly considering their own rural roots, Ian and Sylvia quickly became caught up in the new sounds coming out of north-central Tennessee. The "Nashville Sound" itself—characterized by a heavy use of "strings" as backup—permeated commercial country music during the 1960s, one of its chief promoters being RCA-producer Chet Atkins. While finishing up their recording commitment to Vanguard with 1968's country-jazz fusion entitled *Nashville*, Ian and Sylvia incorporated some of these country influences into a new stage show, put together a country band dubbed the Great Speckled Bird, and began touring in 1969. The two albums they would later record for Capitol—*Full Circle* and *Ian and Sylvia*—each show-cased the duo's avant garde country western repertoire.

Unfortunately, Ian and Sylvia's now heavily instrumental live performances and "countrified" recordings rapidly alienated them from their original fans. In fact, many folk-music purists were offended by the injection of what they saw as derivative Nashville pop into a folk concert. "People even got up and walked out," Sylvia is quoted as commenting in *Encyclopedia of Country and Western Music.* "They would have a violent reaction to the steel guitar. They'd walk out on the first bars that the steel player would hit." Although the group's sound grew increasingly accepted—in 1970 they were given a standing ovation at a Calgary folk music festival—their new audience wasn't enough to win back their U.S. audience. The pair's 1970 recording, the Todd Rundgren-produced *Great Speckled Bird*, was unsuccessful. After Tyson's 1972 arrest for marijuana possession made travel into the United States impossible, the couple disbanded their touring show.

Follow Separate Paths

The following year, while searching for a new direction, Tyson and Fricker were invited to co-host *Nashville North*, a weekly television series planned for broadcast throughout Canada by the Canadian Broadcast System (CBC). The show provided the couple with an excellent opportunity to take the time to reevaluate their direction. Although Ian and Sylvia continued to perform together on *Nashville North*, it became increasingly clear that their paths had begun to diverge, both personally and professionally. Ian and Sylvia announced their decision to separate in 1974; Tyson and Fricker divorced a decade later.

Although each would chart a separate course, both halves of Ian and Sylvia have since maintained strong ties to the folk music genre. In addition to writing and performing on stage, Fricker recorded her first solo album, *Woman's World*, for Capitol, with Tyson acting as producer. From 1977 to 1982 she hosted the CBC-Radio music program *Touch the Earth*. The program, which showcased folk, pop, and country music artists, eventually spun off into a television series called *Country in My Soul*, which was broadcast on Canadian television from 1983 to 1984. In addition to forming her own record label—Salt Records—Fricker helped organize and perform in a 1984 television special for the CBC.

Meanwhile, after extending the popular *Nashville North*'s run on television for a few years as *The Ian Tyson Show*, the other half of Ian and Sylvia turned his back on the celebrity lifestyle and returned to his rural roots. "I wanted to train horses, live on a ranch, and possibly get a ranch if I could make enough money," Tyson told Fusco-Giacobbe of his decision to leave music during the late 1970s. Devoting several years to working his 160-acre spread in southern Alberta's Canadian Rockies, Tyson began to reintegrate music into his life during the early 1980s. The songs he now began to write and record related his experiences as a cattle rancher and rodeo rider; the musical trail he has since followed has joined him with such cowboy traditionalists as Michael Martin Murphey, Red Steagall, and Chris LeDoux. While, as historian Bill C. Malone notes, such traditional cowboy songs "seldom become big commercial successes," Tyson's 1987 release, *Cowboyography*, went platinum in Canada and sold more than 100,000 copies. The recording also earned Tyson a Juno award, Canada's equivalent to a Grammy award.

In 1993 Tyson signed with Vanguard as a solo artist and recorded the critically acclaimed *Eighteen Inches of Rain*, his first album released in the United States in over two decades. Ian and Sylvia reunited briefly in 1986, performing with fellow artists Emmylou Harris, Linda Ronstadt, and Judy Collins in concert on stage in Toronto, the city where they first raised their voices in folk-inspired harmony over two and a half decades earlier.

Selected discography

As Ian and Sylvia

Ian and Sylvia, Vanguard, 1962.
Four Strong Winds, Vanguard, 1964.
Northern Journey (includes "You Were on My Mind"), Vanguard, 1964.
Early Morning Rain, Vanguard, 1965.
Play One More, Vanguard, 1966.
So Much for Dreaming, Vanguard, 1967.
Nashville, Vanguard, 1968.
Full Circle, MGM, 1968.
Lovin' Sound, Columbia, 1969.

Ian and Sylvia, Columbia, 1969.
(With Amos Garrett and Buddy Cage) *Great Speckled Bird*, Ampex, 1970.
(With others) *Folk Music at Newport, Volume 1* Vanguard, c. 1980.

Solo albums by Sylvia Fricker

Woman's World, Capitol, c. 1976.

Solo albums by Ian Tyson

Ol' Eon, A & M Canada, 1975.
Cowboyography, Vanguard, 1987.
Eighteen Inches of Rain, Vanguard, 1993.

Sources

Books

Bufwack, Mary A., and Robert K. Oermann, *Finding Her Voice: The Saga of Women in Country Music*, Crown, 1993.
Basselaar, Kristin, and Donald Milton, *Folk Music Encyclopedia*, Omnibus Press, 1977.
Basselaar, Kristin, and Donald Milton, *Folk Music: More than a Song*, Crowell, 1976.
Editors of *Country Music* magazine, *Comprehensive Country Music Encyclopedia*, Random House, 1994.
Malone, Bill C., *Singing Cowboys and Musical Mountaineers: Southern Culture and the Roots of Country Music*, University of Georgia Press, 1993.
Stambler, Irwin, and Grelun Landon, *Encyclopedia of Folk, Country & Western Music*, St. Martin's Press, 1983.

Periodicals

Country Music, May 1994, p. 30.
Country Song Roundup, August 1994, pp. 62-63.
Rolling Stone, September 10, 1988.
—Pamela Shelton

Blind Lemon Jefferson

Guitarist, singer, songwriter

Archive Photos/Frank Driggs Collection

Blind Lemon Jefferson emerged in the 1920s as one of the most popular and imitated blues guitarists of the decade. As an early exponent of the Texas blues style, Jefferson's recorded performances exhibited an array of unique and inventive musical ideas. His sides for the Paramount label found their way into the repertoires of numerous bluesmen, influencing both country and urban blues stylists throughout the 1930s and 1940s. Despite Jefferson's musical contribution, information regarding his life—limited to one surviving photograph and scant recollections by local eyewitnesses and fellow musicians—has left little to reveal the man behind the music. Sixty years after his death, Jefferson's catalogue of nearly one hundred recordings reveal the musical power and poetic storytelling ability of an American folk music legend.

Lemon Jefferson—the 1900 Freestone census lists one member of the Jefferson family as Lemmon B. Jefferson—was born the youngest child of Alec Jefferson and Classie Banks near Couchman, Texas on July 11, 1897. Believed to be blind at birth, Jefferson was able to offer little help to his farming family. Without an education he took up music and worked as an itinerant musician, performing on streets and local functions outside Wortham, Texas. He also appeared as a singer at local church events such as the General Association of Baptist Churches in Buffalo, Texas.

Played for Tips as Street Musician

Jefferson later traveled through towns along the H & TC Railroad—Groesbeck, Martin, and Kosse—and around 1912 performed in the Deep Ellum section of Dallas. With a tin cup wired to the neck of his guitar, he played for tips on the streets, often performing slide guitar numbers, a technique which utilized a small metal or glass cylinder on a finger of the chord hand to produce voice-like chords and melodies. While in Dallas in 1912, Jefferson joined up with an older musician, Huddie "Leadbelly" Ledbetter. Years later, Leadbelly recalled, in *The Life and Legend of Leadbelly*, his experiences performing with Jefferson: "Him and me was buddies. Used to play all up and around Dallas-Fort Worth. In them times, we'd get on the Interurban line that runs from Waco to Dallas, Corsicana, Waxahacie, from Dallas." For an intermittent period of several years the pair traveled extensively, sometimes taking in $150 each weekend. While Jefferson sang and played slide, Leadbelly accompanied his younger companion on accordion, guitar, or mandolin.

In 1917 Jefferson worked at Al Bonner's Place in Gill, Arkansas, and continued to hobo around the deep

South, often returning to his home base of Dallas. In *Meeting the Blues*, Bluesman Mance Lipscomb, who encountered Jefferson in Dallas around 1917, told how the guitarist's popularity on the street led whites to prohibit him from performing downtown: "They gave him the privilege to play in a certain district in Dallas, and they call that 'on the track.' Right beside the place where he stood 'round there under a big old shade tree, call it a standpoint, right off the railroad track. And people started coming in there, from nine thirty until six o'clock that evening, then he would go home because it was getting dark and someone [led] him home." The spot described by Lipscomb was located on the corner of Elm and Central Tracks in Dallas's ethnic enclave known as Deep Ellum.

Played with "T-Bone" Walker in Early Days

A few years after Lipscomb's encounter with Jefferson, Aaron "T-Bone" Walker also accompanied the blind guitarist around Deep Ellum. In *Meeting the Blues* Walker stated, "I used to lead Blind Lemon Jefferson around playing and passing the cup, take him from one beer joint to another. I liked hearing him play. He would sing like nobody's business ... People used to crowd around so you couldn't see him." "Afterwards," as Walker related to Helen Dance in *Stormy Monday*, "I'd guide him back up the hill, and Mama would fix supper. She'd pour him a little taste."

Around 1922 Jefferson married a woman named Roberta. At that time, "he'd gotten so fat," wrote Samuel

Charters in *The Country Blues*, "that when he played, the guitar sat up on his stomach, the top just under his chin." In the slum areas of Dallas he emerged as the city's most popular street singer. As a songster he entertained crowds by performing a wide musical repertoire such as vaudeville songs, rags, Tin Pan Alley tunes, spirituals, and blues numbers. In the mid 1920s pianist Sam Price brought Jefferson to the attention of his employer, R.T. Ashford, the owner of a Dallas record store and a talent scout for several recording companies (other accounts contend that Price wrote to Paramount's recording director and informed him about Jefferson). Ashford then brought the guitarist to the notice of a Paramount record executive A.C. Bailey. After locating Jefferson on a street in Deep Ellum, Bailey invited the guitarist to attend a recording at the company's Chicago studio.

Debuted on Paramount Label

In the 1920s, when most other major labels sent field units to the South to record blues artists, Jefferson attended out-of-town sessions in the cities of Chicago, Atlanta, and Richmond Indiana. During his first trip to the studio in 1926 he cut his first side, "That Black Snake Moan," in Chicago's Paramount studio. The number became a immediate commercial success and prompted the recording of many more sides. In February 1926 Paramount released the 78 featuring "Got the Blues" and "Long Lonesome," rumored to have sold over one hundred thousand copies. Because of the company's extensive mail order system, there were few African-American folk musicians from Texas to the eastcoast who were not aware of Jefferson's music. As Paul Oliver stated in *The New Grove*, Jefferson's "Lone Lonesome Blues" brought the "authentic sound of rural blues to thousands of black homes." Jefferson's "Matchbox Blues" was recorded twice by Paramount in 1927, and several decades later found its way into the repertoires of Carl Perkins, Elvis Presley, and the Beatles. Another of Jefferson's popular numbers, "See That My Grave is Kept Clean," was re-recorded by numerous blues artists throughout the South. This number, observed John Cowley in *The Blackwell Guide*, "has lyrical antecedents to several earlier pieces, among them 'Old Blue,' the nineteenth-century sea shanty 'Stormalong,' the British folk song 'Who Killed Cock Robin' and several spirituals."

Recorded Final Songs in 1929

In 1927 Jefferson also recorded for the Okeh label in Atlanta, Georgia. Though sales of Jefferson's records waned by the late 1920s, he continued to wear immaculate suits and employed a full-time chauffeur. In 1929 Jefferson recorded his last sides for the Paramount at the Gennett label in Richmond, Indiana. Among the numbers recorded for the Gennett session were "Pneumonia Blues," "The Cheater's Spell," and "Southern Women Blues."

In December 1929, Jefferson died of a heart attack and exposure on a Chicago street, reportedly after his chauffeur abandoned him and his automobile during a snow storm. His body was brought back to Texas and interned in the Negro burying ground of Wortham cemetery. For decades, while Jefferson's unmarked and weed-ridden gravesite existed in small country cemetery, enthusiasts around the world formed societies and publications in his honor. In October 1967 the Texas State Historical Society placed a plaque marking the resting place of one of America's most enduring folk music legends.

Influenced Generations of Music-Makers

Jefferson is considered a musical idol by musicians such as B.B. King, and his recordings continue to awe listeners. In the *New Grove*, British music writer Paul Oliver described Jefferson's enduring vocal sound: "His voice was high, piercing the traffic noise, but could also have a low, moaning quality extended by 'bending' the notes on his guitar to produce crying sounds or imitative passages on the strings." Jefferson's intricate and erratic guitar work followed broken-time patterns with standard four-four measures and tempo altered to fit spontaneous vocal lines or guitar.

Apart from his stunning and inventive guitar work, Jefferson authored many songs that found their way into the repertoires of musicians from John Lee Hooker to Bob Dylan. "Lemon sang things he wrote himself about life—good times and bad. Mostly bad, I guess," stated T-Bone Walker in *Stormy Monday*. "Everyone knew what he was singing about." Over a half century after his death, Jefferson's music still haunts listeners with descriptions of a time and culture that existed outside the popular and glamorous images of America's roaring twenties.

Selected discography

Singles

"That Black Snake Moan," Paramount, 1926.
"Broke and Hungry Blues," Paramount, 1926.
"Match Box Blues," Paramount, 1927.
"See That My Grave is Kept Clean," Paramount, 1928.
"Prison Cell Blues," Paramount, 1928.
"That Crawling Baby Blues," Paramount, 1929.
"Big Night Blues," Paramount, 1929.
"Tin Cup Blues," Paramount, 1929.
"Mosquito Moan," Paramount, 1929.
"Pneumonia Blues," Paramount, 1929.
"Cheater's Spell," Paramount, 1929.
"Southern Woman Blues," Paramount, 1929.

Albums

Blind Lemon Jefferson, Milestone.
King of the Country Blues, Yazoo.

Compilations

The Story of the Blues, Columbia, 1969.
The Blues: A Smithsonian Collection of Classic Blues Singers, Sony, 1993.
Blues Masters Vol. 3: Texas Blues, Rhino.

Sources

Charters, Samuel B., *The Country Blues*, Da Capo, 1975.
Dance, Helen Oakley, *Stormy Monday: The T-Bone Walker Story*, Da Capo, 1987.
Govenar, Alan, *Meeting the Blues, The Rise of the Texas Sound*, Taylor Publishing, 1988.
Kennedy, Rick, *Jelly Roll, Bix, and Hoagy: Gennett Studios and the Birth of Recorded Jazz*, Indiana University Press, 1994.
Oliver, Paul, Max Harrison, William Bolcom, *The New Grove Gospel, Blues and Jazz with Spirituals and Ragtime*, W.W. Norton, 1986.
Wolfe, Charles and Kip Lornell, *The Life and Legend of Leadbelly*, Harper Collins, 1992.

—John Cohassey

Jon Spencer Blues Explosion

Rock band

Combining the dejected airs of the blues with punk's sneering energy, the Jon Spencer Blues Explosion makes records that are often ignored by commercial radio but adored by critics and a hardcore legion of fans alike. Spencer leads his band, together since the early 1990s, into new and innovative musical territories that run the gamut from collaboration with an old-style Mississippi blues artist to incorporating a Theremin for live performances, an odd synthesizer-type instrument developed in the Soviet Union in the 1920s and later used for American horror films and the Beach Boys' hit, "Good Vibrations." Its eerie sound and the gore-matinee mood it evokes seem to dovetail perfectly with Spencer's essence and artistic vision. As *Melody Maker*'s John Robb explained, "Spencer is a sharp blade who knows that the feel of rock 'n' roll was far better in the deadly Fifties than in the overrated Sixties."

Spencer grew up in New Hampshire and went to Brown University, but dropped out his sophomore year after meeting guitarist Julia Cafritz. He had originally wanted to pursue filmmaking, but "then I realized it would be easier to be onstage and playing music than going through the long, drawn-out hassle of making a movie," he recalled in a *Rolling Stone* interview with Christina Kelly. In 1985 he joined New York City-based Pussy Galore with Cafritz; another member was Christina Martinez, who eventually married Spencer. Within a year the band had developed a cult following, though record sales always remained low. "At their '86-'87 peak, Pussy Galore were the finest American punk band going, the jagged side of early Fall/Neubauten filtered through a uniquely U.S. hardcore postgrad sensibility," wrote Gerard Cosloy in the *Village Voice.*

Launched Blues Explosion

Pussy Galore disbanded in 1990, a year after Martinez and Spencer had formed Boss Hogg. Spencer busied himself with the new band and another New York City-based outfit called the Honeymoon Killers, and eventually made the acquaintance of drummer Russell Simins. The two began playing together and were later joined by Simins's roommate, guitarist Judah Bauer. The trio officially formed the Jon Spencer Blues Explosion in 1991 and recorded their first effort under this name, 1992's *Crypt Style,* in just five hours, and released it on Crypt Records. In this band without a bassist, either Spencer or Bauer will play a rhythm line on their guitar; Spencer is partial to a cheap Japanese-made guitar that his wife bought for under twenty dollars. Eventually the Blues Explosion signed with Caroline and an eponymous debut on the label was released that same year. Joe Levy reviewed it for *Rolling Stone* and found that "at his best, Spencer cross-wires the menacing emptiness of early country blues with the compulsive overload of Nineties noise." More succinctly, *Melody Maker*'s Cathi Unsworth called it a record "reeking of blood, sex and vicious jazz."

By 1993 the Blues Explosion had switched to the Matador label, and their second effort, *Extra Width,* was released that year. Again, they finished in near-record time. On it, wrote *Melody Maker*'s Dave Simpson, they "manage to sound *possessed,* as if there's actually something *in* them, throwing this stuff out." Spencer later said that though he was initially happy with the finished product, when he heard the record played in clubs he discerned its flaws clearly. When it came time to record again—1994's *Orange*—he took a different approach, and he and Bauer and Simins rehearsed the songs live over a period of weeks. "It used to be that we would go into the studio every three or four months and just record basic tracks in an afternoon," Spencer said of the previous releases in an interview with *Spin*'s Jac Zinder.

Strove for Perfection

Orange—named in homage to a vivid backdrop behind soul singer James Brown in some 1960s footage they had seen—prompted Spencer to admit to *Spin* that "we tried so hard to get the sound full and make a technically superior record to *Extra Width* that it nearly drove us

Members include **Jon Spencer** (born c. 1965, in New Hampshire; son of a university professor and a cardiology technician; attended Brown University, mid-1980s), vocals and guitar; **Russell Simins**, drums; **Judah Bauer** (born in Wisconsin), guitar.

Group formed c. 1991 in New York City.

Addresses: *Home*—New York City. *Record company*—Matador Records, 676 Broadway, New York, NY 10012-2319.

---

crazy." The results were evident. *Orange* included experimentation with synthesizers and odd production tricks as well as a spoken-word bit that alternative-rapper Beck contributed by phone from Australia. Like other critics, *Melody Maker*'s Robb enthused over *Orange,* calling it an "unholy, godlike surge of excitement." *Rolling Stone*'s Jon Wiederhorn called it "an emotional clash of stormy blues, passionate soul and noisy garage rock punctuated at various points by the sounds of lush strings, distorted vocals, DJ scratching and galactic sound effects."

After touring in support of *Orange,* the Blues Explosion played some dates with Mississippi blues singer R.L. Burnside. They also appeared on his album, *A Ass Pocket Full of Whiskey,* and wrote "RL Got Soul" in homage to him for their next project, 1996's *Now I Got Worry.* Despite this—and its guest appearance by legendary rhythm 'n' blues singer Rufus Thomas—*Rolling Stone*'s Kelly noted, "the album is largely devoid of the black cultural signifiers that have previously worked the nerves of some critics of the Blues Explosion." She termed *Now I Got Worry* "darker and even more raucous than...*Orange,*" and Spencer confirmed that impression in their interview. "There is a lot more personal stuff on the album, just about living, trying to get along," he said.

Spellbinding Shows

The Blues Explosion's live shows are legendary performances. "Bauer sounds like he and Jon have been writing and playing together since birth," wrote Cosloy in the *Village Voice.* In an interview with *Rolling Stone*'s Wiederhorn, guitarist Bauer admitted: "I think the amount of energy we put into one show with the Blues Explosion is easily equal to a 40-hour work week." Wiederhorn's colleague Christina Kelly was also enraptured. His "stage presence is unmatched in indie rock," Kelly wrote. "He screams and gyrates as if he just can't help himself." Spencer closes each live number by shouting "Blues Explosion!" Yet he and his collaborators have also suffered because of that name; journalists ask if they consider themselves an actual "blues" band, or seem confused as to why three white musicians boldly appropriate African American cultural influences. Spencer tried to explain it to James Rotondi in *Guitar Player.* "We're certainly not a blues band in a strict formal sense," he admitted, "but in the sense that it's raw and true and honest, I think we *are* a blues band."

Selected discography

Crypt Style, Crypt, 1992.
The Jon Spencer Blues Explosion, Caroline, 1992.
Extra Width, Matador, 1993.
Mo Width, Au-Go-Go, 1994.
Orange, Matador, 1994.
Now I Got Worry, Matador, 1996.

Sources

Books

Spin Alternative Record Guide, edited by Eric Weisbard with Craig Marks, Vintage Books, 1995.

Periodicals

Guitar Player, March 1995, pp. 29, 34.
Melody Maker, September 25, 1993, p. 34; October 23, 1993, p. 8; October 15, 1994, p. 38; October 22, 1994, p. 43; October 14, 1995, pp. 52-53.
Musician, March 1995, p. 18.
Rolling Stone, November 26, 1992, p. 74; January 26, 1995; October 17, 1996, pp. 31, 36.
Spin, December 1994, p. 30.
Village Voice, May 19, 1992, pp. 74, 87; February 21, 1995, p. 66.

—Carol Brennan

The
Klezmatics

Klezmer music band

What do you get when you throw together a collection of gifted musicians from such diverse musical worlds as rock, experimental jazz, Balkan folk, and classical, and get them to play a hip, updated version of traditional Eastern European Jewish party music? If you're lucky, you might get the Klezmatics, one of the bands most responsible for the surging popularity of klezmer music during the last several years. Klezmer is music for celebration, historically played at weddings and other events at which Jews—both Old World and New—felt like dancing.

Rather than merely reviving a branch of music from the past, the Klezmatics have taken old-time klezmer and made it their own, drawing from the various forms and influences that have been relevant to their own lives. By doing so, the band has helped bring klezmer to the attention of a wide audience that includes Jews and non-Jews. This infectious brand of Jewish roots music frequently has senior citizens and teenage punkers dancing in a shared aisle. Many people had pronounced klezmer dead as early as the 1950s, as second genera-

Photograph by Lloyd Wolf

For the Record . . .

Members include **Lorin Sklamberg,** lead vocals, accordion; **Frank London,** trumpet; **Alicia Svigals,** violin; **David Licht,** percussion; **David Krakauer,** clarinet (replaced by **Matt Darriau,** clarinet, saxophone, 1996); **Paul Morrissett,** bass.

Sklamberg is vice president of Living Traditions, Inc., sponsors of the Yiddish Folk Arts Program and has performed with clarinetist Don Byron and on various Yiddish song recordings; London is a member of Les Miserables Brass Band, has performed with John Zorn, Lester Bowie, L.L. Cool J, and Mel Torme, has composed music for film, theater, and dance projects; Svigals has composed and performed traditional Greek music and has performed with classical and rock artists, including Led Zeppelin's Robert Plant and Jimmy Page; Licht has been a member of Shockabilly and Bongwater and has played with various klezmer ensembles; Darriau leads the Balkan rhythm quartet Paradox Trio, composes for a variety of media, and has performed with, among others, David Byrne and Charlie Haden; Morrissett has performed and recorded traditional Balkan and Scandinavian folk music with many groups in many venues.

Awards: Deutsche Schallplatten Kritikspreis for *Rhythm + Jews,* 1992; nominated for best group at First Annual Gay & Lesbian American Music Awards (GLAMA), 1995.

Addresses: *Record company*—Xenophile Records, 43 Beaver Brook Road, Danbury, CT 06810. *Management*—151 First Ave., Suite 59, New York, NY 10003.

klezmer work, London's resume has covered just about every inch of musical turf, from Mel Torme to LL Cool J.

At first, the band was essentially a jazz outfit that drew from its members' eclectic musical pasts. Within a couple of years, however, the Klezmatics became firmly entrenched in the klezmer idiom. Apparently, the new music scene of Manhattan's Lower East Side was more than ready for its own klezmer group, as the Klezmatics quickly built a healthy following in their home territory.

Added Chutzpah to Klezmer

Through painstaking research, the Klezmatics became experts in traditional klezmer, exploring the nuances of each instrument and song type. Some members even learned the Yiddish language to facilitate their education. At the same time, they infused the material with a politically and artistically charged attitude that reflected their own ideas about music and the world. The result was something that was both familiar and new, and it was effectively captured on the Klezmatics' first recording *Shvaygn = Toyt*—Yiddish for Silence = Death, a motto of the militant AIDS awareness group Act Up—released on the German label Piranha Records in 1988.

Appearing often at Bar Mitzvahs and fashionable downtown nightclubs, the Klezmatics played to increasingly larger audiences as the 1990s began. The group's commitment to dogged research never flagged, as members spent hours scrutinizing scratchy 78s for stylistic clues and new material. In 1992 the second Klezmatics recording, *Rhythm + Jews,* was released on Flying Fish. Among other things, the CD gave voice to the Klezmatics' gay activism, a philosophical stance that has appeared in the band's work repeatedly. *Rhythm + Jews* made it into the top ten on *Billboard* magazine's World Music chart.

The Klezmatics continued to both master klezmer the way the old-timers played it, and to incorporate more outside elements, including rock and hip-hop, into their approach. The idea was that klezmers—meaning musicians—have always absorbed the popular music of their neighbors, whether it be gypsy melodies from Rumania or big band swing in America. As violinist Svigals noted in the *Village Voice,* "Yiddish music is *our* music, but so is Led Zeppelin. What we're playing reflects exactly who we are: Jews in New York in 1991."

Penetrated College Audience

As their popularity grew, the Klezmatics began to collaborate on projects with an assortment of nationally-

tion Jewish-Americans assimilated into the American mainstream. The Klezmatics and other newer bands, however, have proven that far from being extinct, klezmer remains a living, evolving musical form with broad and current appeal.

The Klezmatics formed in 1986, when several of its original members answered a classified ad seeking musicians to play klezmer. Of those individuals, only trumpet player Frank London had an extensive background in klezmer, having performed with the Klezmer Conservatory Band, based in Boston. Violinist Alicia Svigals, for example, specialized in Greek traditional music and composition for theater, while percussionist David Licht was a veteran of such cutting edge rock acts as Bongwater and Shockabilly. In addition to his and internationally-known musicians from a wide variety of musical genres. Their 1995 recording *Jews With Horns* (Xenophile) included guest appearances by pop star Elvis Costello and guitarist Marc Ribot, a fixture on the Manhattan new music scene. On *Jews With Horns* the Klezmatics reaffirmed their pro-gay stance, particularly with the first track, "Man in a Hat," a homosexual pick-up story with a rollicking beat and rapid-fire wordplay. *Jews With Horns* reached the top ten on *College Music Journal*'s World Music chart and also appeared on the *Village Voice*'s 1995 Best of the Year list.

By this time, the list of well-known artists—both musicians and nonmusicians—with whom the Klezmatics had collaborated included poet Allen Ginsberg, composer/saxophonist John Zorn, choreographer Twyla Tharp, and award-winning playwright Tony Kushner. The band had also appeared on several television shows by this time, including *Late Night with David Letterman*, *CBS Nightwatch*, *MTV News*, and the BBC's *Rhythms of the World*.

Fiddled with Perlman on TV

As the 1990s continued, new projects came in bunches for the Klezmatics. Among the band's 1995 projects were the presentation of its performance piece *The Third Seder* at New York's Jewish Museum; and a collaborative effort with the Los Angeles Modern Dance and Ballet Company called *Klezmania*. The band's most visible project, however, was its appearance, along with three other prominent klezmer ensembles, with classical violinist Itzhak Perlman in the Emmy Award-winning PBS television special "In the Fiddler's House." Perlman's involvement in klezmer helped to dramatically increase the American public's awareness of klezmer, and as a result the "In the Fiddler's House" tour played to capacity audiences everywhere it went, through much of 1996.

The success of the Perlman collaboration led to plans for a second recording to be released in 1996, as well as a European tour. That year, the Klezmatics participated in another, perhaps more intriguing collaborative project, teaming with the 4,000-year old Moroccan ensemble The Master Musicians of Jajouka for a performance at New York's Central Park. In the fall of 1996, the Klezmatics went into the studio to begin work on their own next recording project, which promised to include a suite from their score for Tony Kushner's adaptation of the classic Yiddish play *The Dybbuk*, as well as the usual assortment of klezmer originals, standards, nonstandards, neostandards, and hybrids. With bands like the Klezmatics leading the way, it seems likely that klezmer, in spite of the premature reports of its demise 40 years ago, is here to stay.

Selected discography

Shvaygn = Toyt, Piranha, 1988.
Rhythm + Jews, Flying Fish, 1992.
Jews With Horns, Xenophile, 1995.
(With Itzhak Perlman and others) *In the Fiddler's House*, Angel, 1995.

Sources

Economist, April 6, 1996.
New York Times, July 4, 1996.
Sound Views, December 1995.
Village Voice, February 12, 1991.
Washington Post, June 9, 1996.

Additional information for this profile was obtained from Xenophile Records press material, 1996, and a conversation with Klezmatics member Frank London.

—*Robert R. Jacobson*

KMFDM

Industrial music band

Despite any rumors to the contrary, KMFDM is an acronym for the German phrase, *kein Mitleid fuer die Mehrheit,* or "no pity for the majority." It was shortened to an acronym after one of the group's founding members, English musician Raymond Watts, had trouble pronouncing the German words. The sentiment behind their name reflects KMFDM's beginnings as an eighties art-terrorist group with links to fellow German band Einsturzende Neubauten, who used actual machinery such as jackhammers in their music, giving rise to the term "industrial" music; KMFDM became one of the first such European ensembles to find success on American shores. Even after several albums and the co-opting of the industrial-noise ethos by numerous imitators, KMFDM's output manages to remain, according to *Rolling Stone* critic Sandy Masuo, "insidiously arty and intellectually sassy."

KMFDM has boasted an impressive roster of musicians since its inception, but has always been centered around Sascha Konietzko. Born in 1961, he grew up in the German port city of Hamburg and often worked odd

Courtesy of Wax Trax Records

For the Record . . .

Founding members include **Sascha Konietzko** (born c. 1961 in Hamburg, Germany), **En Esch**, and **Raymond Watts**; later members include **William Reifman**, drums; **Chris Connelly**, vocals; **Guenter Schulz**, guitar; **Mark Durante**, guitar; **Svet Am**, guitar; **Dorona Alberti**, vocals; and **F. M. Einheit**, percussion.

Band formed in Hamburg, Germany, c. 1985, with Konietzko, Watts, and En Esch; released first LP, *What Do You Know, Deutschland?*, in December of 1986; signed with Chicago's Wax Trax record label, 1990.

Addresses: *Home*—Chicago, IL. *Record company*—Wax Trax Records, 1657 N. Damen Ave., Chicago, IL 60647.

jobs to help support his family after his parents' divorce. As a teenager, Konietzko verged on juvenile delinquency until he saw a 1976 Sex Pistols concert that literally changed his life. "The next day I shaved off my hair and became a punk," he told *Rolling Stone*'s Jon Wiederhorn. He played in a series of bands before winding up in Paris in early 1984 collaborating with a multimedia German artist named Udosturm. Inside an avant-garde art exhibition in the city's Grand Palais, the duo blasted synthesizer-generated noise with rumbles from several bass guitars; it also included demonstrations of machinery by four Polish coal miners Konietzko and Udosturm had met in a Paris whorehouse.

Formed as Trio

Konietzko eventually moved back to Hamburg and began working with an American musician, Peter Missing, and a German drummer, En Esch. Eventually Konietzko and Esch officially formed KMFDM with Raymond ("Pig") Watts around 1985. Their first release came at the end of 1986, *What Do You Know, Deutschland?* Early the next year a second work appeared, *Kickin' Ass*, which was picked up by a British distributor. The sound was at the forefront of a new wave of northern European music that was assaultive and brutal in spirit, with leaden guitars competing against rapid, headache-inducing beats emanating from computer-programmed synthesizers; vocals were screamed above the chaotic musical backdrop. KMFDM soon began performing in clubs throughout Europe, where their live shows included tossing animal guts at the audience, exploding television sets, and fire-eaters onstage.

By 1988 their reputation had attracted the attention of Chicago's Wax Trax label, who picked up the record *Don't Blow Your Top* for distribution. *UAIOE* followed in 1989, a record that marked the end of the joint collaboration between Konietzko and Esch, though the two would remain friends and continue to work together on KMFDM releases. Konietzko described Esch as being defined by doctors as "mad," and in an interview with Simon Reynolds for *Melody Maker*, Esch said little to counteract that. "I destroy myself. I'm fighting every minute. Fighting with myself. My mind is out of control. Your body should control your mind. That's healthy, that's cool. But my mind went weird somewhere along the way." *UAIOE* also marked the beginning of a studio relationship with famed producer Adrian Sherwood. "Digitally mutated voices rise out of hollow bass and ooze through walls of sampled guitar and computer blips," noted a *Melody Maker* review. "It's a slow, mean, vicious thing."

Debarked from Euro-Industrial Wave

Yet by 1989, lighter-weight industrial bands broke into the German charts; Meat Beat Manifesto and Front 242 became wildly popular; it was also the year that the Berlin Wall fell and the process of reunification began, a historical event that seemed to bring out the worst in the West Germans. An aborted tour with Chicago band My Life with the Thrill Kill Kult also made them increasingly dissatisfied with the European music scene. Konietzko called Wax Trax for rescue; the label gave them the opening slot for a series of Ministry concert dates in the United States.

The following year they officially signed with the Chicago-based label, and Konietzko relocated there. A series of KMFDM records ensued, including 1990's *Naive* and *Money*, released in 1992. The latter included samples from television and radio broadcasts, "all mangled guitar noise, sampled classical bursts and rhythms programmed by sadists," declared *Melody Maker* critic Paul Lester. Konietzko explained his motivations to *Billboard* writer Carrie Borzillo in 1996. "Every album is like a photograph...," he said. "A lot of people tend to think of albums as something written in stone and are really thoughtful about it. I'm not very thoughtful about it. The main incentive behind the band and probably always will be, is that as long as it's fun, it's good."

Invited Numerous Others Aboard

In 1993 KMFDM released *Angst,* and continued to tour intermittently, though they no longer threw animal entrails at audiences. Konietzko remained the mastermind behind KMFDM, with contributions from Esch and a host of others throughout the decade. Despite the studio wizardry needed to create the band's recorded aura, Esch loves performing live. "It's unbelievable, the feeling that you get when you have contact with the crowd," he told *Melody Maker*'s Simon Reynolds. "Prostituting yourself. But in a positive way."

Various other KMFDM members have included guitarists Svet Am, Guenter Schulz, and Mark Durante while William Reifman and F.M. Einheit, a member of Einsturzende Neubauten, have numbered among the percussionists. Almost all of the album covers since 1988 have been executed by Brute, an artist Konietzko has said he considers a virtual member of the band; the 18 different covers are a cohesive narrative that tie in with KMFDM's own visions.

Aging, but Gaining

Surprisingly, Konietzko seems at home in Chicago. When Wax Trax label ran into financial problems, KMFDM stayed aboard—even though most of the other original Wax Trax bands such as Front Line Assembly went on to larger labels. The 1995 release *Nihil* became the first KMFDM record to chart, and within the year Konietzko was remixing KMFDM tracks for inclusion on movie soundtracks such as *Mortal Kombat*. Like the previous records, 1996's *Xtort* was done in Chicago; Konietzko assembles the collaborators and demands that they be available for recording for 13 hours of the day. This release featured vocals by Dorona Alberti as well as horns and a Hammond organ on certain tracks. *Rolling Stone*'s Wiederhorn described *Xtort* as essentially Konietzko's "most cohesive diatribes to date. Combining computerized beats and samples with blazing metallic riffs, soaring female background vocals and even a horn section on one track, KMFDM have assembled a collection of songs that range from the ecstatic dance-floor surge of 'Power' to the apoca-

lyptic, spoken-word electrolysis of 'Dogma.'"

Technology remains an integral element of KMFDM's music. Konietzko uses various Macintosh computers to compose and record music, and personally maintains the KMFDM internet site on the World Wide Web. Surprisingly, the band's music seems to be gaining new adherents after a decade in existence. Konietzko talked with *Keyboard* writer Robert L. Doerschuk about some recent encounters. "People are turning to us and saying, 'Oh, you're the new hot band.' And we're like, 'No, we're an old and untrendy band.' A lot of people are trying to jump on this bandwagon. So I don't know. Maybe it's time to go, because we've made our mark."

Selected discography

What Do You Know, Deutschland?, Z Records, 1986, Skysaw Records, 1987.
Don't Blow Your Top, Wax Trax, 1988.
UAIOE, Wax Trax, 1989.
Naive, Wax Trax, 1990.
Money, Wax Trax, 1992.
Angst, Wax Trax/TVT, 1993.
Nihil, Wax Trax/TVT, 1995.
Xtort, Wax Trax/TVT, 1996.

Sources

Billboard, June 22, 1996, pp. 1, 97.
Details, July 1996, p. 159.
Keyboard, August 1995, p. 12.
Melody Maker, August 26, 1989, p. 12; October 20, 1990, pp. 50-51; February 8, 1992, p. 32; August 6, 1994, p. 32.
Rolling Stone, July 11, 1996, p. 90; August 8, 1996, p, 24.

Additional information for this profile was obtained from the KMFDM site on the World Wide Web.

—*Carol Brennan*

Annie Lennox

Singer

AP/Wide World Photos

She has appeared on stage as a blonde glamour queen, a sideburned Elvis imitator, and a dominatrix Minnie Mouse; but unlike some pop stars who hide a lack of talent behind their controversial costuming, Annie Lennox is also a gifted and powerful singer. The Scottish-born, classically trained performer first gained national attention in the duo the Eurythmics, one of the most influential pop acts of the 1980s. Together with partner Dave Stewart, Lennox created an eerie, brooding music that embraced passion and detachment, optimism and despair. After the demise of the Eurythmics, Lennox proved her talent as a solo performer with the platinum-selling albums *Diva* and *Medusa*. Although her stage presence is commanding, the often-contradictory Lennox describes herself as a retiring person, whose ultimate goal is to drop out of the public eye. "There's so much I haven't done," Terry Smith quoted her as saying in *People*. "I'd like to paint. I'd like to study philosophy. I'd like to bake."

Lennox has traveled a long road to fame and fortune. She grew up in the port city of Aberdeen, Scotland, where her family lived in a working-class neighborhood. Her father, a shipyard worker, loved music and was a talented bagpipe player. He encouraged his daughter to study flute and piano, and by the age of 17, she had won a scholarship to the prestigious Royal Academy of Music in London. Her three years there were not happy ones, however. "I hated it," she was quoted as saying in *Rolling Stone*, and to a *Spin* contributor, she confided, "All the boys were gay and all the girls thought they were Maria Callas." In her London flat, she worked on her own compositions and singing, and explored new musical territory. She discovered the work of two musicians who would greatly influence her: Joni Mitchell and Stevie Wonder. She told Barbara Pepe in *Ms.* that she aspired to "that depth of subtlety and profound statement through music" such as that created by Wonder. Lennox also continued to listen to the Scottish folk songs she'd loved since childhood.

"She Was Straight from Classical"

Three days before her final exams at the Academy, Lennox suddenly walked out, never to return. For the next few years, she worked a series of odd jobs—mostly waitressing—while singing with numerous groups, none of them well-known. By 1977, she was close to abandoning her dreams of making it as a singer-songwriter; instead, she planned to start a career as a music teacher. Just before she made that change, however, a man named Dave Stewart came into the London restaurant where Lennox was working.

For the Record . . .

Born December 25, 1954, in Aberdeen, Scotland; daughter of a shipyard worker and a cook; married Radha Raman, March, 1984 (divorced, 1985); married Uri Fruchtman (a filmmaker), 1987; children: Daniel (deceased), Lola, Tali. *Education:* Studied flute, piano, and harpsichord at Royal Academy of Music, London, England, for three years.

Member of musical groups Catch and The Tourists, 1977-80; founder and member of musical group Eurythmics, 1980-90; solo performer, 1990—. Appeared in film *Revolution.*

Awards: Grammy Award nominations for best new artist, 1984, and, with the Eurythmics, for best rock performance by a duo or group, 1986; three Grammy Award nominations, 1992, for *Diva;* voted best female singer in a *Rolling Stone* readers' poll.

Addresses: *Home*—London, England; and Majorca, Spain. *Office*—c/o RCA Records, 1133 Avenue of the Americas, New York, NY 10036-6710.

Stewart was another struggling musician, whose experience ranged from medieval music to the songs of Bob Dylan. Dedicating himself to music at the age of 15, he had succeeded in working with several moderately successful groups, but his career stalled after problems with drugs and a serious automobile accident. At the time he met Lennox, he and a singer-songwriter named Peet Coombs were trying to find work in London. There was instant chemistry between Lennox and Stewart, and she invited the two men back to her apartment and began to play for them on her wooden harmonium. "She was straight from classical," Stewart recalled to *Rolling Stone.* "She didn't know anything about pop groups. But I heard her sing and we started celebrating. Then we went out to this club, and from that moment on, Annie and I lived together, and we made music together, for about four years."

With Coombs, Lennox and Stewart started a group called Catch, later renamed the Tourists. The Tourists were fairly successful in some respects, recording three albums and touring all over the world. They made no money, however, and their only big hit was a 1979 remake of Dusty Springfield's "I Only Want to Be with You." Strangely enough, that one hit led to the demise of the Tourists. Critics savaged them, believing that the group had sold out to the oldies market. Disillusioned

and embroiled in disputes with their recording label, they disbanded in 1980.

Conflict Leads to "Sweet Dreams"

The romantic relationship between Stewart and Lennox was also crumbling, and they took up separate residences at about the same time that the Tourists ceased to exist. They agreed that their musical relationship was as intense as ever, however, and they remained good friends; accordingly, they made a fresh start as a duo. They named themselves the Eurhythmics and recorded their first album in a West German studio. Their album titled *In the Garden* was never released in the United States and failed to do much on the English charts. Stewart had undergone lung surgery at the time of its release and was unable to promote the album.

Unhappy with their management, Lennox and Stewart next decided to create their own recording studio. It was first housed in an attic warehouse, but eventually moved to a sixteenth-century church in London. There, Stewart began experimenting with unusual musical sounds and a wide variety of instruments and synthesizer techniques. One day, after a nasty argument, the pair was working in their studio, not speaking to each other. Stewart began programming a drum rhythm into his synthesizer, and the music he produced caught Lennox's ear. Words came to her and she began to sing, and their first top ten hit was born. "Sweet Dreams (Are Made of This)" became the title track to their second album, released in 1983, and was the song that shot the Eurhythmics to international celebrity. The sound bore the mark of New Wave and funk influences, and Lennox's vocals were brooding and piercing. Stewart explained to Stephen Holden in the *New York Times,* "In our music we like to have the sense of two things battling at once. You have to have something that sounds nice on the surface, but underneath there's an ominous side." "Sweet Dreams" embodied this philosophy.

Touch, released in 1984, yielded more hit singles, including "Here Comes the Rain Again" and "Right by Your Side." That was also the year Lennox shocked many with her appearance at the Grammy Awards. Through videos, she had become known for her short, orange-dyed hair—an onstage look she had adopted after an audience member had snatched a long, black wig from her head at a London nightclub. At the Grammys, she walked onstage to sing "Sweet Dreams" dressed as Elvis Presley, complete with sideburns. Lennox has explained that her transvestism, often compared to that of David Bowie, is simply a reaction to the tacky, sex-kitten image so frequently exploited by female singers. Although she established herself with a mannish look, in later years she also explored glamorous, more typically feminine presentations, and was named one of the "ten most beautiful women in the world" by *Playboy* magazine in 1983.

Depression and Creativity

Lennox had long been troubled by serious bouts of depression. In 1984, she also developed a recurring problem with her vocal cords, forcing her to rest her voice as much as possible. While in Germany on a world tour, she met Radha Raman, a German man attached to the Hare Krishna movement. He and a group of other Krishnas served the Eurhythmics a special vegetarian dinner and gave Lennox a homeopathic cure for her throat, then began accompanying the duo through Europe. In New York the following year, Lennox and Raman were married, but the union lasted just 14 months.

Despite her personal problems, Lennox's creativity was at a high point. Known at first for her cold, detached sound, the Eurhythmics' music demonstrated more soul with each album they released. *Be Yourself Tonight* featured Lennox holding her own in a duet with Aretha Franklin in the feminist anthem "Sisters Are Doin' It For Themselves." David Gates, writing in *Esquire*, named Lennox "one of the great white soul singers: out of Aretha by way of such Seventies disco divas as Donna Summer." *Touch* and *Be Yourself Tonight* both went platinum, but although critics continued to laud the Eurhythmics' work, their popularity began to decline after 1985.

"Eurythmics was a very changeable beast," Lennox was quoted as saying in a *Rolling Stone* article by David Sinclair, "and in America, when things change too much, they don't know what to make of it. Because one minute they might get 'Would I Lie to You?'—which they can put in an R&B slot or heavy rock—and then we'd do another song, like 'Beethoven (I Love to Listen To)' [from *Savage*], which was a lot different, and they didn't quite know how to deal with us." Lennox's partnership with Stewart was also deteriorating, and although the duo never officially disbanded, after their 1990 tour, Lennox "simply went home to her London townhouse, got pregnant [with second husband, filmmaker Uri Fruchtman, whom she married in 1987], and began writing songs by herself for the first time since hooking up with Stewart," according to Gates.

No Emotional Regressions

Regarding the end of the Eurhythmics, Lennox said to Sinclair: "Who cares if a group is together or not? Does it matter? To me, making a big, elaborate statement like 'We have broken up'—we never discussed it. We haven't written it down in blood or ink....[But] I don't want to go back. I don't want to retread. I was there for ten years. Why should I go back? It would be like an emotional regression." Her first solo album was the 1992 release *Diva*, described by Gates as "a stylized self-portrait, a moody piece of work that can fasten onto and color a few months of your life." Discussing her work on the album with Gates, Lennox remarked on the difficulties of working without her former partner. Despite the frictions between them, he had always given her a great deal of encouragement and constructive criticism. "I was the one wandering around saying, 'Never, never, never,'" she recalled, "and he'd be going, 'Oh come on, this is great.'"

"Fortunately, she thought positively enough to get the job done," Gates related, "but not so positively as to screw up what could turn out to be one of the canonical soundtracks to the century's end game." A *Nation* reviewer offered a less enthusiastic assessment of *Diva*, dismissing it as "pricey radio-ready schlock" even while admitting that the singer's "vocal instrument is still awesome and outsized." Lennox's fans showed what they thought of her solo effort by buying enough copies to make it go platinum, even though she refused to tour to support the album—partly because of her continuing throat problems, but mostly because of her commitment to her daughter Lola, then an infant. "I don't want to have my child trailing around with me," she asserted to Gates. "It's just unfair."

Stable, Secure, Content

That decision was indicative of the great change that Lennox's second marriage had worked in her life. Once known as moody, rootless, and unhappy, she became increasingly stable, secure, and content, even in the face of such challenges as the stillbirth of her first child, Daniel. "My children are the focus of my life," she declared to Terry Smith in *People*, but music remained enough of a force for her to put out a second solo album, *Medusa*, in 1995. It was made up of cover versions of songs by artists as diverse as Neil Young, Bob Marley, and the Temptations.

Numerous reviewers credited Lennox with bringing fresh insights to the tunes. "The fact that she didn't write any of the songs on *Medusa* will likely be taken as a sign that she has mellowed," predicted a *Vanity Fair* writer. "Far from it. For although *Diva* revealed her to be a great songwriter—capable of both melancholy and self-mockery—*Medusa* shows her finally without guise. It is Annie Lennox stripped down. The only thing you hear is the imprint of her voice on the music of Bob Marley, Joni Mitchell, Paul Simon, Neil Young, and the Temptations. The choices ... are alternately surprising and obscure. And her vocal stylings are so distinctive that she transforms the songs into personal statements." "*Medusa* is more than just diva worthy," concurred Elysa Gardner in *Rolling Stone.* "It's proof that a great singer doesn't need a pen or a computer to be creative."

With her success as a solo performer well established, Lennox remains vague about her plans for the future. Emphasizing again in *Vanity Fair* that "having children does really shed a different light on things," she went on to say: "First of all, you have to stop putting yourself as number one, because you're not anymore. Somebody else is for a while. Their needs are more important at three A.M." She concluded, "It could be that after this album [*Medusa*] I do nothing.... I like that. I don't want to put myself in this category of saying, Well, my life depends on being a creative person."

Selected discography

With the Eurythmics

In the Garden, RCA (United Kingdom), 1982.
Sweet Dreams (Are Made of This), RCA, 1983.
Touch, RCA, 1984.
Eurythmics: 1984 (For the Love of Big Brother), 1984.
Be Yourself Tonight, RCA, 1985.
Revenge, RCA, 1986.
Savage, RCA, 1988.
We Too Are One, Arista, 1989.
Greatest Hits, RCA, 1991.

Solo albums

Diva, Arista, 1992.
Medusa, Arista, 1995.

Sources

Books

Hill, Dave, *Designing Boys and Material Girls: Manufacturing the '80s Pop Dream,* Blandford Press, 1986.
Stambler, Irwin, *The Encyclopedia of Pop, Rock and Soul,* revised edition, St. Martin's, 1989.
White, Timothy, *Rock Stars,* Stewart, Tabori, and Chang, 1984.

Periodicals

Creem, July 1984; August 1985; September 1985; December 1986.
Esquire, July 1992, p. 82.
High Fidelity, April 1985; May 1988.
Los Angeles Times, August 2, 1986.
Maclean's, May 11, 1992, p. 54.
Melody Maker, January 29, 1983; July 9, 1983; November 19, 1983; May 4, 1985; November 22, 1986.
Ms., February 1986.
Musician, November 1983; July 1985; November 1985; August 1986.
Nation, July 6, 1992, p. 31.
New Yorker, March 14, 1988, p. 82.
New York Times, July 17, 1983; February 5, 1984; August 3, 1984; September 3, 1989; November 12, 1989.
People, August 22, 1983; December 19, 1983; March 12, 1984; May 20, 1985; November 27, 1989; June 10, 1985; August 7, 1995, p. 103.
Playboy, April 1984.
Q, May 1991.
Rolling Stone, June 23, 1983; September 29, 1983; June 20, 1985; October 24, 1985; September 11, 1986; March 4, 1993, p. 58; April 20, 1995, p. 70; November 2, 1995, p. 28.
Spin, August, 1985.
Stereo Review, October 1984; September 1985; January 1990.
Time, June 23, 1984; September 30, 1985.
Vanity Fair, March, 1995, p. 170.
Wall Street Journal, January 19, 1984.
Washington Post, March 21, 1984; January 10, 1985.

—Joan Goldsworthy

Tommy LiPuma

Record company executive

While Tommy LiPuma's name may not be a familiar one to record buyers, it is an esteemed one within the music industry, particularly in the overlapping boundaries between pop, R&B, and jazz. A record company executive in name but a studio producer at heart, LiPuma has worked with some of the biggest acts of recent decades with behind-the-scenes efforts that have helped recording stars like George Benson and Natalie Cole earn 30 Grammy Award nominations. LiPuma was appointed president of his own label, GRP—a division of industry giant MCA—in 1995; his office oversees a large roster of both new and old talent, but LiPuma asserts he is in his element when working in the studio with the artist—"in the trenches," as he terms it.

Like his contemporary Quincy Jones, another producer with a knack for producing hit records, LiPuma began his career as a musician. The young Cleveland, Ohio resident was a saxophone player who took more interest in the way his favorite records were put together. He gained entry at the ground floor of the record industry in the early 1960s as a shipping clerk for a distributor in the city. "That really gives you a sense of what's going on," LiPuma said of the grunt work in an interview with Michael Bourne in a *Billboard* tribute issue. "Just pack orders for a couple months and you start seeing what's going out—and what's not going out—not only the hits, but in the catalog." He eventually became a promoter with Liberty Records, a label with an eclectic roster that included the Neville Brothers as well as Slim Whitman.

Internal struggles at Liberty spurred LiPuma to seek work elsewhere; when an offer came from another company, LiPuma was on the verge of quitting until his boss offered him another position within the company as a producer. The first record he made was with fellow Cleveland natives the O'Jays; the song, "Lipstick Traces," did moderately well when released in 1964. From there, LiPuma jumped ship to A&M Records at the behest of Jerry Moss and Herb Alpert, two musicians just gaining fame as the Tiajuana Brass.

During his tenure with A&M LiPuma first encountered gravel-voiced piano player Mac Rebennack, also known as blues legend Dr. John. LiPuma spoke of hearing an early demo tape of him back then: "I think it was called 'Ju Ju Man.' I'd never heard anything like it. It was insane. I dug it," LiPuma recalled in *Down Beat.* Dr. John's first recordings with A&M did not do well, but the friendship between the two would lead to later, more successful collaborations.

In 1968 a friend of LiPuma's, Bob Krasnow, was thinking of starting his own label and invited LiPuma to sign on as an executive and producer. Together they founded Blue Thumb Records, revered by some music aficionados as a unique force in progressive rock for its issuance of some of the most avant garde jazz and rock music of the era from the likes of T. Rex, Captain Beefheart, the Mark-Almond Band, Hugh Masekela, and Ike and Tina Turner. Richard Henderson assessed the company's impact in the *Billboard* tribute issue, wryly noting the label "was home to a collection of artists that, to any sensible record exec with the bottom-line in mind, appeared to be composed of anti-matter."

Wore Several Hats around Label Headquarters

At Blue Thumb LiPuma's job was to work with artists such as Sun Ra in the studio, but he also wound up playing an instrument or two on various projects and even appearing on some album covers. One of his first jobs with Blue Thumb was the making and marketing of an album from English singer and guitarist Dave Mason, formally of the supergroup Traffic. The 1974 record *Alone Together* went on to great success; other coups followed. The Pointer Sisters, signed by LiPuma, also launched their career on the label with the LP *Yes We Can Can.* "The late '60s/early '70s was a time when radio play could cut across most categories, and Blue Thumb was one of the few labels to recognize that this was a cultural statement as well as a shift in formats," wrote Ben Sidran in *Billboard.* "This artist-orientation was carried through down to the marketing and distribution of the product as well."

For the Record . . .

Born c. early 1940s; married; wife's name, Gill; children: Jennifer, Danielle.

M.S. Distributors, Cleveland, OH, local promotions representative, c. 1960; Liberty Records, Los Angeles, CA, worked in promotions department, then transferred to Liberty's New York City office to work in the publishing department; A&M Records, staff producer, 1965-69; Blue Thumb Records, cofounder and executive, 1968-74; Warner Brothers Records, producer, 1974-77; Horizon Records (a division of A&M), president, 1978; Warner Brothers Records, vice-president for jazz and progressive music, 1979-90; Elektra Records, senior vice-president for A&R, 1990-94; GRP Records, president, 1995—.

Addresses: *Office*—GRP Records, 555 W. 57th St., New York, NY 10019.

After LiPuma and Krasnow sold Blue Thumb in 1974, LiPuma moved on to industry giant Warner Brothers as a producer. There he collaborated with more accessible artists and helped them achieve almost unheard-of success at that time. LiPuma worked with Barbra Streisand as a producer for the soundtrack to her 1974 film *The Way We Were*, one of the top-selling releases of that year and done live in the studio with an orchestra. "You set up an atmosphere in the room that puts people in a comfortable position where they can forget themselves," LiPuma told *Billboard*'s Bourne. "And when they forget themselves, that's when you get the *stuff*."

Achieved Mainstream Success as a Producer

Yet LiPuma's biggest achievement at Warner Brothers during this era came with jazz guitarist George Benson, for whom he produced the album *Breezin'*, a work significant for its jazz/pop crossover success. Originally planned as an instrumental work, since Benson never sang, LiPuma—having heard him belt out a few bars once off the cuff—convinced the musician to give it a try, and Benson wound up singing on several of the tracks. *Breezin'* became one of the best-selling albums of 1976, bolstered by the success of singles like "This Masquerade," which earned a Grammy for record of the year; *Breezin'* also took home the Grammy for album of the year.

LiPuma left Warner Brothers briefly around 1978 to head Horizon, a division of A&M Records where he produced two albums by Dr. John, but returned in 1979 to become Warner's vice-president of jazz and progressive music. Over the next decade LiPuma worked with a roster of acclaimed artists that included Al Jarreau, Miles Davis, Jennifer Holliday, Earl Klugh, and Everything But the Girl. In 1990 he became senior vice-president at Elektra Records, and his association with this label was crowned by his involvement in Natalie Cole's *Unforgettable* album. He coproduced the 1990 work, which utilized recordings laid down decades earlier in the studio by her father, Nat King Cole. The much-lauded recording went on to win the Grammy for album of the year.

Named Chief Executive of His Own Label

LiPuma's long list of achievements in the music business earned him a top executive slot in 1995 when MCA named him president of its GRP division. In his new position, LiPuma attempts to strike a balance between his executive duties and his responsibility for making hit records in the studio. Shortly after LiPuma signed on with GRP, MCA moved its entire jazz catalog over to the division, including the Blue Thumb back catalog. The label had lay dormant for several years, and much of its output had never been reissued and was becoming increasingly hard to obtain.

Dr. John became the resurrected Blue Thumb's first release with 1995's *Afterglow.* While LiPuma was busy adding new artists like Jonatha Brooke to its roster, older fans were hopeful that some of his most avant garde works as a producer would become available again. Under his direction GRP has also put new money and energy into the Impulse! label, home of more traditional jazz, and has scheduled a number of reissues for the late 1990s. Standard jazz efforts by artists such as George Benson—one of the first to sign when LiPuma came on board—will be released under the GRP label, as well as re-releases from the label's vaults of the famed Chess and Decca catalogs.

Industry insiders and well-known artists alike praise LiPuma for his know-how and ear for music, as well as his interpersonal skills. Natalie Cole told *Billboard* that LiPuma "has no ego. The music is the star. We are the vessels." Record industry colleague Sal Licata, a longtime friend and former roommate who worked with LiPuma during the Blue Thumb days, explained that LiPuma "knows that there's flesh and blood behind the product. Not every president understands this. He's the kind of guy, were Tommy to walk up to you and slap you in the face, you'd thank him because you probably deserved it on some level." Dr. John, also quoted in the *Billboard* tribute issue, described LiPuma as "a conscientious musician, a thinking cat who cared about the music first....There've been a few guys like that, but not too many."

Sources

Billboard, September 16, 1995, pp. L1-L28.
Down Beat, July 1995, p. 20.

—*Carol Brennan*

Luna

Rock band

Luna has suffered over much of its career from comparisons to other bands, initially to founding member Dean Wareham's previous group, Galaxie 500, but more regularly to the Velvet Underground. Yet far from being shamelessly derivative of legendary avant-noise relics, the four-member, New York City-based Luna instead appropriates the detached musical mood set by the Velvets and expands on it through a variety of modern devices. Luna has even managed to attract a former member, Sterling Morrison, as a guest musician on one of their releases, and Morrison's famed colleague, singer Lou Reed, liked Luna's sound so much he chose them as an opening act for one of his concert tours.

Luna was formed in the wake of the break-up of Galaxie 500, a much-vaunted but little-heard indie rock band whose ethereal songs often lacked any discernible thread of rhythmic consistency. Rob Sheffield, writing for the *Spin Alternative Record Guide*, called their music "breezy and content-free even at its most stately," with some songs "luxuriating in melodies and textures for the sake of sweet sonic sensationalism." Wareham, a New Zealand native, had fronted Galaxie 500 through three releases during the late 1980s to little success, yet still received mail from devastated fans when the group disbanded. A chance meeting between he and fellow New Zealander Justin Harwood, the former bass player for the Chills, was the genesis. Before the Chills, "I used to play bass in several bands back home," Harwood admitted in a 1992 interview with Everett True of *Melody Maker*. "Wedding bands, bar bands, bands with 'Pine-

apple' in their name." Like Galaxie 500, the Chills made several records but achieved little success.

The final member of Luna would be drummer and New Jersey resident Stanley Demeski, a veteran of the Feelies. Like Galaxie 500, the Feelies were another vaunted eighties group that evoked comparisons to the Velvet Underground; director Susan Seidelman even made an early film, *Smithereens*, around one of their albums, *Crazy Rhythms*. With the three members, Luna coalesced in 1992 in New York, but then discovered there was already a singer in the area using that name; legal reasons forced them into putting a "2" in superscript after their name for a time. The numeral was silent, but served as a rebuke to legal restrictions, as in "we're Luna too," Wareham told *Melody Maker*'s True.

Luna's debut was released the same year on Elektra Records. The band titled it *Lunapark* after an amusement park located near Coney Island, and enlisted Fred Maher to produce it. Maher had previously produced the hit album *Girlfriend* for Matthew Sweet in 1991. Together the band and Maher mined the ethereal mood of Wareham's Galaxie 500 and added more of a cohesive rhythm thread inside the new songs. "Wareham came up with the last thing anybody expected," wrote Sheffield in the *Spin* book: "discrete songs with a brisk beat and a surprising new sense of humor." Upon its release, Wareham admitted to *Guitar Player*'s Mike Mettler "this is the slickest-sounding record I've done, but it's really warm and crisp—and it doesn't feel processed. Hey, *I* like it." Charles Aaron of the *Village Voice* described as "lucid, hypnotic pop-rock." Later, *Voice* colleague RJ Smith termed *Lunapark* "resentful and crunchy, a set of panoptic views of boho guilt."

When it came time to tour in support of the record, Luna was forced to hire a fourth member as second guitarist, which they did through an ad in the *Village Voice*. Canadian Sean Eden signed on, and things clicked so well he became a full-fledged member. In 1993 they released the EP *Slide*, and for their next effort they were able to recruit former Velvet Underground guitarist Sterling Morrison to sit in on the track for their third record, 1994's *Bewitched*; a Hammond organ and trumpet make appearances elsewhere. Critics continued to laud Wareham's songwriting talents as demonstrated in the arch, meandering lyrics, but *Bewitched* would be their least successful record.

Nevertheless, the *Village Voice*'s Smith asserted its "words isolate fractional moments that go on forever, and the music even more so." More comparisons to the Velvet Underground sound were inevitable, but Steve Simels of *Stereo Review* explained the relationship in more specific terms, asserting that Luna's "angelic

For the Record . . .

Members include **Dean Wareham** (born in New Zealand), vocals; **Stanley Demeski**, drums; **Sean Eden** (born in Canada), guitar; and **Justin Harwood** (born in New Zealand), bass.

Group formed in 1992 as Luna2; became "Luna" with 1993 release *Slide*.

Addresses: *Record company*—Elektra Records, 75 Rockefeller Plaza, New York, NY 10019.

natural-sounding envelope." The critic also praised the group's mastery of unusual technologies, including the Theremin and Mellotron, two early types of electronic instruments. Such unusual production techniques "give *Penthouse* a rich, hypnotic texture," Sherlock asserted.

Luna is forthright about their fascination with the Velvet Underground. "I just love their mix of noise and melody," Wareham told *Guitar Player*'s Mettler. Yet Wareham's talents go far from unappreciated. Wareham, wrote *Stereo Review*'s Simels, has "also got a Velvets-like fondness for inserting the most homicidally atonal guitar outbursts imaginable into otherwise convention-al (and attractive) melodic structures."

harmonies, chiming guitars, and delicate, almost folk-ish songs" are reminiscent of the albums the Velvet Underground did after dark visionary John Cale left the group. *Musician*'s Roy Trakin echoed this sentiment in his review of *Bewitched*: "The emphasis here is on melodies, always an underrated aspect of the Velvets' legacy," Trakin wrote.

Luna's live performances have been as lauded as their mastery of dream-world evocations through studio tech-nology, and they've even played as support for a brief reunion tour the Velvet Underground embarked upon. "Wareham is one of the most casually virtuosic guitarists around," noted *Rolling Stone*'s David Sprague, in a review of a live Luna show, further asserting they've "staked out a strip of terrain bordered by the Velvet Underground's intense desolation and Television's stud-ied indifference."

Sprague was referring to legendary late-seventies New York scenesters Television, fronted by Tom Verlaine, and once again, the very acts that Luna pays homage would return the admiration: Verlaine played guitar for two songs, "23 Minutes in Brussels" and "Moon Palace," on *Penthouse*, the group's 1995 release. Stereolab vocalist Laetitia Sadier sings a duet with Wareham in "Bonnie and Clyde." The track is a cover of a song originally done by Brigitte Bardot and Serge Gains-bourg, sung entirely in French. "The recording is pris-tine," enthused Dev Sherlock of *Musician*, "a warm,

Selected discography

Lunapark, Elektra, 1992.
Slide, (EP), Elektra, 1993.
Bewitched, Elektra, 1994.
Penthouse, Elektra, 1995.

Sources

Books

Spin Alternative Record Guide, edited by Eric Weisbard with Craig Marks, Vintage Books, 1995, pp. 83, 162.

Periodicals

Billboard, March 12, 1994, p. 52D.
Guitar Player, January 1993, p. 13.
Melody Maker, September 26, 1992, p. 37.
Musician, April 1994, pp. 90-91; October 1995, p. 81.
Rolling Stone, February 22, 1996, p. 64.
Stereo Review, November 1992, p. 118.
Village Voice, September 22, 1992, p. 84; June 1, 1993, p. 68; April 26, 1994, p. 74; November 14, 1995, p. 82.

Additional information for this profile was obtained from Epic Records publicity materials, 1995.

—Carol Brennan

Marilyn Manson

Rock band

Over the years, rock and roll music has witnessed several "shocking" artists, including Ziggy Stardust (David Bowie), Alice Cooper, KISS, and others who frightened parents while exciting and intriguing their fans. Marilyn Manson fit the slot of "shock" rock for the 1990s. Admittedly, singer and band founder Marilyn Manson derived his musical and performance influences from the above artists, as well as Iggy Pop, Black Sabbath, and the Beatles. Jim Farber wrote in *Entertainment Weekly:* "He sings about scabs, sodomy, and urine. He enjoys ripping his skin with broken bottles. And compares his music to an act of murder. Any authorities who don't like it, he says, 'should kill themselves.'"

Manson was born Brian Warner in Canton, Ohio, raised by his mother, a nurse, and his father, Hugh Warner, a furniture salesman. He began writing lyrics in the late 1980s with no intention of becoming a singer or forming a band. But in 1990, he did both. He invented the name Marilyn Manson, which he adopted as his own name, by watching and reflecting on American propaganda and sensationalism. After viewing talk shows and other entertainment sources, he came to the conclusion that Marilyn Monroe and Charles Manson stood out as the most popular personalities of the 1960s.

"As I got into the idea further," Manson told Jim Rose in *RIP*, "I started realizing the extreme positive and negative that I was trying to outline with these two names. There was a lot of beauty to be found in Manson. There was a lot of ugliness to be found in Monroe. The lines crossed. I resided in that gray area; that what I was doing transcended morality and sexuality."

Immediate Criticism Sparked Interest

Not long after Manson formed the group, he met Nine Inch Nails' Trent Reznor, also from Ohio. The two singer/songwriters hit it off and when Reznor started his own record label, Nothing Records, Marilyn Manson became its first signing.

Marilyn Manson released its debut album in 1994. Within the year, the group was banned from playing in Salt Lake City, Utah, after Manson ripped apart a Mormon Bible onstage. "Marilyn Manson is a bit of a challenge to people's intelligence," Manson told Rose. "It's almost a little bit of a science project to see how far I can push you, and see exactly what kind of reaction I can get." Marilyn Manson also received censorship requests and disapproval from organizations such as the People for the Ethical Treatment of Animals, the Christian Coalition, and members of the British Parliament.

"My rules and moralities are probably different from a lot of other people's," Manson told Jim Farber in *Entertainment Weekly.* The band did compromise on some occasions to continue to have their music published and their live shows scheduled. "Compromise is inevitable sometimes," bassist Twiggy Ramirez told John Pecorelli in *Alternative Press.* "I mean, if you're banned in 23 states, you're not accomplishing much. No one's going to hear your message."

Cover Song Lured More Listeners

Marilyn Manson released their second effort, an EP called *Smells Like Children*, in 1995. The album included a cover version of the Eurythmics' hit "Sweet Dreams," which launched the EP to No. 31 on *Billboard*'s album chart and racked up platinum sales.

"It was quite obvious to us from the beginning that the song was going to have a broader appeal than the rest of the material on the album," Manson told *MTV News "From the Buzz Bin."* "I felt like it was a piece of cheese on a rat trap to a lot of people who normally wouldn't listen to Marilyn Manson. They thought, 'Well, this is an innocuous little song and they ended up getting their necks snapped because they were introduced to this whole world that they weren't expecting." However, Tom Sinclair, a reviewer for *Entertainment Weekly*, saw

For the Record . . .

Members include **Ginger Fish**, drums; **Madonna Wayne Gacy**, keyboards; **Marilyn Manson** (born Brian Warner in Canton, OH); **Twiggy Ramirez**, bass; **Zim Zum** (replaced **Daisy Berkowitz**), guitar.

Band formed by Manson, 1990; signed with Nothing/Interscope, 1993; released debut, *Portrait of an American Family*, 1994; released *Smells Like Children* EP, 1995; released *Antichrist Superstar*, debuted at number three on *Billboard's* Top 200 albums, 1996.

Addresses: *Record company*—Nothing/Interscope, 2337 West 11th Street, Suite 7, Cleveland, OH 44113.

the band as talentless rather than shocking: "On this artlessly assembled excuse for an album, these minor-league White Zombie wannabes throw together pointless remixes, irritating skits, and lame covers of songs by Eurythmics, Screamin' Jay Hawkins, and Patty Smith."

By the end of 1995, Manson had reorganized the band. He fired guitarist Daisy Berkowitz and hired Chicago-native Zim Zum. Manson and Zum, along with bassist Twiggy Ramirez, keyboardist Madonna Wayne Gacy, and drummer Ginger Fish, released *Antichrist Superstar* on Nothing/Interscope in 1996. The LP debuted at No. 3 on *Billboard's* Top 200 Albums, and included the singles "The Beautiful People" and the title track. Within the first weeks of the album's release, the American Family Association from Mississippi, released a statement to warn American families against Marilyn Manson and its new album. "This should serve as a wake-up call to parents everywhere," the press release stated.

Concept Album Pushed Limits

Manson claimed *Antichrist Superstar* directly attacked Christianity's "weak value system," stating that he had recorded it in an attempt to "bring on the apocalypse." He derived the idea for the album from his own experiences and the influence of concept albums such as Pink Floyd's *The Wall* and David Bowie's *Ziggy Stardust*.

"Marilyn Manson would have fit just fine right alongside Ziggy Stardust and Alice Cooper, the Stooges, T.

Rex—any of that back then," Manson told Pecorelli in *Alternative Press*. "And apparently, I'm gonna be the one that has to break my back to make rock music exciting again, because not too many other people are making the effort." John Pareles wrote about Manson's similarities to Alice Cooper in the *New York Times*. "Mr. Manson is the 1990's version of Alice Cooper," he wrote. "He uses a woman's name, leads a hard-rock band, and provides a stagey spectacle."

On the tour for *Antichrist Superstar*, Manson, a self-proclaimed Satanist, would often lead the crowd in a chant of "We hate love! We love hate!" Adam Tepedelen wrote in a live review in *The Rocket*: "Manson is one sick little doggy; a writhing, taut body like Iggy Pop, a stage persona ('Antichrist Superstar') equal to Ziggy Stardust, Alice Cooper's flare for showbiz shock tactics, and G.G. Allin's bent for self-destruction. Love him or hate him (he'd prefer the latter), there's no denying he's a spectacle." In 1997, Marilyn Manson appeared on the Trent Reznor-produced soundtrack for David Lynch's film *Lost Highway*, with the song "The Apple of Sodom."

Though Manson claimed the album *Antichrist Superstar* would either bring the end of the world or the end of his band, the crowds clamored for more. So what did Manson have to look forward to after the retirement of his music career? He claimed he'd like to do a stint as a Christian television evangelist...always pushing the limits.

Selected discography

Portrait of an American Family, Nothing/Interscope, 1994.
Smells Like Children, Nothing/Interscope, 1995.
Antichrist Superstar, Nothing/Interscope, 1996.

Sources

Alternative Press, February 1997.
Entertainment Weekly, November 24, 1995; December 15, 1995; June 28, 1996; October 11, 1996; October 25, 1996.
MTV News "From the Buzz Bin," January 1997.
New York Times, October 31, 1996.
RIP, February 1995.
Rocket, January 29-February 12, 1997.
Rolling Stone, October 17, 1996.

—*Sonya Shelton*

Katy Moffatt

Singer

MICHAEL OCHS ARCHIVES/Venice, CA

In the liner notes to her 1996 album *Midnight Radio*, Katy Moffatt's longtime collaborator Tom Russell wrote: "Folk, Country, Blues, Rock... Roots? She erases the boundaries. They call the music 'Americana' now. Well, close your eyes and listen to The Voice. It's midnight in Fort Worth; the radio glows a magic yellow-orange...." Along the highways and byways of an itinerant musician's life, Moffatt's singing acquired a complexity and passion transcending the "folk" category where many of America's lyric songwriters are buried. Bill Bell of *The New York Daily News* compared Moffatt to Iris Dement, another soulful Texan with a cult following. Bell described her voice as sometimes forceful, sometimes caressing, and praised her lyrics as "bright and biting." Moffatt was a pioneer in the style that later infiltrated the popular culture through singers such as Alanis Morrisette: the female troubadours, spiritual heirs to Bob Dylan, Kris Kristofferson, and John Lennon. Like Iris Dement, Moffatt may have been too "country" for the mass audience, yet her songs relate a genuine spiritual journey. The songs are bracing as a cup of spring water on a hot Texas afternoon.

Moffatt was born and raised in Fort Worth, Texas. Her grandmother was a concert pianist who taught Moffatt and her brother Hugh to play the piano. Hugh Moffatt also became a songwriter, well-known in the Nashville, Tennessee music business. Moffatt listened to blues and the top forty on the radio. She credits Leonard Cohen's "Dress Rehearsal Rag" for making her want to perform. Like many others, when the Beatles and the British invasion stormed the United States, she was inspired to learn guitar. Those were heady times when music seemed to be a royal road to the imagination for young rebels. Moffatt started playing anywhere she could in Fort Worth: a Neiman-Marcus fashion show, a small coffeehouse, and the Fireside Lodge Rest Home (where her audience included Willie Nelson's grandmother). She modeled herself on folk singers like Judy Collins, Phil Ochs, and Dave Van Ronk. Another key influence was Tracy Nelson of Madison, Wisconsin.

Folksinger and Actress Playing a Folksinger

Moffatt left Fort Worth to attend Tulane University in New Orleans, then went to St. John's College in Santa Fe, New Mexico. At college she sang in her one and only musical, *The Fantasticks*. Her voice and attractive appearance made her a popular act in Santa Fe nightspots. When actor Tom Laughlin came to town to shoot the movie *Billy Jack*, her local fame helped her land a role as, naturally, a folk singer. Moffatt managed to develop an interesting sideline "moonlighting" in films off and on throughout her career. She later ap-

For the Record . . .

Born November 19, 1950, in Fort Worth, TX; sang in local events during her teen years. *Education:* Attended Tulane University, then St. John's College in Santa Fe, New Mexico.

Appeared in movie *Billy Jack,* 1971; signed by CBS Records 1975; released debut album, *Katy,* 1976; contributed to album *A Town South of Bakersfield;* performed at Kerrville Music Festival, 1986; toured nationally and extensively in Europe and Great Britain; signed with Watermelon Records, 1994.

Addresses: *Record company*—Watermelon, P.O. Box 402088, Austin, TX 78704.

peared in *Hard Country, Honeymoon in Vegas,* and *The Thing Called Love.*

After Santa Fe, Moffatt lived in Austin and Corpus Christi, Texas. In 1971, she moved to Colorado. Denver and Boulder were becoming counterculture meccas—good spots for an aspiring songwriter to find an audience. Unfortunately, her music jobs were not steady enough to support her. Just when she was ready to quit and go home to Texas, she got a regular cocktail hour engagement at a Denver hotel. There she met Mary Flower and Randy Handley, who, along with Lon Ephraim, formed a band called Flower, Handley, and Moffatt. They developed a following and traveled all over the state, with Mary Flower and Katy Moffatt eventually becoming a duo that toured nationally. Moffatt's next job as a solo performer at Denver's top rock club, Ebbets Field, opened an avenue into the mainstream recording industry. The club's owner, Chuck Morris, became Katy's manager, and Morris' efforts helped her to land a contract with Columbia Records.

A Man without a Country

Moffatt's first two albums were promising. Her initial album for Columbia, *Katy,* was country flavored; her second album, *Kissin' in the California Sun,* took more of a pop direction. The second album achieved moderate critical acclaim, including positive reviews in *Rolling Stone* and *Newsweek.* She recorded for Columbia Records from 1975 to 1979, making several singles to go with the two albums. However, the glimmer of commercial success faded. According to Watermelon Records, which signed her years later, Moffatt had mixed feelings about her experience with Columbia. "I

had a very strange history with CBS. I started six albums, finished three, and two were released. They simply didn't know what to do with me. At that time, you either had to be pop or country, and I didn't fit into either of those categories. I was a hybrid. I was always a man without a country, so to speak. I would go in and start a new project with a new producer, then they would stop it and not release anything. It was very frustrating because they obviously did not know what they wanted from me."

In 1976, Moffatt had the opportunity to appear with bluesman Muddy Waters, opening for him on the road. She moved to California in 1979 and joined the country rock scene developing there, typified by bands such as the Eagles, The Byrds, and The Flying Burrito Brothers. The scene produced the memorable album *A Town South of Bakersfield,* which featured Katy and many other new country voices, Dwight Yoakam and Rosie Flores among them. Her voice was much appreciated by other musicians, leading to brief singing stints with Warren Zevon, Roy Orbison, the Everly Brothers, and Don Williams. For the next few years, Moffatt toured as a backup singer for many acts, including Lynn Anderson, Tanya Tucker, Hoyt Axton, and Jimmy Buffett. A duet with her brother Hugh on his song "Rose of My Heart" received a lot of play, and the song was later covered by Johnney Rodriquez and Nicolette Larson. She also received some comforting recognition for her solo work when she was nominated for a Country Music Association Award for best new female vocalist in 1985.

Meanwhile, Moffatt's movie career continued. In 1980, she had a small part in *Hard Country,* an "urban cowboy"-type movie starring Jan-Michael Vincent and Kim Basinger. In 1991, she appeared as a backup singer for a string of Elvis impersonators in *Honeymoon in Vegas* with Nicholas Cage and James Caan. She also appeared in River Phoenix's last movie, *The Thing Called Love* (1993), as a dancer in an outdoor scene. She recorded sporadically, but could not get much to market, even recording an album for an MCA subsidiary that folded before the album was released. Two albums in 1989 on Rounder/Philo, *Walkin' on the Moon* and *Child Bride,* received excellent reviews, and she released an album with her old singing partner, brother Hugh called *Dance Me Outside* (1992). In addition, Moffatt cut a studio live album, *Indoor Fireworks* (1992) on Red Moon Records.

Moffatt's career blossomed in the 1990s as she began to work with smaller but more personally involved record companies. She exhibited the variety of talents she had acquired over the years. *Dance Me Outside* demonstrates her impressive harmonic skills in duets. *Indoor Fireworks* brought in a full band from Austin with electric instruments and a more driving sound. *The Greatest Show on Earth* (1993) displayed a range of instrumentation with acoustic folk and country rock elements. The songs on this album were co-written with Tom Russell, who met Moffatt at the Kerrville Music Festival in 1986. Russell also helped her produce the album. Although *The Greatest Show on Earth* received complimentary reviews, the producers subsequently received a brusque legal notice from the Barnum and Bailey Circus that their choice of album title violated the circus' trademark rights. Rounder Records was forced to recall the album and change the title and album cover. It became *The Evangeline Hotel*. The content remained the same, however, and *The Evangeline Hotel* was released in the United States, Canada, and Europe.

Never Mind the Weather

Like many American singer/songwriters, Moffatt is more honored abroad than in her own country. She is celebrated in both Europe and Canada and has toured there often. Moffatt undertook an extensive tour of the United States in 1995, playing more than 220 days on the road, despite a bout of tuberculosis in January and back surgery in December. Always a hard worker, Moffatt released several albums in the mid-1990s: *Hearts Gone Wild* (1994) was highly successful, reaching the top ten on some lists; *Sleepless Nights*, a collaboration with fellow songwriter Kate Brislin, debuted in January 1996. *Midnight Radio* was recorded during the 1996 New York City blizzard, a metaphorical triumph over odds typical of Moffatt's progress. The complexly textured *Midnight Radio* came out later in 1996. Nat Hentoff, the legendary pop music critic, reviewing the album in the *Wall Street Journal*, considered her eclecticism the result of a "naturally protean" streak. He noted: "In all her albums and her appearances, Katy Moffatt is indeed a storyteller. Her voice has many shades of meaning as well as memory. She illuminates—in natural light—the characters and the places in her songs, and even the weather."

Throughout her travels, Moffatt has maintained an artistic quest. She takes her trials and tribulations with a grain of salt, according to Watermelon Records: "It's only through those things that you become who you are. That's what all those years have been for; there's an appreciation for literacy and a desire to go a little deeper because of the years survived and the years given, and this is inextricably bound to and hopefully reflected in the music made." Holly Gleason observed, "There are plenty of good singers in the world: singers with lovely voices and lots of technique, singers with impeccable taste, singers who know how to turn a song inside out. But, singers who know how to get inside the songs, to inhabit them and make them their own are very rare indeed."

Selected discography

Katy, CBS, 1976.
Kissin' in the California Sun, CBS, 1978.
Walking on the Moon, Rounder/Philo, 1989.
Child Bride, Rounder/Philo, 1989.
Dance Me Outside, Rounder, 1992.
Indoor Fireworks, Rounder, 1992.
The Greatest Show on Earth, Rounder/ Round Tower, 1993.
Hearts Gone Wild, Watermelon 1994.
(With Kate Brislin) *Sleepless Nights*, Rounder, 1996.
Midnight Radio, Watermelon, 1996.

Sources

Periodicals

Audio, April 1995.
Billboard, October 28, 1989.
Folk Roots, June 1990; August 1992; April 1993; September 1993; March 1995.
Melody Maker, February 3, 1990.
New York Daily News, November 18, 1994.
Rolling Stone, June 15, 1978.
Sing Out!, Number 2, 1993.
Stereo Review, August 1992; September 7, 1993.
Variety, April 19, 1978.

Internet

Katy Moffatt Home Page: http://members.aol.com/klmoffatt/

—Paul Anderson

Hugo Montenegro

Composer

Hugo Montenegro earned the moniker "The Quad father" in the early 1970s as a pioneering composer for quadrasonic recording. He rose to recognition through his work as a film and television composer and introduced the use of synthesizers to movie and television soundtracks.

Montenegro was born in New York in 1925. He began his music career during his two years in the U.S. Navy, where he arranged music for Service bands. After the Navy, Hugo Montenegro studied composition at the Manhattan College in New York. Once he graduated, he decided to work in the music industry. In 1955, he worked with Andre Kostelanetz as a staff manager. He went on to serve as both a conductor and arranger for several artists, including Henry Belefonte.

During the mid-1960s, Montenegro moved to California, where he began composing and recording music for film and television. He released the soundtracks *Original Music from "The Man from UNCLE"* and *More Music from "The Man from UNCLE"* in 1966. The following year, he wrote the musical score for the Otto Preminger film *Hurry Sundown* starring Michael Caine and Jane Fonda.

Popularized Western Film Soundtracks

The same year, Hugo Montenegro released the record that would launch his name and cement his popularity. His recording of Ennio Morricone's theme for the "spaghetti western" *The Good, The Bad, and The Ugly*, directed by Sergio Leone and starring Clint Eastwood, climbed to number two on the U.S. charts and became number one in the U.K., selling well over a million copies. Arthur Smith played the ocarina, and Muzzy Marcellino provided the whistling. The theme included some unusual instruments for the time, such as the electric violin, electric harmonica, and a piccolo trumpet. "The instrumental contrasted with Montenegro's big romantic sound, and the effects were startling," one writer commented in *The Guinness Encyclopedia of Popular Music*. Montenegro later released *Music from "A Fistful of Dollars" & "For a Few Dollars More" & "The Good, The Bad, and The Ugly,"* a compilation of music from the three movies, which made the Top 10 albums in the U.S. in 1966. He also provided the score for Matt Helm's film *The Ambushers* starring Dean Martin.

Montenegro wrote the theme and soundtrack for *Hang 'Em High* in 1969, another Clint Eastwood western that attempted to match the style of the "spaghetti" originals. During the same year, Montenegro either contributed to the score or wrote the entire soundtrack for four other films: Matt Helm's *The Wrecking Crew*, starring Dean

Martin; a Western with Elvis Presley called *Charro!*: *The Undefeated*, featuring John Wayne; and *Viva Max!* In addition, Montenegro released his own album on RCA Victor called *Moog Power*—the first in a series of "space-age" pop stylings.

Pioneered Quadrasonic Composition

Hugo Montenegro made his mark on the future of film music in 1972 with his work in quadrasonic recording. The technique, an early version of surround sound, involved recording for four speakers instead of two so that the listener would hear sounds from the front and back, as well as left and right. RCA Records wanted a pop quadrasonic album to debut at the International Music Industry Conference that year in Acapulco, Mexico. When the label asked Montenegro to write and produce it, he began to do research into psychoacoustics. He had realized the potential of quadrasonic sound the very first time he heard an example of it. He believed he could use the technique to create a complete circle of sound, motion in every direction, as well as a feeling of spaciousness.

Montenegro studied with Dr. Archer Michael, who helped him gain an understanding of how the ear and the brain process interact to "create" sound. Montenegro began recording the album for RCA, but wasn't happy with the quadrophonic medium until he met with RCA's Red Seal division executive producer Jack Pfieffer, who had a background in electronics. Pfieffer explained the technical aspects of the four-channel recording process along with the concept of ambiance.

"It wasn't until the end of my research at RCA that I found Jack Pfieffer, and he told me why I felt gaps in the music," Montenegro told Eliot Tiegel in *Billboard*. "He began expounding concepts and words new to me.

The problem was I wasn't aware of psychoacoustics and how people react and perceive sound phenomenon around them."

Birth of "The Quadfather"

After he went back to the recording process to test and experiment with his new knowledge, Montenegro discovered the tricks and techniques to composing music for quadrasonic sound. His work resulted in the first ever four-channel pop album, *Love Theme from the Godfather*. The title of the album became the source of his new nickname "The Quadfather." The LP included the tracks "Norwegian Wood," "I Feel the Earth Move," and "Baby Elephant Walk." Montenegro soon communicated his discoveries to other producers and composers interested in the quadrasonic process. He had set the stage for the future of surround sound. "The new generation of electronics oriented musicians will have it easier than we did," Montenegro told Tiegel in *Billboard*.

The year after releasing *Love Theme from the Godfather*, JVC, a manufacturer of the four-channel system, asked Montenegro to come to Japan to promote the quadrasonic concept. He went on to produce other quadrasonic albums, including *Neil's Diamonds*, a collection of covers of Neil Diamond's hits. In the 1970s and early 1980s Montenegro continued to write, arrange, and produce music for film and television. He provided music for the film *The Farmer* in 1977, and wrote background music for *I Dream of Jeannie* and *The Partridge Family* television shows.

Toward the end of his life, Hugo Montenegro fought with emphysema. RCA released a compilation of his work in 1980, *The Best of Hugo Montenegro*, and his final LP *Plays for Lovers* came out in 1981. Montenegro lost the fight with his lung condition and died on February 6, 1981. Yet, his prolific compositions for film and his mark on the future of sound recording have established him as an enduring figure in the history of modern music.

Selected discography

Original Music from "The Man from UNCLE," RCA Victor, 1966.
More Music from "The Man from UNCLE," RCA Victor, 1966.
Hurry Sundown, RCA Victor, 1967.
The Good, The Bad, and The Ugly, RCA Victor, 1968.
Music from "A Fistful of Dollars" & "For A Few Dollars More" & "The Good, The Bad, and The Ugly," RCA Victor, 1968.
Hang 'Em High, RCA Victor, 1969.
Moog Power, RCA Victor, 1969.
Love Theme from the Godfather, RCA Records, 1972.

The Best of Hugo Montenegro, RCA Records, 1980.
Plays for Lovers, RCA Records, 1981.

Sources

Books

The Guinness Encyclopedia of Popular Music, edited by Colin Larkin, Stockton Press,1995.

Periodicals

Billboard, August 5, 1972; August 4, 1973; February 21, 1981.
International Musician, April 1981.
Newsweek, February 16, 1981.

—Sonya Shelton

The Moody Blues

Rock band

In the unstable world of rock and roll music, the lifetime of a band can usually be measured by the number of weeks they spend on the charts with a top ten single. The rare exceptions are the few groups that can consistently maintain a steady stream of hits, produce numerous top ten albums, and generate a devoted fan base. The Moody Blues have achieved all of this, while at the same time sustaining widespread commercial and critical success since 1965—all without compromising their dedication to a unique sound and trademark lyrics.

Formed in 1964 by Denny Laine, Clint Warwick, Mike Pinder, Ray Thomas, and Graeme Edge in Birmingham, England, the Moody Blues began as a rhythm and blues band, their name adapted from the style of music they performed. They immediately rose to fame with the number one single "Go Now," and seemed poised to become another British supergroup following on the heels of the wildly popular Beatles and Rolling Stones. Their place in musical history seemed assured when, in 1965, after seeing a live performance, the Beatles'

Archive Photos

manager Brian Epstein signed the band and Coca-Cola enlisted them to sing on several radio commercials. The following year, "Go Now" was released in the United States, became a hit single, and *The Magnificent Moodies,* their first full album, was received favorably in Britain.

In late 1966, a major upheaval in the band's lineup occurred as both Denny Laine (who later performed with Paul McCartney's Wings) and Clint Warwick left the group; they were replaced by Justin Hayward and John Lodge. The new membership permanently altered the direction of the band, as they ended their relationship with Epstein, began recording with Decca Records, and fashioned a new sound that blended 1960s rock and roll elements with classical overtones.

Bloomed with New Members

The first release of the new lineup, the groundbreaking *Days of Future Passed,* produced two instant top ten hits—"Nights in White Satin" and "Tuesday Afternoon,"—and is often cited as their best album. The album's sound was influenced by the experimentalism in instrumentation and lyrics that the Beatles had popularized with albums like *Revolver* and which other bands were beginning to mimic. *Days of Future Passed* is a sumptuous description of sunrise to sunset in an almost operatic fashion. The album begins with an overture highlighting all of the main musical themes, is followed by recitation of poetry, and ends again with poetry. As the album progresses, several more traditional songs, like "The Day Begins," "Peak Hour," and "Evening," are interspersed with musical interludes which serve to tie together the previous and next stage of the album/day. *Days of Future Passed* was one of the first popular music recordings to feature a classical performance, which was completed by the London Festival Orches-

tra and orchestrated by Peter Knight after the group had finished the main songs.

The album ends with one of the Moody Blues' biggest hits and what quickly became their trademark song: "Nights in White Satin." The song contains many romantic elements—which were to became an important part of the band's image—combined with a complex set of lyrics. The word "nights" becomes a double entendre for the more mythic "knights." "Tuesday Afternoon" also hit the charts immediately as well, and the album itself remained on the charts for two years after its release.

Days of Future Passed is an excellent example of a "concept" album, with its circular nature and narrative structure. The band also used elements from *Days* in their 1968 follow-up *In Search of the Lost Chord.* The latter album begins and ends with poetry, but this time the band wanted more control over the overall sound, so they decided to play each of the 30 featured instruments themselves. The result is a diverse production with a wide range of instrumentation, including 12-string guitar, harpsichord, tabla, flute, and mellotron. The mellotron, an early form of synthesizer, reproduced sampled music from a prerecorded magnetic tape and became a favorite instrument of keyboardist Mike Pinder, further defining the early sound of the Moody Blues. *In Search of the Lost Chord* was the tale of a band searching for their own identities both spiritually and musically; appropriately, after the release of the album the group decided to take a major developmental step.

Sought Creative Control

Following the lead of the Beatles creation of Apple Records, the Moody Blues formed the Threshold label in 1969, not only for themselves but also as a venue for the promotion of new and rising talent. Justin Hayward told *Melody Maker* that the label was born out of frustration and dissatisfaction: "After we'd completed each of our albums we found that we had so many ideas left over....we felt that we weren't able to exercise sufficient control over our material." Threshold still came under the wings of Decca, allowing the band to use Decca's recording facilities and distribution network. In 1969 they released *On the Threshold of a Dream* and also *To Our Children's Children's Children,* which was the first album on the Threshold label.

The Moody Blues' albums had all been received well, and the 1970 release *A Question of Balance* was no exception. By now the group had developed a full, rich characteristic sound that incorporated solid songwriting with cutting-edge instrumentation. Their songs varied thematically, but always presented a kind of philosophical exploration. Hayward told *Melody Maker* that these philosophies "are a lot of people's opinions, not just our own. I think and hope that we are expressing what a lot of people feel." The string of hits continued with 1971's *Every Good Boy Deserves Favour* and 1972's *Seventh Sojourn,* featuring the hits "The Story in Your Eyes," "Isn't Life Strange," and "I'm Just a Singer (in a Rock n' Roll Band)."

Parted Ways to Regroup Later

After their rapid rise to fame, seven gold albums, and a long tour, the band separated in 1974. During the break, each band member recorded at least one solo album; Graeme Edge formed a new band; and John Lodge and Justin Hayward collaborated for *Blue Jays,* a very well-received album. The band reunited in late 1977 and began recording 1978's aptly named release *Octave.* The success of the album convinced them to embark upon a major tour, excepting Mike Pinder; the keyboardist and founding member declined and left the band. Pinder did not reappear on the music scene until 1993, when he released a solo recording, followed by a several children's albums. Pinder was replaced by Patrick Moraz, formerly of the band Yes, who stayed with the group until 1991.

Although Pinder's departure did have an effect on the Moody Blues, the band was fully recovered by the 1981 recording of *Long Distance Voyager.* The album became a huge hit, and the single "The Voice" introduced the Moody Blues to a new generation of listeners. Their rebirth was greeted with praise, but the 1983 follow-up *The Present* performed poorly on the charts. The group fired the producer of both albums, claiming a lack of support for their material on these efforts.

Subsequent releases, including *The Other Side of Life* (1986), *Sur La Mer* (1988), and *Keys of the Kingdom* (1991), brought the band around full circle by updating their sound and producing yet another string of popular singles. *Billboard* hits off these albums included "Your Wildest Dreams" and "I Know You're Out There Somewhere," while the video from the latter won the *Billboard* Video of the Year Award. In 1992 the band recorded a live concert with the Colorado Symphony Orchestra at the popular Red Rocks venue in Colorado. The record-ing was released a year later as *A Night at Red Rocks,* and the band followed with a well-attended tour of the United States in support of the recording.

The immense popularity of the Moody Blues has persisted over several generations of fans despite long periods of dormancy and personnel turnovers. Their longevity can be attributed to several factors, including solid songwriting techniques, unique and often progressive instrumentation, and a distinctive sound which they have never sacrificed in pursuit of trendiness. Throughout the years, the band's simple approach to making music allowed them to remain true to themselves. As John Lodge told *Guitar Player* in 1995, "With everything we've written and recorded, we've wanted the music to last forever. We wanted to be proud of what we did years and years later....Of course, I don't think any of us thought we'd still be talking about it 30 years later."

Selected discography

The Magnificent Moodies, Polydor, 1966.
Go Now, 1966.
Days of Future Passed, Decca, 1967.
In Search of the Lost Chord, Decca, 1968.
On the Threshold of a Dream, Decca, 1969
To Our Children's Children's Children, Threshold, 1969.
A Question of Balance, Threshold, 1970.
Every Good Boy Deserves Favour, Threshold, 1971.
Seventh Sojourn, Threshold, 1972.
Octave, Threshold, 1978.
Long Distance Voyager, Threshold, 1981.
The Present, Threshold, 1983.
The Other Side of Life, Polydor, 1986.
Sur La Mer, Polydor, 1988.
Keys of the Kingdom, Polydor, 1991.
(With the Colorado Symphony Orchestra) *A Night at Red Rocks,* Polydor, 1993.
Time Traveler, 4-cd box set greatest hits, Polygram, 1994.

Sources

Guitar Player, September 1995.
Melody Maker, January 21, 1967; October 19, 1968; November 1, 1969; February 7, 1970; July 15, 1978.

—*Debra Power*

Maria Muldaur

Singer, guitarist

Photo by Caroline Greyshock; reproduced by permission of Telarc International

Maria Muldaur has managed to retain a core of loyal fans over the years with her distinctive mix of soul, blues, jazz, and roots music. She is best known for "Midnight at the Oasis," a major hit that made her an overnight star in the early 1970s. "I was the Tracy Chapman of the time," she told the *Washington Post* in 1989. "Not that I sound anything like Tracy, but like her I was so different from everything else that was going on at the time and the music so pure that it just rose to the top." Throughout her career, Muldaur has been cited for her "love affair" with the music she performs, which many feel makes even old standards seem new again. As Mike Joyce remarked in his *Washington Post* review of a 1994 Muldaur performance at Tornado Alley in Washington, D.C., "As familiar as many of the songs were, Muldaur treated them as if they were still fresh and meaningful to her."

Although her mother preferred classical music, Muldaur grew up as a fan of blues and big band tunes. She immersed herself in the active music scene of New York City's Greenwich Village where she spent her childhood years, often joining in on impromptu jam sessions there. After forming an all-female group called The Cashmeres, she declined the opportunity to sign a recording contract at age sixteen because she wanted to stay in school. By then she was becoming more interested in rhythm and blues, especially the music of Fats Domino, Little Richard, Clyde McPhatter, and Ruth Brown.

Developed Interest in Roots Music

A key influence on Muldaur's musical career was her early exposure to roots music. She frequently got involved with weekend jams in Greenwich Village with blues singers such as Reverend Gary Davis, Mississippi John Hurt, Son House, and Victoria Spivey. She also become affiliated with The Friends of Old Timey Music, a group that traveled to the rural South to find such legends of roots music as Doc Watson and Mississippi John Hammond Jr. Muldaur was especially interested in the music of Watson, and at one time went to North Carolina to learn how to play the fiddle. While there she developed a deep appreciation of Appalachian music and culture while attending get-togethers on Watson's porch. At the same time she was expanding her repertoire of blues songs, especially those of Bessie Smith and Ma Rainey.

In the early 1960s Muldaur became part of the Even Dozen Jug Band with John Sebastian, Stefan Grossman, Joshua Rifkin, and Steve Katz, which recorded an album for Elektra in 1964. After the group broke up, Muldaur became part of the Jim Kweskin Jug Band in

For the Record . . .

Born Maria Grazia Rosa Domenica d'Amato, September 12, 1943, in New York, NY; married Geoffrey Muldaur (divorced 1972); children: Jennie.

Formed group the Cashmeres in high school; became involved with the Friends of Old Timey Music and met Doc Watson, early 1960s; played with Even Dozen Jug Band and Jim Kweskin Jug Band, mid-1960s; recorded *Pottery Pie* and *Sweet Potatoes* albums with husband Geoff Muldaur; contributed to film soundtrack of *Steelyard Blues* with Paul Butterfield and Mike Bloomfield, 1972; recorded first solo album, *Maria Muldaur*, on Reprise label, 1973; had U.S. Top Ten single, "Midnight at the Oasis," 1973; toured U.S. and Europe, 1975; released albums on Takoma, Spindrift, and Myrhh labels, 1980s; signed contract with Blacktop Records, 1992; created and starred in *Developing Your Vocal and Performing Style,* an instructional video, 1990s.

Addresses: *Management*—Steve Hecht, Piedmont Talent, 1222 Kenilworth Ave., Charlotte, NC 28204.

Boston and recorded her first version of "I'm a Woman," which later became her theme song. While with the group Muldaur met and married bandmate Geoff Muldaur. The couple recorded two favorably reviewed albums, *Pottery Pie* and *Sweet Potatoes,* with Reprise while living in Woodstock, New York, during the same time that Bob Dylan, The Band, Paul Butterfield, Janis Joplin's Full Tilt Boogie Band, and other noteworthy music makers were living there.

Fame Established by Hit Song

Muldaur's marriage ended in divorce in 1972 as her husband was forming the group Better Days with Butterfield. After Mo Ostin, president of Reprise Records, gave her the go-ahead for a solo album, Muldaur came out with *Maria Muldaur,* which soared to number three on the U.S. charts and went platinum. On the album was the soon-to-be legendary "Midnight at the Oasis," a sultry song with an acclaimed guitar solo by Amos Garrett that made it to number six on the U.S. charts. Her next album, *Waitress in a Donut Shop,* featured songs by writers such as Kate and Anna McGarrigle and horn arrangements by Benny Carter that gave the album more of a jazz feel. This release made it into the U.S. Top 30, and the album's "I'm a Woman" single rose into the U.S. Top 20 in 1975. "Maria Muldaur's first two solo albums still stand up today as sterling examples of American roots music," wrote Geoffrey Himes in the *Washington Post.*

Riding the wave of her new fame, Muldaur toured the U.S. in 1975 and then took her act to Europe. Although her next two albums, *Sweet Harmony* and *Southern Winds,* made the charts, she lost her recording contract in 1979 because album sales had not lived up to her label's expectations. During the late 1970s she recorded with smaller labels and kept active as a performer, showing up at concerts with artists ranging from Jerry Garcia to Benny Carter. In the early 1980s she ventured into Christian music. She also recorded two critically acclaimed jazz albums and an album of swing music with frequent collaborator Dr. John.

Ventured into Video

In 1992 Muldaur signed with Black Top Records and began devoting herself more to roots music, recording *Louisiana Love Call* in New Orleans. The album included contributions by Dr. John, Charles Neville, accordionist Zachary Richard, and guitarist Garrett, and received major appreciation from magazines such as *Rolling Stone* and *Billboard.* The release was also awarded the "Best Adult Alternative Album of the Year" by the National Association of Independent Record Distributors. In the *Washington Post,* Charles Himes called the album "an attractively sung, user-friendly guide to roots music," averring that "Muldaur brings her steady summer night languor to [these songs]...." In her *Meet Me at Midnight* album, released in the mid 1990s, Muldaur continued her exploration of roots music. Himes wrote: "Muldaur has a smokey voice and slippery sense of phrasing that made Meet Me at Midnight a satisfying return to '70s-style roots-rock."

In recent years Muldaur also created her own instructional video for aspiring singers called *Developing Your Vocal and Performing Style.* She remains popular on the club circuit today, and has recently recorded a tribute to Southern blues music on Telarc Blues called *Fanning the Flames.* "She [Muldaur] has never been able to completely match the success of 'Midnight at the Oasis,' but her soulful style of blues tinged with jazz is still in demand," claimed the *Guinness Encyclopedia of Popular Music.*

Selected discography

Maria Muldaur, Reprise, 1973.
Waitress in a Donut Shop, Reprise, 1974, reissued, 1993.
Gospel Nights, Takoma, 1980.

There Is a Love, Myrhh, 1982.
Live in London, Making Waves, 1987.
On the Sunny Side, Music for Little People, 1991.
Meet Me at Midnight, Blacktop, 1994.

Sources

Books

Clarke, Donald, editor, *The Penguin Encyclopedia of Popular Music*, Viking, 1989, p. 836.
Larkin, Colin, editor, *The Guinness Encyclopedia of Popular Music, Volume 1*, Guinness Publishing, 1992, p. 2956.

Periodicals

New York, December 5, 1988, p. 48.
People, October 15, 1990, pp. 15–17.
Variety, November 15, 1989, p. 51.
Washington Post, September 15, 1989, Section WW, p. 27; April 16, 1993, Section WW, p. 10; May 30, 1994, Section C, p. 7; April 21, 1995, Section WW, p. 17.

Additional information for this profile was obtained from the *All Music Guide* website on the Internet (http://www.cduniverse.com).

—*Ed Decker*

Me'Shell
Ndegéocello

Singer, songwriter

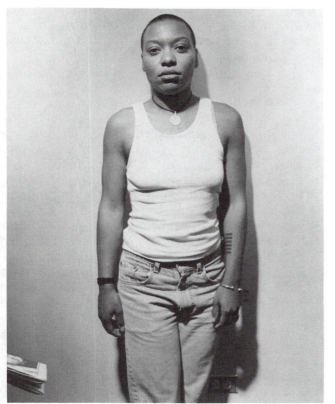

Singer/songwriter and multi-instrumentalist Me'Shell Ndegéocello wrote, "I love music," in a brief essay distributed by her publicist in 1996. "It's like a lover that I can't commit to, but I seem to always find myself in bed with. With music, I free myself from myself." Yet freedom has not always been easy to come by for the acclaimed performer. Despite having released two critically acclaimed albums and scoring some hit songs, Ndegéocello has exhibited such restlessness that it appeared she might leave her "lover" music in the lurch. Yet whatever her ultimate choice, her intimate, dense fusion of funk, soul, jazz and rock and consistently bold lyrical stance had already made her, according to *Rolling Stone,* "one of the few artists who really matter" in the R&B world.

She was born Michelle Johnson in Berlin, Germany, and grew up in Washington, D.C. Her father was in the U.S. Army, and played tenor saxophone; she has recalled in interviews that he played at several presidential inaugurations. His musical aptitude and appreciation for jazz played a huge role in her development. Yet he and her mother, a health care worker, had a troubled relationship, the musician later reflected. "It was horrible watching the way my father treated my mother and not feeling I could help her," she told the *Los Angeles Times.* "I've seen my father cheat on my mother several times in front of my face, and I wasn't strong enough to tell my mother that. Even though I knew she knew, I felt like I betrayed her by not telling her."

Running from the Devil

Her sense of isolation was compounded during her adolescence by sexual feelings she recognized as outside the mainstream. Though she has mostly addressed male lovers in her songs, Ndegéocello identifies herself as a bisexual. This and a sense of musical mission helped form her unique creative identity. At 12, she related in *Rolling Stone,* she had "a dream where I was running from the devil. I kept on reciting the Lord's Prayer in my brain, begging myself to wake up. It seemed like the dream lasted days; finally I woke up, covered in sweat. I didn't sleep again for four days." Like pioneering blues artist Robert Johnson, who was alleged to have signed a pact with the devil, Ndegéocello has made her flight from various demons the focal point of her work.

Inspired by funk, soul and rock records in her brother's collection, she picked up the bass and began writing songs at age 16. Performing in local bands, she focused more intensively on music, and went on to study for a music history degree at Howard University. She then

For the Record . . .

Born Michelle Johnson, August 29, 1968, in Berlin, Germany; daughter of a musician and a health-care worker. *Education:* Received music degree from Howard University. Children: Askia, born c. 1989.

Musician and singer-songwriter, c. 1980s—. Signed with Maverick Records and released album *Plantation Lullabies,* 1993; appeared on recordings by Madonna, John Mellencamp, Marcus Miller, and others, 1994-95; contributed music to theatrical productions *What's Behind Door 1,* 1994, and *Whispers of Angels,* 1995; opened for The Who, 1996; joined H.O.R.D.E. music festival, 1996.

Awards: *Plantation Lullabies* was nominated for three Grammy Awards in 1994; also received Grammy nomination for duet with John Mellencamp; named "Brightest Hope for 1994" by a *Rolling Stone* Critics Poll; best bass player award, Gibson Guitar Awards, 1996.

Addresses: *Home*—Los Angeles, CA. *Publicist*—Mitch Schneider Organization, 14724 Ventura Blvd., Ste. 410, Sherman Oaks, CA 91403.

moved to New York, honing her chops in various bands; she also had a son, Askia, by a father whom she has elected not to name in interviews.

Crafted "Mesmerizing" Soul Music

Choosing the name Ndegéocello, which she identified as the Swahili phrase for "free like a bird"—though some observers have claimed that only part of the word is actually Swahili—she began crafting her own approach. Working in the melodic, groove-oriented idiom of such soul music luminaries as Curtis Mayfield, Stevie Wonder and Marvin Gaye, she avoided the "retro" tag by adding elements of pop and jazz and exploring painful and often controversial subject matter in her lyrics.

In 1993, a tape of her material found its way to some music industry figures in Los Angeles, who arranged for her to perform a special "showcase" gig there. One of those in the audience was Freddy DeMann, co-head of Maverick Records, the label founded by pop megastar Madonna. "She was incredible, mesmerizing," DeMann recalled in the *Los Angeles Times* of Ndegéocello's performance. She chose Maverick over other labels because it offered her creative freedom.

Ndegéocello entered the recording studio and began work on her record, but the pressures of her career began to weigh heavily. "Everything happened so fast," she averred in the *Los Angeles Times.* "I was playing a club and within a week or two weeks, I was signed. Then I was in a studio, working 18 hours a day. I thought I could handle it, but I couldn't." She vanished briefly from her own project, taking refuge in crack cocaine. She quit shortly thereafter, however, and completed the album. "Actually, I think I was having a spiritual death," she later told *Entertainment Weekly.* "I had thought that making a record would solve my problems—lift my self-esteem, make people from my past love me the way I wanted to be loved. But instead I felt as if every bit of joy I had was dying." She added that she understood the 1994 suicide of rock star Kurt Cobain and felt kindred self-destructive tendencies.

Released in 1993, *Plantation Lullabies* demonstrated her range and ambition. One of its songs, the playful "If That's Your Boyfriend (He Wasn't Last Night)," became a hit; other tracks covered more serious territory. *Essence* described her as "sonically and spiritually the daughter of [Sixties jazz-folk singer] Nina Simone and [political rapper and Public Enemy leader] Chuck D." With her shaved head and deep, sultry vocals, Ndegéocello presented a striking departure from the manicured sirens of the R&B world, and her open bisexuality challenged virtually everyone. "People see me as a heretic," she ventured in the *Los Angeles Times.* "Homophobia is rampant in the black community, so I am a traitor to my race, and gay people don't like me because I'm not gay enough."

Reached Masses with Mellencamp

Ndegéocello impressed audiences with her live performances, which showed her stretching into jazzy improvisation. Playing bass and vocalizing in a husky style influenced by both rap and classic soul, she demonstrated a range reminiscent of such genre-busting pop innovators as Prince. *Los Angeles Times* critic Robert Hilburn saw in one performance "a sense of freedom and sweep in her music that was nothing short of intoxicating in its best moments," and felt that despite the artist's occasional lapses, her show "rests on a foundation of potential greatness." A *Rolling Stone* Critics Poll named her "Brightest Hope for 1994."

Yet it was in a duet with a white rock star on a cover tune that Ndegéocello reached her biggest audience. In 1994 she joined pop hitmaker John Mellencamp for a version of the Van Morrison song "Wild Night," lending both her smoky voice and fancy fretwork to the track; it became a hit and helped both their careers substantially. But Ndegéocello didn't restrict herself to such high-profile enterprises. She collaborated with writer-choreographer David Rousseve on a theatrical production titled *Whispers of Angels,* and worked with her life partner, choreographer Winifred Harris, on the production *What's Behind Door 1,* for Harris's Between Lines dance company.

Provocative *Peace*

Ndegéocello's searching—which included obsessive reading of the Bible and perusal of the Koran, Islam's holy book—led to her introspective second album, 1996's *Peace Beyond Passion.* The sophomore set combines her relentless, atmospheric grooves with lengthy meditations on religion, freedom, and sensuality. "This album is all my questions and all my fears," she asserted in *Rolling Stone.* "And sometimes I find peace." The record ignited some controversy with its lead single, "Leviticus: Faggot." A pro-tolerance song detailing the persecution and eventual death of a gay man, the track's repeated use of such a homophobic term ruffled some feathers. Yet the record company worked carefully with gay leaders and radio personnel, conveying its belief in the song's positive message. These efforts paid off, and helped earn the single and the album some glowing reviews. "Some records just leave you speechless—filled with emotion and perspective but grappling for coherent words of expression," wrote *Billboard* columnist Larry Flick. He dubbed the single "an intense, brutally honest cut that has us driven to distraction and reaching for words that are worthy of the song's potentially revolutionary impact."

Peace Beyond Passion, though not universally admired, attracted some raves itself. "With intimacy and purposefulness," declared Ernest Hardy of *Rolling Stone,* "Ndegéocello fulfills the promise of her first album and puts the pop, hip-hop and R&B worlds on notice: She's one of the few artists who really matter." Scott Frampton of *College Music Journal (CMJ)* observed that "her bass is still the prominent force in her music, but more as an anchor for a more soulful sound that reaches back, successfully," to her R&B influences. *Details,* however, offered a slightly dissenting opinion in its assertion that "occasionally the religious concept-album trappings get too heavy for the music to carry the load."

Ndegéocello was invited by Pete Townshend of English rock legends The Who to open three dates of their *Quadrophenia* tour, after which she joined the high-profile H.O.R.D.E. festival. Yet despite such honors, she expressed continued doubts about her career, declaring that *Peace* would be her last solo album and that she might either leave her pop career behind or join a band. "I want some sort of collective experience," she claimed in the *Los Angeles Times,* adding, "I've seen what can happen to you if you think you are invincible in this business" and concluded, "I know one thing: I'm not willing to let it destroy me." Yet in her 1996 essay accompanying the release of *Peace Beyond Passion,* she declared "I no longer spend my days in worry of tomorrow; instead I keep the thought of God ever present, in hope that my days are filled with love for myself and others."

Selected discography

Plantation Lullabies (includes "If That's Your Boyfriend (He Wasn't Last Night)"), Maverick, 1993.
(Contributor) Madonna, *Bedtime Stories,* Maverick, 1994.
(Contributor) John Mellencamp, *Dance Naked* (appears on "Wild Night"), Mercury, 1994.
(Contributor) Marcus Miller, *Tales,* PRA, 1995.
(Contributor) Boney James, *Seduction,* Warner Bros., 1995.
Peace Beyond Passion (includes "Leviticus: Faggot"), Maverick, 1996.

Sources

Amsterdam News (New York), November 25, 1995.
Billboard, May 18, 1996, p. 26.
College Music Journal (CMJ), July 1996, p. 13.
Details, July 1996.
Entertainment Weekly, June 21, 1996, p. 63.
Essence, January 1994, p. 36.
Gannett News Service, March 25, 1994.
Los Angeles Times, August 30, 1994; November 6, 1994; May 18, 1996; August 25, 1996, p. 8.
Musician, August 1996, p. 86.
Rolling Stone, July 11, 1996, p. 86; September 5, 1996, p. 33.

Additional information was provided by publicity materials from The Mitch Schneider Organization, 1996.

—*Simon Glickman*

Mike Oldfield

Guitarist, composer

Popular entertainers who purchase flashy cars have been a common occurrence as long as automobiles have been available to celebrities with disposable income. Mike Oldfield is an exception to the rule. During one of his infrequent interviews with *Melody Maker*, writer Steve Lake was interrupted by an appointment with a car salesman. After test driving a Ferrari, Oldfield told the harried salesman eager to close the deal, "Well, I don't want a fast car so much as a quiet one. That one seems very noisy."

The introverted Oldfield has always been an anomaly to the outlandish side of pop music superstardom. He was born on May 15, 1953, in Reading, England. He began playing the guitar as a youth, forming a folk duo called Sallyangie with his older sister Sally. Following the commercial failure of their album *Children of the Sun* he formed a short-lived band called Barefeet.

Joins The Whole Wide World

In 1970, Mike Oldfield joined former Soft Machine vocalist Kevin Ayers' band The Whole Wide World as lead guitarist. Mike would eventually collaborate extensively with Whole Wide World pianist and arranger David Bedford. During his tenure with the Whole Wide World, Oldfield had conceived a peculiar piece of music he called "Tubular Bells." Kevin lent his tape recorder for Mike to record demos.

Upon the dissolution of The Whole Wide World, Mike Oldfield finished his demos at The Manor, a sixteenth-century house that entrepreneur Richard Branson was converting into a recording studio in the Oxford countryside. After every record company in England turned down *Tubular Bells*, Branson scraped together the capital to release it on his fledgling company Virgin Records. With the help of a few musicians and a vocal choir, and narration by Bonzo Dog Band frontman Viv Stanshall, Oldfield overdubbed himself playing 28 instruments.

Tubular Bells Becomes a Smash Hit

Mike Oldfield promoted the album with a single concert at Queen Elizabeth Hall in London. His backing musicians included Rolling Stone Mick Taylor, Mike Ratledge from the Soft Machine, David Bedford, and Kevin Ayers. The audience was enthusiastic, and the album sold moderately well. When part of *Tubular Bells* was used in the film *The Exorcist,* it turned into a blockbuster hit, topping the British charts and peaking at number three in the United States.

Hergest Ridge, the follow-up to *Tubular Bells*, was somewhat similar in concept but differed in feeling to its famous predecessor. Where *Bells* reflected the urban environment in which it was created, *Ridge* reflected the influence of Oldfield's peaceful new country manor. Oldfield's response in a *Melody Maker* interview to critics who took his romanticism to task was, "Silly boys....The problem of the world today is that there's not enough romance."

Ommadawn, released in 1975, featured Paddy Moloney from the Chieftains on uillean pipes, as well as African percussionists. The same year, in addition to playing on Robert Wyatt's highly acclaimed *Rock Bottom* and albums by David Bedford and Virgin house engineer Tom Newman, Oldfield had a British Christmastime hit with "In Dulce Jublio." He finished the seventies with an orchestral adaptation of *Tubular Bells* and the albums *Incantations* and *Exposed*, a live set recorded during an expensive tour that featured over fifty musicians.

Oldfield's Songs Get Shorter

Throughout the eighties, Mike Oldfield's albums relied less and less on extended instrumental compositions and more on shorter pop songs. His records continued to sell in great quantities in Britain. Although he hadn't had a major American hit since *Tubular Bells*, his song "Family Man" from 1982's *Five Miles Out* was a top ten hit for the popular duo Hall and Oates. Inspired by a treacherous airplane ride over the Pyrenees Mountains,

the album prompted Oldfield's first tour of the United States.

Licensed pilot Oldfield told *Billboard:* "We flew into a thunderstorm in an unpressurized plane. We couldn't come down and land because of the mountains....The wings started icing up, and ice on the propellers was coming off in big chunks, smashing against the windowscreen.... It was about an hour but it felt like five years. It actually got to the stage of praying. At least it was an inspiration for an album."

In 1984 Oldfield scored Roland Joffe's film "The Killing Fields," the tragic story of a naturalized American journalist trapped in Cambodia during the early 1970s. The following year, Paul Hardcastle's hit record "19," with lyrics concerning the draft age during the Vietnam War, featured samples from *Tubular Bells*.

Oldfield's 1987 album *Islands* featured vocal cameos by two progressive rock veterans, Kevin Ayers and former Family vocalist Roger Chapman. During the late eighties, Oldfield's records weren't selling in quantities they once had, a fact he tacitly acknowledged to *Billboard:* "Perhaps [*Islands*] is an attempt to be a little more commercial than in the past, but that's all right."

Tubular Bells Peal Again

With the release of *Tubular Bells II* in 1992, Oldfield reconnected with the record-buying public. Soon after its live debut at the Edinburgh Festival in September, the album entered the British charts at number one. Rob Dickins, Warner Music U.K. chairman, countered the notion that Oldfield's releasing a sequel to his most famous work was an exploitative move. "Fifteen years ago, [the idea of] *Tubular Bells II* probably had nothing to do with entertainment philosophy. But whether you take the artistic side or the success side, a sequel doesn't necessarily mean a cash-in. 'Godfather 2' was a better film than 'The Godfather' for instance."

Oldfield followed the success of the second installment of *Tubular Bells* with 1995's *Songs of Distant Earth*, the first music album to contain computer programs. His 1996 album, *Voyager*, marks a return to his Celtic roots. It features Mike's reworking of seven Scottish, Irish, and Spanish folk songs, as well as several Celtic-inspired originals. Since the early 70s, the introverted Mike Oldfield has quietly carved his own niche in popular music. Along the way he has been at the forefront of utilizing new technology available for musicians and has been rewarded with an appreciative fan base on both sides of the Atlantic.

Selected discography

Tubular Bells, Virgin, 1973.
Hergest Ridge, Virgin, 1974.
Ommadawn, 1975.
Orchestral Tubular Bells, Virgin, 1975.
Boxed, Virgin, 1976.
Incantations, Virgin, 1978.
Exposed, Virgin, 1979.
Platinum, Virgin, 1979.
QE2, Virgin, 1980.
Five Miles Out, Virgin, 1982.
Crises, Virgin, 1983.
Discovery, Virgin, 1984.
The Killing Fields Original Film Soundtrack, Virgin, 1984.
Islands, Virgin, 1987.
Earth Moving, Virgin, 1989.
Amarok, Virgin, 1990.
Heaven's Open, Virgin, 1991.
Tubular Bells II, Reprise, 1992.
Elements, The Best of Mike Oldfield, 1993.
Songs of Distant Earth, Reprise, 1995.
Voyager, Reprise, 1996.

With Kevin Ayers and The Whole Wide World

Shooting at the Moon, Harvest, 1970, reissued, Beat Goes On, 1991.
Whatevershebringswesing, Harvest, 1971, reissued, Beat Goes On, 1991.

With David Bedford

Nurses Songs with Elephants, Dandelion, 1972, reissued, Voiceprint, 1993.
Star's End, Virgin, 1975.
Song of the White Horse, Voiceprint, 1994.
Variations on a Rhythm of Mike Oldfield, Voiceprint, 1995.

With Tom Newman

Fine Old Tom, Virgin, 1975, reissued Voiceprint, 1995.
Live at The Argonaut, Voiceprint, 1995.

Ozymandias, Voiceprint, 1996.

With others

(With Sallyangie), *Children of the Sun*, Transatlantic, 1968, reissued Line, 1989.
(With Lol Coxhill), *Ear of the Beholder*, Dandelion, 1971.
(With Kevin Ayers and the Soporifics), *June 1, 1974*, Island, 1974.
(With Robert Wyatt), *Rock Bottom*, Virgin, 1975.
(With Kevin Ayers), *Kevin Ayers BBC in Concert* (recorded 1972), Windsong, 1993.

Sources

Books

Frame, Pete, *The Complete Rock Family Trees*, Omnibus Press, 1993.
Hardy, Phil and Dave Laing, *The Faber Companion to 20th Century Popular Music*, Faber and Faber, 1990.
Joynson, Vernon, *The Tapestry of Delights: The Complete Guide to British Music of the Beat, R & B, Psychedelic, and Progressive Eras 1963-1976*, Borderline Productions, 1994.
Murrells, Joseph, *Million Selling Records from the 1900's to the 1980's*, Arco Publishing, 1984.
Palmer, Tony, *All You Need Is Love: The Story of Popular Music*, Grossman Publishers, 1976.
Schaffner, Nicholas, *The British Invasion*, McGraw-Hill, 1983.

Periodicals

Billboard, April 24, 1982; February 13, 1988; August 22, 1992; September 26, 1992.
Down Beat, June 5, 1975.
Melody Maker, March 16, 1974; August 24, 1974; October 30, 1976.
Rolling Stone, November 8, 1973; December 20, 1973.
Variety, November 24, 1982.

—*James Powers*

The Orb

Ambient/techno band

The Orb defies conventional classifications at nearly every turn. Less a group than an ongoing project headed by Alex Paterson, the Orb's recordings weave textures taken from synthesizers, guitar, and drum machines into computer-generated sounds and sampled bits of other music. The result is compositions that are orchestral in nature, with singles that are notorious in length. Such tactics have made the Orb synonymous with the term "ambient techno," and Paterson's music remains among the most acclaimed and successful in Europe—though he has yet to achieve such accolades in the United States. The Orb sometimes evokes comparisons to Pink Floyd for its epic and arty opuses, as well as to the work of ambient-music pioneer Brian Eno. Paterson has spoken of both Pink Floyd and Eno as more than influential to his work. "Groups like the Orb...take seriously Brian Eno's dictum that music can, and sometimes should, be as forgettable as it is thrilling," wrote Frank Owen in the *Village Voice*.

Paterson began his career in the music business as a roadie for the influential English band Killing Joke,

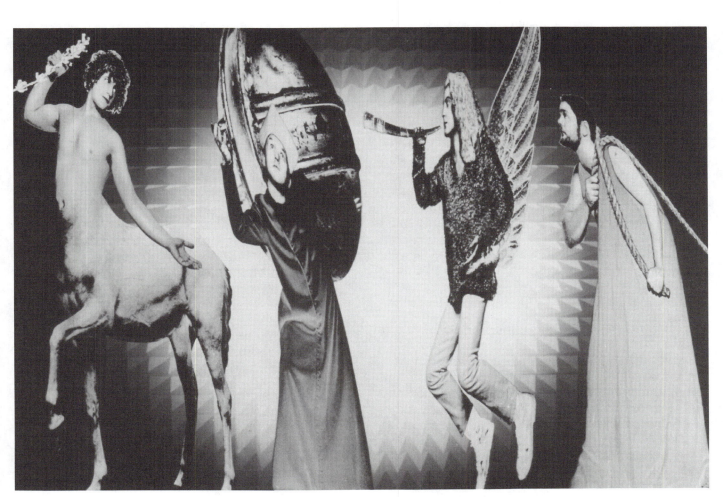

Photograph by Vincent MacDonald; courtesy of Island Records

signing on to their crew in the late 1970s when he was just eighteen. "This was the major turning point in my life," he told *Melody Maker*'s Ian Gittins. "If Killing Joke hadn't formed, The Orb would never have existed." Afterward, Paterson became a DJ inside England's thriving techno/house/rave club scene, and by the late 1980s was spinning records inside one room of a London club called The Land of Oz. This room was designed to soothe danced-out clubgoers in need of a break from the frenetic beats on the main floor, and Paterson's airy, floating mixes soon earned a tag: ambient house. The ambient part had been coined by studio expert Eno, who created lulling, textured melodies under his own name between producing such bands as Roxy Music and U2. Paterson knew the Eno ethos well; at this point in the late Eighties period he was working as an A&R person for Eno's home label, EG Records.

Released First Singles

In 1989, Paterson's interest in creating new sound forms led to the creation of his first single in collaboration with Jimmy Cauty, who was one-half of the equally successful DJ/remixers known as KLF; Paterson had done some uncredited remixes for KLF's early LPs. The single was entitled "A Huge, Ever-Growing and Pulsating Brain That Rules the World from the Centre of the Ultraworld" and clocked in at an equally lengthy 24 minutes. A second single, "Little Fluffy Clouds," followed in 1990, another dreamy and long track most notable for its overdub of Rickie Lee Jones waxing poetic about her childhood in Arizona.

"Little Fluffy Clouds" became the first Orb single to chart, and the success led Paterson to put together a full-length album, *Adventures Beyond the Underworld.* Released in England in 1991, the work paid homage to Pink Floyd with its cover photograph of the famous English power station at Battersea, which Pink Floyd had also used on the cover of their 1977 release *Animals.* One track was called "The Back Side of the Moon," a reference to Pink Floyd's enduring 1973 release *The Dark Side of the Moon.* The sound engineering difficulties involved in putting Paterson's complex compositions onto vinyl or CD form forced him to take the master tapes to a German classical recordings production plant to achieve the perfection he sought.

Adventures Beyond the Underworld, which *Melody Maker* termed "the definitive 'ambient House' album," was released as a a double CD in Britain, but sliced down to a single disc for American release. Both "Little Fluffy Clouds" and "Perpetual Dawn" became successful club hits. An essay on the Orb in the *Spin Alternative Record Guide* called the double version "an ambient opus—an exploratory space probe using the latest computer technology, incorporating elements of Chicago house music, Jamaican dub, television samples, and huge chunks of Brian Eno-like moods." Paterson had originally planned it as a three-CD work, but instead released the extra tracks as *The Aubrey Mixes: The Ultraworld Excursions.*

Gave up Day Job

Around this time Paterson quit his post at EG records. "I realised that I had to direct my efforts at my own career rather than at anybody else's," Paterson told *Melody Maker* writer Push in 1991. "It's weird because a lot of what I do is just for [kicks], it's just me and some mates having fun, so I never expected it to turn out this way." Paterson's next effort enlisted the help of legendary British bass player Jah Wobble. He also began a collaboration with Kristian "Thrash" Weston, a young mixing prodigy on the techno/house scene, as well as Steve Hillage, a guitarist from the band Gong. The result was the single "The Blue Room," which Paterson named after a mysterious room at an Ohio air force base where alien remains are allegedly stored. The single was just two seconds short of forty minutes, which was the maximum length of time allowed for a song to be eligible for the charts. *Melody Maker* writer Mat Smith called it their "most subtle" to date, "a huge ambient meisterwerk and the first to work entirely as a set piece rather than a mere series of clever effects."

In response to the chart success of "The Blue Room," Paterson made adamant to Smith his refusal to go along with the usual industry hype. "The last thing we want to do is go on *Top of the Pops*," he said, referring to a long-running staple of British television in which pop bands lip-synch to their chart-topping singles. "How degrading can you actually get?" Within time, however, the Orb did appear on *Top of the Pops*, with members playing a boring round of chess while the song played in the background. "The Blue Room" was included on another LP released in 1992, *UFOrb*, a record which explored the alien theme further. This release reached number one on the British charts, but after disputes with their British label, Big Life, the Orb moved to Island Records. In 1993 came their first release for Island as well as their first live work, *Orb Live '93*.

Baffled Audiences

Late the same year, the Orb embarked upon their first tour of the United States, continuing their promise to provide concertgoers with an unusual experience. Previously, they had played in Denmark's Copenhagen harbor and the nearby airport had to be temporarily shut down because the lights were bothersome to incoming planes. In the American performances Paterson and Thrash were sometimes obscured by a giant sheet hung just below waist-level, or by smoke and strobe lights. "This is what we want to put across," Paterson told Push in *Melody Maker* concerning the live shows. "We're not a band, we're not four people onstage projecting a traditional image. We're two people with all kinds of images around us."

The 1994 record *Pomme Fritz* marked the entry of yet another collaborator onto the Orb roster, Thomas Fehlmann. The German techno artist contributed the track "Alles Ist Schon." The record was much more industrial sounding than previous releases, and—perhaps buoyed by the success of the previous year's tour—*Pomme Fritz* became the onset of some nominal success for the Orb in the United States. Jon Wiederhorn of *Rolling Stone* termed it "a jumbled, disorienting miasma of misfiring neurons and overloaded synapses." Compared to other groups of the genre, Wiederhorn maintained, Paterson and company "inspire awe by splashing a profusion of unfocused noises and samples across a grid of billowing, textured synth lines." Robert L. Doerschuk, critic for *Keyboard* magazine, also gave the recording a favorable review, noting that its melding of diverse musical styles yields "complex patterns glistened by textural showers."

Paterson and Thrash eventually parted ways around the time of the Orb's sixth release, 1995's *Orbus Terrarum*.

The work's title reflected Paterson's move away from the otherworldly, space-rock moods evoked on previous releases and a figurative return to the earth; its title came from a medieval map he keeps on his wall. Sampled bits were more often than not taken from nature. *Musician*'s Ken Micallef wrote that "the sounds tumble from one song to the next, building a seamless whole that leaves you in a dreamlike state." Wiederhorn of *Rolling Stone* asserted that "much of the album is orchestral in design, with songs that ebb and flow like symphonic movements....*Orbus Terrarum* is a dense, convoluted record, for sure, but it's not difficult or pretentious. Credit this to the Orb's oddball sense of humor—a quality that further separates the band from the horde of computer geeks that holds every keyboard bleep sacred."

Writer Mark Prendergast of venerable British political journal *New Statesman & Society* contended that "the Orb's approach—which links turntable to samplers to effects machines and mixing desk, then feeds in as many exotic found sounds as possible via computer discs—is the best electronic version of popular music for years." Paterson, however, has said that he knows there are indeed limits to the Orb. "I'll do The Orb until I'm 40, which will be the year 2000, and that will be it," Paterson told *Melody Maker*'s Gittins. "After that I'll run a label. I'll let other people make music."

Selected discography

Adventures Beyond the Ultraworld, Big Life/Mercury, 1991.
The Aubrey Mixes: The Ultraworld Excursions, Big Life, 1991.
UFOrb, Big Life, 1992.
Orb Live '93, Island/Red, 1993.
Pomme Fritz, Island/Red, 1994.
Orbus Terrarum, Island/Red, 1995.

Sources

Books

Spin Alternative Record Guide, edited by Eric Weisbard with Craig Marks, Vintage Books, 1995.
The New Encyclopedia of Rock and Roll, edited by Patricia Romanowski and Holly George-Warren, Fireside/Rolling Stone Press, 1995.

Periodicals

Down Beat, September 1995.
Keyboard, April 1994; October 1994.
Melody Maker, April 20, 1991; June 6, 1992; October 24,

1992; March 27, 1993; June 4, 1994; June 25, 1994; March 25, 1995.

Musician, July 1995.

New Statesman & Society, April 9, 1993.

Rolling Stone, December 9, 1993; October 20, 1994; April 20, 1995.

Stereo Review, March 1994.

Village Voice, September 17, 1991; November 9, 1993.

Further information for this profile was obtained from promotional material provided by Island Records, 1995.

—Carol Brennan

Pentangle

Folk group

The five members of Pentangle were established solo performers when they came together as a group in 1967 at the club Les Cousins in Soho, London. Guitarists Bert Jansch and John Renbourn were highly esteemed folk musicians, double-bassist Danny Thompson and drummer Terry Cox were session players who had been members of Alexis Korner's Blues Incorporated, and singer Jacqui McShee, according to disc jockey John Peel's liner notes on the band's first album, had "survived a prolonged baptism of fire in clubs, concert halls, and pubs." As Pentangle, these individuals fused traditional British folk music styles with the jazz leanings of its rhythm section.

The group didn't consciously set out to create such unique music. According to Renbourn, "Unlike the more archly traditionalist clubs, the Cousins had no musical policy to speak of. The place stayed open all night, which meant a cheap kip for the punters, but a long haul for the musicians. We played anything we knew and much that we didn't to spin it out until morning. Everybody came up with ideas. When the repertoire eventually stabilized, it was a fairly mixed bag." For a brief time Jansch and Renbourn experimented with electric guitars but returned to acoustic instruments when Danny Thompson refused to switch from double bass to electric bass guitar. As Karl Dallas noted in *Melody Maker,* "The rich, fat tone [Danny] can get out of it, and the sensitive slurs and dynamics of his playing, compared with the rather synthetic tone of most bass guitars, shows that he has a point."

Pentangle earned rave reviews from their first major concert at London's Royal Festival Hall. Reviewer Tony Wilson enthused in *Melody Maker,* "With five individually talented people, the Pentangle has flexibility not only in types and styles of music but in the combinations of group members who play them. Thus with the interplay of performers and music types the evening never lagged and gave a true picture of what the Pentangle can actually do." In a *Melody Maker* interview, Jansch acknowledged the group's chemistry: "It's really fantastic, the way we all think together. Anything we do is a really co-operative effort." Having won over the music press, Pentangle's first single "Traveling Song" received significant airplay, propelling the self-titled debut album to number 21 on the British album charts.

Album Made Top Five

Pentangle's 1970 album *Basket of Light* became its biggest seller. The band continued to tour the world to great acclaim; a 1971 *Melody Maker* review likened Pentangle's performance to an imaginary kingdom, "a

For the Record . . .

Original members include **Terry Cox** (drums), **Bert Jansch** (born November 3, 1943; from Glasgow, Scotland; guitar and vocals), **Jacqui McShee** (vocals), **John Renbourn** (guitar), and **Danny Thompson** (born April, 1939; double bass). Later members include **Gerry Conway** (born 1947; from King's Lynn, Norfolk; drums; joined band c. 1985), **Peter Kirtley** (guitar; joined band c. 1985), and **Nigel Portman-Smith** (from Sheffield, England; bass; joined band c. 1985).

Band formed in 1967, in London; recorded first album, *The Pentangle*, 1968, on Reprise; disbanded in 1973; reformed in 1985.

Addresses: *Record company*—Green Linnet, 43 Beaver Brook Road, Danbury, CT 06810.

quiet, reflective place...where the enthusiasm of the populace putting their hands together at the conclusion of each more delicate construction comes as a rude interruption."

Some critics complained of Pentangle's music becoming consistent and dull. *Rolling Stone*'s review of the group's album *Solomon's Seal* opined, "No surprises here, either plus or minus, just the same light, airy ensemble sound. You get the feeling they'll go on for decades like this, making pretty, well-played, unstartling albums, enjoying themselves in their own mild way, and not causing any commotion." However, *Melody Maker*'s perennial Pentangle supporter Karl Dallas commented, "It has always surprised me that those who have failed to look beyond the surface of their music have failed to be aware of the incredible powerhouse that purrs away, like a tiger with claws sheathed in velvet, at the very heart of Pentangle. What is now beginning to happen, I think, is that the tiger is going to be allowed more length to its chain." Guitarist Jansch addressed the criticisms of the band's consistency, "I'd like to see the band not so tight, even if we created other bands. Not that we'd fold Pentangle, but there's no reason why Danny shouldn't also have a jazz band of his own, or a group of some description. From this, musically we'd also begin to get a lot looser because of it."

Bassist Thompson Departed

Jansch's predictions were partially seen through in March of 1973 when bassist Danny Thompson left the band due to stress following an arduous British tour. Thompson told *Rolling Stone*, "...my head was very mixed up; I was exhausted from the tour, and eventually a mixture of depression and anxiety—because I just couldn't take any more—caused this heart flutter." The remaining members folded Pentangle because, as Jansch told *Rolling Stone*, "Danny is an essential part of Pentangle. Take him away and replace him with something else, and you might have something, but you wouldn't have Pentangle."

The split confirmed rumors and denials that had been passed around over the last two years of the band's existence. *Melody Maker*'s Karl Dallas summed up the group's influence thusly, "Where would [the British electric-folk scene] have got without the trailblazing of Pentangle and Bert Jansch in particular, whose superb 'Jack Orion' solo album itself anticipated so much that was to come later?"

Reunited after Decade Apart

Pentangle's breakup would not be a permanent one. Over a decade later, in 1986, a new edition of Pentangle formed with original members McShee, Jansch, and Cox joined by guitarist Mike Piggott and bassist Nigel Smith. When *Washington Post* writer Mike Joyce asked why the group reunited, Jansch replied, "Some bloke just asked us if we could get together again for a show, and we did." The new Pentangle featured electric guitars and bass which Jansch said gave the music "a lot of new colors now." Jacqui McShee and Bert Jansch are currently anchored by guitarist Peter Kirtley, bassist Nigel Portman, and drummer Gerry Conway, a veteran of Jethro Tull, The Incredible String Band, and Steeleye Span. Reviewing the band's 1992 album *Think of Tomorrow, Folk Roots* said, "[It] certainly isn't going to set the roots music scene alight, but the warm and tasteful sounds created by a bunch of class musicians at ease go down very nicely at the end of a long day."

Although Pentangle has had difficulty recently living up to its own reputation, the band continues to delight audiences with its mix of traditional and original material. Pentangle's innovations continue to influence today's folk musicians.

Selected discography

The Pentangle, Reprise, 1968.
Sweet Child, Reprise, 1968.
Basket of Light, Reprise, 1969.
Cruel Sister, Reprise, 1970.
Reflections, Reprise, 1971.

Solomon's Seal, Reprise, 1972.
Open The Door, Varrick, 1985.
In The Round, Varrick, 1986.
So Early In The Spring, Green Linnet, 1990.
Think of Tomorrow, Green Linnet, 1991.
Early Classics (recorded 1968-73), Shanachie, 1992.
A Maid That's Deep In Love, Shanachie.
(By Bert Jansch) *Best of Bert Jansch,* Shanachie, 1992.
"Let No Man Steal Your Thyme" on *Troubadours of British Folk,* vol. 1, *Unearthing The Tradition,* Rhino, 1995.

Sources

Books

Joynson, Vernon, *Tapestry of Delights: The Comprehensive Guide to British Music of the Beat, R & B, Psychedelic, and Progressive Eras,* Borderline Productions, 1995.

Periodicals

Audio, December, 1990.
Billboard, February 22, 1969.
Folk Roots, July, 1992.
Guitar Extra, Fall, 1990.
Jazz & Pop, July 1970; September 1970.
Melody Maker, May 18, 1968; July 6, 1968; August 23, 1969; January 16, 1971; October 30, 1971; September 30, 1972; March 31, 1973.
Rolling Stone, January 18, 1973; March 1, 1973.
Washington Post, July 22, 1986; October 19, 1990; November 5, 1990.

Additional information was obtained from the liner notes to *Troubadours of British Folk,* vol. 1, *Unearthing the Tradition* and Folklore Productions, Inc., press materials.

—*James Powers*

Art

Pepper

Saxophonist

Archive Photos/Frank Driggs Collection

Straight Life would seem to be an ironic title, no doubt deliberately so, for the memoir of Art Pepper. For though he lived to see himself regarded as one of the great alto sax players in the world—a unique voice in the post-Charlie Parker era—Pepper lived most of his life as it began, in turmoil and trouble. That he lived to his mid-50s is little short of miraculous, given his self-destructive behavior, as chronicled in the book that was produced in collaboration with his third wife, Laurie, about three years before his death.

Essentially the unwanted child of a rebellious, high-living mother and a traveling seaman father, Pepper found himself being raised by a well-meaning but cold grandmother. Musical talent emanated from his mother's Italian family and nine-year-old Art persuaded his father to buy him a musical instrument and provide a teacher, Leroy Parry, who assigned the clarinet as his first instrument. His proud father would showcase his son playing popular tunes of the day, earning spending money and adulation, as they made the rounds of local bars. By the age of twelve, Pepper switched to alto sax which was to become his major instrument throughout his professional career.

Self-Taught through Intensive Listening

Largely self-taught through intensive listening, Pepper began jamming and sitting in on Central Avenue, Los Angeles's home of black jazz and the West Coast's answer to New York's 52nd Street. In 1941 the Ritz Club and the Club Alabam were the places to be as the blooming altoist jammed and sometimes earned money playing with the likes of trumpeters Louis Armstrong and Roy Eldridge, bassist Jimmy Blanton, alto stylist Johnny Hodges, and tenor saxophonists Coleman Hawkins, Ben Webster and Dexter Gordon. Gordon introduced the upstart to drummer Lee Young, brother of tenor legend Lester "Prez" Young. The drummer served as a mentor and eventually introduced Pepper to Benny Carter, the legendary saxophonist and bandleader.

Pepper recalls his 1943 experience in the Carter band in his autobiography, *Straight Life:* "I had never played much lead alto, so with Benny I played second alto, he played lead, but in my book I had two parts written in most of the arrangements and sometimes, if there wasn't a large audience, Benny would just get off the stand and let me play his parts. I'd get all his solos. I learned that way how to play lead in a four-man saxophone section. And I learned a lot following Benny, listening to his solos, what he played against the background." With a southern tour pending, Carter decided not to take the promising white musician with his "col-

Born Arthur Edward Pepper, Jr.; September 1, 1925, in Gardena, CA; died of complication from a stroke, June 15, 1982, Panorama, CA; son of Arthur, Sr. (a longshoreman/seaman/machinist) and Mildred Bartold; married Patricia (Patti) Madeleine Moore, 1943; Diane Suriago, 1957; Laurie La Pan Miller, 1974; children: Patricia Ellen.

Began clarinet lessons at age nine, moving principally to alto saxophone at age 12; played with important jazz figures on Los Angeles's Central Avenue at age 15; while still in teens, played with bands of Gus Arnheim, Lee Young, Benny Carter, Stan Kenton; drafted into Army in 1943; re-joined Kenton, 1947-52; recorded widely, in concert and studio settings mostly with small groups, 1953-1982.

Awards: *DownBeat* Readers' Poll, second (to Charlie Parker), best altoist, 1951-52; *DownBeat* Critics' Poll, best altoist deserving wider recognition, 1957 and 1977; *DownBeat* Critics' Poll, best established altoist, 1980; *Swing Journal* record of the year, 1980.

ored" band. Instead, Carter arranged for Pepper to audition successfully with the upcoming Stan Kenton band, for whom Art began playing lead alto at age 17. Kenton's highly stylized arrangements convinced Pepper that he needed to know more about theory and chord structure in order to solo effectively. Kenton's tenorman, Red Dorris, provided help at this stage of Pepper's development.

Though he had been a sickly and weak child, Pepper developed into a strong and handsome teen-ager. Virtually unsupervised and becoming street-wise, he began fighting, drinking, and experimenting with a variety of "soft" drugs, largely ignoring school. In mid-1943, while working his way through the bands of Gus Arnheim, Young, and Carter, the 17-year-old Art Pepper married his 16-year-old girlfriend, Patti Moore. While with Kenton, Pepper received his draft notice shortly after his eighteenth birthday and was inducted into the army in February of 1944. Just before going overseas, where he served as both a musician and as an unlikely member of the military police, Pepper became a father for the only time. His daugher, Patricia Ellen, was born on on January 5, 1945.

Through much of 1947, after his discharge, Pepper struggled for jobs and dug deeper into drinking and

drugs. Kenton, with whom Pepper had made his first recording in 1943, summoned, and from that point until the end of 1951 the altoist was a featured soloist with the band that spawned an all-star list of jazz greats, including trumpeters Maynard Ferguson and Shorty Rogers, trombonists Kai Winding and Milt Bernhart, saxophonists Bob Cooper and Bud Shank, and drummer Shelly Manne. It was during this on-the-road period that Pepper—lonely, insecure and musically unsatisfied at times—became addicted to heroin, a substance that would dominate his life until about 1969.

Continued Playing Despite Heroin Habit

Pepper left the Kenton band at the end of 1951, as did several of the other players who were tired of the nine months of grinding touring and bus living. Deeply into heroin and alcohol use, Pepper formed his own quartet and began recording with his own band as well as with other groups led by Kenton alumni. His own highly acclaimed early 1952 combo featured pianist Hampton Hawes, bassist Joe Mondragon and drummer/vibist Larry Bunker. Shorty Rogers and His Giants and the Shelly Manne Septet also provided recording exposure, and irregular gigs supplemented his income, but not enough to support his growing heroin habit.

With the encouragement of his father, Pepper committed himself to a sanitarium in order to kick his dependence. Immediately upon release, however, he sought out a dealer and began using again. Now often using borrowed instruments, the altoist staggered through a series of minor jobs until his arrest for possession of heroin in early 1953. During this 15-month incarceration at the Fort Worth U. S. Public Health Service Hospital, Patti divorced Art and remarried.

Returned to Jail Time and Again

Upon his release in May of 1954, Pepper resumed his now-familiar behavior. This led to his December arrest and further stops in the Los Angeles County Jail and at Terminal Island, totaling somewhat over a year. In mid-1960, he spent 90 days in jail, then in October was sentenced to San Quentin and Tehachapi where he served four and one-half years. Three months after this release, Pepper failed a drug test, for which he served six months at the Chino Institute for Men, receiving counseling and "rehabilitation." Once again violating parole upon release, Pepper was again assigned to San Quentin, leaving there for the last time in 1966.

During this turbulent period Pepper's 1957 marriage to Diane Suriago, who became a fellow addict, and his subsequent attachments to other co-dependent women were of little help to him. Often, he worked at various odd jobs, including helping to run a bakery. Upon his 1966 release from San Quentin, he had no horns and limited funds. As Pepper wrote in his liner notes for the *Living Legend* album, "I had switched to tenor for two reasons. Rock was in vogue, and only tenor players seemed to be working. But the major reason was that after all my years of playing, I had been influenced to the point of imitation by another musician, [tenor] John Coltrane. I felt what I wanted to say I could only say with the tenor."

Embodied West Coast "Cool" Jazz

Pepper grew away from his natural style, intensity became more evident, he became freer in his solo playing, introducing a rough, stabbing, searing quality. He soon returned to the alto and his identifiable voice on that instrument, but with a much more emotional component. Despite the extreme pathological behavior in his personal life, Pepper's playing, at least on record, rarely reflected these difficulties. Originally an extremely melodic, swinging player sometimes compared to Lee Konitz and Paul Desmond, Pepper was the embodiment of the West Coast "cool" style. As Shelly Manne put it, "He's very individual. You can hear it. You know it. Art was a very lyrical player. Especially at a time when most of the alto players were in a Charlie Parker bag, Art had a distinct style of his own." Another fellow Kenton alumni, tenorist Bob Cooper added, "I always felt that Art's major influence was Lester Young; that came out more clearly when I heard him playing tenor a few times.... And to transfer that beautiful sound to the alto!... I think his sound was by far the best alto sound at the time."

Devoted to Mastering Technique

In addition to his unique sound, Pepper also astounded jazz listeners with his apparently effortless technique. Though he sometimes denied studying and practicing, Pepper details in his memoir two periods of intensive devotion. The first was in England when he was in the army. A friend and musician, Alan Dean, recalled Pepper going off duty and securing himself in a rehearsal room to "practice his instrument for hours and hours on end with very little sleep." Pepper also recalled a time during his stay at Fort Worth in *Straight Life:* "I'd go to the band room in the morning, sweep the floor, clean the place, and make sure everything was locked up, and then I'd get out my horn. I'd close the door in this little room and just sit there and practice. I did that every day...and I really got down with music."

In 1968 Pepper received an invitation to play lead alto in the band of Buddy Rich. There was a small problem: Pepper's alto had long ago been hocked. Don Menza, the great tenorman then with Rich, loaned Pepper his alto, with which Pepper made his first recordings in more than seven years. Pepper fit in immediately and, but for his physical condition, this could have been an agreeable long-term association. However, his spleen ruptured, followed by other complications. After three months of hospitalization, he returned to the Rich band briefly, playing the less demanding third alto chair. With his health deteriorating still further, Pepper eventually enrolled himself in Synanon, a California drug rehabilitation center, in 1969. There he met Laurie Miller who became a very positive influence on Pepper, and, in 1974, his third wife. It was Miller who helped him return to a successful music career and introduced some stability to his personal life.

Straight Life

From 1968 to 1975 Pepper recorded only one album. In 1975, however, he returned to the Contemporary studios to begin a series of albums that signaled his renaissance. One sustaining musical activity during his recording hiatus was provided in 1972 by Ken Yohe who, representing the Buffet instrument company, gave Pepper a set of instruments and arranged for him to conduct teaching clinics at colleges all over the country. After resuming his recording career, the altoist also made concert and club appearances, mostly with his own quartet, with the major exception of a 1975 stint with the experimental big band trumpeter Don Ellis. Included were several tours of the United States, Europe and Japan, where the enthusiastic reception buoyed Pepper and his group. Often his groups played such stellar Pepper compositions as, "Straight Life," "Diane," "Patricia," "Zenobia" and "Las Cuevas de Mario."

Pepper eventually succumbed to years of abuse and died of complications from a stroke in 1982. It is principally through his recordings as leader, with Kenton, and in a variety of settings with Marty Paich that Pepper will be best remembered. Marty Paich, is the leader/composer/arranger who utilized Pepper so often in accompaniments of Mel Torme and other singers and whose recordings with Pepper included the highly acclaimed, *Art Pepper + Eleven.* Paich praises Pepper in this way, "He had the notes, and he was swinging all the time. That's very important.... Art always swung. And he played all the instruments...exactly the same. He put them in his mouth and it was Art Pepper."

Selected discography

The Early Show: A Night at the Surf Club, Vol. 1, Xanadu, 1952.
The Art Pepper Quartet, 1956; reissued, Fantasy, 1994.
Art Pepper Meets the Rhythm Section, Contemporary, 1957.
Art Pepper + Eleven, Modern Jazz Classics Original Jazz Classics CD, 1959.
The Complete Pacific Jazz Small Group Recordings of Art Pepper, Mosaic, 1956-57.
Intensity, Contemporary, 1960; reissued, Fantasy, 1989.
Living Legend, Contemporary, 1975; reissued, Fantasy, 1990.
The Trip, Contemporary, 1976; reissued, Fantasy, 1990.
Friday Night at the Village Vanguard, Contemporary, 1977; reissued, Fantasty, 1992.
Today, Galaxy, 1978; reissued, Fantasy, 1990.
Landscape, Galaxy, 1979; reissued, Fantasy, 1991.
Straight Life, Galaxy, 1979; reissued, Fantasy, 1990.
One September Afternoon, Galaxy, 1980; reissued, Fantasy, 1991.
Winter Moon, Galaxy, 1980; reissued, Fantasy, 1991.
The Complete Galaxy Recordings, 1978-82, Galaxy, 1989.
Tokyo Debut, Galaxy, 1995.
The Complete Village Vanguard Sessions, Galaxy, 1995.
The Complete Pacific Jazz Small Group Recordings of Art Pepper, Mosaic.

Sources

Books

Erlewine, Michael, and others, editors, *All Music Guide to Jazz,* Miller Freeman Books, 1996.
Feather, Leonard, *The New Edition of the Encyclopedia of Jazz;* Bonanza Books, 1965.
Lyons, Len and Don Perlo, *Jazz Portraits: The Lives and Music of the Jazz Masters,* William Morrow, 1989.
Pepper, Art and Laurie Pepper, *Straight Life: The Story of Art Pepper,* Schirmer Books, 1979.

Periodicals

DownBeat, September 1982.
New York Times, June 16, 1982.

Additional information for this profile was obtained from the liner notes to *Friday Night at the Village Vanguard,* Contemporary; *Intensity,* Contemporary; *Living Legend,* Contemporary; *The Complete Pacific Jazz Small Group Recordings of Art Pepper,* Mosaic; *and Smack Up,* Contemporary.

—Robert Dupuis

Astor Piazzola

Bandleader, composer, instrumentalist

Although the tango had been a way of life as well as an expressive form of music and dance for a number of years before his birth, the legendary Argentinean bandoneon master Astor Piazzolla took the romantic, dangerous, and sultry traditional tango, added a healthy mix of jazz and classical styles, infused his own ideas, and created the *nuevo tango.* When Piazzolla was born in 1921 in Mar de Plata, Argentina, the tango was starting its meandering journey from bordellos and back streets to respectability all around the world. Nowhere was it more revered and worshiped than its birthplace—Buenos Aires. Soon after their only son's birth, Vincent Piazzolla and wife Asunta Menetti moved the small family to New York City's Little Italy. Attempting to maintain their cultural roots, Astor's father gave his son a bandoneon, a version of the accordion with buttons and a deeper sound. By the age of nine, Astor had mastered the bandoneon and began to perform in public. Early musical influences included jazz masters Cab Calloway and Duke Ellington, with a hearty infusion of Bach, Mozart, and Chopin. Many classical piano compositions were rearranged by a neighbor so the young musician could play them on the bandoneon.

At age 13, Piazzolla got his big break when Carlos Gardel, a famous Argentinean singer and actor, came to the United States to make a movie and records. Astor's father presented his son to the celebrity, and Gardel was so impressed by the boy's bandoneon talents that he invited him to accompany him on his current world tour. Because of his tender age, Astor was not allowed to go on the tour, but he did make his first recording with Gardel and the NBC Symphony. Piazzolla ultimately benefited from passing on the offer—Gardel's plane crashed a year later and the great musician perished.

Studied Composing with a Master

Before he turned 20, Astor and his family returned to Argentina for good. The young man made a meager living by playing his bandoneon in tango clubs, but what he really wanted to do was create and perform his own compositions. After boldly introducing himself to the famed Arthur Rubinstein, the pianist introduced Astor to musical maestro and composer Alberto Ginastera. Astor studied with Ginastera for six years, during which time the composer not only taught Piazzolla the fundamentals of music and composition, but the importance of intertwining all of the various arts.

In between studying, Piazzolla spent time with his children, Diana and Daniel, and their mother, painter

Dede Baralis. Around this time, the bandoneon player had also begun playing with the best tango orchestra in Buenos Aires, Anibal Troilo's Orquesta Tipica. He played second bandoneon to Troilo for eight years.

The New Tango Was Born

By 1944 Piazzolla was ready to act upon the musical instincts that had been simmering in him for years. He broke off with Anibal Troilo and focused more of his time on composing. Still deeply interested in classical music, Piazzolla took courses on conducting. Many of his earlier pieces are decidedly influenced by Bach, Stravinsky, and other classical composers. His music began to take on a sound of its own as Piazzolla began to incorporate unusual elements into traditional tangos. In 1946 Piazzolla formed the band Orquesta del 46 so that he could perform his nuevo tango. Although he didn't receive much support from tango traditionalists, he did garner interest from outsiders like American composer Aaron Copland. One of his first pieces, *Sinfonia Buenos Aires*—which received a first place award in the international Fabien Sevitsky Competition in Indianapolis—was met with boos and insults elsewhere. The people of Argentina were not yet ready for the sounds of the new tango.

In 1954 Astor took his family and musical talents to Paris, where he received a warm welcome. The French government offered Piazzolla and his wife fellowships specifically because of his prize winning *Sinfonia.* Astor

began studying under the direction of composer Nadia Boulanger, who had worked with such impressive composers as Bernstein and Copland. While she marveled at his intricate compositions, Boulanger encouraged Piazzolla to search for himself in his music and to reach for his Argentinean roots.

According to legend, Boulanger one day persuaded Piazzolla to perform one of his tangos on the piano and promptly proclaimed, "*This* is Piazzolla, not *that.* Throw the rest away!" After doing so, Piazzolla found peace for himself and his music. "I promised myself I'd write a tango a day and that's what I did," the musician was quoted in *Americas*.

Old Traditions Died Hard

Although he was gaining respect and popularity around the world, the artist was still not accepted in his native country. Returning to Buenos Aires in 1955, Piazzolla received death threats and mistreatment from tango extremists. At one point, a gun was pointed at his head by a disgruntled Argentinean who didn't appreciate his use of jazz and non-traditional instruments. Undaunted, Piazzolla returned to the United States, where he spent an unproductive three years. "Colleagues in the United States urged him to compromise by writing 'marketable' stuff, especially for the movie industry, but he resisted and finally withdrew," noted Caleb Bach in *Americas*.

After returning to Argentina, Piazzolla made his homeland breakthrough with *Tango-operita* in 1968. The folk opera was directly influenced by the works of George Gershwin, whom Piazzolla had admired for many years. Prior to this success, Piazzolla formed a new Quinteto Nuevo Tango that performed at his club, Jamaica. Many musicians, eager to work with the composer, often stopped by for a jam session.

During the 1970s Piazzolla's music began to experience critical acclaim in his beloved Argentina. Early in the decade his hard work, extravagant lifestyle, jet setting and chain smoking gave Piazzolla a massive heart attack. The 54-year-old musician attempted to quiet his habits, but his resolutions lasted only a year before he was traveling around Europe, writing compositions feverishly. It was also during that decade Piazzolla's mentor, Anibal Troilo, of the Anibal Troilo Orchestra, died.

Attained Lifelong Dreams

Not one to stop working, Piazzolla began taking his musical efforts to the film stage and beyond. Some claim this final period of Piazzolla's musical career was his finest. Music for the Roman Polanski film *Frantic* was scored by Piazzolla, along with *Armagedón, Henri IV,* and many others. In 1986 his compositions were featured in *Tango Argentina,* a Broadway musical. Even while concentrating on commissions for other artists, like the Kronos Quartet, Piazzolla never forgot his first love—the bandoneon. Piazzolla's favorite bandoneon was inherited from Troilo. He used the instrument on *Five Tango Sensations,* a series of moody pieces for bandoneon and string quartet, played by the Kronos Quartet. His own tour of North America began in 1989 but was cut short on account of his deteriorating health. He was able, however, to see Placido Domingo play the leading role in his tango-opera *Gardel.*

Following many serious health ailments, including a debilitating stroke, Astor Piazzolla died a national hero in his beloved Argentina in 1992. No longer shunned by his countrymen and tango traditionalists, Piazzolla was revered as the man who brought life to the tango. He uncovered a new experience for the tango through his compositions. "For me," he is often quoted as saying, "tango was always for the ear rather than the feet."

Selected discography

The Vienna Concert, American Clavé, 1986.
Tango: Zero Hour, American Clavé, 1986.
The Rough Dancer and the Cyclical Night, American Clavé, 1987.
The New Tango with Gary Burton, Atlantic, 1987.

La Camorra: La Soledad de la Provocacion Apasionada, American Clavé, 1989.
Tangos (3) for Bandoneon & Orchestra, Milan, 1990.
Maria De Buenos Aires, Milan, 1991.
Five Tango Sensations, Electra Nonesuch, 1991.
Lumiere, Tropical Storm, 1992.
The Lausanne Concert, Polygram Latino, 1992.
Sur, Milan, 1992.
The Central Park Concert, Chesky, 1994.
Piazzolla Boxed Set, Just a Memory, 1995.

Sources

Books

World Music: The Rough Guide, Rough Guides, Ltd., 1994.

Periodicals

Americas (English Edition), September-October 1991.
Chicago, May 1989.
El Mercurio, July 1989.
Esquire, May 1991.
High Fidelity, September 1986

Online

http://www.ee.ucl.ac.uk/~hread/astor/history.html, http://www.tango.montreal.qc.ca, and egsve@cc.uab.es

—Gretchen VanCleave

Pizzicato Five

Contemporary dance/pop band

Pizzicato Five leader Yasuharu Konishi told the *San Jose Mercury News*, "I always think about pop not as pop music but just as pop art." Konishi, the musical director of the Japanese group—which makes a collage of obscure samples, dance beats, noise, movie chic and fashion absurdity—added, "Whenever I compose, I just imagine, in my mind, what to wear for the song." This celebration of surface pleasures has resonated strongly with international audiences, and has helped P5, as the group is called for short, to surmount the language barrier. Assisted by singer-model Maki Nomiya and a rotating crew of musicians, DJs and dancers, Konishi has brought his "smile pop" to a growing cult audience in the United States as well. An attempt by Barry Walters of the *San Francisco Examiner* to describe the P5 concert experience was typically lengthy: "Imagine every great record you've ever heard stuck in a blender overlaid with the most experimental heavy metal guitar you've *never* heard combined with the most outstanding montage of video clips you *can't* imagine *plus* superadorable camp fashions, all synthesized through a demented Japanese consumerist impression of America," he wrote. "Then try to imagine something better than that and you might be begin to understand what happened Thursday night at the Great American Music Hall."

The group formed during the early 1980s. Konishi, who grew up adoring his family's lounge and jazz records, met Keitaro Takanami while the two were at Aoyama University in 1979; the pair started a band with another friend, Ryo Kamomiya. After several years the group enlisted vocalist Mamiko Sasaki. The group released its debut single, "Audrey Hepburn Complex," in 1985. The personnel shifted numerous times in the ensuing years; in 1988, Kamomiya and Sasaki departed and Takao Tajima joined the group, only to be replaced by Nomiya in 1990. Takanami eventually departed to do solo work; guitarist Bravo Kmatsu brought his thrashing, metallic theatricality to the group in 1995. P5 became increasingly popular in Japan; based in the hip Tokyo neighborhood of Shibuya, they continued to hone Konishi's eclectic vision.

"Pervasive" Pop Knowledge

This vision has a great deal to do with his enormous record collection, which boasts the now-hip "bachelor pad" recordings of Les Baxter and Juan Esquivel, the orchestral pop of Burt Bacharach, along with soul jazz, hippie folk, spy movie soundtracks, electronic dance music, and virtually everything in between. "I have thousands of records," Konishi told *BAM*. "I pick up stuff mostly from records of the `60s and `70s—music before the digital age." He further commented that his favorites "have atmosphere or some kind of smell."

What binds these widely divergent styles together into P5 has as much to do with their retro charm as their musical reach. "We don't like to limit ourselves with one type of music," was Konishi's understated admission in *Billboard*. "When I first saw them," Atlantic Records executive Michael Krumper added in the same article, "it struck me that they're what Andy Warhol would create if he were putting together a band for the '90s." Krumper further noted that P5 "sample from every area of pop culture, reflecting their pervasive knowledge of pop music."

Fashion Sense, U.S. Appeal

Nomiya, meanwhile, helped crystallize the group's visual aspect. A veteran of the bands Hot Pink and Portable Rock, she has for the most part left the songwriting to Konishi so as to maximize her main task: "I choose the costumes, wigs, and makeup," she informed *Puncture*, and told *Paper*'s Marisa Fox, "I love 60's fashion because it is so colorful and the materials, like polyester, are so new." Her frequent outfit changes during P5 concerts adds to their circus-like unpredictability. "Through myriad costume changes," observed *Mercury News* writer Yoshi Kato, "Nomiya takes on many personas—Diana Ross and all three Supremes, a Swiss mountain girl, a 1930s nightclub diva." Walters of the

San Francisco Examiner characterized the singer as "[Japanese cartoon hero] Hello Kitty reborn as a drag queen." Konishi and P5's fans clearly view her as a major pop icon. "I have three superstars: [French avant-garde filmmaker Jean-Luc] Godard, Warhol, and Maki," Konishi asserted in *Puncture.* Reviewers have repeatedly cited a P5 song lyric that seems to capture her stylistic outlook: "cute, gorgeous, and in bad taste."

P5's records were largely unavailable to American audiences except as foreign imports until the group signed with Matador Records. Their first album for the label, *Made in USA,* a compilation of tracks from their substantial catalog of Japanese recordings, was released in 1994. Reviewing it, Johnny Ray Huston of the *San Francisco Weekly* dubbed them "easily the smartest, most stylish import concoction to hit the States this year." Thanks to heavy video and radio rotation for the single "Twiggy Twiggy/Twiggy Vs. James Bond," the group was able to garner an American following. "I think Matador has intelligent listeners," Konishi reflected in *Puncture.* "In Japan they have more sense of humor, and Matador has a sense of humor. Pizzicato Five is a joke. It means nothing."

"Hip Like Sushi"

Their second U.S. release, *The Sound of Music by Pizzicato Five,* was released jointly by Matador and its parent company, Atlantic; the group also landed a song on the soundtrack to the film *Unzipped,* a documentary about fashion designer Isaac Mizrahi. Indeed, the group's style-obsessed eclecticism seemed to epitomize the post-MTV fashion universe. "They're about costumes and dressing up, full theatricality and spectacle," insisted Matador's Patrick Amory in *Billboard.* "They're all about style." Konishi claimed in *Spin* that the whole package made sense in performance: "Without the visuals," he asserted, "people wouldn't understand us." According to *Paper's* Fox, the group's "intention was never to be a straightforward band. Think of them instead as more of a conceptual band, part theater of the absurd, part veritably loopy musical outfit."

BAM described P5's appeal in terms of novelty: "They're hip like sushi; bubbly like imported champagne; strange and kitschy like Japanimation; theatrical like Kabuki, and fun like [fellow dance-pop internationalists] Deee-Lite." For Konishi, however, his group provides not so much a trip across cultural borders as unlimited travel through different eras. "Today, we have a time machine," he told *Puncture.* "It's called a sample machine." Sampling from all over the map, the group can rightfully regard the world as its oyster.

Selected discography

Singles; on Teichiku

"Audrey Hepburn Complex," 1985.
"In Action," 1986.

On CBS/Sony (Japan)

Couples, 1987.
"Pizzicatomania," 1987.
Bellisima, 1988.
On Her Majesty's Request, 1989.
Soft Landing on the Moon, 1990.
Lover's Rock, 1990.

On Columbia/Seven Gods (Japan)

Hi Guys! Let Me Teach You, 1991.
This Year's Model, 1991.

London-Paris-Tokyo, 1991.
Readymade Recordings, 1991.
This Year's Girl, 1991.

On Columbia/Triad (Japan)

Sweet Pizzicato Five, 1992.
Pizzicato Free Soul, 1992.
Instant Replay, 1993.
Sweet Soul Revue, 1993.
Bossa Nova 2001, 1993.
Free Soul 2001, 1993.
Expo 2001, 1993.
The Night is Still Young, 1993.
A Children's Workshop, 1994.
Happy Sad, 1994.
Overdose, 1994.
TYO: Big Hits and Jet Lags, 1995.
Romantique '96, 1995.

On Matador and Matador/Atlantic

Five by Pizzicato Five, 1994.
Made in USA (includes "Twiggy Twiggy/Twiggy Vs. James Bond"), 1994.

The Sound of Music by Pizzicato Five, 1995.
Quickie EP, 1995.

Sources

BAM, March 24, 1995, p. 21.
Billboard, September 30, 1995.
Interview, September 1994.
Melody Maker, April 1, 1995.
Option, March 1995.
Paper, October 1994, p. 87.
Puncture, Fall 1994.
Raygun, May 1995.
San Francisco Examiner, February 24, 1995, p. D14.
San Francisco Weekly, September 28, 1994.
San Jose Mercury News, February 17, 1995, p. 23.
Spin, October 1994.
Vogue, May 1995.

Additional information was provided by Matador Records publicity materials, 1995, and materials from Ed's Pizzicato Pages on the World Wide Web.

—Simon Glickman

Louis Prima

Singer, bandleader

During the peak of his career in the mid-1950s, Louis Prima summed up the appeal of his act to *Down Beat* in one word—variety. "The audience never knows what comes next," explained Prima, "and to tell the truth, neither do we. We're always throwing 'em surprises, and they love it!"

By the time Prima uttered those words, he had been a veteran of show business for three decades. Louis Leo Prima was born on December 7, 1911 in New Orleans, the city with the most Italian and Sicilian immigrants in the United States. Young Louis took examples from both of his parents that would eventually serve him well; his father Anthony was a hardworking beverage distributor, and doting mother Angelina was a strong-willed house-wife, church activity organizer, and amateur performer. Her advice to Louis was to "always smile, people want to see that you're having a good time."

Angelina insisted that the Prima children take music lessons. Older brother Leon and younger sister Eliza-beth took piano lessons and Louis took violin lessons. Louis didn't enjoy playing the violin, despite winning an amateur fiddling contest. The violin's fate was sealed when Leon gave up the piano for the cornet. New Orleans was teeming with jazz musicians; once the elder Prima joined the fold, his younger brother soon followed, also playing the cornet.

By 1931, Louis Prima was becoming well known in his hometown, playing in the orchestra of the Saenger Theatre, where elaborate stage productions filled time between the new talking motion pictures. In 1934, Louis impressed visiting orchestra leader Guy Lombardo, who easily persuaded the impressionable young Prima to move to New York, despite having a wife and child in New Orleans.

Louis spent his first six months fruitlessly seeking em-ployment despite Lombardo's connections. Racial prej-udice prevented him from being hired by Leon and Eddie's on 52nd Street, because, according to Lombar-do, "[Club owner] Eddie Davis, on first seeing olive-skinned and swarthy Louis Prima and knowing that he came from New Orleans, had simply assumed that he was a black man. The shame is not so much that he lost a gold mine, but that he capitulated to the prejudice of the times."

"The Famous Door" Opens to Success

Prima's fortunes improved when he played opening night at the Famous Door. The after-hours musicians' club was named for the door signed by the establish-ment's famous investors. Louis packed the house and earned glowing reviews. During this time, Prima recorded several hit singles and wrote "Sing Sing Sing," a 1938 hit for Benny Goodman. He also made cameo appearances in films and toured the United States.

Has Big Hits during Wartime

By the mid-1940s, Prima became one of the most popular entertainers in the country, performing sell-out engagements across America. During this period, he discovered a new formula for hit records with "Angelina," a song laden with Italian-American slang phrases about a waitress in a pizza parlor. Despite the national sentiment against Italy as a result of World War II, the record became a big hit, and was followed by similar titles like "Please No Squeeza Da Banana," and "Josephine, Please No Lean On The Bell."

Following a series of recordings for the Majestic label, Prima moved to RCA Victor. After he released a Top Ten hit, "Civilization," in 1947, dynamics within the music business caused many big bands' fortunes to plummet. Many disbanded after the war as television gained popularity. Newly married to his third wife, Louis was able to sustain his orchestra through the lean times by concentrating on recording.

During auditions for a female vocalist in Norfolk, Virginia, Louis found the woman who would be his partner for the most successful years of his life. Dorothy Jacqueline Keely, better known as Keely Smith, struck Louis with her lack of movement while she sang. She would prove to be the ideal foil for the hyper-animated Prima. In no time, Prima divorced his third wife Tracelene and married Keely, as the pair began their ascent to stardom. With Keely, Prima did a complete transition from his previous sound to a renewed career using the beat of the latest popular music—rock n' roll.

This revitalization began in the fall of 1954 at the lounge of the Sahara in Las Vegas. As his fame grew he unleashed a new backing combo, the Witnesses, led by Sam Butera, an old sax-playing crony from New Orleans. The line up proved to be a smash hit nationwide. One *Variety* review in 1956 noted that "Prima's uninhibited verve on stage is instantly communicated to his audience" while Smith's "deadpan makeup is used solely as a foil for spouse Prima as he affectionately kids her." Another *Variety* review esteemed the "zing and zip Butera and the bandsmen added to the place." The band recorded for Capitol Records and enjoyed a major hit in 1959 with "That Old Black Magic".

Keely Smith Files For A Divorce

All seemed to be going well until the usually private Prima took out an angry advertisement in several newspapers denying rumors that his health was failing. Prima also denied having marital problems with Keely, stating that they were "a preposterous lie started by some imbecile." In 1961, however, Keely filed for a divorce. Although Louis continued to perform with the Witnesses, his days with Keely were the yardstick by which his performances were measured.

Prima's final moment in the spotlight was providing the voice for the character King Louie in Disney's animated feature "The Jungle Book". He continued to perform across the United States until he was diagnosed with a brain tumor in 1975. After an operation, Louis slipped into a coma that would last almost three years until his death on August 24, 1978.

The man who "learned to swing before [he] learned to talk" left an impressive musical legacy as well as a reputation as a consummate showman. His music, being revived on lounge music releases, out-hips much associated with that genre. Prima would be happy to swing and groove for whatever audience welcomed him.

Selected discography

"Chasin' Shadows" on *The 1930's—The Singers*, Columbia, 1987.

"Angelina," Majestic, 1944.

"Please No Squeeza da Banana," Majestic, 1945.

"Josephine, Please No Lean On The Bell," Majestic, 1946.

"Civilization (Bongo, Bongo, Bongo)," RCA Victor, 1947.

"Oh Florence (The Thousand Islands Song)," RCA Victor, 1947.

Capitol Collectors' Series, Capitol, 1991.

"Jump, Jive, and Wail," "Closer To The Bone" on *Ultra Lounge Volume 5: Wild, Cool, & Swingin'*, Capitol, 1996.

Swing With Louis Prima & His Orchestra, Fat Boy, 1996.

With others

(With Keely Smith), "That Old Black Magic" on *Cocktail Mix Volume 3: Swingin' Singles*, Rhino, 1996 and *Ultra Lounge Volume 5: Wild, Cool, & Swingin'*, Capitol, 1996.

(By Sam Butera), "The Boulevard of Broken Dreams/Fever," on *Ultra Lounge Volume 4: Bachelor Pad Royale*, Capitol, 1996.

(By Sam Butera & The Witnesses), "I Love Paris" and "La Vie En Rose" on *Ultra Lounge Volume 10: A Bachelor In Paris*, Capitol, 1996.

(By Louis Prima & Sam Butera), "Harlem Nocturne" on *Ultra Lounge Volume 12: Saxophobia*, Capitol, 1996.

Sources

Books

Boulard, Garry, *Just A Gigolo: The Life and Times of Louis Prima*, University of Southern Louisiana, 1989.

Lombardo, Guy, and Jack Altshul, *Auld Acquaintance*, Doubleday, 1975.

Murrells, Joseph, *Million Selling Records*, Arco Publishing, 1984.

Whitburn, Joel, *Pop Memories 1890-1954*, Record Research, Inc., 1986.

Periodicals

Down Beat, November 1, 1939; December 1, 1940; July 2, 1947; June 30, 1954; October 31, 1957; February 19, 1959.

International Musician, November 1959.

Melody Maker, September 7, 1968.

Time, September 7, 1959.

Variety, October 10, 1956; September 11, 1957; December 25, 1957; April 8, 1959.

—James Powers

Pulp

Pop band

The English pop band Pulp soldiered away in obscurity through the 1980s and part of the 90s, before achieving fame in their home country and some measure of recognition elsewhere. Fronted by the flamboyant Jarvis Cocker, the band merged everything from classic pop melodies to disco beats. In the words of National Public Radio commentator Mark Jenkins, "The sextet's musical style is flexible and eclectic so as to best suit the lyrics, which are clearly the most important element." Those lyrics often sketch seedy, ambivalent tales of London's restless working-class. "A standard Pulp song," declared *Newsday,* "is a cocoon of catchiness wrapped around a larva of verbal irony and storytelling." Cocker himself has noted that he values the pop form for its lack of pretense. "It's cheap and it's throwaway," he told *Face,* "but somehow—and nobody really knows exactly how—a song can crystallize a certain moment and a certain feeling."

A native of Sheffield, in England's industrial north, Cocker had a difficult childhood. He was nearly killed by a bout of meningitis, which severely affected his vision. Tall and skinny, fitted with huge glasses, he felt doomed to be unpopular for the rest of his life. His father left the family when the boy was only 7, running off to Australia to pursue a music career. As a teenager, Jarvis himself decided to form a band; first known as Arabacus Pulp, the embryonic project first performed at his school, where fellow students paid for the privilege of seeing them perform during lunch hour. The group made an impression on John Peel, the BBC radio host who had helped many British acts achieve stardom. With Peel's encouragement, Cocker and his mates decided to continue—though the singer has since noted that if he'd known how long it would take, he probably wouldn't have invested the effort.

Struggled for Years

A panoply of musicians have passed through the group's ranks over the years. After a 1983 debut EP, *It,* on the Red Rhino label, and a follow-up album in 1986, most of the lineup that would survive into the 90s came together. This included guitarist-violinist Russell Senior, keyboardist Candida Doyle, and drummer Nick Banks. Bassist Steve Mackey signed on in 1988, while Mark Webber—who participated as a part-time guitarist starting in 1992, would not become a full-fledged member of Pulp until 1995.

The band struggled through the 1980s, working low-paying jobs or living on welfare (also known as "the dole") and scraping by. Senior met Cocker when the singer was working in a Sheffield market selling crabs.

For the Record . . .

Members include **Nick Banks** (joined group 1986), drums; **Jarvis Cocker** (born September 19, 1963, Sheffield, England), vocals, guitar; **Candida Doyle** (joined 1984), keyboards; **Steve Mackey** (joined 1988), bass; **Russell Senior** (joined 1983), guitar and violin; **Mark Webber** (part-time member, 1992-95; became full member, 1995), guitar; various other musicians.

Band formed c. 1981, Sheffield, England. Recorded EP *It* for Red Rhino, 1983; signed with Fire Records and released album *Freaks,* 1986; signed with Gift Records and released single "O.U.," 1992; signed with Island Records, 1993, and released first album exclusively for that label, *His 'N' Hers,* 1994; Cocker and Mackey co-directed film to accompany single "Do You Remember the First Time?," 1994, and directed videos for other groups, including Aphex Twin; group performed at Glastonbury music festival, 1995; Cocker appeared on Barry Adamson album *Oedipus Schmoedipus,* 1996.

Awards: Mercury Music Prize, 1995; named BBC Radio One and *Melody Maker*'s "Band of the Year," 1995.

Addresses: *Record company*—Island Records, 825 Eighth Avenue, New York, NY 10019; 8920 Sunset Blvd., 2nd Floor, Los Angeles, CA 90069. *Internet*—http://ns.ph.liv.ac.uk/~mbs/pulp. *E-mail*—pulp@trade2.demon.co.uk. *Fan club*—Pulp People, P.O. Box 87, Sheffield S10 14Q United Kingdom.

Doyle had trouble keeping her job in a toyshop. "I was on the dole for six years in Sheffield," she told the 'zine *Pulpfreak,* in an interview reprinted on one of Pulp's unofficial Internet websites. "The first few years were hard because I was working at the same time," she added. "We never got money for being in Pulp—in fact, I spent more money on the band than I made from it."

Landed on Island

Cocker sustained serious injuries when he fell from an upper-floor window in the course of trying to impress a female acquaintance and was forced to perform several shows in a wheelchair. The singer referred to the experience as "a major watershed, a point at which my life changed course" in an interview with *Rolling Stone.* "I

really believe," he added, that "whatever doesn't kill you makes you stronger." He moved to London in 1988 and enrolled in art school, studying film—a skill he would later utilize in making videos for his own and other groups. The group's third album was completed in 1989, but for various reasons wasn't released for 3 years.

After a handful of releases on the independent label Gift, Pulp were at last offered a major label deal, signing with Island Records. Island then put out a compilation of the group's work on Gift, titled *Pulpintro.* It was with the 1994 album *His 'N' Hers,* however, that the band began to achieve widespread recognition in England—and the beginnings of a substantial cult following in the U.S. Rather than release a video to accompany their successful single "Do You Remember the First Time?" Jarvis and Mackey instead collaborated on a 26-minute film, in which various personages—some relatively famous—were asked the song's title question.

English Fame, Stateside Obscurity

Pulp had at last arrived in the U.K. "If somebody told me in 1981 that it would take 13 years to get recognized, I would have been horrified," reads a quote from Cocker in the band's Island Records biography. "I guess it was self-belief that kept it going all the time, because for a long time nobody else seemed to like it. But we thought we were doing something that was worth doing, so we kept doing it and hoped that the world would come round to our way of thinking." This "coming round" had much to do with the ascendance of "Britpop," practiced most successfully by international hitmakers Oasis and the more parochial Blur. "I don't know what it's like in America," Cocker noted in *Musician,* "but in England, there's a bit more personality coming back into the music." And along with this personality came a renewed interest in rock fashion, of which Cocker was an accomplished practitioner.

Pulp's 1995 release *Different Class* enjoyed mass success in England and earned the band a higher profile in the U.S. With its trenchant single "Common People"— the story of an upper-class girl who "slums" among the less privileged for the sake of artistic authenticity—the album made a marked impression on American critics. *Newsday* deemed *Different Class* "perhaps the best British pop album of the last year," though he admitted that "it may just be too culture-specific for the American mainstream." He was correct; the album didn't sell well stateside. But in England, Pulp were heroes. *Different Class* debuted at the top position on the British charts, and BBC Radio One and *Melody Maker* deemed Pulp "Band of the Year"; after filling in for their friends the

Stone Roses at the Glastonbury rock festival that year, they won the Mercury Music Prize.

Rained on Jackson's Parade

The Mercury award was a particularly sweet plum for the group, which had been shut out of the Brit awards earlier that year. Even so, Pulp were the stars of the Brits ceremony, thanks to Cocker's disgust with Michael Jackson. The American pop megastar was in the midst of a performance that involved his Messianic deliverance of Third-World children, among others. Cocker, appalled at the egotism of the display—particularly given accusations of child molestation that Jackson had averted but never disproved—leapt onstage and frolicked sacreligiously.

At that point, wrote producer-composer Brian Eno, in a letter to London's *Independent,* "Jarvis, here seen as the voice of the people, pricked the balloon [of Jackson's pomposity], and the beg men on stage disguised as deprived Third Worlders jumped him." In the ensuing melee, some children were mildly hurt; Jackson's people accused Cocker of "attacking" them, and the singer was briefly detained by authorities. Ultimately, however, he was hailed by many as a hero for daring to deflate what observers considered Jackson's megalomaniacal display. The incident only reinforced Cocker's defiantly down-to-earth stance. "People go along with [Jackson's Messianic self-presentation], even though they know it's a bit sick," the singer griped to *Musician's* Mac Randall. "I just couldn't go along with it anymore."

It was an impetuous outburst from someone capable of immense patience. "We've already existed for 16 years," he told Randall, "and most groups are long gone by that time." In *Spin,* he marked his own progress: "I'm really well-adjusted now," he ventured. "It just took me a long time." That the story of Pulp has so often been the story of Jarvis Cocker is not lost on his bandmates. "I'm glad that so much of the attention is focused on Jarvis," Doyle asserted in *Pulpfreak.* "But that leads people to say Pulp is Jarvis' band, that we wouldn't exist if it wasn't for him—and that's not true. We all have a say in what happens in Pulp." Even so, she mused, "I would worry if I got as famous as him."

Selected discography

It, Red Rhino, 1983.
Freaks, Fire, 1986.
Separations, Fire, 1989.
Pulpintro, Island, 1993.
Masters of the Universe, Fire, 1994.
His 'N' Hers (includes "Do You Remember the First Time?"), Island, 1994.
Different Class (includes "Common People"), Island, 1995.

Sources

College Music Journal (CMJ), November 1994.
Face, July 1995.
Independent, February 22, 1996.
Los Angeles Times, February 18, 1996.
Musician, July 1994; July 1996; December 1996.
Newsday, March 24, 1996; June 5, 1996.
Rolling Stone, April 18, 1996.
Spin, March 1996.

Additional information was provided by Island Records publicity materials, 1995, a transcript of the National Public Radio program *All Things Considered* from April 22, 1996, and materials from various Pulp sites on the Internet.

—Simon Glickman

Rage Against the Machine

Rock/rap band

Greek philosopher Plato once wrote, "The introduction of a new kind of music must be shunned as imperiling the whole state, since styles of music are never disturbed without affecting the most important political institutions." It is this idea that fueled the inspiration behind Rage Against the Machine. Combining the aggressiveness of metal with the vocal styling of rap, the band decided to use this hybrid to broadcast their societal message to anyone who would listen. Their self-titled debut album sold more than four million copies worldwide, and the musical message reached ears all over the world. "We're trying to do something most bands don't do," guitarist Tom Morello told Katherine Turman in *Spin*, "which is combine music and activism. The lofty goal would be bringing down an oppressive, racist, capitalistic system that feeds on the exploited and repressed."

Singer Zack de la Rocha met bassist Timmy C. (a.k.a. Tim Bob) in the sixth grade. De la Rocha and Timmy C. grew up in Orange County, California, an area known for its suburban conservatism. As a child, de la Rocha's

© Ken Settle

For the Record . . .

Members include **Tim Bob** (a.k.a. Timmy C.), bass; **Tom Morello** (graduated from Harvard University, 1986), guitar; **Zack de la Rocha**, vocals; **Brad Wilk**, drums.

Band formed in Orange County, California, 1991; self-produced 12-song cassette, 1992; toured U.S. and Europe; signed with Epic Records and released self-titled debut, 1992; toured worldwide and organized benefits, 1993-94; video for "Freedom" reached Number One, 1994; released *Evil Empire* on Epic, 1996.

Addresses: *Record company*—Epic Records, 550 Madison Ave., New York, NY 10022-3211.

parents put him in the middle of a heavy custody battle. He moved back and forth between his mother's home in Irvine, California, and his father's in East Los Angeles. His mother worked as a teacher's aide at the University of California at Irvine, while his father was a first-generation Mexican muralist.

De la Rocha compared his own career to his father's in an interview with Timothy White in *Billboard*. "Back in 1974, my father's paints were part of the first Chicano art exhibit ever organized at the L.A. County Museum of Art ['Los Four: Almarez, de la Rocha, Lugan, Romero']. That accomplishment was really something to be proud of. I want to make music that gives people that same sense of identity, and lets them see that human rights, civil rights, and spiritual rights are part of the same struggle we all face: to take the power back."

Birth of a Revolution

De la Rocha and Timmy C. met guitarist Tom Morello and drummer Brad Wilk in the early 1990s. Morello's father served as a member of the Mau Mau guerrilla organization that freed Kenya from colonial rule in the 1960s. His mother, Mary Morello, was a schoolteacher and later founded the anti-censorship organization Parents for Rock & Rap. Before moving to Los Angeles, Morello, originally from Libertyville, Illinois, graduated from Harvard University in 1986 with a degree in Social Services. He played in a punk band called Lock-Up, then co-founded Rage Against the Machine in 1991.

The group recorded and released a self-produced, 12-song cassette in 1992, which included the song "Bullet in the Head," which later became a single from the band's debut album. The members sold the tape through their fan club and at live shows in the area, and ended up selling more then 5,000 copies. Rage Against the Machine had received its first contract offer from a major label after its second club performance. However, the group wanted to make sure they had the freedom to express their message and took their time before inking a deal with Epic Records.

Before *Rage Against the Machine* ever hit the stores, the band had played with Porno for Pyros on that band's debut performance, a European tour with Suicidal Tendencies, and performances on the second stage of the Lollapallooza II tour. On November 6, 1992, Epic released the record, which included the singles "Killing in the Name," "Freedom," and "Take the Power Back."

Reinforced Message with Activism

Timothy White wrote of Rage Against the Machine in *Billboard*, "On the strength of the Epic album, they must be viewed as one of the most original and virtuosic new rock bands in the nation, capable of a latticed wall of stridor so deftly woven that it's destined to be the standard for any audacious headbangers who dare follow." Despite the band's obvious rap and hip hop influences, they stayed true to their name and shunned electronic keyboards, samples, and drum machines. "You'd assume there was a DJ in the band if you didn't know better," Morello told Chuck Crusafulli in *Guitar Player*, "but all the sounds we make are guitar, bass, drums, and vocals."

Rage Against the Machine's first video for "Killing in the Name" did not receive any airplay in the U.S. because of the language in the song's refrain. However, it did receive substantial airplay in Europe and boosted the group's popularity and sales overseas far above its home country.

Right out of the gate, Rage Against the Machine stood behind its activist message by participating and producing many benefits for political organizations. On January 23, 1993, the band headlined a Rock for Choice show in support of pro-choice abortion organizations. On July 18, 1993, Rage Against the Machine created a silent protest onstage at Lollapallooza III in Philadelphia. Each member of the band stood naked without singing or playing a note for 25 minutes in a statement against censorship. With duct tape sealing their mouths, they each wore a letter spelling "P-M-R-C," for the Parents Music Resource Center. They also headlined a sold-out Anti-Nazi League benefit at Brixton Academy in London, England, to raise money and promote an anti-Nazi march that took place the next month.

Nearly a year after the album's release, *Rage Against the Machine* reached No. 70 on *Billboard*'s Top 200 albums chart without much radio or video exposure. On December 19, 1993, Rage Against the Machine released its first MTV-aired video, "Freedom." Directed by Peter Christopherson, the video mixed live footage of the band with scenes from Robert Redford's 1992 documentary *Incident at Oglala* and text from Peter Matthiessen's *In the Spirit of Crazy Horse*. The video argued for the innocence of American Indian Movement leader Leonard Peltier.

Sophomore Release Even More Political

In 1994, Rage Against the Machine released the song "Year of tha Boomerang" on the soundtrack for the John Singleton film *Higher Learning*. The following year, the group organized and headlined a benefit concert at the Capitol Ballroom in Washington, D.C. The show raised more than $8,000 for the International Concerned Friends and Family of Mumia Abu-Jamal, an activist sentenced to death. In 1996, Rage Against the Machine released their second effort, *Evil Empire* on Epic Records. Evelyn McDonnell wrote in *Rolling Stone*, "Rage's second album, *Evil Empire*, may be the most politically radical album ever to hit No. 1 on the pop charts." This album again focused on political and social commentary.

"We're able to make music that can reach a lot of people and contains a really potent message," Morello told James Rotondi in *Guitar Player*. "It's not merely about thinking for yourself, or supporting the occasional feel-good cause. It's about revolutionary values.... But there is a depth and importance to our message which completely transcends the artist side of it."

Selected discography

Rage Against the Machine, Epic, 1992.
Evil Empire, Epic, 1996.

Sources

Anti-Matter, April 1993.
Billboard, December 26, 1992; July 3, 1993; July 10, 1993; February 5, 1994; March 23, 1996.
Desert Sun, June 6, 1996.
Entertainment Weekly, July 16, 1993; January 13, 1995; April 19, 1996.
Guitar Player, July 1993; June 1994; June 1996.
Los Angeles Times, October 31, 1993.
New York Times, November 8, 1993.
People, May 20, 1996.
Playboy, February 1993.
Rolling Stone, March 10, 1994; June 16, 1994; April 18, 1996; October 3, 1996.
Spin, November 1993; February 1994.
Stereo Review, August 1996.
Time, September 23, 1996.

Additional information for this profile was obtained from Epic Records press material, 1996.

—*Sonya Shelton*

The Roches

Folk trio

The Roches—Maggie, Terre, and Suzzy Roche—are a singing trio of sisters who are best known for their three-part harmony, quirky lyrics, and otherwise unconventional approach to music. Holly Crenshaw described their music in *The Performing Songwriter:* "The Roches' art is filled with flashes of unexpected beauty, weird turns of phrase that suddenly veer off to the left, self-deprecating humor tinged with an edge of seriousness, and choir-like, three-part harmonies that dip and soar with an easy grace. It's a one-of-a-kind commodity that confounds categorization—and consequently, their ten albums have often fallen outside the safe parameters of commercial pop music." The group, which is most often given a folk-pop tag, has largely maintained its status as a cult or campus phenomenon, although it has had mainstream media exposure, having made guest appearances on Saturday Night Live, The Tonight Show, The Late Show with David Letterman, and VH-1. More importantly, however, the Roches's loyal and enthusiastic following has continued to grow over the span of their career as a trio—which is approaching the 20-year mark.

It is the Roches's idiosyncrasies, perhaps, that seem to guarantee their continued cult status. Their 1995 release *Can We Go Home Now* includes a musical anomaly, an eight-minute song about Maggie's favorite possession, "My Winter Coat." When the group performed on the Johnny Carson show, they chose to sing the song "Big Nuthin'"—which deals with the disappointments they had faced following other events that were supposed to be big career breaks—to the obvious consternation of their host. Also, otherwise complementary critics reveal why the group may not agree with everyone's tastes. In *Stereo Review* Brett Milano quoted a friend who said, "They sound just like a female version of the Chipmunks." Daniel Gewertz commented in the Boston *Herald,* "The Roches' modus operandi has been to write songs about life's weird little details, making the mundane seem funny. The strange harmonies and purposefully flat melodies can get too aimless. But at their best, the Roches aren't just clever nihilists: their quirks shed light on the plight of the heart."

A Musical Childhood

The Roche sisters grew up in Park Ridge, New Jersey, singing in Catholic choirs. Maggie and Terre also performed at political rallies; their father, John Roche, wrote the songs' lyrics to fit popular melodies. When they were in their teens, Maggie introduced herself to Paul Simon at a New York University songwriting class, which he invited the two older sisters to attend. Eventually, the pair dropped out of high school to go on tour, performing in college towns. They sang backup vocals on

Members include **Maggie Roche**, born October 26, 1951, in Detroit, Michigan; **Terre Roche**, born April 10, 1953, in New York City; **Suzzy Roche**, born in New York City; daughters of John (a teacher) and Jude Roche (an advertising copywriter). *Education:* Suzzy Roche graduated from the State University of New York at Purchase with a degree in dramatic arts.

Maggie and Terre Roche began performing professionally in their teens, sang back-up vocals for Paul Simon on *There Goes Rhymin' Simon* and recorded an album as a duo, *Seductive Reasoning*, 1975; formed the Roches with the addition of sister Suzzy, c. 1976; recorded debut album, *The Roches*, in 1979.

Awards: Parent's Choice Gold Award for *Will You Be My Friend?*.

Addresses: *Record company*—Rykodisc, Shetland Park, 27 Congress Street, Salem, MA 01970.

Simon's *There Goes Rhymin' Simon* and, in 1975, they recorded an album, *Seductive Reasoning,* for CBS. However, the thrill of being signed by a big-name label was counteracted by difficulties in the recording studio. The young women were given an impressive backup band but had to fight for the right to play their own instruments. The project with CBS thoroughly soured the sisters' taste for the music industry; they soon dropped out altogether and moved (with Suzzy) to a kung fu temple in Hammond, Louisiana.

Six months later the three sisters were back in New York City, singing Christmas carols in the streets. Having graduated from college with a degree in dramatic arts, it was Suzzy who reinvigorated Maggie and Terre's desire to sing. Maggie later explained to the *San Francisco Examiner*, "We have always been really close, so when she joined us it wasn't like her joining our duo. It was like we became a whole new thing." After performing, and also tending bar, at a Greenwich Village club, the sisters started identifying themselves as the Roches.

It was at a New York club that the sisters met Robert Fripp, the guitarist of the temporarily-disbanded art rock band King Crimson, who would produce their first album, *The Roches,* for Warner Brothers. Not only did they enjoy the experience and Fripp's emphasis on a "live" sound, the record also proved to be a critical success.

The Roches made more albums for Warner Brothers, during which time they learned to incorporate conventional rock instrumentation and synthesizers into their work. Following their 1985 release *Another World*, the band began shopping around for a new recording contract. In the meantime, the sisters released a four-cut EP and contributed four songs to the soundtrack of *Crossing Delancy*; Suzzy also made her screen debut in the 1988 film, playing Amy Irving's friend. The Roches did not release a new album until 1989, when they produced *Speak* for MCA. Two of the group's subsequent albums, the Christmas collection *We Three Kings* and the children's recording *Will You Be My Friend?*, gave the group an opportunity to revisit old favorites and to reach back into their own childhood for musical inspiration. The band's final recording for MCA was *A Dove,* an album produced in the in-home studio of Stewart Lerman.

Returned to Earlier Sound

When the Roches left MCA for Rykodisc in 1995 they continued to work with Lerman, producing *Can We Go Home Now?* In one way the album is a throwback to the group's early sound, with its absence of keyboards and computerized effects. Writing for *New Country*, Brett Milano commented that Lerman "is their first producer since Robert Fripp to understand how to record the sisters' voices, not smoothing out the natural roughness...it recalls the freshness of the first album and throws more depth into the bargain." It is also the Roches most serious album to date; it deals with themes such as lost friendship, jealousy, and their father's struggle with Alzheimer's Disease. Terre Roche told the *Washington Post* that the album was indeed a tribute to their father, who shared their love of words and sense of humor—and who supported their careers from the first; she said, "I remember it'd be 3 o'clock in the morning, and he'd be there with his 15-year-old daughters waiting to play three songs at the Gaslight in the city. All those memories came flooding back this past year, so making the record was a very emotional process."

Formed a Democracy

Like all of their previous albums, *Can We Go Home Now?* consists of equal contributions from each sister. Some Roches songs are written collaboratively, others come from an individual point of view. The Roches operate as a democracy, with each providing a different sensibility and style to their songs. The process of selecting songs for an album is part diplomacy, part sibling intuition. "You've got this real bank of communication that goes back to when you were babies," Terre explained to the *Washington Times.* "You really know what each other is talking about." In August of 1996 the sisters agreed that it was time to take a break from being the Roches, and announced that they were going on a six-month hiatus to work on solo projects. As Terre told the Providence *Journal-Bulletin,* "All of us have songs we've written that have never been on Roches albums....There are times when you express something that isn't really appropriate for the Roches."

Selected discography

(Maggie and Terre Roche) *Seductive Reasoning,* CBS, 1975.
The Roches, Warner Brothers, 1979.
Nurds, Warner Brothers, 1980.
Keep On Doing, Warner Brothers, 1982.
Another World, Warner Brothers, 1985.
No Trespassing (EP), Rhino, 1986.
Speak, MCA/Paradox, 1989.
We Three Kings, MCA/Paradox, 1990; reissued, Rykodisc, 1994.
A Dove, MCA/Paradox, 1992.
Will You Be My Friend? (children's album), Baby Boom, 1994.
Can We Go Home Now?, Rykodisc, 1995.

Sources

Boston Globe, February 27, 1996.
Boston Herald, June 6, 1994.
Dirty Linen, October/November 1995.
Journal-Bulletin (Providence, Rhode Island), March 15, 1996.
Los Angeles Times, June 27, 1995.
New Country, September 1995.
New York Times, November 10, 1995.
Performing Songwriter, September/October 1995, pp. 73-75.
San Francisco Examiner, January 14, 1990.
Times-Picayune (New Orleans, LA), January 19, 1990.
Village Voice, December 26, 1995.
Washington Post, September 22, 1995.
Washington Times, July 2, 1990.

—*Paula Pyzik Scott*

Ryuichi Sakamoto

Composer, keyboardist

Archive Photos Inc.

Ryuichi Sakamoto cites Debussy and Kraftwerk as his biggest influences but his style is far more than a peculiar hybrid of classical impressionism and technopop. He is known for his combination of melodic touch and technological mastery, but the depth of his work is derived from his comprehensive interest in multicultural sources. His work combines musical influences from Asia, Indonesia, the West Indies, Latin America, and other cultures with the classicism of Europe and American pop. Some see this cultural integration as an influential precursor to the world music of the 1990s, arguing that his electronic lyricism broke ground for contemporary ambient and new age movements.

Ryuichi Sakamoto was born in Japan in 1952. By age 11, his musical interests ranged from the Beatles to Beethoven and he began to study under Professor Matsumoto at the Tokyo University of the Arts. In 1971, he entered the university, where he earned a bachelor of arts in composition and a master's degree with a concentration in electronic and ethnic music. In 1977, he began work as a composer, arranger, and studio musician with some of Japan's most popular rock, jazz, and classical artists. Within a few years, he became a noted producer, arranger, and keyboardist. "Piano is my main instrument. It is like the extension of my body and brain." he said during an America Online chat, qualifying his classical leanings with the comment: "I'm basically a gadget victim, I always like new things!" In the 1970s and 1980s, Sakamoto became known as an innovator in electronic keyboard work and worked with such equipment as Fairlight 2, Prophet 5, and Arp Odyssey.

Formed Group; Began Recording and Touring

In 1978, Sakamoto released his first solo album, *Thousand Knives*, and, along with Haruomi Hosano and Yukihiro Takahashi, formed Yellow Magic Orchestra (YMO). In 1979, YMO's second album sold well over a million copies, leading to the first of many world tours. While touring, Sakamoto witnessed firsthand the origin of those influences that had fascinated him as a youth.

YMO released 13 albums between 1978 and 1984, also releasing another 13 albums of other material and remixes over the over next 12 years. YMO remains popular to this day, with several Internet Web sites devoted to the group. YMO's music shows Sakamoto's influence by such diverse sources as jazz, classical, Jamaican dub, Latin Bossa Nova, and Indonesian gamelan, as well as his interest in pioneering electronic equipment. YMO continues to have a devoted following and its influence on technopop and ambient new age music is still widely recognized.

In 1983, Sakamoto left YMO to begin writing film scores. He created his first soundtrack for the film *Merry Christmas Mr. Lawrence,* in which he also had an acting role. This experience led to a number of other film scores. In 1984, Sakamoto formed his own publishing company Hon Hon Doh and published Long Calls, a dialogue with Yuji Takahashi.

In 1987, Sakamoto's score for Bertolucci's *The Last Emperor,* written in collaboration with Cong Su and Talking Heads founder David Byrne, won an Oscar, a Grammy, a Golden Globe, and The New York, Los Angeles, and British Film Critics Association awards for Best Original Score. He also had an acting role in the film. "The director asked me to act first, then I asked to compose the music so it was a good trade," he said in an America Online chat. Since that time Sakamoto has worked twice with Bertolucci, as well as Oliver Stone (*Wild Palms*), Almodovar (*High Heels*) and other films. Of his working relationship with Bertolucci, he told America Online, "We're friends, but when we work, we, of course, fight. I'm always the loser, because it's his film. That's what he says, 'It's my film.'"

Sakamoto's film roles also led to an appearance in Madonna's "Rain" music video, and as a celebrity model for Barney's New York fashion designer Antonio Miro and the Gap. He has even appeared as a menswear model in some of the world's most prestigious magazines. Sakamoto's film scores have led to work with such iconic musicians as David Bowie (who also acted in *Merry Christmas Mr. Lawrence),* Iggy Pop, and Jamaican reggae artist Sly Dunbar on his 1987 album Neo Geo.

Other collaborators include Beach Boy Brian Wilson, the Band's Robbie Robertson, Talking Head's David Byrne, David Sylvain, and Caetano Veloso, as well as writer William Burroughs and cyberpunk trailblazer William Gibson. Between 1979 and 1996, Sakamoto played on, arranged, or produced 13 albums and 15 singles in collaboration with other artists. He also composed and conducted El Mar Mediterano for the Opening Ceremony of the 1992 Barcelona Olympics, and composed music for the opening ceremony of The World Athletic Championships in Tokyo, in 1991.

New Times, New Media

In addition to his work with YMO, film soundtracks, and collaborative efforts, Sakamoto has engaged in a weighty solo career. Between 1978 and 1996, he released 23 solo albums. His musical interests, always geographically expansive, have broadened in a conceptual sense as well. His solo musical career is not limited to CDs and live performance. Three of his live performances—July 26, 1996 at London's Royal Festival Hall—June 16, 1996 at the Knitting Factory in New York—and August 28, 1996, at Orchard Hall in Tokyo—were broadcast on the Internet. He also has a radio program in Japan, and his guest lecture at Keio University is available on the Internet as well.

Sakamoto continues to explore new musical concepts and anticipates the music of the next century. In his online diary for September, 1996, he wrote, "I ask myself what the sound of music originating from something as immense as the Internet would sound like. The music would be without a center. Perhaps a key in understanding of what this kind of music would sound like lies in the music of the Pygmy tribes in Africa or in sounds made by whales." With close to a hundred singles and albums to his credit since 1973, Sakamoto is one of the more prolific artists around. His diversity in style and medium is impressive as well. He has done work in film, video, vinyl, CD, on the radio and Internet. His style encompasses the technopop he pioneered as well as the multi-cultural idioms he has always embraced—Latin, Asian, European Classical, American pop, and a wide variety of constantly evolving interests. Sakamoto's range, productivity, and ability to constantly grow and explore continue to make him a prominent feature on the musical landscape of the 1990s.

Selected discography

Solo albums

Thousand Knives, Nippon Columbia, 1978.
B-2 Unit, Alfa, 1980.
Left Handed Dream, Alfa, 1981.
Coda, London, 1983.
Illustrated Musical Encyclopedia, Midi 1984.
Esperanto, Midi, 1985.
Future Boy, Midi, 1986.
Media Bahn Live, Midi, 1986.
Neo Geo, CBS Sony/Epic, 1987.
Playing the Orchestra, Virgin, 1988.
Beauty, Virgin, 1988.
Gruppo Musicale, Midi, 1989.
Ryuichi Sakamoto in the 90's, Mark Plati remix, Alfa, 1991.
Heartbeat, Virgin, 1992.
Gruppo Musicale II, Midi, 1993.
Ryuichi Sakamoto Soundtracks, Toshiba EMI 1993.
Ryuichi Sakamoto Virgin Tracks, Toshiba EMI 1993.
Sweet Revenge, For Life/Gut-Elektra, 1994.
Hard Revenge, For Life/Gut, 1994.
Sweet Revenge Tour 1994, For Life/Gut, 1994.
Smoochy-Japanese Version, For Life/Gut, 1995.
Snooty, For Life/Gut, 1996.
1996, For Life/Gut, 1996.
Smoochy, Milan/BMG, 1997.
Stalker: Nigekirenu Ai, For Life/Gut, 1997.

With Yellow Magic Orchestra

Yellow Magic Orchestra, Alfa, 1978.
Yellow Magic Orchestra U.S. Remix, Alfa, 1979.
Solid State Survivor, Alfa, 1979.
Public Pressure from Live Performance, Alfa, 1980.
Multiples—with Snakeman Show—10 inch vinyl, Alfa, 1980.
Multiples—Album Version, Alfa, 1980.
BGM, Alfa, 1981.
Technodelic, Alfa, 1981.
Naughty Boys, Alfa, 1983.

Naughty Boys—Instrumental, Alfa, 1983.
Service, Alfa, 1983.
Sealed limited edition compilation, Alfa, 1984.
After Service from Live Performance, Alfa, 1984.
YMO Mega Mix, Alfa, 1990.
YMO in the 90's—Peter Lorimar remix, Alfa, 1991.
Faker Holic, YMO World Tour Live, Alfa, 1991.
Techno Bible YMO, Alfa, 1992.
YMO vs. The Human League, Alfa, 1993.
Technodon, Toshiba EMI, 1993.
Technodon Remixes remix by Tei Towa and Go Hotoda, Toshiba EMI, 1993.
Technodon Remixes remix by the Orb, Toshiba EMI, 1993.
Technodon Live, Toshiba EMI, 1993.
Live at Budhokkan 1980, Alfa, 1993..
YMO—Winter—Live—1981, Alfa, 1995.
YMO/Over Seas Collection, Alfa, 1995.
YMO World Tour 1980, Alfa, 1996.

Collaboration albums

Summer Nerves, with The Kakutogi Session, CBS Sony, 1979.
The End of Asia, with Danceries, Nippon Columbia, 1982.
The Arrangement, with Robin Scott, Alfa, 1982.
Hope in a Darkened Heart, (Producer/Arranger) Virginia Astley, WEA, 1986.
Let It Be, with Aki Takahashi, Toshiba EMI, 1992.
A Chance Operation—A Tribute to John Cage, Koch Classics, 1993.
Asian Games, with Yosuke Yamashita and Bill Laswel, Mercury, 1993.
Dreamland, (Producer/Arranger) Aztec Camera, Sire/WEA, 1993.
The Geisha Girls—Remix, with The Geisha Girls, For Life/Gut, 1994.
The Geisha Girls Show, (Producer) The Geisha Girls, For Life/Gut, 1995.
The Geisha "Remix" Girls Show, with The Geisha Girls, For Life/Gut, For Life/Gut, 1995.
Syokumotsu-rensa, (Producer) Miki Nakatani, For Life/Gut, 1996.
E Preciso Perdoar—Red Hot + Rio, with Caetano Veloso and Cesaria Evora, Antilles/Verve, 1996.

Soundtrack albums

Merry Christmas Mr. Lawrence, London/Milan, 1983.
Kitten Story (Koneko Monogatari), Midi, 1986.
Aile De Honneamise, Midi, 1987.
The Last Emperor, Virgin, 1988.
The Handmaid's Tale, Japan Record, 1990.
The Sheltering Sky, Virgin, 1990.
High Heels, Island/Virgin, 1992.
Peach Boy (Momotaro), Rabbit Ear Productions, 1992.
Wuthering Heights, Capitol, 1992.

Wild Palms, Capitol, 1992.
Little Buddha, Milan, 1993.

Sources

Books

Murakami, Ryu and Ryuichi Sakamoto, *A Writer's Sonata; A Musician's Story,* Shinchosha, 1996.

Periodicals

Billboard, June 29, 1996.

Online

Web site: http://www.kab.com./m/siteskmt, November 21, 1996.
American Online, transcript from chat with Ryuichi Sakamoto, June 13, 1996.

Other

Tokyo Melody, documentary by French National TV, 1985.

Additional information for this profile was obtained from RZO advisory press material, 1996.

—*Link Yaco*

The
Skatalites

Reggae/ska band

Although many people today would associate ska with bands like The Specials, The English Beat, and Crawdaddy, it was actually The Skatalites, formed in 1963, that pioneered this musical sound. Lasting only 14 months after their original inception, this ground-breaking band has made some major comebacks. In 1984 they performed at The Reggae Sunsplash Festival in London and released the album *Return of the Big Guns* that same year. More recently, The Skatalites have composed two more albums accompanied with live performances. The 1990s marked the group's fourth decade together, during which they have gained wide-spread popularity since their reunion. In an effort to meet the demand for their colorful, electrifying shows, The Skatalites continue to tour year round.

"When I came back to Jamaica in 1962, there was this tune there, 'Schooling the Duke.' It was tearing down the airwaves," recalled original Skatalites leader Tommy McCook in a 1984 interview with David Rodigan of Capital Radio London. He was impressed by the jazzy sounds of Johnny "Dizzy" Moore and Don Drummond, who both played on the tune. A jazz musician himself, McCook was peforming one night when he was approached by Moore and Drummond and asked to record with them. McCook initially refused but eventually joined the band that would later become The Skatalites.

During the 1960s, members of the band were heavily involved with recording sessions in Jamaica. They are also credited with inspiring the Britsh two-tone movement of the late seventies and early eighties. While recording primarily for producer Clement "Sir Coxsone" Dodd of Studio One, they performed with other acts such as the Charms, the Maytals, the Wailers, and the Heptones.

The Last Gig

Although band members continued to perform with other artists, The Skatalites officially broke up in the summer of 1965. "Our last gig was at the Runaway Bay Hotel, Police Dance," one Skatalite remembered in the 1984 interview. However, a new band, Soul Vendors, was subsequently formed and included the likes of Johnny Moore, Jackie Mittoo, Lloyd Brevette, and Bunny Williams.

Tragedy struck the band on May 6, 1969, when one of the founding Skatalites members, Don Drummond, died mysteriously while in a mental hospital. He had been plagued with mental problems for years, which perhaps influenced his music. "He was great, the sounds he produced," commented McCook in his interview with Rodigan. "And the way he played his horn...would make you wonder you know...it was all so moonfull, sometimes you could cry inside." McCook also suggested that Drummond's death involved foul play—possibly as the result of a 1965 incident in which Drummond, in an angry rage, stabbed his girlfriend Marguerita to death. She was the daughter of an alleged mafia family.

Drummond's Music Lives On

Drummond had written some songs that were posthumously recorded, allowing his music to survive. McCook acquired the compositions after one bandmember collected them during Drummond's arrest. For years he retained the music as a memory, but McCook eventually decided to record it. "I took the music...to the piano," he told Rodigan, " and started to put the changes to it and things like that and it came out nice." Before his death, Drummond had won several jazz trombonist awards.

One of the first Jamaican acts to sign with Island records, The Skatalites reached the British Top 40 with "Guns of Navarone" in 1967. The same year the Skatalites

ceased recording under that name, although most members remained involved in Jamaican music. Some pursued solo careers, while others moved to England and became session musicians. One member, Rico Rodriguez, played horns on The Specials self-titled debut album in 1979, which incidentally was produced by the legendary Elvis Costello.

"Synergy" Reunited the Band

But it was "synergy" that reunited the band, as McCook declared to Rodigan. Playing for a whole new generation, The Skatalites released *Ska Voovee* in 1993, which contained 11 new instrumental songs, including a tribute to Drummond called "The Don," featuring his replacement in the band, jazz trombonist Steve Turre. Reunited band members include Tommy McCook, Ron Wilson, Lester Sterling, Lloyd Knibbs, and Lloyd Brevette. According to Geoffrey Himes of the *Washington Post*, "The two Lloyds once again serve up the push-and-pull rhythms—with their emphasis on the off-beat— that first defined ska as something different from North American R&B and set the stage for reggae." This "off-beat" sound has influenced the music of many modern artists, who have sampled Skatalites rhythms to blend with their own.

Although The Skatalites defined the ska sound in the 1960s, most of the original members began their careers as jazz musicians, and with the 1994 release of *Hi-Bop Ska*, the band seems to have come full circle. The founding members "at the core of this reformed ensemble reaffirm their jazz roots in vibrant style here," opined *Down Beat*'s Larry Birnbaum. "New compositions blend easily with classics like 'Guns of Navarone' and 'Man in the Street.'" In 1995 McCook suffered a heart attack and was forced to take a hiatus from his busy touring schedule. But this didn't prevent him from returning to the studio to record 1996's *Greetings from Skamania*. A biography released by Shanachie Entertainment asserted that the result of this effort is "a lava-hot album that exemplifies the best the Skatalites have to offer. Pounding ska beats and blistering jazz solos blend seamlessly together to create an album that feels simultaneously cutting-edge fresh and tempered-steel classic. Greetings from Skamania!"

Selected discography

Ska Authentic, Studio One, 1963.
Legendary Skatalites, Top Ranking, 1975.
African Roots, United Artists, 1977.
Scattered Lights, Aligator, 1984.
Ska Voovee, Shanachie, 1993.

Hi-Bop Ska, Shanachie, 1994.
Greetings from Skamania, Shanachie, 1996.

Sources

Books

Rolling Stone Encyclopedia of Rock and Roll, edited by Jon Pareles, Rolling Stone Press/Summit Books, 1983.

Periodicals

Down Beat, June 1995.
Washington Post, March 4, 1994.

Online

The Boston Ska Home Page: http//www.dataweb.nl/ ~vanbreda/Skatalites.HTML.

Additional information was obtained from Shanachie Entertainment press materials, 1996.

—*Maria L. Munoz*

Otis Spann

Pianist

Archive Photos

In the early 1950s Otis Spann gained fame as the pianist for the Muddy Waters band and as house pianist for Chicago's Chess records, the record label of Waters and other blues legends such as Willie Dixon, Howlin' Wolf, Etta James, and Buddy Guy. Playing in a style rooted in boogie-woogie piano tradition, he developed a unique and formidable blues approach. Though a talented singer and soloist with many fine recordings to his credit, Spann's career saw him primarily in the role of accompanist, recording with such bluesmen as Sonny Boy Williamson and Howlin' Wolf, and rock 'n' roll pioneers Bo Diddley and Chuck Berry. His work with Muddy Waters contributed to one of the most celebrated ensembles in the history of the blues. By the 1960s Spann's solo career brought audiences a refined barrelhouse sound unequaled among postwar blues pianists.

Otis Spann was born on March 21, 1930 in Jackson, Mississippi. One of five children, Spann was reared by his stepfather Frank Houston Spann, a preacher, and his mother Josephine Erby. As a youth he heard the blues at house parties and, at an early age, learned the rudiments of keyboard from Friday Ford, a pianist based in nearby Belzoni. Despite the fact that his student's fingers had yet to attain the proper reach between the keys, Ford sat young Otis on his knee and taught him the basics of blues piano. In *Conversation with the Blues*, Spann described Ford as "a great man and a wonderful player," a musician who had a lasting impact on his musical development.

Started Career Early, Thanks to Contest

With his stepfather's purchase of a piano, Spann earnestly pursued his musical studies. In *Jazz Journal* he noted the influence of Ford and several other blues musicians: "My biggest influence was [local pianist] Coot Davis and also Tommy Johnson, Leroy Carr, Big Maceo [Merriweather]. Maceo could play just as good as he could sing." At age eight, Spann won a talent contest at the Alamo Theatre where the owner subsequently hired him to perform behind vaudeville acts dressed in a hat and tails.

As a teenager, in the early 1940s, Spann fought in the Golden Gloves and claimed to have twenty-eight knock outs in a string of forty-eight fights. He also played pro football and eventually became a pro fighter, but his sports career was interrupted by his induction in the Army in 1946. Discharged from the service in 1951, he moved north to Chicago where he supported himself as a plasterer by day and as a pianist at nightly house parties. He eventually formed his own combo and took a job at the Tick Tock Lounge where he performed steadily between 1950 and 1953. In the vibrant Chicago blues scene he encountered many older and established blues pianists such as Roosevelt Sykes, Little Brother Montgomery, and Sunnyland Slim.

After Spann recorded with Muddy Waters in 1952, he performed in Chicago clubs with the band of guitarist and harmonica player Louis Meyers. In 1953, after a stint with Louisiana-born guitarist Morris Pejoe, he replaced Big Maceo as Waters's regular pianist. "Spann was the natural successor to Big Maceo," observed Mike Rowe in *Chicago Blues*. "In the band Otis was a tower of strength. Never obtrusive (in fact Spann believed the harmonica to be the most important instrument), he was the perfect accompanist and ensemble player and every note he hit seemed just right."

With the hiring of Spann, wrote Jas Obrecht in *Blues Guitar*, "Muddy finally actualized his dream of a blues `big band' when pianist Otis Spann, whom Muddy lovingly referred to as his half-brother, was an unobtrusive sideman who could accommodate styles ranging from subtle fills to thunderous boogies. His admission into the band completed Muddy's move away from the intimate Delta-inspired sound."

Chicago Studio Musician

In 1953 Spann accompanied Waters on the Chess hits "Blow Wind Blow" and "Mad Love (I Want You to Love Me)" and appeared on such Waters classics as "Hoochie Coochie Man" and "I Just Want to Make Love to You"— numbers greatly enhanced by Spann's tastefully executed piano lines. Taking note of Spann's talent, the Chess brothers and the label's in-house bassist and producer, Willie Dixon, called upon the pianist to back a number of the label's artists. In *Nothing But the Blues*, Dixon described Spann as "a good musician ... who knew "how to make other fellows sound good. Otis was the type of guy who could play with anybody." In 1954 Spann recorded on Howlin' Wolf's first Chess hit, "No Place to Go." Describing Spann's contribution to the number, Paul Garon wrote in *The Blackwell Guide*, "Otis Spann adds considerable solo demonstrating a remarkable sensitivity for the potential intricacy of the piece." Spann also appeared on Howlin' Wolf's 1954 sides "How Long," "Forty-Four" and the haunting blues classic "Evil (Is Goin' On)."

In April of 1954, Spann and Muddy Waters took part in Junior Wells's second session for the States label. Spann also made several J.O.B label recordings with saxophonist J.T. Brown and a side for Checker entitled "It Must Have Been the Devil." In February of 1955, Spann appeared on Bo Diddley's famous Chess sides "Bo Diddley" and "I'm a Man." In the same year, Spann recorded on Chuck Berry's Chess hit "You Can't Catch Me" and Sonny Boy Williamson's "Don't Start Me to Talkin."

On Tour in England with Muddy Waters

As a member of the Muddy Waters band Spann appeared on the 1956 Chess sides "Don't Go No Further" and "I Live the Life I Love." In October of 1958 Waters accepted an invitation to tour England. Without funds to bring his entire group, Waters took along Spann as his only accompanist. Critics and writers, accustomed to skiffle music and the live performances of acoustic bluesmen such as Big Bill Broonzy and Sonny Terry and Brownie McGhee, voiced their negative reaction to Waters's amplified guitar sound. One local publication summed up one of the duo's performances by displaying the headline "Screaming guitar and howling piano." One of the surviving recordings of the tour, *Collaboration, Muddy Waters & Otis Spann*, reveals an intimate performance by Waters and Spann greeted by spirited applause with little evidence of the cacophonous volume that initially outraged English critics. As the only harmonic support behind Waters's voice and guitar, Spann, despite the poor recording quality, is heard with full creative force, his right hand delivering trademark syncopated runs and trills.

Back In Chicago, Spann continued to record with Waters, producing such Chess sides as the 1959 cut "Mean Mistreater." During the same year, Spann and guitarist Robert Junior Lockwood backed Sonny Boy (Rice Miller) Williamson for his Chess releases "Let Your Conscience be Your Guide" and "Cool Disposition." Though a strong vocalist possessing a soothing whiskey-soaked voice as well as a gifted pianist, Spann was overlooked by the Chess brothers as a potential solo artist. It wasn't until 1960 that Spann, joined by Junior Lockwood, recorded his first major solo work, *Otis Spann is the Blues*, on the Candid label. As Mike Rowe noted in *The Blackwell Guide*, the album emerged as "the definitive postwar piano solo album for a small jazz label...with blues piano playing and singing of the highest order." During the same year, English researcher and scholar Paul Oliver recorded two numbers by Spann, "Peoples Calls Me Lucky" and Friday Ford's "Poor Country Boy," which appeared on the Decca LP *Conversation With the Blues*.

Considered Boogie-Woogie Master

Spann's performance on his 1960 cut "This is The Blues" was described by Peter J. Silvester in *A Left Hand Like God* as "an impressive tour de force, using a variety of boogie-woogie bass figures against a scintillating and dazzling display of pyrotechnics in the right hand (which, however, rely heavily on repeated chords with crashing force). Some may regard this piece—not without just foundation—as the ultimate development of the boogie-woogie piano; others may consider that the 'modernity' of its musical language and style place it beyond the confines of the boogie-woogie idiom."

During the same year, Spann displayed his talents with the Muddy Waters band at the 1960 Newport Jazz Festival. Appearing at the Sunday afternoon blues program of the festival—a performance later released as the now-classic Chess album *Muddy Waters at Newport*—Spann joined Waters and bandmembers drummer Francis Clay and bassist Andrew Stevenson for a set which featured a rousing version of "Got My Mojo Working." For the show Spann contributed one vocal number "Goodbye Newport Blues," a slow blues written by African American poet Langston Hughes which lamented the Newport City Council's decision to cancel

the concert series, after a Saturday night riotous crowd attempted to gain entrance to the sold-out festival.

In 1962 Spann provided the piano accompaniment for several of Buddy Guy's Chess sides including "First Time I Met The Blues" and "Stone Crazy." In the following year, while on tour in London with the Muddy Waters band, he recorded with Waters's unit and several guest horn players for the solo effort *The Blues of Otis Spann*. While in Europe he also attended a Copenhagen recording session with Sonny Boy Williamson. Spann then released the 1965 Prestige solo album which featured Waters under the alias "Dirty Rivers."

Continues as a Force in Chicago Scene

The prominence of Spann's talent in the Chicago scene was celebrated on the Vanguard label's 1966 blues series, *Chicago/The Blues Today! Vol. I*. One of the featured artists on the album, Spann performed in duo setting with drummer S.P. Leary. In his original review of the album for *Jazz* magazine, John F. Szwed commented, "Spann's full-handed piano approach is in great tradition of classic blues pianists the easy rolling beat, the surprising flights of the right hand—and one is fooled into believing that a four piece band is backing him." On the second volume of the Vanguard's series, Spann, along with guitarist J. Madison, and drummer S.P. Leary, comprised the "Jimmy Cotton Blues Quartet." The session produced a fine rendition of Cotton's 1954 Sun recording "Cotton Crop Blues" and a remake of Jackie Brenston's 1951 Sun hit "Rocket 88."

With the Muddy Waters band, Spann backed John Lee Hooker for the 1966 LP *Live at the Cafe Au-Go-Go*. Recalling the collaboration Hooker stated, as quoted in *Blues Guitar*, "I really enjoyed when we did the *Cafe Au-Go-Go* in New York, me and Otis Spann and Muddy Waters. Otis was one of the greatest piano players of the blues ever...A good man, too. Loyal, friendly, no ego...just a perfect gentlemen." Inspired by Hooker's *Cafe' Au-Go-Go* album, Bluesway invited Spann to record his 1966 solo album, *The Blues is Where it's At*. Recorded in front of a live studio audience and backed by the Muddy Waters band, the album captured many fine moments, especially the opening number, "Popcorn Man," written by Waters.

In 1967 Spann married singer Lucille Jenkins and featured her, along with the Muddy Waters band, on the Bluesway LP *The Bottom of the Blues*. That same year, he recorded with the Waters band for the Muse album *Muddy Waters/Mud In Your Ear* and Buddy Guy's Vanguard release, *A Man and The Blues*. In 1969 Spann performed on Muddy Waters's half-studio and half-live double-album, *Fathers and Sons,* a critically acclaimed recording which showcases Spann, the fine harmonica of Paul Butterfield, and guitarist Michael Bloomfield.

Spann left the Waters band in 1969 and released his Vanguard solo album *Cryin' Time,* backed by the gifted Chicago blues guitarist Luther Tucker, who was relegated to playing rhythm guitar, leaving the lead guitar work to Barry Melton of the rock group Country Joe and the Fish. Spann also guested on the 1969 all star blues LP *Super Black Blues* and toured the college circuit and various nightclub venues with his wife Lucille. That same year saw the release of Spann's album *Cracked Spanner Head*—with vocal material culled from the album *The Blues of Otis Spann*—complete with pseudo-abstract cover art intended to promote sales among the psychedelic rock audience.

Recorded Final Album in 1970

In 1970 Spann took part in his last recording session for Junior Wells's Delmark LP *South Side Blues Jam,* which captured Spann, Wells, and Buddy Guy in a relaxed afterhours atmosphere. Spann was responsible for selecting several of the album's traditional cover songs, and his rolling piano work added drive and intensity to such numbers as Wells's rendition of Robert Johnson's "Stop Breaking Down" and the Waters hit "I Just Want to Make Love to You." In the early spring of 1970, writer and music researcher Peter Guralnick visited Spann's Chicago apartment and found the pianist in good spirits, but extremely underweight with a "painfully emaciated face." A few weeks later, Spann entered Cook County Hospital where he died of cancer on April 24, 1970. Scheduled to play the 1970 Ann Arbor Blues Festival, Spann received a posthumous tribute by the event's organizers who renamed the festival site "Otis Spann Memorial Field."

A decade after his death, Spann was inducted into the Blues Hall of Fame. Musicians and critics alike have continued to hail Spann's piano talent. In the late 1960s Muddy Waters told Sheldon Harris, in *Jazz Journal,* that he considered Otis Spann "the best blues piano player we have today. There is no one left like him who plays the real, solid, bottom blues." Samuel Charters, in his liner notes to *Chicago/The Blues Today!,* stated that Spann "without argument or qualification, is one of the greatest blues piano men who ever lived." In an age dominated by guitarists and harmonica soloists dependent on excessive volume, Spann's thundering piano style, with its vibrant expression and articulate attack, represents a vital contribution in the shaping of postwar Chicago blues.

Selected discography

Otis Spann/Lightin' Hopkins Sessions, Mosaic.
Otis Spann is the Blues, Candid, 1960.
The Blues Never Dies, Prestige.
Chicago/The Blues/ Today! Vol. 1, Vanguard, 1966.
Otis Spann's Chicago Blues, Testament.
The Blues Is Where It's At, Bluesway.
The Bottom of the Blues, Bluesway.
Cryin' Time, Vanguard, 1969.
The Greatest Thing Since Collosus (with Fleetwood Mac), Blue Horizon.
Raw Blues, London.
Down to Earth, The Bluesway Recordings, MCA, 1995.

With others

Muddy Waters, *Live at Newport,* 1960, Chess.
Muddy Waters, *Chess Box,* Chess.
Muddy Waters, *Sail On,* Chess.
Muddy Waters, *Trouble No More, Singles 1955-1959,* Chess, 1989.
Muddy Waters, *Rare and Unissued,* Chess, 1991.
Muddy Waters, *Mud in Your Ear,* Muse.
Howlin' Wolf, *Real Folk Blues,* Chess, 1967.
Howlin' Wolf, *Chess Blues Masters Series,* Chess, 1972.
Chuck Berry, *The Great Twenty-Eight,* Chess, 1984.
Buddy Guy, *I Was Walking through the Woods,* Chess.
Buddy Guy, *A Man and the Blues,* Vanguard.
Sonny Boy Williamson, *One Way Out,* Chess, 1984.
Sonny Boy Williamson, *Final Sessions 1963-1964,* Blue Night.
John Lee Hooker, *Live at the Cafe' Au Go-Go,* Bluesway.
Johnny Young and His Chicago Blues Band, Arhoolie.
Junior Wells, *Blues Hit Big Town,* Delmark.
Junior Wells, *Southside Blues Jam,* Delmark, 1970.

Compilations

Conversation with The Blues, Decca, 1960.
The Story of the Blues, Columbia.
The Great Bluesmen, Vanguard.
The Best Of Chicago Blues, Vanguard.
The Blues Guitar Box 2, Sequel.

Sources

Books

The Blackwell Guide, edited by Paul Oliver, Blackwell Reference, 1989.
Blues Guitar: The Man Who Made the Music from the Pages of Guitar Player Magazine, Miller Freeman Books, 1993.
Cohn, Lawrence, *Nothing but the Blues,* Abbeville Press, 1993.
Guralnick, Peter, *Lost Highway: Journeys and Arrivals of*

American Musicians, Harper & Row, 1979.

Oliver, Paul, *Conversation with the Blues,* Horizon Press, 1965.

Rowe, Mike, *Chicago Blues, The City and the Music,* Da Capo, 1975.

Silvester, Peter J., *A Left Hand Like God,* Da Capo, 1988.

Periodicals

Jazz, October 1966.

Jazz Journal, March, 1968.

—*John Cohassey*

Sparks

Rock band

MICHAEL OCHS ARCHIVES/Venice, CA

Sparks, a quirky rock band consisting mainly of brothers Ron and Russell Mael, have found popularity overseas by consistently creating clever, satirical, and often catchy songs since their debut in the early 1970s. Despite some early success, however, the U.S. charts and critics remained more or less indifferent to the duo over the next several decades, regardless of their international fame.

Brothers Ron and Russell Mael were born in southern California and began their careers in show business at an early age. At their mother's urging, both modeled for clothing catalogs for over a year as teenagers. Their combined artistic talents found a musical outlet in 1970, when the brothers and some friends from school formed the band Halfnelson, with Ron writing the songs and playing keyboards and Russell providing vocals. While studying graphic design, literature, and film at UCLA, the group recorded a demo tape and presented it to every major and minor record label, only to be met with indifference. A friend then mailed one of their tapes to rock artist Todd Rundgren, who had just recently began to explore music from the production side. Rundgren was sufficiently impressed to agree to go to Los Angeles to produce Halfnelson's first album.

From a Cardboard Box to a Top Ten Hit

The band's formative years were characterized by rough-edged guitar and primitive instrumentation. Ron Mael described some of their early percussive effects to *Melody Maker:* "We used to beat on cardboard boxes with reverb on and run it through amps." Their first album was completed in 1972, but was virtually ignored until their label recommended that they change their name and put a photo of the band members on the cover. Thus Sparks were born. Sparks included the Billboard U.S. top ten hit "Wondergirl," and the band was invited to perform on American Bandstand to promote the single. Unfortunately, American audiences were disinterested with their 1973 follow-up *A Woofer in Tweeter's Clothing,* so, at their label's urging, Sparks traveled to Europe.

The band embarked on a whirlwind tour of England, France, Germany, and Switzerland, where they were met with open arms. The visit left an indelible mark, and Sparks would eventually find that their unique sound could only find true success in the open-minded European market. Following the tour some of the original band members moved on to new projects, and Sparks became simply Ron and Russell backed by different set musicians for each album. In 1974 the duo signed with Island Records and released *Kimono My House* and

For the Record . . .

Members include **Ron Mael,** born August 12, 1948, in Culver City, CA; and **Russell Mael,** born October, 1953, in Santa Monica, CA.

First album as Halfnelson produced by Todd Rundgren, 1971; released U.S. Top Ten hit "Wonder-girl" and were invited to perform on *American Bandstand,* 1972; embarked on a whirlwind tour of England, France, Germany, and Switzerland, where they attracted a considerable following, 1973; signed with Island Records and released *Kimono My House* and *Propaganda,* the first of many albums to become hits in Europe but little notice in the U.S.; released *No. 1 in Heaven,* an album often credited with having planted the seed for the New Wave sound of the 1980s, 1979; began a trend toward New Wave, dance-oriented tunes, 1980s; reemerged in Europe with *Gratuitous Sax and Senseless Violins,* 1994.

Addresses: *Fan club*—Sparks International Fan Club, P.O. Box 25038, Los Angeles, CA, 90025; *Management*—D.E.F., P.O. Box 2477, London NW6 6NQ, England.

Propaganda, produced by Muff Winwood (brother of Steve). In a pattern that repeated itself throughout their career, both albums became hits in Europe but barely received notice in the U.S. Sparks were beginning to develop a cult American following, however, that would remain devoted to them over the years.

Quirky Songs Did Not Lead to Airplay

The band's lack of recognition in the U.S. may have been attributable to Sparks often off-the-wall lyrics and Russell's falsetto, which, when combined with traditional rock instrumentation, was too unusual for American tastes. Songs like "Talent Is An Asset," which viewed Albert Einstein's genius from the vantage point of his overbearing relatives, or "Reinforcements," a love song in the guise of military maneuvers, were BBC favorites but never received airplay in Sparks' home country.

Undaunted by American critics, Sparks went on to release *Indiscreet* (1975) and *Big Beat* (1976), both of which featured a sound that predicted the widespread use of keyboards and drum machines. They had hoped that the more straightforward *Big Beat* would be more accessible for American audiences, but their appear-

ances on BBC's "Top of the Pops" still vastly outnumbered those on U.S. radio. Russell later opined to *Melody Maker:* "You need the sledgehammer approach here (in the U.S.) and people had to think a little too much about what Sparks were doing....The quaintness was really acceptable in England,...[where] that charming sound was what people came to expect from us."

At each stage of their development the Maels found themselves on the forefront of the next big pop trend. In the late 1970s, after hearing a disco album produced by Giorgio Morodor, they recruited his assistance for 1979's *No. 1 in Heaven.* One of the first albums to utilize synthesizers to create a dance beat, *No. 1 in Heaven* is often credited with having planted the seed for the New Wave sound of the 1980s and arguably influenced groups such as Depeche Mode, the Pet Shop Boys, Erasure, and Morrissey. Although some in the British press decried the band for converting to disco, their public still loved such quirky, catchy tunes as "Beat the Clock" and the album's title track, which both hit the charts immediately.

Finally Get Critical Recognition in U.S.

The next decade of Sparks's career was characterized by a feverish pace of releases. 1980's *Terminal Jive* (featuring the No. 1 French hit "When I'm With You") and 1981's *Whomp That Sucker* finally created a stir amongst U.S. critics. New songs like "Tips for Teens" ("Soon, you will lose all your zits/Tight sweaters no longer fit") garnered the band a reappearance on American Bandstand, and even one *Rolling Stone* reviewer sent a wake up call: "These guys should be someone's heroes by now.... These borderline wacko cases are probably the most intriguing yin-yang brother duo in rock & roll."

1982's *Angst In My Pants* furthered Sparks' conversion to New Wave dance-oriented tunes and featured some of their most literate and rhythmic songwriting. The hit title track, a classic tale of sexual frustration, is cleverly contrasted with "Sextown U.S.A.," where if "you try to abstain, they'll send you to the prison for the criminally insane." "I Predict" derides the often overzealous tabloids ("Lassie will prove that Elvis and her/Had a fleeting affair") and "Moustache" profiles Ron's controversial facial hair ("When I trimmed it real small/My Jewish friends would never call"). Their next releases, *Sparks In Outer Space* (1983) and *Pulling Rabbits Out of a Hat* (1984), didn't produce as many hits, but were still well-received in Europe.

By now Ron and Russell were well established as a two-man band, so for *Pulling Rabbits Out Of A Hat* and 1986's *Music That You Can Dance To* the brothers decided to maintain firm control over their recordings by becoming their own producers. They took some of the best elements from their previous albums and produced dance-club hits like "Music That You Can Dance To" and "Modesty Plays," which earned them a place on the hip Fright Night soundtrack. After setting up their own home studio for 1988's Interior Design, the brothers took an extended break before returning in 1994 with Gratuitous Sax and Senseless Violins. The band's reemergence on the music scene was well-received in Europe, where listeners found the trademark Sparks sound still intact in satirical songs like "Now That I Own the BBC" and the self-reflexive "When Do I Get to Sing 'My Way,'" which can be read either as a send-up of Frank Sinatra, or, more significantly, of Sparks themselves.

"When Do I Get to Sing 'My Way'" became the ninth Sparks single to hit the Top 40 overseas. The U.S. continued to elude them, mainly due to their resolve in maintaining the dance-club sound, which was at the time very unpopular with American radio programmers. Still, the British and German press welcomed their return to the music world. Q called Gratuitous Sax and Senseless Violins a "triumph," adding that "this majestically punned collection is further proof of the injustices of their continued lack of commercial success." Melody Maker referred to the album as a "wicked fantasy of revenge for years of unforgivable airplay deprivation" and "a magnificent flight of berserk imagination."

Sparks represent a rarity in the popular music industry. Although they were never successful in their native country, they found immense popularity in Europe and continued to release offbeat, enigmatic albums despite commercial pressures to conform. The duo's tongue-in-cheek lyricism and unfailing ear for hummable melodies have allowed them to survive several decades of record-industry turbulence without sacrificing their commit-ment to themselves or their music. The Mael brothers' imperturbable, self-mocking wit has prevailed over any disappointment they felt regarding their lack of success in the U.S. top 40. As Russell told Attitude in 1994: "We must be the only band to reach their sixteenth album and still be trying to crack it."

Selected discography

(As Halfnelson) Halfnelson, Bearsville, 1971.
Sparks, Bearsville, 1971.
A Woofer in Tweeter's Clothing, Bearsville, 1972.
Kimono My House, Island, 1974.
Propaganda, Island, 1974.
Indiscreet, Island, 1975.
Big Beat, CBS, 1976.
Introducing Sparks, CBS, 1977.
No. 1 in Heaven, Virgin, 1979.
Terminal Jive, Virgin, 1980.
Whomp That Sucker, RCA, 1981.
Angst in My Pants, Atlantic, 1982.
Sparks in Outer Space, Atlantic, 1983.
Pulling Rabbits Out of a Hat, Atlantic, 1984.
Music That You Can Dance To, MCA/Curb, 1986.
Interior Design, Fine Art/Rhino, 1988.
Profile: The Ultimate Sparks Collection, Rhino, 1991.
Gratuitous Sax and Senseless Violins, Logic/Arista, 1994.

Sources

Attitude, November 1994.
Melody Maker, April 13, 1974; June 8, 1974; January 8, 1977; November 27, 1993; March 2, 1996.
Q, October 22, 1994.
Rolling Stone, October 29, 1981.

—Debra Power

Sponge

Rock band

AP/Wide World Photos

It's a classic music industry tale: musicians who have been struggling for years at success in the business are suddenly "discovered" and considered an "overnight sensation." "This doesn't feel like an overnight sensation to me," Vinnie Dombroski told *Rolling Stone.* Dombroski is the front man for the band Sponge, who exploded onto the music scene in 1994 with their debut album *Rotting Piñata.* The five members of Sponge have worked hard to find their place in the spotlight and know that in this fickle world they could just be a flash in the pan. However, they plan to be much more than that.

Sponge hails from Detroit, Michigan, a city that for a while bred many star musicians. But as Dombroski explained in *Circus,* "There's a real lack of opportunity [in Detroit]. Because of that people turn to music as a form of sustenance." That's exactly what all of the members of Sponge did starting in the mid 1980s. Growing up in the same working-class area, they've known each other most of their lives, although they played in different bands on the local scene.

As a band, Sponge's roots go back to the late 1980s when the Cross brothers—Mike on guitar, Tim on bass—and Dombroski, on drums, were in a band called Loudhouse. "The music was nothing like what we're doing now," Tim told *Addicted to Noise*'s Gillian G. Gaar. "It was a lot heavier, a lot more obscure; we were springing off in different directions trying to find ourselves. But we just never did."

Rose from the Ashes of Loudhouse

Loudhouse signed with Virgin Records in the early 1990s, but was dropped from the label after only one album. "That was five years of hard work," Dombroski told Steve Appleford of *Rolling Stone.* And Tim admitted to Gaar, "That was a pretty low point in my life." Loudhouse gave it one more try, going back into the studio to record an album, but they disbanded before it was far off the ground.

Sponge guitarist Joey Mazzola, also a Detroit native, spent five of the hardest years of his life on the Los Angeles club circuit. When he decided to return home he hooked up with Dombroksi, with whom he had played earlier in his career. Almost a year after the Loudhouse breakup, around the end of 1992, Mazzola sat in on a jam session above a Detroit drugstore with Dombroski and the Cross brothers. The four clicked and Sponge was formed. Since Sponge had already formed before actually finding a singer, Dombroksi filled in at the mike temporarily. "And to my and my brother's amazement, and to Joey's as well," Tim enthused to

For the Record . . .

Members include **Mike Cross** (born in Detroit, MI), guitar; **Tim Cross** (born in Detroit), bass; **Vinnie Dombroski** (born in Detroit, 1962), vocals; **Charlie Grover** (born in Detroit, December 1967; joined band, 1995), drums; **Joey Mazzola** (born in Detroit, c. 1962); and **Jimmy Paluzzi** (left band, 1995), drums.

Band formed in Detroit, MI, c. 1993; signed with Columbia Records, 1993; released *Rotting Piñata*, 1994.

Addresses: *Record company*—Columbia Records, 2100 Colorado Ave., Santa Monica, CA 90404.

Gaar, "it was like, 'Man, this guy sounds great! We don't need to look for a singer, let's look for a drummer!'"

Drummer Jimmy Paluzzi was added to the line up and the band began sending out their demo. Record labels were immediately interested. By October of 1993 Sponge was recording *Rotting Piñata*, although they didn't even ink their deal with Columbia Records until December of 1993—the label was so enthusiastic about the band, they fronted the money for recording before plans were final.

Buzz Built

Rotting Piñata was released in 1994. Their first single, "Plowed," caught on very quickly. MTV put the video for the song in their "Buzz Bin"—videos by new artists whom the cable network finds worthy of developing a "buzz" for. Popularity formed on the basis of that video, making the song a top track on Alternative and Album Oriented Rock (AOR) radio. The single "Molly" soon followed, and the album eventually went platinum. They had a relentless touring schedule in support of *Rotting Piñata*, which delayed their follow-up album until 1996.

However, by that time, drummer Jimmy Paluzzi had been replaced by another Detroit native, Charlie Grover. As the young band's style began maturing during constant touring, it became apparent that Paluzzi's style was no longer in sync with the band's. Grover, who blended in more smoothly, joined Sponge in early 1995.

The 1996 album *Wax Ecstatic* "was going to be this whole concept through song of the experiences of this fictitious type of character," Dombroski told *Circus*'s Vinnie Penn. It was to have a "Memphis-type slant, a la old Stax Records, Memphis-sounding R & B, Al Green meets Ziggy Stardust." The band eventually abandoned the project, deciding it was too confining. Several of the songs did remain, however, placed among an entirely new set of tunes.

Sophomore Effort Praised

Rolling Stone's Jon Wiederhorn noted that, with *Wax Ecstatic*, "the group is making an effort to shatter the grim-faced grunge image that shoe-horned Sponge into the same category as acts like Bush, Everclear and the Verve Pipe...the music is more daring and mature this time." And *RIP*'s Tom Lanham wrote, judging by *Wax Ecstatic*, "The pop strategies of *Rotting Piñata*...won't prepare listeners for the sheer sonic delight of this sophomore disc."

With all the praise from critics, however, *Wax Ecstatic* did not explode among fans as Sponge's first album had. But even with *Rotting Piñata* selling so well, and long before the release of *Wax Ecstatic*, the band knew that big labels count numbers. As Dombroski told Gaar, "Well, make no mistakes. We need to sell more records."

Sponge would just like to keep making music until they're old men. Dombroski confided in *Music Connection*, "I don't want to give off the impression that I think that we've made it.... We've come a long way, but we've got a long way to go." But Sponge does have confidence in their abilities. Dombroski went on to say, "I think that whatever this business can do with us, wherever it'll take us, it'll all happen as long as we've got the tunes. And we have got the tunes!"

Selected discography

Rotting Piñata (includes "Plowed" and "Molly"), Work Group/ Columbia Records, 1994.
Wax Ecstatic, Work Group/Columbia Records, 1996.

Sources

Addicted to Noise, October 1995.
Circus, September 1996.
iMagazine, 1996.
Music Connection, May 29, 1995.
RIP, August 1996.
Rolling Stone, April 20, 1995; September 5, 1996.

Additional material for this profile was obtained from Columbia Records press materials, 1996, and from the World Wide Web.

—*Joanna Rubiner*

Stereolab

Pop band

Stereolab singer Laetitia Sadier told *Pulse!:* "We're a pop band in the sense that being pop is about knowing how to steal from the past and bring your own personality and ideas into it." Stereolab established itself as a cult favorite, partly because the band "stole" from an eclectic combination of largely ignored musical forms. But while other acts that share their passion for "Space-Age Bachelor Pad Music," easy listening, and other previously debased styles—mostly from the 1950s and '60s—Stereolab have refused to indulge in camp. Instead, they have taken the adventurous thread of such recordings and followed it into new sonic territory. Meanwhile, Sadier's lyrics have explored political and social issues with a surrealist's sense of poetry. "The whole effect is one of a shiny silver bubble," ventured Kathy Mancall in *Addicted to Noise*, "an erotically charged Jetsonian 60s vision of the future."

The band began in 1988, when Sadier met British guitarist-songwriter Tim Gane in Paris. Gane, then a member of the moody pop band McCarthy, used some translated lyrics of Sadier's on his band's final album, and the two were both musically and romantically involved shortly thereafter. By 1991 they formed Stereolab, which took its name from a record company of the "hi-fi" era that specialized in recordings designed to exploit the sonic capabilities of stereo equipment. Gane and Sadier also created their own label, Duophonic. Fascinated by the inventive, atmospheric recordings of such composers as Juan Esquivel and Martin Denny,

who fused "exotic," symphonic, and avant-garde textures as well as such pop innovators as Brian Wilson of the Beach Boys, Stereolab began searching for new sounds.

"A Bit of Spillage"

The group's approach leaned heavily on out-of-date keyboards, especially old organs. Gane and company took the already spooky tone of such vintage gear and further modified it with other musical effects. "That roughed-up organ, put through an amp and distorted—I don't know why, but I'm always attracted to that kind of sound," Gane told the *Los Angeles Times.* "I don't like things too clean. I like a bit of spillage." Sadier noted to the newspaper's Lorraine Ali that the ensemble "didn't look for that particular sound, we kind of stumbled on it. We happened to find this Farfisa organ, a great big plastic thing from the '70s, in a thrift shop," she added. The sound of this organ—generally considered "cheesy" since its long-vanished heyday--appealed strongly to the Stereolab sensibility. "This incredible, heavy, compressed and loaded sound was like a huge shaver—Whaaah!" Sadier elaborated. "That's just something you can't premeditate."

With a shifting crew of personnel that has included vocalist-guitarist Mary Hansen, bassist Duncan Brown, drummer Andy Ramsay, keyboardist-singer Katharine Gifford, multi-instrumentalist Sean O'Hagan, and a score of guest performers, Stereolab began constructing their idiosyncratic sound. "Basically, Tim writes the music on a 4-track (tape machine) and gets a very thin, sort of skeleton of a song," Sadier noted of their approach in *Grip.* "And I write some lyrics on top of that, and then we have the bones of the song. And then we either take time to practice it and then take to the studio, or we go straight to the studio and bring flesh to it there. Basically, when we record we've not really worn the songs in, it's really the birth of them."

Rode "Elevator Music" to Major Label

After a couple of indie releases began to generate a cult following, Stereolab were signed to Elektra Records. Their major-label debut, *Transient Random-Noise Bursts with Announcements,* stunned critics and suggested that the group's ambitions were expanding. Sadier recalled in *Pulse!* that the album "was a nightmare to record--even talking about it brings a pain to my stomach." Yet by the time of 1994's follow-up, *Mars Audiac Quintet,* she added, Stereolab "were much more in control. You always need to f--- up somewhere to then be able to do something that's right."

At the time of the *Mars* release, Gane outlined some of his musical preferences to Lorraine Ali of the *Los Angeles Times.* "I like music made for utilitarian reasons, like elevator music," he asserted. "You can take it out of its original purpose, then it's just strange and very avant-garde. It's like an odd little art world, but the people who made that music didn't think it was strange at the time." In *Addicted to Noise,* he argued that "People are ready to look for something else [besides] mainstream rock music, and trying to find something for themselves, taking a chance and finding things that aren't forced down your throat." Ali of the *Los Angeles Times* characterized the group's work as "easy-listening music for a generation raised on [alternative noise-rockers] Sonic Youth." This proved accurate; Stereolab toured on the second stage of the traveling alternative music festival Lollapalooza. Yet such widespread exposure didn't prevent them from providing music for an art exhibit by a little-known sculptor, Charles Long.

Rather than exploit the kitsch value of "hi-fi" eccentrics like Esquivel, Denny, Les Baxter, and others—as a burgeoning circle of indie "lounge" bands had done—Stereolab took their influences seriously. "There's

supposedly a trashy quality to it," Sadier told *Pulse!,* "but to us it actually means a lot. We don't feel it's kitsch. Some of these records are actually really good, with good music and ideas. Things that take you somewhere. These records were looking into the future with enthusiasm and great hope, and we like to look at the future that way."

Lyrics Have Sociopolitical Content

Meanwhile, over sonic collages inspired by such eclectic sources, Sadier wrote lyrics—in French and English—of social confusion and loss. She was nonetheless bemused that critics persisted in labeling her a Marxist. However, her questioning stance did suggest a politically subversive agenda. "I'm not coming up with answers," she claimed in *Strobe,* "but surely there are answers to our problems. After having asked all the right questions, you'll want to take action. It's up to us, there's no big written solution, there's no God, and no ideologies either. There's only ourselves that we can rely on."

Stereolab expanded its following considerably with its subsequent releases, especially the much-praised *Emperor Tomato Ketchup.* Newly inspired by European progressive rock and the avant-jazz of Sun Ra and Don Cherry, the group once again explored new sonic territory. "The new songs are similar to what we always do with repetition and minimalism," Gane told *Newsday.* "But this time I wanted them to be bouncy, more rubbery. I wanted to have more of a swing." *Musician* deemed *Emperor* "extraordinary," while England's *Melody Maker* called it "bloody essential." *Entertainment Weekly* proclaimed that "They may be influenced by obscure German groups, they may sing partially in French, but Stereolab's kitsch pop is enjoyable even without a foreign language degree."

Selected discography

Switched On Stereolab, Too Pure, 1992.
Peng!, Too Pure, 1992.
The Groop Played Space Age Bachelor Pad Music, Too Pure, 1993.
Transient Random-Noise Bursts with Announcements, Elektra, 1993.
Mars Audiac Quintet, Elektra, 1994.
Refried Ectoplasm, Duophonic, 1995.
Emperor Tomato Ketchup, Elektra, 1996.

Sources

Addicted to Noise, June 1996.
College Music Journal (CMJ), April 1996.

Grip, June 1996.

Los Angeles Times, August 6, 1994; April 24, 1996; April 27, 1996.

Melody Maker, March 16, 1996.

Musician, June 1996.

Newsday, May 20, 1996.

Option, July 1993.

Pitchfork, June 1996.

Progressive, July 1, 1996.

Pulse!, September 1994.

Spin, August 1996.

Strobe, September 1994.

—*Simon Glickman*

Syd Straw

Singer, songwriter

AP/Wide World Photos

Jim DeRogatis in *Rolling Stone* described Syd Straw's voice as "alternately soaring and angelic, and gruff and gravelly." To Steve Rosen of the *Denver Post,* "Her voice is forceful and dynamic with a self-assured twang," while *Interview* waxed rhapsodic about her "honey-suckle of a voice." Despite such accolades, Straw has remained mostly in the pop background. A rootsy singer-songwriter, she has released two albums to critical acclaim but little mainstream success; most of the recognition she's earned has been for her work with other artists. Nonetheless, she noted in several interviews that she felt she'd grown, both musically and emotionally, in a satisfying direction. "My life is a lot like some weird movie," she quipped in her Capricorn Records biography. "Boy, would I hate to have to edit it!"

She was born to actor parents in Vermont; after they divorced, she moved with her mother to Los Angeles. She sang in her high school choir. "I would be quite welcome in all the little cliques and clubs," she recalled to *Rolling Stone*'s DeRogatis. "I didn't really join all the clubs, but when people were having their school yearbook pictures taken, the track and field team, or the chess club or whatever would always wave me over to get in the picture. It's kind of like that with my music," she added wryly, referring to her longtime status as everyone's favorite guest artist.

Landed Gig with Pat Benatar

Her upbringing, she stated in the *Denver Post,* prepared Straw for her nomadic adulthood. "I could say that, as a reflection of the chaos that happened in our family when I was growing up, I think I got used to a lack of security," she told Rosen. Poor scores on her SAT's—which, DeRogatis reported, she took while stoned—frustrated her hopes of attending college. Therefore, she headed for New York, arriving there "during a weird transitional period in 1978," as she put it in her Capricorn bio. "I didn't know anyone or where anything was happening, so I just hung around at open-mike nights or out-of-the-way comedy clubs and bars. My first musical job was singing harmonies for Pat Benatar."

And it was behind Benatar, who became a pop superstar over the next several years, that she found herself providing "whoa-hoos," as she told Brett Milano of the *Boston Phoenix,* in a reggae version of Led Zeppelin's classic rock anthem "Stairway to Heaven." Straw admitted to Milano that she "felt a little funky about that, because I wasn't sure it was the right way to do that song. She'd be up there with her leather spandex sequined outfits. And I was the back-up chick in the washed-out jeans, standing there going 'whoa-hoo.'"

For the Record . . .

Born c. 1958 in Vermont; grew up in Los Angeles; married c. 1993 (divorced).

Singer, songwriter, actress, 1978—. Worked as backup singer for singer Pat Benatar, c. late 1970s; member of group Golden Palominos, 1984-87; appeared as guest artist on recordings by Van Dyke Parks, Evan Dando, Phranc, Rickie Lee Jones, Freedy Johnston, Richard Thompson, Leo Kottke, Loudon Wainwright III, Vic Chesnutt, James McMurtry, Dave Alvin, and others, 1984–; contributed to soundtrack of film *Heathers,* 1989; signed with Virgin Records and released debut album, *Surprise,* 1989; appeared on television series *Tales of the City,* 1993, and *The Adventures of Pete and Pete,* c. 1990s; produced album *It Must Have Been Something I Said* by comedian-songwriter Harry Shearer, 1994; signed with Capricorn Records and released album *War and Peace,* 1996; contributed song "People of Earth" to *Party of Five* television soundtrack, 1996.

Addresses: *Home*—Chicago, IL. *Record company*—Capricorn Records, 2205 State St., Nashville, TN 37203. *Internet*—Syd Straw Fan Page: ourworld.compuserve. com/homepages/gregoryp/syds.htm#.

others. At last, in 1989, she released a solo recording for Virgin Records. The album, *Surprise,* featured an all-star supporting cast, including Stipe, Thompson, Parks, John Doe of X, Marshall Crenshaw, Dave Alvin, Daniel Lanois, Ry Cooder, and Palomino alums Fier, Jody Harris and Bernie Worrell. Recorded over a year in a variety of studios, the album was, Straw joked to DeRogatis, "an excuse to travel all over the world and visit people, and I called it a record." Critics were kinder to the mix of collaborative originals and well-chosen cover tunes on *Surprise*—Ray Rogers of *Interview* called it "dazzling," and *Entertainment Weekly'*s Tony Scherman dubbed it a "first-rate debut"—but it sold poorly. Bill Wyman, a columnist for the Internet music site *Addicted to Noise,* described Straw's debut as "one of the buried classics of the pre-Alternative era."

Hoping to compensate for this disappointment with her next record, Straw asked producers to work with her, but found the process rather lengthy. Virgin, concerned about another potential commercial failure, began to convey what the singer characterized to Wyman as "ideas that didn't have anything to do with the record I wanted to make." She eventually left the label, focusing on guest spots and the occasional acting job. She appeared in the PBS miniseries *Tales of the City,* and appeared as the math teacher, Miss Fingerwood, on the acclaimed kids' program *The Adventures of Pete and Pete.* "That was a nice job," she recollected of the latter in her interview with DeRogatis, "because the producers said to the director, 'For the role of the math teacher, we want someone just like Syd Straw.' I didn't even have to audition, which is my favorite way to win work."

Recorded Follow-Up with Skeletons

Straw then entered a difficult period. She continued to write songs without a record deal, the advantage of which, she told the *Los Angeles Times,* was that "You can just do whatever you want. It's kind of fun." Yet without a contract, she was unable to make her own records. She also experienced a short-lived marriage in Athens, Georgia. But a new relationship and relocation to Chicago lifted Straw's spirits. She eventually decided to make a record with the Missouri band Skeletons, whose accompaniment brought just the right energy to her compositions. "It's a record that I spent six years thinking about and just about a month to make," she said in her record company bio.

The result was *War and Peace,* which was released by Capricorn in 1996. Straw, who had continued to enjoy the admiration of critics, earned some glowing notices for the album. David Okamoto of the *Dallas Morning News* hailed it as "a resilient country-rock concept

More dignified work followed, notably a collaboration with pop innovator Van Dyke Parks, who has been a longtime supporter of Straw's. But it was making the acquaintance of cutting-edge drummer and bandleader Anton Fier that set the course for much of her work during the 1980s. Fier led the collective known as the Golden Palominos, a rotating crew of artists from all ends of the pop world eager for a collaborative, experimental side project. Straw sang on two of the group's albums, providing distinctive lead work and backing up such guest Palominos as ex-Cream bassist Jack Bruce, R.E.M.'s Michael Stipe, and acclaimed singer-songwriters Matthew Sweet and T-Bone Burnett. "The coolest thing that came out of my time with the Palominos was a desire to begin writing my own songs," she related in her Capricorn bio. "For the first time, I started thinking of myself as a writer, and not just an interpreter."

Backup Work, Solo Debut

Straw worked steadily as a background singer, and has appeared on recordings by Richard Thompson, Rickie Lee Jones, Phranc, Leo Kottke, Evan Dando, and many album about doomed relationships and their caustic, but ultimately cathartic, aftershocks." *Entertainment Weekly* reviewer Scherman called it "proof of what she can accomplish when she focuses. The melodies lilt, the band rocks, and Straw's reedy voice is an addictive blend of country warmth and urban jitters."

While her admittedly quirky singing and songwriting did not catapult her to superstardom, Straw summarized her awareness of her strengths to *Boston Phoenix* writer Milano. "Hell, I can tell a story, you know?" she said. "I am trying to be emphatic and empathic and direct and absorbing as I can possibly imagine being." Whatever her fate commercially, Straw seemed guaranteed of a rapt audience for whatever stories she chose to tell.

Selected discography

With the Golden Palominos

Visions of Excess, Celluloid, 1985.
Blast of Silence, Celluloid, 1986.

Solo recordings

Surprise, Virgin, 1989.
War and Peace, Capricorn, 1996.

Other

Chris Stamey and Friends, *Christmas Time* (appears on "Presents, Dear (I'm Always Touched By Your"), ESD, 1986.
"People of Earth," *Party of Five* television soundtrack, Reprise, 1996.

Also appeared on recordings by Van Dyke Parks, Evan Dando, Phranc, Rickie Lee Jones, Freedy Johnston, Richard Thompson, Leo Kottke, Loudon Wainwright III, Vic Chesnutt, James McMurtry, Dave Alvin, and others.

Sources

Boston Phoenix, June 13, 1996.
Dallas Morning News, July 4, 1996.
Denver Post, June 20, 1996.
Entertainment Weekly, May 10, 1996.
Interview, May 1996.
Los Angeles Times, February 23, 1995.
Rolling Stone, May 16, 1996.

Additional information was provided by Capricorn Records publicity materials, the *Addicted to Noise* Internet site, and the Syd Straw Fan Page Internet site.

—*Simon Glickman*

The Subdudes

Rhythm and blues band

The Subdudes's signature sound was always rooted in a gospel-inspired, relaxed R&B rhythm that was ignited by the music of New Orleans. In the decade they were together, their music stretched from simple harmonies to hard-hitting tunes, running the instrumental gamut from tambourine to accordian to mandolin. The band initally developed a cult following in New Orleans and throughout Colorado, then garnered a larger audience through their eclectic albums.

Three of the members grew up in the small sugarcane town of Edgard, Louisiana, while John Magnie hailed from Denver, Colorado. All four migrated to the musical mecca of New Orleans. Malone, Allen, and Amedee began working with bands like Lil' Queenie & The Percolators. Their original band, the Continental Drifters, was formed in 1981 and performed mostly covers in New Orleans bars. The Subdudes emerged there in 1987, taking their name for a gig at Tipitina's. At Magnie's prompting, the group headed to Denver in late 1987, where they played ski resorts and area clubs. They were discovered when they placed second in

© Waring Abbott/MICHAEL OCHS ARCHIVES/Venice, CA

For the Record . . .

Original members include **Johnny Ray Allen** (born in Edgard, Louisiana), bass; **Steve Amedee** (born in Edgard, Louisiana), tambourine and other percussions and vocals; **John Magnie** (born in Denver, Colorado), vocals, accordion, and keyboard; and **Tommy Malone** (born in Edgard, Louisiana), vocals and acoustic/electric/slide guitars.

Group formed in 1987 in New Orleans; signed with Atlantic Records, released first album, *Subdudes*, 1989; signed with High Street Records, 1994; disbanded, 1996.

Addresses: *Record company*—High Street Records, 1540 Broadway, 33rd Floor-Times Square, Dept. 290, New York, NY 10036-4021. *Internet site*—www.the-subdudes.com. *Fan club*—305 W. Magnolia, #217, Ft. Collins, CO 80521.

Musician magazine's "Best Unsigned Band" contest, after which Atlantic Records signed them. Their self-titled debut album was released in 1989.

"Joyous, Sexy, Full-Bodied Songs"

This first recording effort revealed the band's distinctive mix of blues, country, and New Orleans soul. In an age of music reflecting upon issues of the time, the Sub-dudes instead focused on simple, passionate love songs. Elizabeth Wurtzel wrote in *New York* magazine, "...a New Orleans band that creates joyous, sexy, full-bodied songs that are so good, they sound like classics even though they're brand-new." The music indeed stood the test of time, as the album was re-released by High Street Records in 1996.

By the time they released their second album, *Lucky*, the Subdudes had developed a cult following. This 1991 release coincided with their proven success in Colorado. The "Dude-heads" were likened to Deadheads—ardent followers of the band The Grateful Dead—dancing wildly in the front rows at their concerts. The band's sound took a new direction, as drummer Amedee fervently played tambourine. Their move toward a more acoustic performance on *Lucky* was a definite deviation from their earlier electric bar sound. The New Orleans blues was still very much evident, but a stronger country twang and Southern soul rang in their songs as they broke into a genre all their own. Gil Asakawa stated in

Rolling Stone, "*Lucky* was recorded in New Orleans and is imbued with the city's rhythmic pulse, but it defies typecasting. Malone's, Allen's and Magnie's original tunes mix R&B and country, and the best of their efforts sound familiar in the best sense of the word."

Unfortunately, the Subdudes were dropped by Atlantic Records in 1992. However, they remained busy in 1993, touring in Europe with Bonnie Raitt and performing with Steve Winwood on the Traffic tour. That same year, they also recorded with Shawn Colvin.

A Religious Departure

High Street Records, a subsidiary of Windham Hill Records, picked up the Subdudes and released their third album, *Annunciation*, in 1994. The album was named for the street on which it was recorded, specifically at Chez Flames Recordings in New Orleans. In religious terms, the Annunciation refers to the angel Gabriel's proclamation that the Virgin Mary would give birth to the Christ child. In regards to this biblical reference, Adele Sulcas stated in *Rolling Stone*, "The four Subdudes have more modest ambitions, but the album does delve into spiritual territory and does so without, mercifully, a hint of preachiness and with an abundance of high spirits."

This album marked the resurrection of their recording career and took the Subdudes beyond their previous cult status in New Orleans and Colorado. *Annunciation* has also been credited with generating a new celebrity following, including Huey Lewis & The News, Joni Mitchell, Rosanne Cash, and Shawn Colvin.

Guest musicians on *Annunciation* added new depth to the Subdudes' R&B sound. The band was joined by guests Howard Levy on harmonica, harp, and mandolin, Willie "Bootsy" Williams on electric guitar, and David Torkanowsky on crank organ. Alanna Nash wrote in *Stereo Review* that "the playing here is uniformly fine, with affecting slide-guitar work, memorable harmonica solos from guest Howard Levy, and the astonishing tambourine work of Steve Amedee."

Eclecticism

Their next effort, a musically ambitious album titled *Primitive Streak*, was released in 1996. The album's eclecticism reached from the Subdudes' earliest simple sound to a dark and moody beat. Several songs, such as "Sarita" and "Love Somebody," sounded more mainstream, which led to more play on the radio and further popularity outside of their cult following. Lead singer

Tommy Malone said in High Street Records' promotional material, "We cover a wide range on this record.... So I really feel that this album represents some kind of expansion away from that original feel that we had on the first couple of albums. I personally like this more eclectic approach."

Once again, the addition of guest musicians enhances the Subdudes' sound. Bonnie Raitt lent her voice on "Too Soon To Tell," while "fifth Subdude" Willie Williams joined in the music on his Zion Harmonizers. Reminders of New Orleans legend Professor Longhair are evident in the rumba-intoned song "Why Do You Hurt Me So."

The recording session for *Primitive Streak* at the Egyptian Room in New Orleans was preceded by a period of isolation. The band spent a week in a cabin in the picturesque town of Red Feather Lakes in Colorado putting the finishing touches on the album's 13 songs.

Although members of the Subdudes live in different cities, they claimed the magic of their music bridged the geographic gap. Amedee said in a 1996 High Street promotional piece, "We find it a little harder to collaborate now because of where we all live, but whenever we do get together to work on new material, whether it's in New Orleans or Colorado, it just instantly clicks. It's all very intuitive and natural." The distance may have inevitably proven to be too much for the band to endure, however, as the Subdudes disbanded in September of 1996. Things had changed since the times when they lived in two houses on the same block in New Orleans.

Selected discography

Subdudes, Atlantic Records, 1989, reissued, High Street Records, 1996.
Lucky, Atlantic Records, 1991.
Annunciation, High Street Records, 1994.
Primitve Streak, High Street Records, 1996.

Sources

Periodicals

New York, January 8, 1990.
Rolling Stone, June 13, 1991; June 30, 1994.
Stereo Review, October 1994.

Online

Subdudes' Official Internet Site, www.the-subdudes.com, 1997.

Additional information for this profile was obtained from promotional material for the Subdudes' album *Primitive Streak*, released by High Street Records.

—Alison Jones

Big Mama Thornton

Blues singer, instrumentalist

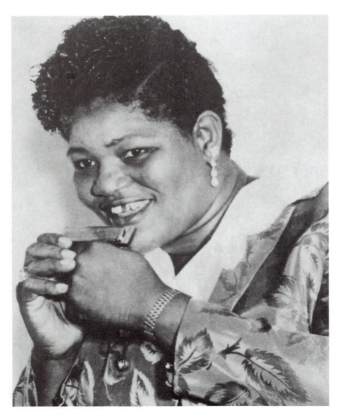

Earning the nickname "Big Mama" because of her broad girth, Willie Mae Thornton continued the tradition of the great female blues singers who made their mark a few decades before their heyday. She was a popular performer on the rhythm-and-blues circuit from the 1950s until her death in 1984 and is best-known for "Ball and Chain," a composition of her own that was also a hit for Janis Joplin. "Her booming voice, sometimes 200-pound frame, and exuberant stage manner had audiences stomping their feet and shouting encouragement in R&B theaters from coast to coast from the early 1950s on," remarked Irwin Stambler in the *Encyclopedia of Pop Rock & Soul.*

Robert Santelli wrote in the *Big Book of Blues* that Thornton "was a direct descendant of such classic blues singers as Ma Rainey, Bessie Smith, and especially Memphis Minnie, the '30s blues woman whose style Thornton's most strongly resembled." Concurring with this opinion in his review of Thornton's *Ball 'N' Chain* album in the *Grove Press Guide to the Blues on CD,* Frank-John Hadley noted, "Willie Mae Thornton, full throated and aggressive, was a gale wind of passion in the fashion of her foremothers Bessie Smith and Ma Rainey." Thornton never received formal training as a singer or musician. "No one taught her how to sing or how to play the harmonica and drums," wrote Chris Strachwitz in the liner notes for *Big Mama Thornton: Ball N' Chain.* "Willie Mae just watched others and tried things."

Hit the Blues Circuit

One of seven children of a minister in Alabama, Thornton sang in church choirs along with her mother as a child. She was forced to begin working at age 14 when her mother died, and got her first chance to sing in public at a saloon where she scrubbed floors after the regular singer quit her job one night. After joining Sammy Green's Hot Harlem Review of Atlanta, Georgia, in 1941, she hit the road on the blues circuit throughout the South. While on tour she was treated to live performances by blues legends such as Bessie Smith, Memphis Minnie, and Big Maceo.

After settling in Houston in 1948, Thornton met Junior Parker, Lightning Hopkins, Lowell Fulson, and Gatemouth Brown, all of whom influenced her style. Her first recording was released in Houston under the name Harlem Stars. Next she signed a contract with the Peacock label and headed to Los Angeles to appear with bandleader Johnny Otis, who was well known on the pop music scene at the time. His tour included famous performers such as Little Esther and Mel Walker. With the Otis band on the Peacock label, Thornton recorded some 30 songs in the early 1950s that were "remarkable for the vocal presence and total cohesiveness," according to Gérard Herzhaft in the *Encyclopedia of Blues*.

Made Reputation with "Hound Dog"

Thornton's big break came in 1953 when, according to Bob Shannon and John Javna in *Behind the Hits*, Johnny Otis asked composers Jerry Lieber and Mike Stoller to write a song especially for Thornton. The song was "Hound Dog," and it climbed to number one on the R&B charts, making Thornton a national star. "They [Lieber and Stoller] were just a couple of kids then and they had this song written on a paper bag," Thornton told a columnist in New York City, claimed Stambler. "So I started to sing the words and join in some of my own. All that talkin' and hollerin'—that's my own." Three years later, the song became a monster hit for Elvis Presley, with an arrangement similar to the original. Thornton always felt that she was cheated out of the success she deserved from "Hound Dog." *The Penguin Encyclopedia of Popular Music* noted that some people thought Thornton rather than Lieber and Stoller should have received credit for writing it. "I never got what I should have," she was quoted as saying by Stambler. "I got one check for $500 and I never seen another."

After "Hound Dog," Thornton kept busy at R&B showcases across the country. She traveled the circuit with friends Junior Parker and Johnny Ace in 1953 and 1954, then with Gatemouth Brown in 1956 before returning to California and taking up residence in Los Angeles the next year. As blues music declined in popularity in the late 1950s, Thornton was no longer in such demand, and she lost her recording contract in 1957. However, she continued to perform, playing drums and harmonica with small bands at local blues clubs in San Francisco. Thornton regained some of her lost limelight in 1961 with "Ball and Chain," which became a modest hit for her. Her star status continued to rise during the 1960s as white audiences began embracing blues music.

Popularity Surged in 1960s

After appearing at the Monterey Jazz Festival in 1964, Thornton toured Europe as part of the American Folk Blues Festival. Her increasing popularity led to a new recording contract in 1965 with the Arhoolie label, an association that lasted into the 1980s. Her first Arhoolie album was recorded in Europe and featured a noteworthy lineup of James Cotton on harmonica, Otis Spann on piano, and Muddy Waters on guitar. Her visibility increased as she performed at Monterey again in 1966 and at various other jazz and blues festivals in the 1960s and 1970s. Her live appearances at two penitentiaries were also recorded In the 1970s.

Years of heavy drinking and hard-living had taken their toll on Thornton by the 1980s. But she continued to perform and remained popular in West Coast clubs up until the end of her life. "Emaciated, unable to remain standing, 'Big Mama' was still impressive with her swing during her last performances on stage," contended Herzhaft. She died of a heart attack in 1984 while living in a Los Angeles boarding house.

Selected compositions

"Ball and Chain."
"Sweet Little Angel."
"I'm Feeling Alright."
"Swing it On Home."

Selected discography

Big Mama Thornton in Europe, Arhoolie, 1965.

Big Mama Thornton with the Chicago Blues Band, Arhoolie, 1967.

Big Mama Thornton: Ball N' Chain, Arhoolie, 1968.

Sassy Mama, Vanguard, 1992.

Sources

Clarke, Donald, editor, *The Penguin Encyclopedia of Popular Music,* Viking, 1989, p. 1163.

Hadley, Frank-John, *The Grove Press Guide to the Blues on CD,* Grove Press, 1993, p. 216.

Herzhaft, Gérard, *Encyclopedia of the Blues,* University of Arkansas Press, 1992, pp. 345–347.

Larkin, Colin, editor, *The Guinness Encyclopedia of Popular Music, Volume 5,* Guinness Publishing, 1992, pp. 4155–4156.

Santelli, Robert, *The Big Book of Blues,* Penguin, 1993, pp. 404–405.

Shannon, Bob and John Javna, *Behind the Hits,* Warner Books, 1986, p. 84.

Sonnier, Austin, Jr., *A Guide to the Blues,* Greenwood Press, 1994, p.205.

Stambler, Irwin, *The Encyclopedia of Pop, Rock & Soul,* St. Martin's Press, 1974, pp. 684–685.

Additional information for this profile was obtained from the liner notes to *Big Mama Thornton: Ball N' Chain,* Arhoolie.

—Ed Decker

Ali Farka Toure

Singer, guitarist

© Denise Sofranko/MICHAEL OCHS ARCHIVES/Venice, CA

Malian guitarist Ali Farka Toure has often been referred to as a missing link between the blues and traditional music of West Africa. While Toure's guitar playing and singing have elements in common with both the blues and traditional African music, that statement is an oversimplification.

Ali Farka Toure is actually a mechanic by profession and considers his music secondary. While blues may be a solid foundation for Toure, he has forged a style all his own. Reviewing his album, *The Source, Sing Out!* stated that "his right-hand patterns would drive even the most accomplished bluesman screaming into the night and he seems less interested in singing about rambling, gambling, and fooling around than in chronicling the construction of a new irrigation system for the village of Dofana (a project that took him off the road and out of the studio for more than a year)."

"The Sky Opens Up"

Toure is a native of Niafenke, a small village in a remote region of Northern Mali. The first instrument he learned to play as a child was the single-stringed gurkel, a gourd covered with cowhide and fitted with a neck and rattles. This instrument, which is Toure's favorite, has ritual functions; he told *Guitar Player*, "the sky opens up, and knowledge and power descend on the player." However, he also warned that, "it attacks you fast. If you don't take certain measures, it can even cause mental illness." Toure later taught himself the n'jarka, a single-string fiddle, and began playing the guitar in 1956 after seeing Guinean guitarist Keita Fodeba.

Understanding Ali Farka Toure's music requires an understanding of the differences between his African culture and the culture in which American and European musicians emerge. In some African regions, musical training is passed down from generation to generation among the griots. Author Bill Barlow defines griots as "talented musicians and folklorists designated to be the oral carriers of their people's culture...Griots preserved the history, traditions, and mores of their respective tribes and kinship groups through songs and stories." However, Toure is not a griot, so he is more ambivalent about playing music. He told *Guitar Player* in 1990, "My family weren't griots, so I never got any training. This is a gift I have; God doesn't give everybody the ability to play an instrument. Music is a spiritual thing--the force of sound comes from the spirit."

Ali Farka Toure has been performing primarily in public since the late 1970s, when he backed American blues legend John Lee Hooker on a tour of France. He's had several album releases in Europe before his self-titled American debut. A *Village Voice* article illustrated the difference between the two guitarists' music, "[Toure] doesn't crank out one-chord boogies like his idol. It's as if he merely hints at the possibility before meandering off in other directions." A *Guitar Player* writer eloquently debunked the "missing link" hype with the statement, "While Ali Farka Toure's song point up the shared lineage of the music of the Mississippi Delta and the African savanna, the explanation for these similarities is not nearly as mysterious as some ethnomusicologists would prefer. Toure, like many other Africans, heard [John Lee] Hooker, Ray Charles, Otis Redding, and others on dance-hall jukeboxes."

Cooder and Toure

With his 1992 album *The Source*, Ali Farka Toure began to gain commercial and artistic recognition. It topped the *Billboard* World Music chart for eleven weeks, helped in part by guest appearances from American bluesman Taj Mahal and guitarist Ry Cooder. In a *Billboard* profile, Toure's manager Nick Gold spoke of the logistics involved with recording him. Ali Farka Toure does not have a telephone, so Gold sends faxes to Mali's capital, Bamako, which are helicoptered to Toure's village. As far as getting other musicians, Gold said it was difficult "because the musicians live in various parts of the north of Mali, and travel is not easy. You have to send a messenger out and hope that people will show up."

During a brief American tour in 1994 with Ry Cooder, the rapport between the two guitarists was such that they completed an album together in four days. The result,

Talking Timbuktu, was the 1994 *Down Beat* Critics' Poll's "Beyond Album of the Year" Award. *Sing Out!* praised Cooder's production on the album: "As a producer, Cooder makes few of the mistakes common to this type of venture. He does not try to alter Toure's playing in any way, but takes the songs and builds arrangements around them. And his guitar playing does not intrude."

A Sense of Well-Being

Ry Cooder described the making of *Talking Timbuktu* to *Guitar Player;* "You'd think Ali's just goofing and jamming, but they're all tunes, because these musicians don't jam. Americans do, but Africans don't. They don't just blow; they play a song. And he says his melodies are ancient melodies and they have a purpose." A typical track from *Talking Timbuktu* is "Gomni," a song about an individual's place in the community. Toure describes it in the liner notes, "You have to work hard to achieve a sense of well being. You should dedicate your life to the work which brings you happiness. When the community needs you, you should not turn a blind eye. Every job has its worth and everyone should make their contribution."

Selected discography

Ali Farka Toure, Mango, 1989.
African Blues, Shanachie, 1990.
The Source, Hannibal, 1992.
Talking Timbuktu, Hannibal, 1994.
Bandolobourou, Safari Ambience.
Sabou Yerkoy, Safari Ambience.

Sources

Books

Barlow, William, *Looking Up At Down: The Emergence of Blues Culture*, Temple University Press, 1989.

Periodicals

Billboard, October 16, 1993; October 30, 1993; July 9, 1994.
Down Beat, August 1990; October 1993; August 1994; October 1994.
Guitar Player, August 1990; June 1994.
Sing Out!, Volume 38, number 3; Volume 39, number 2.
Village Voice, May 16, 1989.

—James Powers

The Tragically Hip

Rock band

According to the *Los Angeles Times's* Bill Locey, the Tragically Hip "have long been the biggest band in Canada, where they have won lots of awards and sold even more albums." And although it is not necessarily every Canadian band's goal to be "big in America," critics there wonder why the Hip is not more successful in the United States. Gannett News Service's Daniel Aloi, for example, remarked that the band, "long considered the most popular and beloved band in Canada, are still something of an anomaly to many Americans." His opinion?: "It can't be their music—hard-edged, emotional and carefully wrought songs with as much appeal as any current stateside alternative act. The five-man band produces loud but melodic rock music, with Gordon Downie's emotional lyrics riding out a deep and roiling musical sea."

The members of the Tragically Hip—Bobby Baker, Gordon Downie, Johnny Fay, Paul Langlois, and Gord Sinclair—went to high school together in Kingston, Ontario, which is about three hours east of Toronto. Although some of the members had known each other much longer, they mark their year of formation as 1986. Since all the clubs in town had nothing but cover bands, the Hip "wanted to provide a suitable soundtrack to hang out with their friends and drink beer," according to Locey. They played their first gig at the Kingston Artists Association.

The name of the band was taken from music video pioneer and former Monkee, Michael Nesmith's video called *Elephant Parts.* The video contained a clip asking for contributions to The Foundation for the Tragically Hip—poor, afflicted people in need of jacuzzis, Lamborghinis, and cocaine. The band thought that was very clever. According to guitarist Baker, "We thought our musical taste was far too sophisticated to be successful," he told *Musician's* Jon Young. "In Canada, people loved the name, but when we came to the U.S., everyone hated it. 'One of the worst names in the annals of rock history,' said a critic."

MCA Gets Hip, Thanks to EP

The band self-released a six-song EP entitled *The Tragically Hip* in 1987. On hearing that record in 1988, MCA Records quickly signed on the Hip. *Up to Here,* the band's first full-length album, was released in 1989. Charles Foran of *Saturday Night* wrote that "*Up to Here,* their 1989 breakthrough album, was happily mired in the pathology of an unnamed Kingston ... The album is full of tales of hard-luck Kingston lives." It remains perhaps the most popular recording with fans.

Both *Up to Here* and 1991's *Road Apples* contained some pretty hard rock or "fist-pumping riff-rock," opined the *Los Angeles View.* The *American Statesman* music critic Michael Corcoram loved *Road Apples,* although he "didn't care much for their experimental forays and the way [Downie's] lyrics started getting real artsy." In his opinion, the band "went alternative" with 1993's *Fully Completely* and 1994's *Day for Night.*

Downie, who is generally credited with lyric writing, had wanted to be a poet in college, but eventually decided against it. In 1996 Foran wrote, "[Downie's] lyrics, once scrupulously crafted, are now more free form, more 'trusting of the moment' of creation, and he isn't always sure where they come from."

Continued Developing Sound

The changes Corcoram heard in the band were obvious to listeners, although most were more positive than Corcoram. Foran said, "*Day for Night* ... confirmed the change: gone were the hook-laden FM tunes and compressed, often funny lyrics. In their place were almost reluctant melodies that stuck in the memory and lyrics, set in a psychological landscape of detached emotions and suppressed violence, that crept into dreams."

Although Downie receives most lyrical credit, the rest of the band functions as a democracy, with everyone having input. As they have grown up together, the Hip's music has also grown and developed. Discussing their

For the Record . . .

Members include: **Bobby Baker**, guitar; **Gordon Downie**, vocals; **Johnny Fay**, drums; **Paul Langlois**, guitar, vocals; and **Gord Sinclair**, bass, vocals.

Band formed in 1986 in Kingston, Ontario, Canada; released independently produced, self-titled EP debut, with initial distribution in the Kingston area only, 1987; EP distributed in the rest of Canada and the band signed to MCA Records, 1988; released first full-length album, *Up to Here*, 1989; dropped by MCA Records in the U.S., picked up by Atlantic Records, 1994.

Address: *Record company*—Atlantic Recording Corporation, 9229 Sunset Blvd., Los Angeles, CA 90069.

changes in a 1994 interview with Martin Renzhofer in the *Salt Lake Tribune*, bassist Sinclair said, "It's more a question of evolution. It's been a conscious effort in every sense. In the last three or four years, our songwriting system changed." Renzhofer wrote, "Band members were forced out of an individualist style. Song ideas are now brought into the studio, or are boiled down from 3-minute jam sessions." Sinclair continued, "The songs now reflect the collective nature of the band. It's made for a healthier environment within the band with everyone contributing."

In the *Los Angeles Times* Sinclair offered, "After the first album, everyone thought we were just like the Georgia Satellites; then after the second one, it was the Black Crowes; then after the third one, it was R.E.M. ... [but] I think we have our own original sound." According to Locey "the band puts on a killer live show," and Foran called Downie "one of rock's most charismatic front men."

In 1996 the Hip released *Trouble at the Henhouse.* Downie told Foran, "This is the closest to where the Tragically Hip wants to be as a band." Corcoram agreed. In the *American Statesman* he had admitted, though a huge fan of the band's live shows, "I didn't think that they ever made a truly great album....That was until they released *Trouble at the Henhouse* (three and a half stars), their best album ever."

The *Houston Press's* Greg Barr gave the album 4 stars and stated, "The band once more carries out a musical niche with intriguing moods rather than winning hooks, waving a multilayered, seamless sound much thicker than you'd expect from the standard two guitars, bass and drums line up." "Among the new songs," wrote Foran in *Saturday Night*, "are a few instant favourites, plus others that will need further listenings."

The *Los Angeles View* called the Tragically Hip "the band without a haircut or a gimmick or even a peg that goes much deeper than the all-inclusive 'rock and roll.'" The magazine also advises people not to call the band boring, "not unless you can stand in the middle of their sonic swirl, then walk away without feeling just a little weaker." With praise like that, the Hip just wants to keep playing and developing their music. "Growing up in Canada," Downie told *Musician*, "You see the road to Los Angeles littered with the corpses of bands seeking American acceptance, as if that would make you a legitimate success story back home. The lesson is that it's pointless to do anything differently to attract an American audience."

Selected discography

The Tragically Hip (EP), 1987.
Up to Here, MCA Records, 1989.
Road Apples, MCA Records, 1991.
Fully Completely, MCA Records, 1992.
Day for Night, Atlantic Recording, 1994.
Trouble at the Henhouse, Atlantic Recording, 1996.

Sources

American Statesman (Austin), June 22, 1996.
Gannett News Service, April 27, 1995.
Houston Press, June 20, 1996.
Los Angeles Times, October 6, 1994.
Los Angeles View, August 1, 1996.
Musician, March 1993.
Salt Lake Tribune, July 19, 1996.
Saturday Night, June 1, 1996.

Additional information for this profile was obtained from Atlantic Recording Corporation press materials, 1996, and from the Tragically Hip Web page at http://www.thehip.com.

—Joanna Rubiner

Tricky

Producer, composer, singer, songwriter

Photograph by Paul Ryder, courtesy of Island Records

Despite having been credited with inventing the genre known as "trip-hop"— the spacey, atmospheric variation on hip-hop that began captivating listeners in the mid-1990s—the multi-faceted British artist known as Tricky has worked to distance himself from the label. "People are always making up stupid names for shit," he complained in *Option.* It is this impatience with categories that has driven him, from his early work with the groundbreaking group Massive Attack to his rapidly evolving solo recordings and collaborations with artists both world-famous and obscure. Tricky's passion for new sounds has led him to push aside boundaries with reckless abandon, wielding samples and beats in disorienting new ways. "Sometimes my music don't work on the first listen," he asserted to Dennis Romero of the *Los Angeles Times.* "You could listen to it and think, 'Hmm, what's this all about?' You have to take time and be gentle with it. It don't hit you straightaway."

Adrian Thaws, as Tricky was christened, grew up in Bristol, England to Anglo-Caribbean parents. His mother took her own life when he was only 4; his father departed soon thereafter and left young Adrian in the care of his uncles and grandparents. The underworld activities of his uncles influenced his own adolescent misbehavior. "I was quite violent growing up," he told Romero, "doing it because there was nothing else to do." Though he grew up to a backdrop of reggae, his imagination was captured by ska, the uptempo Jamaican pop that saw a huge resurgence in Britain during the first wave of punk in the late 1970s and early '80s. In particular Tricky Kid, as he was then known—thanks to his skill at petty crime—revered the bi-racial ska-rock of The Specials. He later became enamored of hip-hop storytellers like Slick Rick and Rakim.

From Massive to *Maxinquaye*

Tricky fell in with a posse of Bristol hip-hoppers known as the Wild Bunch, rapping at parties and experimenting with mixing. Soon he found himself rapping with seminal hip-hop innovators Massive Attack. He spent several years working with the group—eventually producing and writing lyrics in addition to contributing vocals—but then found even their relatively open approach too limiting. He had met a teenaged singer named Martina Topley Bird and recorded a track with her titled "Aftermath"; Massive Attack decided not to use it, and Tricky subsequently went solo. While preparing his own musical recipe, he also collaborated with cutting-edge pop artists like Björk. A couple of solo singles became very popular in the underground dance music world. Tricky's subversive, pot-fueled sound—

For the Record . . .

Born Adrian Thaws, c. 1967, in Bristol, England; children: (with Martina Topley Bird) Maisey, born 1995.

Singer, producer, and songwriter, c. 1980s–. Member of group Massive Attack, c. 1990-95; produced tracks for Björk, Neneh Cherry, and other artists, c. 1990s; signed with Island Records and released solo debut album, *Maxinquaye*, 1995; released album under umbrella name Nearly God on own Durban Poison imprint, 1996.

Addresses: *Record company*—Island Records, 825 Eighth Ave., New York, NY 10019; 8920 Sunset Blvd., 2nd Floor, Los Angeles, CA 90069.

alongside the dark vibe of fellow Bristol act Portishead —was declared truly original. Island record tracked him down despite the fact that he had no permanent residence, offering him a unique contract that permitted him to record with other labels and even let him create his own imprint.

This eclectic vision was first unleashed in its unadulterated form on Tricky's debut solo album, *Maxinquaye.* Named after his mother, the album embraces a vast range of styles, and includes "Black Steel," a version of "Black Steel in the Hour of Chaos" by rap agitators Public Enemy. The Tricky version is sung by Bird in a disaffected murmur that undercuts the original's fury. "I knew it was going to work," Tricky said of the track in *Musician.* "I f---ed around with some Indian religious music to make that beat up, and I'd had it for ages. As soon as Martina sang it, I knew we'd gotten it right. And Chuck liked it," he added, referring to Public Enemy leader Chuck D. "He came up to me at a party and said 'Thank you' and all I could say was 'Thank *you.*'" In the wake of the album's release, Tricky described his approach in *Pulse!.* "I take a sample, rip it apart and then replay it on the keyboards," he declared. "I'm just a little kid messing around. It's like throwing paints on the floor and saying it's art." Critics generally felt the album *was* art, and showered the young producer-artist with acclaim.

Dubbed "Revolutionary" Artist

By 1995, the accolades had become nearly religious in their intensity. *Spin* put him at the top of their list of artists who represented "The Future of Rock," calling *Maxin-*

quaye "revolutionary." Tricky himself told the magazine, "I don't try to make a song. I don't use big sounds or melodies." His disavowal of pop song structure was even more decisive on the 1996 release *Nearly God,* a collaboration with a number of well-known artists that included Terry Hall of The Specials—one of Tricky's heroes—as well as Neneh Cherry, Björk, and Alison Moyet. Bird also contributed to the collection, which *Rolling Stone* described as "a set of collaborative vocal-soundscape improvisations" and deemed "fabulous."

"I Want to Control Hip-Hop"

The same year *Tricky Presents Grassroots,* an EP, was released. This effort explored more traditional hip-hop territory with young rappers Hillfiguzes and other relatively untested artists, yet it fared less well with critics, who awaited yet another 1996 album, *Pre-Millennium Tension,* with bated breath. "Oh, it's punk," Tricky said of the latter in *Raygun.* "It's just a punk attitude, a total punk attitude." In the same interview, he expressed a desire for far-flung power in music. "I want to control hip-hop," he declared. "I want to control jungle, I want to control rock music, I just want to keep destroying everybody's illusions. There ain't no point in being in it, unless you're in it that deep."

"Tricky is probably the most spontaneous music person I've met," Björk told *Spin.* "That is very smittening. Affects you on a creative/unconventional level, not on an artificial/musical one." That spontaneity was reflected in Tricky's affinity for wild photo shoots, cross-dressing, and other flamboyant displays. His home life, however, was fairly down-to-earth, much affected by the birth of a daughter, Maisey, whom he had with Bird. "Because of her, I'm more positive," he told the *Los Angeles Times.* Yet he never claimed to have been a former wild man tamed by fatherhood. "I'm completely normal," he claimed in *Raygun.* "I'm like fish and chips. Really normal."

Selected discography

Solo releases

Maxinquaye (includes "Black Steel"), Island, 1995.
Pre-Millennium Tension, Island, 1996.
Tricky Presents Grass Roots, Island, 1996.

With Massive Attack

Blue Lines, Virgin, 1991.
Protection, Virgin, 1995.

Others

Björk, *Post,* Elektra, 1995.
Whale, *We Care,* Virgin, 1995.
Nearly God, *Nearly God,* Durban Poison/Island, 1996.

Sources

Detour, October 1996.
LA Weekly, October 4, 1996.
Los Angeles Times, June 27, 1995; July 28, 1996.
Musician, February 1996; October 1996.
Option, September 1996.
Pulse!, June 1995.
Raygun, October 1996.
Rolling Stone, August 22, 1996.
Spin, June 1995; November 1995; January 1996; October
    1996.

Additional information was obtained from Island Records
publicity materials, 1996.

—Simon Glickman

2 Unlimited

Techno band

Despite its name, 2 Unlimited is actually a quartet, comprised of two behind-the-scenes composer-producers, Phil Wilde and Jean Paul de Coster, and two lyricist-performers, Anita Doth and Ray Slijngaard. The four have worked together since 1991, presenting their audience with regular contributions to the techno sound, the dance club style prevalent throughout Europe in the 1990s. All of the group's 14 singles have broken the top ten charts and achieved gold and platinum sales worldwide. Ironically, the quartet's happy careen through sales and celebrity has been accompanied by relentless scorn from music reviewers; their name has become synonymous with techno at its most commercial.

Phil Wilde and Jean Paul de Coster, both from Antwerp, Belgium, created 2 Unlimited in their studio, initially without any performers or vocalists. Both were already adept with the studio's equipment but, more importantly, they also shared a sensitivity to what will make a crowd dance. Wilde built his reputation deejaying for eight years on the demanding European club scene before investing in his own studio; de Coster ran a successful Antwerp record store. Wilde also provided an experienced background in composition and performance, which he first learned studying classical piano.

Wilde and de Coster first collaborated on a single called "Don't Miss the Party Line" by Bizz Nizz. When the piece made the European top ten in 1990, the producers decided to continue working together. In 1991 they set down the instrumental dance track "Get Ready for This," that would later receive vocals with some additional help. As de Coster recalled in *Billboard*, "We invited rapper Ray Slijngaard to have a go at it. We had worked with him before on 'Money Money,' an unreleased single by Bizz Nizz. By September, he returned the tape to us. To our surprise, he had also added the female vocals of a certain Anita Doth, a traffic warden from Amsterdam. He told us she was a good friend of his out of the city's nightlife. Ray discussed the possibility of forming a duo to front the project." Happy with what they heard, the producers took Slijngaard and Doth on board.

"Give Them Something Visual"

The team quickly worked out a production routine. Wilde and de Coster composed the music, then carefully, deliberately designed the track on the mixing board. Meanwhile, Doth and Slijngaard worked up the lyrics; "Once we have the melody," Wilde told Tony Horkins from *Melody Maker* in 1994, "I give them a cassette—one instrumental, and one with my piano melody....They write the lyrics and they come back to the studio." Even the vocals, the only acoustic element to begin with, could be sampled to carry a particular sound throughout. Explaining the use of Doth's voice, for example, Wilde told Horkins that "she does actually sing all three choruses, say, but if one of them is very good we'll use it all the way through. It's best for the record."

Writing for *Melody Maker* in 1994, Tom Sheehan noted the "widespread suspicion that Slijngaard and [Doth] are brainless puppets." Although Wilde and de Coster deny the charges, they do allow most of the creative and entrepreneurial credit to fall on their own shoulders. Doth and Slijngaard take second place, acknowledged as largely competent collaborators, but never touted as the driving force of the operation or even as vocal divas. They provide the look of 2 Unlimited—faces, vocals, bodies, outfits, dance routines, video style, and even logo—which all involved consider vital to the group's success. "If you want continuity for your projects," de Coster told Flick, "you better give them something visual too....That way, the kids out there can easily relate to it."

Both born in the Netherlands in 1971, the vocalists came to the producers with part-time music backgrounds. Slijngaard supported himself as a chef at the Schipjol Airport in Amsterdam, rapping at night with a friend and dancing at the city's clubs; he had something of a reputation for his skills as a break dancer. Doth belonged to an all-female group called Trouble Sisters and did some modeling, but made her living in the traffic-wardens' division of the Amsterdam police. When "Get Ready for This" came their way, neither one expected it

For the Record . . .

Members include **Phil Wilde** (born in Belgium), synthesizer, sampler, and mixing board; **Jean Paul de Coster** (born in Belgium), synthesizer, sampler, and mixing board; **Ray Slijngaard** (born c. 1971, in Holland), vocals; and **Anita Doth** (born c. 1971, in Holland), vocals.

Wilde and de Coster began as duo, mixing dance single "Get Ready for This," as an instrumental track, 1991; Doth and Slijngaard joined on vocals the same year; group released *Get Ready*, PWL, 1992.

Awards: *Smash Hits* magazine Best Newcomer Award, 1992, and Best Dance Act Award, 1993.

Address: *Record company*—Critique/BMG Records, 1540 Broadway, Times Square, New York, NY 10036.

to really change their lives. Talking with Sheehan, Doth recalled that she hoped to "sell a few in Holland and Belgium, maybe a dance hit in England." Slijngaard added that "At best...I thought maybe I'd get some money to open my own restaurant." When the collaboration proved to be successful enough to make them all professional, Doth and Slijngaard took on more creative roles. Slijngaard told Flick that "Having that kind of input has been key....I could never be a part of a situation that didn't allow for my creative expression and growth."

Dubbed "2 Untalented" by Press

Like their producers, the vocalists also brought with them an intimate knowledge of the techno audience, since both had been regulars on the Amsterdam underground circuit. Despite that background, however, the two ultimately took part in the mainstreaming of techno. Their manager, Michel Maartens, described that phenomenon for Flick: "When they surfaced, many parents feared that house and techno would damage their children....It was associated with pills and nightly escapades. But Ray and Anita proved to be the acceptable faces of techno. When mom and dad saw they were harmless pop stars—which is essentially what they still are—all mistrust was over." The mainstreaming, accomplished by all four artists together, contributed simultaneously to the group's appeal and to its illtreatment. Charging the quartet with superficiality and unoriginality, the press heaped scorn on them, regularly

referring to them as "2 Untalented." Simon Price, for example, reviewing *Real Things* for *Melody Maker* in 1994, declared that "2 Unlimited are—at best—a crude, bastardized assault on tasteful dance standards."

Ironically, however, 2 Unlimited proved at least as irresistible as they were unlikable, as most of the commentators from *Melody Maker* have demonstrated over the years. Reviewing *Get Ready* in 1992, Paul Lester suggested the paradox that 2 Unlimited seemed to pose for music critics: the music's simultaneous shallowness and infectiousness. After noting the "juvenile puerility of the lyrics and rhythms," he concluded that "2 Unlimited stand for energy and excitement. And if you're not thrilled by the lobotomising insistence of 'Workaholic,' 'Contrast' and the rest you're either dead from the toes up, or too grown-up for your own good."

Calvin Bush commented on the same phenomenon in 1993; he told *Melody Maker* readers, "I truly admire the way a nation can unite as one to destroy them and they just have bigger hits than ever before. They're harmless, gormless goons who'll be outta sight shortly. Right now, though, they're Number One Band in Hell by consensus." Band member Slijngaard defended the act to Sheehan with a simple honesty about their motivation: "Underground bands don't *want* to sell records....I respect that, but I want to sell records. I want to make money."

And Sell Records They Did

By 1996, 2 Unlimited had 14 consecutive singles that went top ten in the international market. Their earliest effort, "Get Ready for This," reached Number Two on the charts. By far their greatest achievement was 1993's "No Limits," which hit Number One in 35 countries and sold in excess of two million copies worldwide by 1996. Its attendant album broke three million in sales; *Real Things* debuted at the top of *Billboard's* Hits of the World chart when it came out in 1995. By the time they released a greatest hits compilation in 1996, the record industry had presented them with over 150 gold and platinum records, and MTV had honored the release of *Real Things* with a three-hour television special at Disneyland, Paris.

The 1995 release of *Hits Unlimited* was accompanied by an aggressive American advertising campaign aimed at increasing the group's sales in the United States. Despite their celebrity status in European markets—led first by England, Belgium, Luxembourg, and the Netherlands, later with France and Germany—and Asian and South American markets, name recognition had persistently eluded 2 Unlimited in the United States.

Their music was familiar to any regular club-goer in America; as noted by Larry Flick, their singles had "saturation airplay in nightclubs, television sports programs, malls, boutiques, even aerobic workout sessions." However, that same club-goer would be hard put to name the group behind the tune.

Selected discography

Get Ready (includes "Get Ready for This," "Twilight Zone," "Workaholic," and "Contrast"), PWL, 1992.
No Limits (includes "No Limits"), PWL, 1993.
Real Things, PWL, 1994.
Hits Unlimited, PWL/Radikal, 1995.

Sources

Billboard, September, 1994; March 9, 1996.
Melody Maker, February 22, 1992; July 10, 1993; May 14, 1994; June 4, 1994; February 17, 1996.

—*Ondine Le Blanc*

US3

Jazz/hip-hop group

Though a few traditional voices from the jazz scene cringe at the thought of hip-hop artists delving into the jazz catalog for material, the British duo of Geoff Wilkinson and Mel Simpson managed to prove that the two can be smartly arranged. The Londoners form the nucleus of jazz/hip-hop collective US3, whose 1993 release, *Hand on the Torch*, went platinum largely on the strength of the club hit "Cantaloop (Flip Fantasia)." While US3 is not alone in bringing jazz and hip-hop together, some argue that their sonic concoctions are the best of the bunch. US3 succeeds in retaining jazz's syncopation and meter fluctuations rather than burying them beneath ground-shaking bass beats, much to the delight of the jazz artists whose works surface in US3 material.

Acid Jazz Burns up Clubs, More

Combined with releases from Digable Planets, Incognito, and Brand New Heavies, a genre loosely known as acid-jazz made significant strides in 1994. Acid jazz is now emerging from the dancehalls of London and clubs around the world, bringing its blend of hip-hop rhythms and jazz samples to more and more listeners. Neil Conner, a music industry figure in San Francisco, told *Billboard:* "Acid-jazz has enough of a raw, street feel to attract kids who are into hip-hop. It's a fresh change of pace for all of us—and it's schooling these kids on musical history, whether they know it or not."

Wilkinson and Simpson came together in 1991 with the shared notion of mating jazz and hip-hop. "My partner and I," Simpson told *Rolling Stone,* "spoke of this idea as a way of making jazz more accessible to people who would otherwise give the music a wide berth or consider it inappropriate to them." Wilkinson had been a journalist and member of London's jazz scene while Simpson was a keyboardist with a knack for music production. They had collaborated in staging club events with jazz artists and rappers and then decided the results were worth recording. Once Simspon completed constuction of his London studio, Flame, the pair issued "Where Will We Be in the 21st Century?" Though the record sold only 250 copies, successful gigs at London jazz clubs gave them reason to continue.

Feared a Lawsuit, Offered a Contract

US3 could very easily have never been, due to their illicit use of copyrighted material. When the two released their second effort, "The Band Played the Boogie," in 1991, the single was so laden with takes from Blue Note artists that Columbia Records, Blue Note's proprietors, came looking for them. "We thought it was curtains for us. We thought we were going to be sued out of existence," Simpson told *Request.* Instead of serving them a summons, Columbia offered them a deal. They hit a recording studio after the 1992 meeting and worked out a demo that secured them a contract. "I'd have to say it was the best crime I've ever committed," Wilkinson told the *Sacramento Bee.* As part of the arrangement, Wilkinson and Simpson were given access, this time legitimately, to Blue Note's legendary archives. The pair drew from Art Blakely and the Jazz Messengers, Thelonius Monk, Herbie Jancock, Lou Donaldson, and others for their Blue Note debut.

Wilkinson and Simpson originally conceived of US3 as a studio project and the Blue Note record as a one-time effort. Relying on their sampling and sequencing skills honed as DJs in London clubs, the duo planned to piece together hip-hop beats with bits from the legends of jazz. With Simpson playing keyboards and managing samples and Wilkinson producing, the duo relied on rappers Tukka Yoot, Kobie Powell, and Rashaan Kelly to provide the lyrical content. The two also contracted a horn section comprised of London jazz artists and it is this conglomerate of rappers and musicians that comprise the third pillar in the US3 triumvirate. Going into the project, Wilkinson and Simpson had definite ideas for the record. "We were trying to fuse the two musics together in a way that hadn't been done....We wanted 50 percent of each, a real fusion," Wilkinson explained to the *Sacramento Bee.*

Members include producers **Geoff Wilkinson** (born in Britain, c. 1956) and **Mel Simpson** (born in Britain, c. 1963); rappers **Tukka Yoot** (born in Jamaica, c. 1973), **Rashaan Kelly,** and **Kobie Powell.**

Group formed in 1991 with a jazz-hip hop single titled "Where Will We Be in the 21st Century?"; released "The Band Played the Boogie," 1991, which used samples from the Blue Note archives; released *Hand on the Torch,* Blue Note, 1993. Musicians appearing on the album include Ed Jones, saxophone and flute; Dennis Rollins, trombone; Tony Remy, guitar; Matthew Cooper, piano; Roberto Pia, percussion; Gerard Presencer, trumpet; and Mike Smith, saxophone. Single "Cantaloop (Flip Fantasia)" rose on European and Japanese charts prompting tours of those regions; tour band included Cheryl Alleyne, drums; Geoggrey Gascoyne, bass; Timothy Vine, keyboards; Dominick Glover, trumpet; and Tony Cofie, saxophone; toured with UB40 in England and United States, 1994; "Cantaloop" broke into *Billboard*'s Top Ten and helped make *Hand on the Torch* the most successful Blue Note release ever.

Awards: *Hand on the Torch* named best jazz album of the year by Japan's *Swing Journal,* 1993; group named jazz musicians of the year by Britain's *Independent,* 1993.

Addresses: *Record company*—Blue Note, 1290 Avenue of the Americas, New York, NY 10104.

Sensing that they had a potential chart-topper on their hands, Blue Note contacted parent-label Columbia to request support in promoting the record. Blue Note president Bruce Lundvall told *Billboard,* "We realized we wouldn't have enough resources on our own to take this as far as it could go." With Columbia's industry muscle raising support among urban and alternative radio, "Cantaloop (Flip Fantasia)" steadily climbed through the charts. The song relies on a riff from Herbie Hancock's "Cantaloupe Island," a popular 1960s jazz tune, and hit *Billboard*'s Top Ten in the Spring of 1994. The "Cantaloop" video landed in MTV's Buzz Bin, a rotation normally reserved for emerging alternative bands. John Cannelli, Vice President of music and talent at MTV, told *Billboard,* "Certainly its jazz influence helps with the older demo, while the rap brings it to relevance in the 1990s with a younger demo."

Capitalizing on support from different market segments, the record became the biggest selling Blue Note release ever and helped spark the label to its best sales year in its history. Lundvall told *Down Beat,* "Their music respectfuly transforms the classic of the past into urgent and viable music that speaks to today's listeners." While the sales meant a great deal to US3, the members share a great deal of respect for the musicians who made the Blue Note label synonymous with the best jazz had to offer. "We have mixed feelings about the album being the biggest-selling Blue Note album. It's great to have a hit record, but the other side of it is that not even someone like Herbie [Hancock] sold that many. That's a shame," Tukka Yoot, US3's Jamaican-born rapper, told *Down Beat.*

Grew From Studio Project to Live Band

As the band recorded *Hand on the Torch,* the project moved beyond its original bounds. The group felt the music come together in unanticipated harmony. "Through a couple generations of the band, it became totally live. We realized we didn't really need the samples, since the horn guys knew this stuff and played it in little jazz clubs on the weekends," Simpson told *Request.* In fact, neither Wilkinson nor Simpson tour with the band. The live show, while bearing their mark with its fresh blend of rap and hip-hop, is dominated by the trio of rappers, a drummer, and the horn section. Tukka Yoot is the prime vocalist, rapping with the music rather than over it and using his voice an instrument in the layered whole. Successful American, European, and Japanese tours following *Hand on the Torch* generally showed Root to be the focal point, and the 21-year old has proved himself a quick study in working in jazz. Previously unfamiliar with the genre, Root is the perfect example of the band's goal. "The aim of US3 was to get jazz nonbelievers into jazz, and jazz purists into hip-hop," he told *Entertainment Weekly.*

While the live band took to the road for most of 1993 and 1994, Wilkinson and Simpson remained in London, working on the musical future of US3. Projects such as a collaboration with jazz saxophonist Joshua Redman and an all-out jazz record for Blue Note keep the two busy, while each of the band's three rappers have solo deals with projects in the works. Intended as a rotating collaboration guided by Wilkinson and Simpson, US3 are expected to release their second Blue Note album in 1996. "In the name US3, two are me and Geoff, The third is like the third side of the triangle waiting to be completed. It can be a rapper, singer, maybe a whole orchestra. Who knows what will happen next time," Simpson told *Request.*

Selected discography

"The Band Played the Boogie" (12-inch), Ninja Tune Records, 1991.

"Where Will We Be in the 21st Century?," Ninja Tune Records, 1991.

Hand on the Torch (contains "Cantaloop (Flip Fantasia)," Blue Note, 1993.

Sources

Billboard, January 22, 1994; April 30, 1994; July 2, 1994; July 16, 1994.

Down Beat, August 1994.

Entertainment Weekly, March 18, 1994.

Metro Times (Detroit), August 3, 1994.

Plain Dealer (Cleveland), April 15, 1994.

Providence Jounal-Bulletin, August 4, 1994.

Request, May 1994.

Rolling Stone, March 10, 1994; June 16, 1994.

Sacramento Bee, August 21, 1994.

Salt Lake Tribune, August 19, 1994.

Spin, April 1994.

Time, January 24, 1994.

Vibe, December 1993.

—*Rich Bowen*

The Verve

Eglish alternative act the Verve traveled a long road during their mere half-decade of existence, a path that might be defined by the fact that fellow northern England musicians Oasis once opened for their live shows. A few years later, the Verve were scheduled as Oasis's opening act. Oasis singer Liam Gallagher even admitted in print to liking them—a high honor, given his disdain of most popular music except that of his own band. The Verve's career path was also marked by two well-received albums, debauched nights during the 1994 Lollapalooza tour, the narrow avoidance of a potentially costly lawsuit, and interviews with the press in which they unabashedly proclaimed their talent and high moral standards in the face of relentless pressure to sell out. Despite the misfortunes, the band's spiraling, guitar-driven melodies and complex arrangements won them vociferous critical praise as well as comparisons to the Doors, early U2, and even Pink Floyd. *Musician* writer Aidin Vaziri described their sound as "a wondrous concoction of molten guitars, psychedelic rhythms, and halcyon choruses."

The Verve formed as simply "Verve" around 1990 in the English town of Wigan, near Manchester's famed music scene. Founding members Richard Ashcroft, Simon Jones, Nick McCabe, and Peter Salisbury attended college together, and Ashcroft had long entertained dreams of escaping Wigan's dreary atmosphere, at one time considering a career on the soccer field. His father's death when Ashcroft was just eleven impacted his ambitions: "He'd worked nine to five all his life, and he suffered and got nowhere," the singer told *Melody Maker*'s David Stubbs. "I immediately realised that this wasn't the life for me. Immediately I found out how quickly someone can die and just be wiped out." In high school, he asserted during a career-guidance session that he wanted to be a musician. "I got the classic wry smile that said, 'You're going to be working in a factory in two years, son,'" he recalled in another interview with Andrew Smith for the same publication. "After that, I fluffed my exams and then I really started thinking about doing it."

Success Came Quickly

After the Verve played their first London show and completed a demo tape that cost a mere $90 to record, they were signed to England's Hut label and were playing regular shows around London by 1991. They released three singles in England, but refused to cut their typically eight-to-ten-minute tracks down to a more radio-friendly format. Their music was lauded by critics, but the singles failed to chart—though Ashcroft's resemblance to Mick Jagger did make good press.

The Verve's refusal to become acquiescent performers for their label also seemed a hindrance to greater success. Once, they walked offstage after only two songs (albeit, one lasted 25 minutes) because of poor turnout. Hut released a five-track EP entitled *The Verve EP* in 1992, comprised of their earlier singles and their B-sides; it was also released in the United States on the Caroline label. Sharon O'Connell reviewed it for *Melody Maker* and described the band and their music as "all weightlessness and detachment, their tunes barely-delineated, freeform drifts which refuse definition.... They have a petulant, ragged glamour and there's Ashcroft at their centre, a dark star with a stripling ego who seduces/goads/guides the others toward their transcendental launch pad."

Launched in America

In 1993 the Verve were picked as the first band on the Vernon Yard label, a newly-created American affiliate of British giant Virgin Records. Their full-length debut, recorded in Cornwall, was *A Storm in Heaven*, released that same year on Hut in England and Vernon Yard in the United States. "Slide Away" appeared as the single, and did nominally well, receiving some airplay on American alternative stations. Yet the band remained pegged in the "indie" slot, although having received almost unstinting praise from jaded rock journalists in both countries. Writing about *A Storm in Heaven* for *Melody*

Maker, Smith avowed "it shimmers and drifts, going nowhere beautifully." David Stubbs reviewed it for the same paper and termed it "music to make your head melt." That first single, Stubbs asserted, moves "effortlessly from glittering, turquoise beauty to tempestuous noise." He concluded by enthusing: "Verve have already achieved transcendence—their music sounds like it's been around for centuries waiting to be brought into being and will linger for centuries to come."

American reviewers were equally laudatory, with *Rolling Stone* pegging the band as an up-and-coming alternative act of 1993. The magazine called their first full-length release "an engrossing, atmospheric debut that jams an epic-song spine plus zero-to-ninety-and-back-again dynamics into the hellbent guitar storms of Britain's psychedelic dreamers." The summer of 1993, however, was also the start of numerous troubles for the band. The venerable jazz label "Verve," part of the Deutsche Grammophone company, initiated a lawsuit to order them to stop using the name lest music-buyers become confused. In the initial suit, the label demanded that sales of *A Storm in Heaven* be halted, and in the event of infringement, that all profits be seized. Vernon Yard president Keith Wood issued a statement quoted in *Billboard* that read, in part, "I cannot imagine a record buyer mistakenly coming home with the new Verve album when they've set out to buy a Charlie Parker box set." A compromise was reached which resulted in the band's name change to "The" Verve.

Being launched into the world of American alternative rock had other drawbacks. Tales of unabashed substance abuse and destroyed hotel rooms abounded; Ashcroft earned the nickname "mad Richard" for his misbehavior both off and onstage. "At the start, it was an adventure, but America nearly killed us," the singer told *Melody Maker* writer Dave Simpson in 1995. "My prob-

lem, basically, is that I think too much. Sticking someone who thinks too much on a chrome bus and sending him around America isn't a very good...experiment." Returning to their hometown of Wigan was also difficult. "That's supposed to be your life, but you don't know who you are," bassist Simon Jones explained to Simpson. The group set out to record a follow-up album, but the aforementioned escapades made recording difficult. Additionally, Ashcroft was devastated by the breakup with his girlfriend of six years, and a sense of isolation and despair worked its way onto the recording. Other personal problems surfaced. At one point Ashcroft left the studio, manned at the time by producer Owen Morris, who had also helped craft Oasis's phenomenally successful *Definitely Maybe.*

Constrained by Success

Despite the hindrances to its creation and completion, *A Northern Soul* was released in mid-1995. Again, it was well received by critics—but this time by fans as well; in just two months after *A Northern Soul*'s summer release it sold more copies than *A Storm in Heaven* had in two years. "Listen to *A Northern Soul*...and the recurrent images are of terror, horror, dread, and morbidity," *Melody Maker*'s Simpson wrote. One cut, "History," he called "an epic, windswept symphony of strings, flailing vocals and staggeringly bitter sentiments." *Melody Maker* colleague Victoria Segal contended the record "has a mirror-smashing intensity."

Unfortunately, such intensity ultimately seemed to portend the end of the band. A series of concert dates in the United States, and the attendant round of press interviews that went with it, further exhausted Ashcroft. He quit, and the Verve then officially disbanded in August of 1995. They had been scheduled to play more tour dates, including opening for Oasis, for the coming year, which probably would have launched them into mainstream commercial success—but Ashcroft had long asserted that he despised the "business" side of the music industry. "As far as I'm concerned, if by the second or third single, Verve are getting pressure off men in suits, Verve will fold and we'll just go off and do our own thing," Ashcroft avowed in the 1992 *Melody Maker* interview with Stubbs. His colleague, guitarist Nick McCabe, put it more succinctly: "This band is totally selfish, self-centred and self-indulgent and that's exactly the way it should be."

Selected discography

The Verve (EP), Caroline, 1992.
A Storm in Heaven, Vernon Yard/Virgin, 1993.

No Come Down (EP), Vernon Yard/Virgin, 1994.
A Northern Soul, Vernon Yard/Virgin, 1995.

Sources

Billboard, May 8, 1993, pp. 1, 79; July 3, 1993, pp. 10, 76.
Guitar Player, October 1995, p. 19.
Melody Maker, June 12, 1992, pp. 28-29; December 5, 1992, p. 29; May 15, 1993, p. 43; June 19, 1993, p. 33; May 15, 1994, p. 5; May 28, 1994, p. 34; May 13, 1995, pp. 10-11; July 1, 1995, p. 38; July 15, 1995, pp. 30-32; September 9, 1995, p. 5.
Rolling Stone, July 8, 1993, p. 95; October 5, 1995, p. 32.

—*Carol Brennan*

Steve Wariner

Guitarist, singer, songwriter

AP/Wide World Photos

Since his 1981 recording debut, country guitarist, vocalist, and songwriter Steve Wariner has shown himself to be a resilient talent. Within country music's inner circle, Wariner is respected, not only as a protege of guitar virtuoso Chet Atkins, but as a consummate guitarist in his own right. The close to 30 top ten hits he has achieved during his career—12 of them, including "The Tips of My Fingers" and "Leave Him Out of This," climbing to the number one spot—attest to Wariner's vocal ability and his popularity with country music listeners. And his skill as a songwriter has been attested to by such stellar country performers as Garth Brooks and the late Conway Twitty, both of whom have successfully recorded Wariner-penned tunes. Wariner's mellow tenor vocals have linked him with Glen Campbell and Vince Gill, and his reputation for durable hits on three different record labels has earned him a reputation around Music City as one of Nashville's "nice guys."

Describing his style as a blend of country and pop influences, an interviewer in *Country Guitar* magazine attributes the reason for Wariner's continued success to his overall personality. "His personal manner translates into his playing and singing—sincerity and affability are the qualities that come through most clearly...," the interviewer comments. "He manages, with his soothing guitar and voice, to establish a connection to places in the heart and mind." While some critics have noted that Wariner's relaxed style has been reflected by recordings that have rarely taken risks, all would agree that it has also resulted in his lucrative career as a recording artist.

Premiered with Father's Band at Barn Dance

Born in Noblesville, Indiana, on Christmas Day, 1954, Wariner was raised by parents Roy and Ilene in a musical environment—each of the five Wariner children would become proficient in at least one music-related activity. Roy Wariner, who worked in a local foundry by day, fronted a small country band; by the time he was nine, young Steve was determined to join his dad on stage. Using recordings by Ray Price, Hank Thompson, Jim Reeves, and guitarists Atkins and Merle Travis as a musical backdrop, he tackled his father's Danelectro bass guitar, quickly mastering the instrument. A year later, with Steve now on bass guitar, the new Roy Wariner Band debuted at a barn dance in Russell Springs, Kentucky. They were soon performing on local radio and television shows. While he was a great fan of country stars George "the Possum" Jones and Merle Haggard, Wariner's absolute idol remained six-string guitar whiz Chet Atkins, the gauge against he would measure all other guitar players. Although the young guitarist did not know it at the time, the two musicians' paths were destined to cross.

From bass guitar, the musically inclined teen moved on to electric guitar, and then to drums, continuing to play with country and rock bands composed of various family members. Before he had even graduated from high school, 17-year-old Wariner found himself graduating to a higher level in the country music circuit when he was asked to open a show for the late, great country chanteuse Dottie West at the Nashville Country Club in Indianapolis. West was so impressed with Wariner's easy personality and talent as a singer that she offered him the chance to work as a bass player and backup vocalist in her touring band. Wariner was quick to say yes, despite his mother's concern. "I had never really been out of a two-state area," Wariner recalled in an Arista press release. "[My mom] told Dottie, 'Take care of my boy.' And Dottie put her arm around her and said, 'I'll be his mother when you're not there.' She really lived up to her word. She really was like a mother to me."

After three years travelling with West and her band, Wariner moved to similar duties in the road band for the late rockabilly artist Bob Luman. The bass guitarist would work alongside Luman—the pair formed a publishing company in 1978—until fate intercepted Wariner two and a half years later, in the form of none other than Chet Atkins himself. Then still an acting producer for RCA Records, Atkins heard a demo recording of Wariner performing some of his original material and immediately approached the talented musician with the offer of a "singles" recording contract. Wariner signed with RCA in 1977. In addition to recording several songs with RCA, he would gain the opportunity to work alongside his longtime musical idol, backing up Atkins on tour and soloing with a few of his original songs during Atkins's shows.

Writes for Big Names and Records Solo Hits

Wariner's first recording to reach the number one spot on the country charts was "All Roads Lead to You," which RCA promoted as a single in 1981. The following year marked the release of the artist's self-titled debut album, which placed Wariner's name on the charts once again with such hits as "Your Memory," "Kansas City," and "By Now," which crested in the top five. *Steve Wariner* proved the debut artist to be a talented songwriter as well. His songs have since been recorded by such artists as Garth Brooks, Lou Reed, Clay Walker, Lisa Brokop, and Luman. The first of his original compositions to reach number one was 1985's "You Can Dream of Me," which would reach beyond a country audience as the theme song from the long-running ABC-TV hit sitcom *Who's the Boss?* Other albums followed on the strenth of Wariner's debut effort: 1984's *Midnight Fire* featured several Top Ten hits, and RCA had enough confidence in its new artist to issue Wariner's first *Greatest Hits* album a year later.

Meanwhile, late in 1984 Wariner made the decision to switch recording labels. With *One Good Night Deserves Another*, he came under the tutelage of MCA producer Tony Brown, who also handled the career of successful country artist Vince Gill. Under Brown, Wariner was able to showcase his talents as an instrumentalist—something that MCA had, surprisingly, refused to do in favor of promoting him as a vocalist. Wariner's fiery guitarwork on such hits as "Some Fools Never Learn" and "You Can Dream of Me" would send them blazing up the charts. His MCA debut effort produced several Top Ten hits and built Wariner's momentum as a country act. By the time *Life's Highway* hit record stores in 1986, Wariner seemed to be on his way: four number one singles and a Grammy award nomination for "That's How You Know Love's Right," a duet with

Highway 101 singer Nicolette Larson, were along his path. In 1987 Wariner teamed up with Glen Campbell for the hit duet "The Hand that Rocks the Cradle," and the following year found *I Should Be with You* charting with Number One hits that included the title track, "Baby, I'm Yours," and "Hold On." Another creative recording project with MCA was 1990's *Christmas Memories*, a holiday recording Wariner made with Nanci Griffith, Chet Atkins, Maura O'Connell, and the Chieftans.

A Move to Arista Goes Gold

In 1990, following the release of *Laredo* and *Christmas Memories*, Wariner switched labels again, this time signing with Arista Nashville. With the aptly titled *I Am Ready*, his first Arista release, Wariner finally managed to "go gold." Ballads like "The Tips of My Fingers," "A Woman Loves," and "Like a River to the Sea" sailed *I Am Ready* to gold-record status by 1994. Meanwhile, asked to collaborate on a project with fiddler Mark O'Connor, Vince Gill, and bluegrasser Ricky Skaggs, Wariner found himself slated with the group for a Grammy award for best country vocal collaboration for 1991's "Restless," a single included on *Mark O'Connor & the New Nashville Cats*. The Grammy win would be yet another first for Wariner.

Heading into the 1990s, Wariner's name was rarely absent from the country music countdown; his fifteenth album in over a decade, 1993's *Drive* was carried forward by the momentum of *I Am Ready*, even though the artist had begun to shift his focus from mellow ballads to more rock-inspired rhythms. "I think I'm at a point now where I can take chances a little bit more and stretch out," the singer-guitarist explained to Jennifer Fusco-Giacobbe in *Country Song Roundup*. While Geoffrey Himes noted in *Country Music* that the ten songs on *Drive* "are all tasteful country-pop numbers with pleasant melodies, well sung and well played, but without anything distinctive to remember them by," Wariner sustained his ability to produce hits even while shifting his overall focus. The album produced the top ten hit "If I Didn't Love You," and the hit single "Drivin' and Cryin'."

No More Mr. Nice Guy, which Wariner produced and released in 1996, would be an even more dramatic shift for the artist. Composed of instrumentals rather than the radio-friendly country vocals that had fueled Wariner's career thus far, it showcased such dynamic "pickers" as guitarists Vince Gill, Bryan Austin, Leo Kottke, and Chet Atkins, fiddler Mark O'Connor, mandolinist Sam Bush, and innovative banjoist Bela Fleck, among others. The album was a shift from the kind of country-pop fusion Wariner had been noted for—the rock, swing, blues, semi-classical, and jazz influences in *No More*

Mr. Nice Guy put the album into a broader category than "country" and Arista was quick to market the album to guitar enthusiasts of all persuasions. However, it was also a gamble for Arista, as instrumentals rarely achieve significant airplay on mainstream country radio. While he had been in demand as a guitarist around Nashville for many years—Takamine Guitars had, by now, issued their third "Steve Wariner" signature-edition acoustic guitar—fans of Wariner's country ballads would now discover a new side to this Nashville "nice guy."

Comes Full Circle as a Musician

Regarding *No More Mr. Nice Guy*, Wariner's attitude remained pragmatic. "I've wanted to do a project like this since I was a kid," he admitted to Deborah Evans Price in *Billboard*, but I was always realistic. I knew my voice and the lyrics were my bread and butter, especially in the commercial world." Yet, after 15 successful albums, he felt able to leave the commercial world behind for a while and devote himself to his first love: playing the guitar. Writing or co-writing every song on the release, Wariner's commitment to his music is obvious on every track, according to Edward Morris in *Nashville Scene*. On *Nice Guy*, Morris notes, Wariner "has created a refreshing departure from conventional country fare. It is inventive, mood provoking, enchantingly varied, and soulfully executed throughout." *Country Music*'s Rich Kienzle agrees in a review of *No More Mr. Nice Guy*, commenting that the "near-extinction of [non-bluegrass instrumental albums] will almost surely result in a revival someday soon. If so, Steve Wariner may well deserve some of the credit."

Despite its innovations, recording *No More Mr. Nice Guy* found Wariner also retracing his own musical roots. "A guitar player is all I wanted to be growing up," he noted in an Arista press release. He fell into singing by chance, because the bands he played for early in his career were in need of vocalists. "I received attention for singing, so I did more of it," recalled Wariner. "I never took it that seriously because I always thought of myself as a guitarist. Now, after all the hits and everything, this record brings me back to where I started."

Wariner has also contributed his talents to tribute albums—including *Mama's Hungry Eyes* (a tribute to Merle Haggard), *Keith Whitley: Tribute Album*, and *Come Together: America Salutes the Beatles*. In addition, he has been an active supporter of the American Heart Association and several other charities that aid children with life-threatening illnesses. Although Wariner has performed as far away as Grindelwald, Switzerland, and Kuamoto, Japan, he and his family spend their time at home in the quiet Nashville suburb of Franklin,

Tennessee. As his career continues to mature, Wariner remains confident in his success as a musician. "[R]egardless of sales or success, I'm going to be making music one way or the other," he once told an interviewer. "That's the way I look at it. I love it too much. It's all I've ever done since childhood."

Selected discography

Steve Wariner, RCA, 1982.
Midnight Fire, RCA, 1984.
Greatest Hits, RCA, 1985.
One Good Night Deserves Another, MCA, 1985.
Life's Highway, MCA, 1986.
Down in Tennessee, RCA, 1986.
It's a Crazy World, MCA, 1987.
I Should Be With You, MCA, 1988.
I Got Dreams, MCA, 1989.
Laredo, MCA, 1990.
(With Nanci Griffith, Chet Atkins, Maura O'Connell, and the Chieftans) *Christmas Memories*, MCA, 1990.
I Am Ready (includes "A Woman Loves" and "The Tips of My Fingers"), Arista, 1991.
Drive, Arista, 1993.
No More Mr. Nice Guy, Arista, 1996.

Sources

Books

Comprehensive Country Music Encyclopedia, Random House, 1994, pp. 408-409.

Periodicals

Billboard, February 3, 1996.
Country Guitar, summer 1993, pp. 21-24.
Country Music, September/October 1993, p. 32; May/June 1996, pp. 28-29.
Country Song Roundup, April 1994, pp. 16-18.
Nashville Scene, November 18, 1995.

Additional information for this profile was provided by Arista Records press materials.

—*Pamela Shelton*

Mark Whitfield

Jazz guitarist

One would think a guitarist who had graduated from the prestigious Berklee College of Music would be all technique, no emotion. Mark Whitfield dispels that misconception. Although his guitar work is often fast and flashy, his technical proficiency is driven by his interest in structure and melody, and he constantly strives to reduce the number of notes he plays to get at the deeper emotional truth that jazz and blues can reveal.

Whitfield was born in October of 1966 in Long Island, New York. The youngest of five brothers and sisters, his love for jazz and blues music came early. When he was seven, his brother bought him a guitar and a Lightning Hopkins album; he immediately started playing both. At the age of 15, all his siblings were moving into careers as doctors and lawyers and Whitfield himself, had obtained a medical student internship at Georgetown University. While that's an impressive feat for any 15-year-old, it was the scholarship he won a scholarship to the Berklee College of Music, in Boston, which excited Whitfield even more. After his family moved across the country to a suburb of Seattle, Whitfield convinced his parents to let him attend Berklee after graduating from high school early, at the age of 16. It was while studying guitar at Berklee where Whitfield met a young piano and vocal student from Baton Rouge, Louisiana, named Jody Davis. The two eventually were married and moved to her home state.

Whitfield's tenure at Berklee was not as smooth as his acceptance to the famed school had been. He wanted to play traditional mainstream jazz, which was not in vogue at Berklee at the time. "I was looking for a pure sound, a hollow-body guitar, a small amplifier, no effects," he told *Offbeat.* He found a core of jazz purists that he could jam with. They included Delfeayo, Wynton, and Branford Marsalis.

Stockbroker's Blues

In 1987 at the age of 20, Whitfield graduated, married Jody, and the couple moved to a small studio apartment in Brooklyn, New York. Whitfield's sister was a stockbroker and got him a position as a stockbroker's assistant. More importantly, his brother-in-law, drummer Tory Davis, got him a job playing with the after-hours house band at the famous Blue Note jazz club in Greenwich Village.

Later that same year, he was playing at the club's 25th anniversary party when legendary jazz guitarist George Benson heard him. Benson was impressed and arranged for him to work with celebrated organist Jack McDuff. McDuff was not especially enamored of Berklee graduates but let him play with his band. It was a learning experience for Whitfield who incorrectly assumed he had a sophisticated theoretical and harmonic background; McDuff soon set him straight. "Stop playing those banjo chords," he told Whitfield, who reacted defensively at first, but then listened and learned how to strip away some of the frilly riffs from his playing.

Around the time he was playing with McDuff, Benson often let Whitfield jam with him on many occasions and put him in touch with his record producer, Tommy LiPuma. In 1989 at the age of 23, Whitfield signed his first recording contract with Warner Brothers. His first album, *The Marksman,* was a pure jazz guitar album that while critically well received, failed to make little more than a rumble commercially.

Losing the Pop

In 1990, around the time his debut album came out, Whitfield and Jody discovered they would soon be parents. They decided to move to Jody's home town of Baton Rouge, to raise their child in a more traditional family setting. There, Whitfield met saxophonist Alvin Batiste, head of Southern University's jazz program, who soon became his mentor. He began playing with his old classmate, Delfeayo Marsalis and through him met other members of the New Orleans jazz community.

For the Record . . .

Born in October of 1966; graduated from Berklee College of Music, 1987; married Jody Davis, 1987; children: Mark Jr., Davis.

Student intern at Georgetown University, and considering a medical career when he won a scholarship to Berklee College of Music; graduated high school at 16 and went to Berklee; worked as stockbroker's assistant, 1987; joined the house band at the Blue Note jazz club in New York, 1987; signed with Warner Brothers, 1989; released debut album, *The Marksman,* 1990; switched labels to Verve Records, 1994.

Addresses: *Home*—Baton Rouge, LA; *Record company*—Verve Records, 825 Eighth Ave., New York, NY 10019.

One such player was trumpeter Nicholas Payton. Since then, the two have played on each other's albums and as backing musicians for famed organist Jimmy Smith.

Whitfield's second album, *Patrice,* was released in 1991. More avant garde than his previous album, it again did well with the critics but not in sales. In 1993, his third album, *Mark Whitfield,* swung toward the commercial. He had been persuaded to try a more salable approach and the smooth jazz of his Kenny G-style work produced a modest success. His cover of Stevie Wonder's "That Girl" was a minor hit on modern jazz radio and Whitfield toured with a large band for a few months but found he disliked playing pop songs. He returned to playing more traditional jazz with a trio and in turn confounded the audiences, who were expecting his pop material. "The alternative is, you sell out your musical and artistic vision," he told Keith Spera of *Offbeat.* "If it's not a huge commercial success, then you're a complete failure—you have no recourse. You weren't successful as a jazz musician, you weren't successful as a pop musician. What do you do now?"

In 1994 Whitfield moved to the Verve record label and returned to his jazz and blues interests with *True Blue,* an album that featured seven original compositions and six jazz classics. The combination garnered both critical praise and impressive sales. "The maturation process of this standout jazz guitarist continues unabated,"

wrote Bob McCullough in the *Boston Globe.* It was followed by *7th Ave. Stroll,* in 1995, a collection of mostly original compositions and another commercial and critical success as well. His new life in Louisiana had helped move his playing beyond the styles he learned in Boston and New York but *7th Ave. Stroll* readily calls to mind the eastern urban ambiance of his beginnings at the Blue Note. With this album, it can be said, he has completed a creative circle.

In a commercial landscape that discourages young guitarists from pursing a career in straight-ahead jazz, Whitfield is a rarity. An academically-trained jazz purist, he is aware of the happy union of technical proficiency and soulful, emotive playing. Still, despite his accomplishments, he endeavors to move even farther from his academic background. He told Jonathan Eig of *Jazziz:* "I'm prone to playing a lot of notes.... At some point every jazz musician has to pass his technical audition with the audience. But once you do that, people don't want you to bombard them with technical prowess. They want you to show emotion."

Selected discography

The Marksman, Warner Brothers, 1990.
Patrice, Warner Brothers, 1991.
Mark Whitfield, Warner Brothers, 1993.
True Blue, Verve, 1994.
7th Ave. Stroll, Verve, 1995.

With others

From This Moment, Nicholas Payton, Verve, 1995.
Damn!, Jimmy Smith, Verve, 1995.

Sources

Birmingham News, October 5, 1995; October 9, 1995.
Dallas Morning News, February 10, 1995,
Downbeat, November 1995.
Jazziz, September 1995.
Kansas City Star, February 9, 1995.
Offbeat, October 1995.
San Diego Union-Tribune, October 14, 1995.

Additional information for this profile was obtained from Verve Records publicity materials, 1996.

—Link Yaco

Cumulative Indexes

Cumulative Subject Index

Volume numbers appear in **bold**.

Bernstein, Leonard **2**
Boyd, Liona **7**
Bream, Julian **9**
Britten, Benjamin **15**
Bronfman, Yefim **6**
Canadian Brass, The **4**
Carter, Ron **14**
Casals, Pablo **9**
Chang, Sarah **7**
Clayderman, Richard **1**
Cliburn, Van **13**
Copland, Aaron **2**
Davis, Anthony **17**
Davis, Chip **4**
Fiedler, Arthur **6**
Galway, James **3**
Gingold, Josef **6**
Gould, Glenn **9**
Gould, Morton **16**
Hampson, Thomas **12**
Harrell, Lynn **3**
Hayes, Roland **13**
Hendricks, Barbara **10**
Herrmann, Bernard **14**
Hinderas, Natalie **12**
Horne, Marilyn **9**
Horowitz, Vladimir **1**
Jarrett, Keith **1**
Kennedy, Nigel **8**
Kissin, Evgeny **6**
Kronos Quartet **5**
Kunzel, Erich **17**
Lemper, Ute **14**
Levine, James **8**
Liberace **9**
Ma, Yo-Yo **2**
Marsalis, Wynton **6**
Masur, Kurt **11**
McNair, Sylvia **15**
McPartland, Marian **15**
Mehta, Zubin **11**
Menuhin, Yehudi **11**
Midori **7**
Nyman, Michael **15**
Ott, David **2**
Parkening, Christopher **7**
Perahia, Murray **10**
Perlman, Itzhak **2**
Phillips, Harvey **3**
Rampal, Jean-Pierre **6**
Rostropovich, Mstislav **17**
Rota, Nino **13**
Rubinstein, Arthur **11**
Salerno-Sonnenberg, Nadja **3**
Salonen, Esa-Pekka **16**
Schickele, Peter **5**
Schuman, William **10**
Segovia, Andres **6**
Shankar, Ravi **9**
Solti, Georg **13**
Stern, Isaac **7**
Sutherland, Joan **13**
Takemitsu, Toru **6**
Toscanini, Arturo **14**
Upshaw, Dawn **9**

von Karajan, Herbert **1**
Weill, Kurt **12**
Wilson, Ransom **5**
Yamashita, Kazuhito **4**
York, Andrew **15**
Zukerman, Pinchas **4**

Composers
Adams, John **8**
Allen, Geri **10**
Alpert, Herb **11**
Anka, Paul **2**
Atkins, Chet **5**
Bacharach, Burt **1**
Badalamenti, Angelo **17**
Beiderbecke, Bix **16**
Benson, George **9**
Berlin, Irving **8**
Bernstein, Leonard **2**
Blackman, Cindy **15**
Bley, Carla **8**
Bley, Paul **14**
Braxton, Anthony **12**
Britten, Benjamin **15**
Brubeck, Dave **8**
Burrell, Kenny **11**
Byrne, David **8**
    Also see Talking Heads
Cage, John **8**
Cale, John **9**
Casals, Pablo **9**
Clarke, Stanley **3**
Coleman, Ornette **5**
Cooder, Ry **2**
Cooney, Rory **6**
Copeland, Stewart **14**
Copland, Aaron **2**
Crouch, Andraé **9**
Curtis, King **17**
Davis, Anthony **17**
Davis, Chip **4**
Davis, Miles **1**
de Grassi, Alex **6**
Dorsey, Thomas A. **11**
Elfman, Danny **9**
Ellington, Duke **2**
Eno, Brian **8**
Enya **6**
Esquivel, Juan **17**
Evans, Bill **17**
Evans, Gil **17**
Fahey, John **17**
Foster, David **13**
Frisell, Bill **15**
Galás, Diamanda **16**
Gillespie, Dizzy **6**
Glass, Philip **1**
Gould, Glenn **9**
Gould, Morton **16**
Green, Benny **17**
Grusin, Dave **7**
Guaraldi, Vince **3**
Hamlisch, Marvin **1**
Hancock, Herbie **8**
Handy, W. C. **7**

Hargrove, Roy **15**
Harris, Eddie **15**
Hartke, Stephen **5**
Henderson, Fletcher **16**
Herrmann, Bernard **14**
Hunter, Alberta **7**
Isham, Mark **14**
Jacquet, Illinois **17**
Jarre, Jean-Michel **2**
Jarrett, Keith **1**
Johnson, James P. **16**
Jones, Hank **15**
Jones, Quincy **2**
Joplin, Scott **10**
Jordan, Stanley **1**
Kenny G **14**
Kern, Jerome **13**
Kitaro **1**
Kottke, Leo **13**
Lateef, Yusef **16**
Lee, Peggy **8**
Legg, Adrian **17**
Lewis, Ramsey **14**
Lincoln, Abbey **9**
Lloyd Webber, Andrew **6**
Loewe, Frederick
    See Lerner and Loewe
Mancini, Henry **1**
Marsalis, Branford **10**
Marsalis, Ellis **13**
Martino, Pat **17**
Masekela, Hugh **7**
McBride, Christian **17**
McPartland, Marian **15**
Menken, Alan **10**
Metheny, Pat **2**
Mingus, Charles **9**
Moby **17**
Monk, Meredith **1**
Monk, Thelonious **6**
Montenegro, Hugo **18**
Morricone, Ennio **15**
Morton, Jelly Roll **7**
Mulligan, Gerry **16**
Nascimento, Milton **6**
Newman, Randy **4**
Nyman, Michael **15**
Oldfield, Mike **18**
Ott, David **2**
Palmieri, Eddie **15**
Parker, Charlie **5**
Parks, Van Dyke **17**
Peterson, Oscar **11**
Piazzolla, Astor **18**
Ponty, Jean-Luc **8**
Porter, Cole **10**
Previn, André **15**
Puente, Tito **14**
Pullen, Don **16**
Reich, Steve **8**
Reinhardt, Django **7**
Ritenour, Lee **7**
Roach, Max **12**
Rollins, Sonny **7**
Rota, Nino **13**

Grusin, Dave **7**
Guaraldi, Vince **3**
Hamlisch, Marvin **1**
Hancock, Herbie **8**
Harrison, George **2**
Hayes, Isaac **10**
Hedges, Michael **3**
Herrmann, Bernard **14**
Isham, Mark **14**
Jones, Quincy **2**
Knopfler, Mark **3**
Lennon, John **9**
  Also see Beatles, The
Lerner and Loewe **13**
Mancini, Henry **1**
Marsalis, Branford **10**
Mayfield, Curtis **8**
McCartney, Paul **4**
  Also see Beatles, The
Menken, Alan **10**
Mercer, Johnny **13**
Metheny, Pat **2**
Montenegro, Hugo **18**
Morricone, Ennio **15**
Nascimento, Milton **6**
Nilsson **10**
Nyman, Michael **15**
Parks, Van Dyke **17**
Peterson, Oscar **11**
Porter, Cole **10**
Previn, André **15**
Reznor, Trent **13**
Richie, Lionel **2**
Robertson, Robbie **2**
Rollins, Sonny **7**
Rota, Nino **13**
Sager, Carole Bayer **5**
Sakamoto, Ryuichi **18**
Schickele, Peter **5**
Shankar, Ravi **9**
Taj Mahal **6**
Waits, Tom **12**
  Earlier sketch in CM **1**
Weill, Kurt **12**
Williams, John **9**
Williams, Paul **5**
Willner, Hal **10**
Young, Neil **15**
  Earlier sketch in CM **2**

Flugelhorn
Sandoval, Arturo **15**

Flute
Anderson, Ian
  See Jethro Tull
Galway, James **3**
Lateef, Yusef **16**
Mann, Herbie **16**
Rampal, Jean-Pierre **6**
Ulmer, James Blood **13**
Wilson, Ransom **5**

Folk/Traditional
Altan **18**
America **16**

Arnaz, Desi **8**
Baez, Joan **1**
Belafonte, Harry **8**
Black, Mary **15**
Blades, Ruben **2**
Bloom, Luka **14**
Blue Rodeo **18**
Brady, Paul **8**
Bragg, Billy **7**
Bromberg, David **18**
Buckley, Tim **14**
Bulgarian State Female Vocal Choir, The
  10
Byrds, The **8**
Carter Family, The **3**
Chandra, Sheila **16**
Chapin, Harry **6**
Chapman, Tracy **4**
Chenille Sisters, The **16**
Cherry, Don **10**
Chieftains, The **7**
Childs, Toni **2**
Clegg, Johnny **8**
Cockburn, Bruce **8**
Cohen, Leonard **3**
Collins, Judy **4**
Colvin, Shawn **11**
Cotten, Elizabeth **16**
Crosby, David **3**
  Also see Byrds, The
Cruz, Celia **10**
de Lucia, Paco **1**
DeMent, Iris **13**
Donovan **9**
Dr. John **7**
Drake, Nick **17**
Dylan, Bob **3**
Elliot, Cass **5**
Enya **6**
Estefan, Gloria **15**
  Earlier sketch in CM **2**
Fahey, John **17**
Feliciano, José **10**
Galway, James **3**
Germano, Lisa **18**
Gilmore, Jimmie Dale **11**
Gipsy Kings, The **8**
Gorka, John **18**
Griffith, Nanci **3**
Grisman, David **17**
Guthrie, Arlo **6**
Guthrie, Woody **2**
Hakmoun, Hassan **15**
Hardin, Tim **18**
Harding, John Wesley **6**
Hartford, John **1**
Havens, Richie **11**
Henry, Joe **18**
Hinojosa, Tish **13**
Ian and Sylvia **18**
Iglesias, Julio **2**
Indigo Girls **3**
Ives, Burl **12**
Khan, Nusrat Fateh Ali **13**
Kingston Trio, The **9**
Klezmatics, The **18**

Kottke, Leo **13**
Kuti, Fela **7**
Ladysmith Black Mambazo **1**
Larkin, Patty **9**
Lavin, Christine **6**
Leadbelly **6**
Lightfoot, Gordon **3**
Los Lobos **2**
Makeba, Miriam **8**
Masekela, Hugh **7**
McLean, Don **7**
Melanie **12**
Mitchell, Joni **17**
  Earlier sketch in CM **2**
Moffatt, Katy **18**
Morrison, Van **3**
Morrissey, Bill **12**
Nascimento, Milton **6**
N'Dour, Youssou **6**
Near, Holly **1**
Ochs, Phil **7**
O'Connor, Sinead **3**
Odetta **7**
Parsons, Gram **7**
  Also see Byrds, The
Paxton, Tom **5**
Pentangle **18**
Peter, Paul & Mary **4**
Pogues, The **6**
Prine, John **7**
Proclaimers, The **13**
Redpath, Jean **1**
Ritchie, Jean, **4**
Roches, The **18**
Rodgers, Jimmie **3**
Sainte-Marie, Buffy **11**
Santana, Carlos **1**
Seeger, Pete **4**
  Also see Weavers, The
Selena **16**
Shankar, Ravi **9**
Simon, Paul **16**
  Earlier sketch in CM **1**
Snow, Pheobe **4**
Story, The **13**
Sweet Honey in the Rock **1**
Taj Mahal **6**
Thompson, Richard **7**
Tikaram, Tanita **9**
Toure, Ali Farka **18**
Van Ronk, Dave **12**
Van Zandt, Townes **13**
Vega, Suzanne **3**
Wainwright III, Loudon **11**
Walker, Jerry Jeff **13**
Watson, Doc **2**
Weavers, The **8**

French Horn
Ohanian, David
  See Canadian Brass, The

Funk
Bambaataa, Afrika **13**
Brand New Heavies, The **14**
Brown, James **2**

Burdon, Eric **14**
  Also see War
Clinton, George **7**
Collins, Bootsy **8**
Fishbone **7**
Gang of Four **8**
Jackson, Janet **3**
Khan, Chaka **9**
Mayfield, Curtis **8**
Meters, The **14**
Ohio Players **16**
Parker, Maceo **7**
Prince **14**
  Earlier sketch in CM **1**
Red Hot Chili Peppers, The **7**
Stone, Sly **8**
Toussaint, Allen **11**
Worrell, Bernie **11**

Fusion
Anderson, Ray **7**
Beck, Jeff **4**
  Also see Yardbirds, The
Clarke, Stanley **3**
Coleman, Ornette **5**
Corea, Chick **6**
Davis, Miles **1**
Fishbone **7**
Hancock, Herbie **8**
Harris, Eddie **15**
Lewis, Ramsey **14**
McLaughlin, John **12**
Metheny, Pat **2**
O'Connor, Mark **1**
Ponty, Jean-Luc **8**
Reid, Vernon **2**
Ritenour, Lee **7**
Shorter, Wayne **5**
Summers, Andy **3**
Washington, Grover, Jr. **5**

Gospel
Anderson, Marian **8**
Boone, Pat **13**
Brown, James **2**
Caesar, Shirley **17**
Carter Family, The **3**
Charles, Ray **1**
Cleveland, James **1**
Cooke, Sam **1**
  Also see Soul Stirrers, The
Crouch, Andraé **9**
Dorsey, Thomas A. **11**
Five Blind Boys of Alabama **12**
Ford, Tennessee Ernie **3**
Franklin, Aretha **17**
  Earlier sketch in CM **2**
Green, Al **9**
Hawkins, Tramaine **17**
Houston, Cissy **6**
Jackson, Mahalia **8**
Kee, John P. **15**
Knight, Gladys **1**
Little Richard **1**
Louvin Brothers, The **12**
Mighty Clouds of Joy, The **17**

Oak Ridge Boys, The **7**
Paris, Twila **16**
Pickett, Wilson **10**
Presley, Elvis **1**
Redding, Otis **5**
Reese, Della **13**
Robbins, Marty **9**
Smith, Michael W. **11**
Soul Stirrers, The **11**
Sounds of Blackness **13**
Staples, Mavis **13**
Staples, Pops **11**
Take 6 **6**
Waters, Ethel **11**
Watson, Doc **2**
Williams, Deniece **1**
Williams, Marion **15**
Winans, The **12**
Womack, Bobby **5**

Guitar
Ackerman, Will **3**
Adé, King Sunny **18**
Allman, Duane
  See Allman Brothers, The
Alvin, Dave **17**
Atkins, Chet **5**
Autry, Gene **12**
Baxter, Jeff
  See Doobie Brothers, The
Beck **18**
Beck, Jeff **4**
  Also see Yardbirds, The
Belew, Adrian **5**
Benson, George **9**
Berry, Chuck **1**
Berry, John **17**
Bettencourt, Nuno
  See Extreme
Betts, Dicky
  See Allman Brothers, The
Block, Rory **18**
Bloom, Luka **14**
Boyd, Liona **7**
Bream, Julian **9**
Bromberg, David **18**
Brown, Junior **15**
Buck, Peter
  See R.E.M.
Buckingham, Lindsey **8**
  Also see Fleetwood Mac
Burrell, Kenny **11**
Campbell, Glen **2**
Chesnutt, Mark **13**
Christian, Charlie **11**
Clapton, Eric **11**
  Earlier sketch in CM **1**
  Also see Cream
  Also see Yardbirds, The
Clark, Roy **1**
Cockburn, Bruce **8**
Collie, Mark **15**
Collins, Albert **4**
Cooder, Ry **2**
Cotten, Elizabeth **16**
Cray, Robert **8**

Cropper, Steve **12**
Dale, Dick **13**
Daniels, Charlie **6**
Davis, Reverend Gary **18**
de Grassi, Alex **6**
de Lucia, Paco **1**
Dickens, Little Jimmy **7**
Diddley, Bo **3**
DiFranco, Ani **17**
Di Meola, Al **12**
Drake, Nick **17**
Earl, Ronnie **5**
  Also see Roomful of Blues
Eddy, Duane **9**
Edge, The
  See U2
Ellis, Herb **18**
Etheridge, Melissa **16**
  Earlier sketch in CM **4**
Fahey, John **17**
Feliciano, José **10**
Fender, Leo **10**
Flatt, Lester **3**
Flores, Rosie **16**
Ford, Lita **9**
Frampton, Peter **3**
Frehley, Ace
  See Kiss
Fripp, Robert **9**
Frisell, Bill **15**
Garcia, Jerry **4**
  Also see Grateful Dead, The
Gatton, Danny **16**
George, Lowell
  See Little Feat
Gibbons, Billy
  See ZZ Top
Gill, Vince **7**
Gilmour, David
  See Pink Floyd
Gorka, John **18**
Green, Grant **14**
Green, Peter
  See Fleetwood Mac
Guy, Buddy **4**
Haley, Bill **6**
Hardin, Tim **18**
Harper, Ben **17**
Harrison, George **2**
Hatfield, Juliana **12**
  Also see Lemonheads, The
Havens, Richie **11**
Healey, Jeff **4**
Hedges, Michael **3**
Hendrix, Jimi **2**
Hillman, Chris
  See Byrds, The
  Also see Desert Rose Band, The
Hitchcock, Robyn **9**
Holly, Buddy **1**
Hooker, John Lee **1**
Hopkins, Lightnin' **13**
Howlin' Wolf **6**
Iommi, Tony
  See Black Sabbath
Ives, Burl **12**

Herrmann, Bernard **14**
Horne, Marilyn **9**
McNair, Sylvia **15**
Norman, Jessye **7**
Pavarotti, Luciano **1**
Price, Leontyne **6**
Sills, Beverly **5**
Solti, Georg **13**
Sutherland, Joan **13**
Te Kanawa, Kiri **2**
Toscanini, Arturo **14**
Upshaw, Dawn **9**
von Karajan, Herbert **1**
Weill, Kurt **12**
Zimmerman, Udo **5**

Percussion
Baker, Ginger **16**
    Also see Cream
Blackman, Cindy **15**
Blakey, Art **11**
Bonham, John
    See Led Zeppelin
Burton, Gary **10**
Collins, Phil **2**
    Also see Genesis
Copeland, Stewart **14**
DeJohnette, Jack **7**
Densmore, John
    See Doors, The
Dunbar, Aynsley
    See Jefferson Starship
    Also See Whitesnake
Dunbar, Sly
    See Sly and Robbie
Fleetwood, Mick
    See Fleetwood Mac
Hampton, Lionel **6**
Hart, Mickey
    See Grateful Dead, The
Henley, Don **3**
Jones, Elvin **9**
Jones, Kenny
    See Who, The
Jones, Philly Joe **16**
Jones, Spike **5**
Kreutzman, Bill
    See Grateful Dead, The
Krupa, Gene **13**
Mason, Nick
    See Pink Floyd
Moon, Keith
    See Who, The
N'Dour, Youssou **6**
Otis, Johnny **16**
Palmer, Carl
    See Emerson, Lake & Palmer/Powell
Palmieri, Eddie **15**
Peart, Neil
    See Rush
Powell, Cozy
    See Emerson, Lake & Palmer/Powell
Puente, Tito **14**
Rich, Buddy **13**
Roach, Max **12**
Sheila E. **3**

Starr, Ringo **10**
    Also see Beatles, The
Walden, Narada Michael **14**
Watts, Charlie
    See Rolling Stones, The
Webb, Chick **14**

Piano
Allen, Geri **10**
Allison, Mose **17**
Amos, Tori **12**
Arrau, Claudio **1**
Bacharach, Burt **1**
Ball, Marcia **15**
Basie, Count **2**
Berlin, Irving **8**
Bley, Carla **8**
Bley, Paul **14**
Britten, Benjamin **15**
Bronfman, Yefim **6**
Brubeck, Dave **8**
Bush, Kate **4**
Charles, Ray **1**
Clayderman, Richard **1**
Cleveland, James **1**
Cliburn, Van **13**
Cole, Nat King **3**
Collins, Judy **4**
Collins, Phil **2**
    Also see Genesis
Connick, Harry, Jr. **4**
Crouch, Andraé **9**
DeJohnette, Jack **7**
Domino, Fats **2**
Dr. John **7**
Dupree, Champion Jack **12**
Esquivel, Juan **17**
Ellington, Duke **2**
Evans, Bill **17**
Evans, Gil **17**
Feinstein, Michael **6**
Ferrell, Rachelle **17**
Flack, Roberta **5**
Flanagan, Tommy **16**
Frey, Glenn **3**
Galás, Diamanda **16**
Glass, Philip **1**
Gould, Glenn **9**
Green, Benny **17**
Grusin, Dave **7**
Guaraldi, Vince **3**
Hamlisch, Marvin **1**
Hancock, Herbie **8**
Henderson, Fletcher **16**
Hinderas, Natalie **12**
Hines, Earl "Fatha" **12**
Horn, Shirley **7**
Hornsby, Bruce **3**
Horowitz, Vladimir **1**
Jackson, Joe **4**
Jarrett, Keith **1**
Joel, Billy **12**
    Earlier sketch in CM **2**
John, Elton **3**
Johnson, James P. **16**
Jones, Hank **15**

Joplin, Scott **10**
Kissin, Evgeny **6**
Levine, James **8**
Lewis, Jerry Lee **2**
Lewis, Ramsey **14**
Liberace **9**
Little Richard **1**
Manilow, Barry **2**
Marsalis, Ellis **13**
McDonald, Michael
    See Doobie Brothers, The
McPartland, Marian **15**
McRae, Carmen **9**
McVie, Christine
    See Fleetwood Mac
Milsap, Ronnie **2**
Mingus, Charles **9**
Monk, Thelonious **6**
Morton, Jelly Roll **7**
Newman, Randy **4**
Palmieri, Eddie **15**
Perahia, Murray **10**
Peterson, Oscar **11**
Powell, Bud **15**
Previn, André **15**
Professor Longhair **6**
Puente, Tito **14**
Pullen, Don **16**
Rich, Charlie **3**
Roberts, Marcus **6**
Rubinstein, Arthur **11**
Russell, Mark **6**
Schickele, Peter **5**
Sedaka, Neil **4**
Shaffer, Paul **13**
Solal, Martial **4**
Solti, Georg **13**
Spann, Otis **18**
Story, Liz **2**
Strayhorn, Billy **13**
Sunnyland Slim **16**
Tatum, Art **17**
Taylor, Billy **13**
Taylor, Cecil **9**
Tyner, McCoy **7**
Waits, Tom **12**
    Earlier sketch in **1**
Waller, Fats **7**
Weston, Randy **15**
Wilson, Cassandra **12**
Winston, George **9**
Winwood, Steve **2**
Wonder, Stevie **17**
    Earlier sketch in CM **2**
Wright, Rick
    See Pink Floyd
Young, La Monte **16**

Piccolo
Galway, James **3**

Pop
Abba **12**
Abdul, Paula **3**
Adam Ant **13**
Adams, Bryan **2**

Knight, Suge **15**
Kool Moe Dee **9**
Kris Kross **11**
KRS-One **8**
L.L. Cool J. **5**
MC Breed **17**
MC Lyte **8**
MC 900 Ft. Jesus **16**
MC Serch **10**
Naughty by Nature **11**
N.W.A. **6**
Pharcyde, The **17**
P.M. Dawn **11**
Public Enemy **4**
Queen Latifah **6**
Rage Against the Machine **18**
Riley, Teddy **14**
Rubin, Rick **9**
Run-D.M.C. **4**
Salt-N-Pepa **6**
Scott-Heron, Gil **13**
Shanté **10**
Shocklee, Hank **15**
Simmons, Russell **7**
Sir Mix-A-Lot **14**
Snoop Doggy Dogg **17**
Special Ed **16**
Sure!, Al B. **13**
TLC **15**
Tone-L c **3**
Too $hort **16**
Tribe Called Quest, A **8**
Tricky **18**
2Pac **17**
US3 **18**
Vanilla Ice **6**
Young M.C. **4**
Yo Yo **9**

Record Company Executives
Ackerman, Will **3**
Alpert, Herb **11**
Brown, Tony **14**
Busby, Jheryl **9**
Combs, Sean "Puffy" **16**
Davis, Chip **4**
Davis, Clive **14**
Ertegun, Ahmet **10**
Foster, David **13**
Gabriel, Peter **16**
  Earlier sketch in CM **2**
  Also see Genesis
Geffen, David **8**
Gordy, Berry, Jr. **6**
Hammond, John **6**
Harley, Bill **7**
Harrell, Andre **16**
Jam, Jimmy, and Terry Lewis **11**
Knight, Suge **15**
Koppelman, Charles **14**
Krasnow, Bob **15**
LiPuma, Tommy **18**
Madonna **16**
  Earlier sketch in CM **4**
Marley, Rita **10**

Martin, George **6**
Mayfield, Curtis **8**
Mercer, Johnny **13**
Miller, Mitch **11**
Mingus, Charles **9**
Near, Holly **1**
Ostin, Mo **17**
Penner, Fred **10**
Phillips, Sam **5**
Reznor, Trent **13**
Rhone, Sylvia **13**
Robinson, Smokey **1**
Rubin, Rick **9**
Simmons, Russell **7**
Spector, Phil **4**
Teller, Al **15**
Too $hort **16**
Wexler, Jerry **15**

Reggae
Bad Brains **16**
Black Uhuru **12**
Burning Spear **15**
Cliff, Jimmy **8**
Dube, Lucky **17**
Inner Circle **15**
Marley, Bob **3**
Marley, Rita **10**
Marley, Ziggy **3**
Mystic Revealers **16**
Skatalites, The **18**
Sly and Robbie **13**
Steel Pulse **14**
Third World **13**
Tosh, Peter **3**
UB40 **4**
Wailer, Bunny **11**

Rhythm and Blues/Soul
Abdul, Paula **3**
Adams, Oleta **17**
Alexander, Arthur **14**
All-4-One **17**
Austin, Dallas **16**
Baker, Anita **9**
Ball, Marcia **15**
Ballard, Hank **17**
Basehead **11**
Belle, Regina **6**
Berry, Chuck **1**
Bland, Bobby "Blue" **12**
Blige, Mary J. **15**
Blues Brothers, The **3**
Bolton, Michael **4**
Boyz II Men **15**
Braxton, Toni **17**
Brown, James **16**
  Earlier sketch in CM **2**
Brown, Ruth **13**
Bryson, Peabo **11**
Burdon, Eric **14**
  Also see War
Busby, Jheryl **9**
C + C Music Factory **16**
Campbell, Tevin **13**

Carey, Mariah **6**
Charles, Ray **1**
Cole, Natalie **1**
Cooke, Sam **1**
  Also see Soul Stirrers, The
Cropper, Steve **12**
Curtis, King **17**
D'Arby, Terence Trent **3**
DeBarge, El **14**
Des'ree **15**
Dibango, Manu **14**
Diddley, Bo **3**
Domino, Fats **2**
Dr. John **7**
Earth, Wind and Fire **12**
Edmonds, Kenneth "Babyface" **12**
En Vogue **10**
Fabulous Thunderbirds, The **1**
Four Tops, The **11**
Fox, Samantha **3**
Franklin, Aretha **17**
  Earlier sketch in CM **2**
Gaye, Marvin **4**
Gordy, Berry, Jr. **6**
Green, Al **9**
Hall & Oates **6**
Hayes, Isaac **10**
Holland-Dozier-Holland **5**
Incognito **16**
Ingram, James **11**
Isley Brothers, The **8**
Jackson, Freddie **3**
Jackson, Janet **3**
Jackson, Michael **17**
  Earlier sketch in CM **1**
  Also see Jackson, The
Jackson, Millie **14**
Jacksons, The **7**
Jam, Jimmy, and Terry Lewis **11**
James, Etta **6**
Jodeci **13**
Jones, Booker T. **8**
Jones, Grace **9**
Jones, Quincy **2**
Jordan, Louis **11**
Khan, Chaka **9**
King, Ben E. **7**
Knight, Gladys **1**
Kool & the Gang **13**
LaBelle, Patti **8**
Los Lobos **2**
Mayfield, Curtis **8**
Medley, Bill **3**
Meters, The **14**
Milli Vanilli **4**
Moore, Melba **7**
Morrison, Van **3**
Ndegéocello, Me'Shell **18**
Neville, Aaron **5**
  Also see Neville Brothers, The
Neville Brothers, The **4**
Ocean, Billy **4**
Ohio Players **16**
O'Jays, The **13**
Otis, Johnny **16**

Lateef, Yusef **16**
Lopez, Israel "Cachao" **14**
Lovano, Joe **13**
Marsalis, Branford **10**
Morgan, Frank **9**
Mulligan, Gerry **16**
Parker, Charlie **5**
Parker, Maceo **7**
Pepper, Art **18**
Redman, Joshua **12**
Rollins, Sonny **7**
Sanborn, David **1**
Sanders, Pharoah **16**
Shorter, Wayne **5**
Threadgill, Henry **9**
Washington, Grover, Jr. **5**
Winter, Paul **10**
Young, La Monte **16**
Young, Lester **14**
Zorn, John **15**

Sintir
Hakmoun, Hassan **15**

Songwriters
Acuff, Roy **2**
Adams, Bryan **2**
Albini, Steve **15**
Alexander, Arthur **14**
Allen, Peter **11**
Allison, Mose **17**
Alpert, Herb **11**
Alvin, Dave **17**
Amos, Tori **12**
Anderson, Ian
    See Jethro Tull
Anderson, John **5**
Anka, Paul **2**
Armatrading, Joan **4**
Astbury, Ian
    See Cult, The
Atkins, Chet **5**
Autry, Gene **12**
Bacharach, Burt **1**
Baez, Joan **1**
Baker, Anita **9**
Balin, Marty
    See Jefferson Airplane
Barrett, (Roger) Syd
    See Pink Floyd
Basie, Count **2**
Becker, Walter
    See Steely Dan
Beckley, Gerry
    See America
Belew, Adrian **5**
Benton, Brook **7**
Berg, Matraca **16**
Berlin, Irving **8**
Berry, Chuck **1**
Bjork **16**
    Also see Sugarcubes, The
Black, Clint **5**
Black, Frank **14**
Blades, Ruben **2**
Blige, Mary J. **15**

Bloom, Luka **14**
Bono
    See U2
Brady, Paul **8**
Bragg, Billy **7**
Brickell, Edie **3**
Brooke, Jonatha
    See Story, The
Brooks, Garth **8**
Brown, Bobby **4**
Brown, James **16**
    Earlier sketch in CM **2**
Brown, Junior **15**
Brown, Marty **14**
Browne, Jackson **3**
Buck, Peter
    See R.E.M.
Buck, Robert
    See 10,000 Maniacs
Buckingham, Lindsey **8**
    Also see Fleetwood Mac
Buckley, Tim **14**
Buffett, Jimmy **4**
Bunnell, Dewey
    See America
Burdon, Eric **14**
    Also see War
Burnett, T Bone **13**
Burning Spear **15**
Bush, Kate **4**
Byrne, David **8**
    Also see Talking Heads
Cahn, Sammy **11**
Cale, J. J. **16**
Cale, John **9**
Calloway, Cab **6**
Captain Beefheart **10**
Carpenter, Mary-Chapin **6**
Carter, Carlene **8**
Cash, Johnny **17**
    Earlier sketch in CM **1**
Cash, Rosanne **2**
Cetera, Peter
    See Chicago
Chandra, Sheila **16**
Chapin, Harry **6**
Chapman, Steven Curtis **15**
Chapman, Tracy **4**
Charles, Ray **1**
Chenier, C. J. **15**
Childs, Toni **2**
Chilton, Alex **10**
Clapton, Eric **11**
    Earlier sketch in CM **1**
    Also see Cream
    Also see Yardbirds, The
Clark, Guy **17**
Clements, Vassar **18**
Cleveland, James **1**
Clinton, George **7**
Cockburn, Bruce **8**
Cohen, Leonard **3**
Cole, Lloyd **9**
Cole, Nat King **3**
Collins, Albert **4**

Collins, Judy **4**
Collins, Phil **2**
    Also see Genesis
Cooder, Ry **2**
Cooke, Sam **1**
    Also see Soul Stirrers, The
Collie, Mark **15**
Cooper, Alice **8**
Cope, Julian **16**
Corgan, Billy
    See Smashing Pumpkins
Costello, Elvis **12**
    Earlier sketch in CM **2**
Cotten, Elizabeth **16**
Crenshaw, Marshall **5**
Croce, Jim **3**
Crofts, Dash
    See Seals & Crofts
Cropper, Steve **12**
Crosby, David **3**
    Also see Byrds, The
Crow, Sheryl **18**
Crowe, J. D. **5**
Crowell, Rodney **8**
Daniels, Charlie **6**
Davies, Ray **5**
    Also see Kinks, the
DeBarge, El **14**
DeMent, Iris **13**
Denver, John **1**
Des'ree **15**
Diamond, Neil **1**
Diddley, Bo **3**
Difford, Chris
    See Squeeze
DiFranco, Ani **17**
Dion **4**
Dixon, Willie **10**
Doc Pomus **14**
Domino, Fats **2**
Donelly, Tanya
    See Belly
    Also see Throwing Muses
Donovan **9**
Dorsey, Thomas A. **11**
Doucet, Michael **8**
Dozier, Lamont
    See Holland-Dozier-Holland
Drake, Nick **17**
Dube, Lucky **17**
Duffy, Billy
    See Cult, The
Dulli, Greg **17**
    See Afghan Whigs, The
Dylan, Bob **3**
Earle, Steve **16**
Edge, The
    See U2
Edmonds, Kenneth "Babyface" **12**
Eitzel, Mark
    See American Music Club
Elfman, Danny **9**
Ellington, Duke **2**
Emerson, Keith
    See Emerson, Lake & Palmer/Powell

Jones, Michael
  See Kronos Quartet
Killian, Tim
  See Kronos Quartet
Menuhin, Yehudi **11**
Zukerman, Pinchas **4**

Violin
Acuff, Roy **2**
Anderson, Laurie **1**
Bromberg, David **18**
Bush, Sam
  See New Grass Revival, The
Chang, Sarah **7**
Clements, Vassar **18**
Coleman, Ornette **5**

Daniels, Charlie **6**
Doucet, Michael **8**
Germano, Lisa **18**
Gingold, Josef **6**
Grappelli, Stephane **10**
Gray, Ella
  See Kronos Quartet
Harrington, David
  See Kronos Quartet
Hartford, John **1**
Hidalgo, David
  See Los Lobos
Kennedy, Nigel **8**
Krauss, Alison **10**
Lewis, Roy
  See Kronos Quartet

Marriner, Neville **7**
Menuhin, Yehudi **11**
Midori **7**
O'Connor, Mark **1**
Perlman, Itzhak **2**
Ponty, Jean-Luc **8**
Salerno-Sonnenberg, Nadja **3**
Shallenberger, James
  See Kronos Quartet
Sherba, John
  See Kronos Quartet
Skaggs, Ricky **5**
Stern, Isaac **7**
Whiteman, Paul **17**
Wills, Bob **6**
Zukerman, Pinchas **4**

Cumulative Musicians Index

Volume numbers appear in **bold**.

Beckford, Theophilus
  See Skatalites, The
Beckley, Gerry
  See America
Bee Gees, The **3**
Beers, Garry Gary
  See INXS
Behler, Chuck
  See Megadeth
Beiderbecke, Bix **16**
Belafonte, Harry **8**
Belew, Adrian **5**
  Also see King Crimson
Belfield, Dennis
  See Three Dog Night
Bell, Andy
  See Erasure
Bell, Derek
  See Chieftains, The
Bell, Eric
  See Thin Lizzy
Bell, Jayn
  See Sounds of Blackness
Bell, Melissa
  See Soul II Soul
Bell, Ronald
  See Kool & the Gang
Belladonna, Joey
  See Anthrax
Bellamy, David
  See Bellamy Brothers, The
Bellamy, Howard
  See Bellamy Brothers, The
Bellamy Brothers, The **13**
Belle, Regina **6**
Bello, Frank
  See Anthrax
Belly **16**
Belushi, John
  See Blues Brothers, The
Benante, Charlie
  See Anthrax
Benatar, Pat **8**
Benedict, Scott
  See Pere Ubu
Benitez, Jellybean **15**
Bennett, Tony **16**
  Earlier sketch in CM **2**
Bennett-Nesby, Ann
  See Sounds of Blackness
Benson, George **9**
Benson, Ray
  See Asleep at the Wheel
Benson, Renaldo "Obie"
  See Four Tops, The
Bentley, John
  See Squeeze
Benton, Brook **7**
Bentyne, Cheryl
  See Manhattan Transfer, The
Berenyi, Miki
  See Lush
Berg, Matraca **16**
Berigan, Bunny **2**
Berlin, Irving **8**

Berlin, Steve
  See Los Lobos
Bernstein, Leonard **2**
Berry, Bill
  See R.E.M.
Berry, Chuck **1**
Berry, John **17**
Berry, Robert
  See Emerson, Lake & Palmer/Powell
Best, Nathaniel
  See O'Jays, The
Best, Pete
  See Beatles, The
Bettencourt, Nuno
  See Extreme
Bettie Serveert **17**
Betts, Dicky
  See Allman Brothers, The
Bevan, Bev
  See Black Sabbath
    Also see Electric Light Orchestra
B-52's, The **4**
Biafra, Jello **18**
Big Audio Dynamite **18**
Big Mike
  See Geto Boys, The
Big Money Odis
  See Digital Underground
Bingham, John
  See Fishbone
Binks, Les
  See Judas Priest
Birchfield, Benny
  See Osborne Brothers, The
Bird
  See Parker, Charlie
Birdsong, Cindy
  See Supremes, The
Biscuits, Chuck
  See Danzig
Bishop, Michael
  See Gwar
Biz Markie **10**
Bizzy Bone
  See Bone Thugs-N-Harmony
Bjelland, Kat
  See Babes in Toyland
Björk **16**
  Also see Sugarcubes, The
Black, Clint **5**
Black Crowes, The **7**
Black Francis
  See Black, Frank
Black, Frank **14**
Black, Mary **15**
Black Sabbath **9**
Black Sheep **15**
Black Uhuru **12**
Black, Vic
  See C + C Music Factory
Blackman, Cindy **15**
Blackmore, Ritchie
  See Deep Purple
Blades, Ruben **2**
Blake, Norman

  See Teenage Fanclub
Blakey, Art **11**
Blanchard, Terence **13**
Bland, Bobby "Blue" **12**
Bley, Carla **8**
Bley, Paul **14**
Blige, Mary J. **15**
Block, Rory **18**
Blondie **14**
Blood, Sweat and Tears **7**
Bloom, Eric
  See Blue Oyster Cult
Bloom, Luka **14**
Blue Oyster Cult **16**
Blue Rodeo **18**
Blues, Elwood
  See Blues Brothers, The
Blues, "Joliet" Jake
  See Blues Brothers, The
Blues Brothers, The **3**
Blues Traveler **15**
Blunt, Martin
  See Charlatans, The
Blur **17**
Bob, Tim
  See Rage Against the Machine
BoDeans, The **3**
Bogaert, Jo
  See Technotronic
Bogdan, Henry
  See Helmet
Bogguss, Suzy **11**
Bolade, Nitanju
  See Sweet Honey in the Rock
Bolan, Marc
  See T. Rex
Bolton, Michael **4**
Bon Jovi **10**
Bon Jovi, Jon
  See Bon Jovi
Bonebrake, D. J.
  See X
Bone Thugs-N-Harmony **18**
Bonham, John
  See Led Zeppelin
Bonner, Leroy "Sugarfoot"
  See Ohio Players
Bono
  See U2
Bonsall, Joe
  See Oak Ridge Boys, The
Books
  See Das EFX
Boone, Pat **13**
Booth, Tim
  See James
Bordin, Mike
  See Faith No More
Borg, Bobby
  See Warrant
Borowiak, Tony
  See All-4-One
Bostaph, Paul
  See Slayer
Boston **11**

Cabaret Voltaire **18**
C + C Music Factory **16**
Cachao
    See Lopez, Israel "Cachao"
Caesar, Shirley **17**
Cafferty, John
    See Beaver Brown Band, The
Cage, John **8**
Cahn, Sammy **11**
Cale, J. J. **16**
Cale, John **9**
    Also see Velvet Underground, The
Calhoun, Will
    See Living Colour
Callahan, Ken
    See Jayhawks, The
Callas, Maria **11**
Callis, Jo
    See Human League, The
Calloway, Cab **6**
Cameron, Duncan
    See Sawyer Brown
Cameron, Matt
    See Soundgarden
Campbell, Ali
    See UB40
Campbell, Glen **2**
Campbell, Kerry
    See War
Campbell, Luther **10**
Campbell, Phil
    See Motörhead
Campbell, Robin
    See UB40
Campbell, Tevin **13**
Canadian Brass, The **4**
Cantrell, Jerry
    See Alice in Chains
Canty, Brendan
    See Fugazi
Cappelli, Frank **14**
Captain Beefheart **10**
Carey, Mariah **6**
Carlisle, Belinda **8**
Carlos, Bun E.
    See Cheap Trick
Carlos, Don
    See Black Uhuru
Carlson, Paulette
    See Highway 101
Carnes, Kim **4**
Carpenter, Bob
    See Nitty Gritty Dirt Band, The
Carpenter, Karen
    See Carpenters, The
Carpenter, Mary-Chapin **6**
Carpenter, Richard
    See Carpenters, The
Carpenters, The **13**
Carr, Eric
    See Kiss
Carrack, Paul
    See Mike & the Mechanics
    Also see Squeeze
Carreras, José **8**

Carrigan, Andy
    See Mekons, The
Carroll, Earl "Speedo"
    See Coasters, The
Carruthers, John
    See Siouxsie and the Banshees
Carter, Anita
    See Carter Family, The
Carter, A. P.
    See Carter Family, The
Carter, Benny **3**
    Also see McKinney's Cotton Pickers
Carter, Betty **6**
Carter, Carlene **8**
Carter, Helen
    See Carter Family, The
Carter, James **18**
Carter, Janette
    See Carter Family, The
Carter, Jimmy
    See Five Blind Boys of Alabama
Carter, Joe
    See Carter Family, The
Carter, June **6**
    Also see Carter Family, The
Carter, Maybell
    See Carter Family, The
Carter, Nell **7**
Carter, Ron **14**
Carter, Sara
    See Carter Family, The
Carter Family, The **3**
Caruso, Enrico **10**
Casady, Jack
    See Jefferson Airplane
Casale, Bob
    See Devo
Casale, Gerald V.
    See Devo
Casals, Pablo **9**
Case, Peter **13**
Cash, Johnny **17**
    Earlier sketch in CM **1**
Cash, Rosanne **2**
Cates, Ronny
    See Petra
Catherall, Joanne
    See Human League, The
Catherine Wheel **18**
Caustic Window
    See Aphex Twin
Cauty, Jimmy
    See Orb, The
Cavalera, Igor
    See Sepultura
Cavalera, Max
    See Sepultura
Cave, Nick **10**
Cavoukian, Raffi
    See Raffi
Cease, Jeff
    See Black Crowes, The
Cervenka, Exene
    See X
Cetera, Peter

    See Chicago
Chamberlin, Jimmy
    See Smashing Pumpkins
Chambers, Martin
    See Pretenders, The
Chambers, Paul **18**
Chambers, Terry
    See XTC
Chance, Slim
    See Cramps, The
Chandra, Sheila **16**
Chang, Sarah **7**
Channing, Carol **6**
Chapin, Harry **6**
Chapin, Tom **11**
Chapman, Steven Curtis **15**
Chapman, Tony
    See Rolling Stones, The
Chapman, Tracy **4**
Chaquico, Craig
    See Jefferson Starship
Charlatans, The **13**
Charles, Ray **1**
Chea, Alvin "Vinnie"
    See Take 6
Cheap Trick **12**
Checker, Chubby **7**
Cheeks, Julius
    See Soul Stirrers, The
Chenier, C. J. **15**
Chenier, Clifton **6**
Chenille Sisters, The **16**
Cher **1**
Cherone, Gary
    See Extreme
Cherry, Don **10**
Cherry, Neneh **4**
Chesnutt, Mark **13**
Chevalier, Maurice **6**
Chevron, Phillip
    See Pogues, The
Chicago **3**
Chieftains, The **7**
Childress, Ross
    See Collective Soul
Childs, Toni **2**
Chilton, Alex **10**
Chimes, Terry
    See Clash, The
Chopmaster J
    See Digital Underground
Christ, John
    See Danzig
Christian, Charlie **11**
Christina, Fran
    See Fabulous Thunderbirds, The
    Also see Roomful of Blues
Chuck D
    See Public Enemy
Chung, Mark
    See Einstürzende Neubauten
Church, Kevin
    See Country Gentlemen, The
Church, The **14**
Cinderella **16**

Crash Test Dummies **14**
Crawford, Dave Max
  See Poi Dog Pondering
Crawford, Ed
  See fIREHOSE
Crawford, Michael **4**
Cray, Robert **8**
Creach, Papa John
  See Jefferson Starship
Cream **9**
Creedence Clearwater Revival **16**
Creegan, Andrew
  See Barenaked Ladies
Creegan, Jim
  See Barenaked Ladies
Crenshaw, Marshall **5**
Cretu, Michael
  See Enigma
Criss, Peter
  See Kiss
Croce, Jim **3**
Crofts, Dash
  See Seals & Crofts
Cropper, Steve **12**
Crosby, Bing **6**
Crosby, David **3**
  Also see Byrds, The
Cross, David
  See King Crimson
Cross, Mike
  See Sponge
Cross, Tim
  See Sponge
Crouch, Andraé **9**
Crow, Sheryl **18**
Crowded House **12**
Crowe, J. D. **5**
Crowell, Rodney **8**
Cruz, Celia **10**
Cuddy, Jim
  See Blue Rodeo
Cult, The **16**
Cummings, David
  See Del Amitri
Cure, The **3**
Curless, Ann
  See Exposé
Curley, John
  See Afghan Whigs
Curran, Ciaran
  See Altan
Currie, Justin
  See Del Amitri
Currie, Steve
  See T. Rex
Curry, Tim **3**
Curtis, King **17**
Curve **13**
Custance, Mickey
  See Big Audio Dynamite
Cuthbert, Scott
  See Everclear
Cutler, Chris
  See Pere Ubu
Cypress Hill **11**
Cyrus, Billy Ray **11**

Dacus, Donnie
  See Chicago
Dacus, Johnny
  See Osborne Brothers, The
Daddy G
  See Massive Attack
Daddy Mack
  See Kris Kross
Daellenbach, Charles
  See Canadian Brass, The
Dahlheimer, Patrick
  See Live
Daisley, Bob
  See Black Sabbath
Dale, Dick **13**
Daley, Richard
  See Third World
Dall, Bobby
  See Poison
Dalton, John
  See Kinks, The
Dalton, Nic
  See Lemonheads, The
Daltrey, Roger **3**
  Also see Who, The
Dando, Evan
  See Lemonheads, The
D'Angelo, Greg
  See Anthrax
Daniels, Charlie **6**
Daniels, Jack
  See Highway 101
Danko, Rick
  See Band, The
Danny Boy
  See House of Pain
Danzig **7**
Danzig, Glenn
  See Danzig
D'Arby, Terence Trent **3**
Darin, Bobby **4**
Darling, Eric
  See Weavers, The
Darriau, Matt
  See Klezmatics, The
Darvill, Benjamin
  See Crash Test Dummies
Das EFX **14**
Daugherty, Jay Dee
  See Church, The
Daulne, Marie
  See Zap Mama
Dave Clark Five, The **12**
Dave Matthews Band **18**
Davenport, N'Dea
  See Brand New Heavies, The
Davidson, Lenny
  See Dave Clark Five, The
Davies, Dave
  See Kinks, The
Davies, Ray **5**
  Also see Kinks, The
Davies, Saul
  See James
Davis, Anthony **17**

Davis, Chip **4**
Davis, Clive **14**
Davis, Michael
  See MC5, The
Davis, Miles **1**
Davis, Reverend Gary **18**
Davis, Sammy, Jr. **4**
Davis, Skeeter **15**
Davis, Steve
  See Mystic Revealers
Davis, Zelma
  See C + C Music Factory
Dawdy, Cheryl
  See Chenille Sisters, The
Dayne, Taylor **4**
dc Talk **18**
de la Rocha, Zack
  See Rage Against the Machine
de Coster, Jean Paul
  See 2 Unlimited
DeBarge, El **14**
DeLeo, Dean
  See Stone Temple Pilots
DeLeo, Robert
  See Stone Temple Pilots
dePrume, Ivan
  See White Zombie
de Albuquerque, Michael
  See Electric Light Orchestra
Deacon, John
  See Queen
Dead Can Dance **16**
Deakin, Paul
  See Mavericks, The
Dee, Mikkey
  See Dokken
  Also see Motörhead
Deee-lite **9**
Deep Forest **18**
Deep Purple **11**
Def Leppard **3**
DeGarmo, Chris
  See Queensryche
de Grassi, Alex **6**
Deily, Ben
  See Lemonheads, The
DeJohnette, Jack **7**
Del Amitri **18**
De La Soul **7**
DeLorenzo, Victor
  See Violent Femmes
Del Mar, Candy
  See Cramps, The
Delp, Brad
  See Boston
de Lucia, Paco **1**
DeMent, Iris **13**
Demeski, Stanley
  See Luna
Demos, Greg
  See Guided By Voices
Dempsey, Michael
  See Cure, The
Dennis, Garth
  See Black Uhuru

Densmore, John
See Doors, The
Dent, Cedric
See Take 6
Denton, Sandy
See Salt-N-Pepa
Denver, John **1**
De Oliveria, Laudir
See Chicago
Depeche Mode **5**
Derosier, Michael
See Heart
Desert Rose Band, The **4**
Des'ree **15**
DeVille, C. C.
See Poison
Deschamps, Kim
See Blue Rodeo
Destri, Jimmy
See Blondie
Deupree, Jerome
See Morphine
Devo **13**
Devoto, Howard
See Buzzcocks, The
DeWitt, Lew C.
See Statler Brothers, The
de Young, Joyce
See Andrews Sisters, The
Diagram, Andy
See James
Diamond "Dimebag" Darrell
See Pantera
Diamond, Mike
See Beastie Boys, The
Diamond, Neil **1**
Diamond Rio **11**
Di'anno, Paul
See Iron Maiden
Dibango, Manu **14**
Dickens, Little Jimmy **7**
Dickerson, B. B.
See War
Dickinson, Paul Bruce
See Iron Maiden
Dickinson, Rob
See Catherine Wheel
Diddley, Bo **3**
Diffie, Joe **10**
Difford, Chris
See Squeeze
DiFranco, Ani **17**
Digable Planets **15**
Diggle, Steve
See Buzzcocks, The
Digital Underground **9**
Dilworth, Joe
See Stereolab
DiMant, Leor
See House of Pain
Di Meola, Al **12**
DiMucci, Dion
See Dion
DiNizo, Pat
See Smithereens, The
Dinning, Dean

See Toad the Wet Sprocket
Dinosaur Jr. **10**
Dio, Ronnie James
See Black Sabbath
Dion **4**
Dion, Céline **12**
Dirks, Michael
See Gwar
Dirnt, Mike
See Green Day
Dittrich, John
See Restless Heart
Dixon, Jerry
See Warrant
Dixon, Willie **10**
DJ Domination
See Geto Boys, The
DJ Fuse
See Digital Underground
DJ Jazzy Jeff and the Fresh Prince **5**
D.J. Lethal
See House of Pain
D.J. Minutemix
See P.M. Dawn
DJ Muggs
See Cypress Hill
DJ Premier
See Gang Starr
DJ Ready Red
See Geto Boys, The
DJ Terminator X
See Public Enemy
Doc Pomus **14**
Dombroski, Vinnie
See Sponge
Donovan, Bazil
See Blue Rodeo
Doth, Anita
See 2 Unlimited
Downie, Gordon
See Tragically Hip , The
Doyle, Candida
See Pulp
Dr. Dre **15**
Also see N.W.A.
Dr. John **7**
Doe, John
See X
Dokken **16**
Dokken, Don
See Dokken
Dolby, Thomas **10**
Dolenz, Micky
See Monkees, The
Domingo, Placido **1**
Domino, Fats **2**
Don, Rasa
See Arrested Development
Donelly, Tanya
See Belly
Also see Throwing Muses
Donovan **9**
Doobie Brothers, The **3**
Doodlebug
See Digable Planets
Doors, The **4**

Dorge, Michel (Mitch)
See Crash Test Dummies
Dorsey, Jimmy
See Dorsey Brothers, The
Dorsey, Thomas A. **11**
Dorsey, Tommy
See Dorsey Brothers, The
Dorsey Brothers, The **8**
Doucet, Michael **8**
Douglas, Jerry
See Country Gentlemen, The
Dowd, Christopher
See Fishbone
Downes, Geoff
See Yes
Downey, Brian
See Thin Lizzy
Downing, K. K.
See Judas Priest
Dozier, Lamont
See Holland-Dozier-Holland
Drake, Nick **17**
Drayton, Leslie
See Earth, Wind and Fire
Dreja, Chris
See Yardbirds, The
Drew, Dennis
See 10,000 Maniacs
Drumbago,
See Skatalites, The
Drumdini, Harry
See Cramps, The
Drummond, Don
See Skatalites, The
Dryden, Spencer
See Jefferson Airplane
Dubbe, Berend
See Bettie Serveert
Dube, Lucky **17**
Duffey, John
See Country Gentlemen, The
Also see Seldom Scene, The
Duffy, Billy
See Cult, The
Duffy, Martin
See Primal Scream
Dulli, Greg
See Afghan Whigs
Dunbar, Aynsley
See Jefferson Starship
Also see Whitesnake
Dunbar, Sly
See Sly and Robbie
Duncan, Steve
See Desert Rose Band, The
Duncan, Stuart
See Nashville Bluegrass Band
Dunlap, Slim
See Replacements, The
Dunn, Holly **7**
Dunn, Larry
See Earth, Wind and Fire
Dunn, Ronnie
See Brooks & Dunn
Dupree, Champion Jack **12**
Duran Duran **4**

Durante, Mark
  See KMFDM
Duritz, Adam
  See Counting Crows
Dutt, Hank
  See Kronos Quartet
Dylan, Bob 3
E., Sheila
  See Sheila E.
Eagles, The 3
Earl, Ronnie 5
  Also see Roomful of Blues
Earle, Steve
  See Afghan Whigs
Earle, Steve 16
Earth, Wind and Fire 12
Easton, Sheena 2
Eazy-E 13
  Also see N.W.A.
Echeverria, Rob
  See Helmet
Eckstine, Billy 1
Eddy, Duane 9
Eden, Sean
  See Luna
Edge, Graeme
  See Moody Blues, The
Edge, The
  See U2
Edmonds, Kenneth "Babyface" 12
Edwards, Dennis
  See Temptations, The
Edwards, Gordon
  See Kinks, The
Edwards, Leroy "Lion"
  See Mystic Revealers
Edwards, Mike
  See Electric Light Orchestra
Einheit
  See Einstürzende Neubauten
Einheit, F.M.
  See KMFDM
Einstürzende Neubauten 13
Eitzel, Mark
  See American Music Club
Eklund, Greg
  See Everclear
Eldon, Thór
  See Sugarcubes, The
Eldridge, Ben
  See Seldom Scene, The
Eldridge, Roy 9
  Also see McKinney's Cotton Pickers
Electric Light Orchestra 7
Elfman, Danny 9
Elias, Manny
  See Tears for Fears
Ellefson, Dave
  See Megadeth
Ellington, Duke 2
Elliot, Cass 5
Elliot, Joe
  See Def Leppard
Ellis, Bobby

See Skatalites, The
Ellis, Herb 18
Ellis, Terry
  See En Vogue
ELO
  See Electric Light Orchestra
Ely, John
  See Asleep at the Wheel
Emerson, Bill
  See Country Gentlemen, The
Emerson, Keith
  See Emerson, Lake & Palmer/Powell
Emerson, Lake & Palmer/Powell 5
Emery, Jill
  See Hole
English Beat, The 9
Enigma 14
Eno, Brian 8
Enos, Bob
  See Roomful of Blues
Enright, Pat
  See Nashville Bluegrass Band
Entwistle, John
  See Who, The
En Vogue 10
Enya 6
EPMD 10
Erasure 11
Eric B.
  See Eric B. and Rakim
Eric B. and Rakim 9
Erickson, Roky 16
Erlandson, Eric
  See Hole
Ertegun, Ahmet 10
Esch, En
  See KMFDM
Escovedo, Alejandro 18
Eshe, Montsho
  See Arrested Development
Esquivel, Juan 17
Estefan, Gloria 15
  Earlier sketch in CM 2
Estrada, Roy
  See Little Feat
Etheridge, Melissa 16
  Earlier sketch in CM 4
Eurythmics 6
Evan, John
  See Jethro Tull
Evans, Bill 17
Evans, Dick
  See U2
Evans, Gil 17
Evans, Mark
  See AC/DC
Evans, Shane
  See Collective Soul
Everclear 18
Everlast
  See House of Pain
Everly, Don
  See Everly Brothers, The
Everly, Phil

See Everly Brothers, The
Everly Brothers, The 2
Everman, Jason
  See Soundgarden
Everything But The Girl 15
Ewen, Alvin
  See Steel Pulse
Exkano, Paul
  See Five Blind Boys of Alabama
Exposé 4
Extreme 10
Ezell, Ralph
  See Shenandoah
Fabian 5
Fabulous Thunderbirds, The 1
Fadden, Jimmie
  See Nitty Gritty Dirt Band, The
Fagan, Don
  See Steely Dan
Fahey, John 17
Faithfull, Marianne 14
Faith No More 7
Fakir, Abdul "Duke"
  See Four Tops, The
Falconer, Earl
  See UB40
Fall, The 12
Fallon, David
  See Chieftains, The
Fältskog, Agnetha
  See Abba
Farley, J. J.
  See Soul Stirrers, The
Farndon, Pete
  See Pretenders, The
Farrell, Perry
  See Jane's Addiction
Farris, Dionne
  See Arrested Development
Farriss, Andrew
  See INXS
Farriss, Jon
  See INXS
Farriss, Tim
  See INXS
Fay, Johnny
  See Tragically Hip, The
Fay, Martin
  See Chieftains, The
Fearnley, James
  See Pogues, The
Fehlmann, Thomas
  See Orb, The
Feinstein, Michael 6
Fela
  See Kuti, Fela
Felber, Dean
  See Hootie and the Blowfish
Felder, Don
  See Eagles, Theh
Feldman, Eric Drew
  See Pere Ubu
Fennell, Kevin
  See Guided By Voices

Garrett, Scott
  See Cult, The
Garvey, Steve
  See Buzzcocks, The
Gaskill, Jerry
  See King's X
Gatton, Danny 16
Gaudreau, Jimmy
  See Country Gentlemen, The
Gaye, Marvin 4
Gayle, Crystal 1
Geary, Paul
  See Extreme
Geffen, David 8
Geldof, Bob 9
Genesis 4
Gentry, Teddy
  See Alabama
George, Lowell
  See Little Feat
George, Rocky
  See Suicidal Tendencies
Georges, Bernard
  See Throwing Muses
Germano, Lisa 18
Gerrard, Lisa
  See Dead Can Dance
Gershwin, George and Ira 11
Geto Boys, The 11
Getz, Stan 12
Giammalvo, Chris
  See Madder Rose
Gibb, Barry
  See Bee Gees, The
Gibb, Maurice
  See Bee Gees, The
Gibb, Robin
  See Bee Gees, The
Gibbons, Billy
  See ZZ Top
Gibbons, Ian
  See Kinks, The
Gibson, Debbie 1
Gibson, Wilf
  See Electric Light Orchestra
Gifford, Katharine
  See Stereolab
Gifford, Peter
  See Midnight Oil
Gift, Roland 3
Gilbert, Gillian
  See New Order
Gilbert, Ronnie
  See Weavers, The
Giles, Michael
  See King Crimson
Gilkyson, Tony
  See X
Gill, Andy
  See Gang of Four
Gill, Janis
  See Sweethearts of the Rodeo
Gill, Pete
  See Motörhead
Gill, Vince 7
Gillan, Ian

See Deep Purple
Gillespie, Bobby
  See Primal Scream
Gillespie, Dizzy 6
Gilley, Mickey 7
Gillian, Ian
  See Black Sabbath
Gillingham, Charles
  See Counting Crows
Gilmore, Jimmie Dale 11
Gilmour, David
  See Pink Floyd
Gin Blossoms 18
Gingold, Josef 6
Gioia
  See Exposé
Gipsy Kings, The 8
Glass, Philip 1
Glasscock, John
  See Jethro Tull
Glennie, Jim
  See James
Glover, Corey
  See Living Colour
Glover, Roger
  See Deep Purple
Gobel, Robert
  See Kool & the Gang
Godchaux, Donna
  See Grateful Dead, The
Godchaux, Keith
  See Grateful Dead, The
Goettel, Dwayne Rudolf
  See Skinny Puppy
Golden, William Lee
  See Oak Ridge Boys, The
Goldstein, Jerry
  See War
Goo Goo Dolls, The 16
Gooden, Ramone PeeWee
  See Digital Underground
Goodman, Benny 4
Goodridge, Robin
  See Bush
Gordon, Dexter 10
Gordon, Dwight
  See Mighty Clouds of Joy, The
Gordon, Kim
  See Sonic Youth
Gordon, Mike
  See Phish
Gordy, Berry, Jr. 6
Gordy, Emory, Jr. 17
Gore, Martin
  See Depeche Mode
Gorham, Scott
  See Thin Lizzy
Gorka, John 18
Gorman, Christopher
  See Belly
Gorman, Steve
  See Black Crowes, The
Gorman, Thomas
  See Belly
Gosling, John
  See Kinks, The

Gossard, Stone
  See Pearl Jam
Gott, Larry
  See James
Goudreau, Barry
  See Boston
Gould, Billy
  See Faith No More
Gould, Glenn 9
Gould, Morton 16
Goulding, Steve
  See Poi Dog Pondering
Gracey, Chad
  See Live
Gradney, Ken
  See Little Feat
Graham, Bill 10
Graham, Johnny
  See Earth, Wind and Fire
Gramolini, Gary
  See Beaver Brown Band, The
Grandmaster Flash 14
Grant, Amy 7
Grant Lee Buffalo 16
Grant, Lloyd
  See Metallica
Grappelli, Stephane 10
Grateful Dead, The 5
Graves, Denyce 16
Gray, Del
  See Little Texas
Gray, Ella
  See Kronos Quartet
Gray, James
  See Blue Rodeo
Gray, Tom
  See Country Gentlemen, The
  Also see Seldom Scene, The
Gray, Walter
  See Kronos Quartet
Gray, Wardell
  See McKinney's Cotton Pickers
Grebenshikov, Boris 3
Green, Al 9
Green, Benny 17
Green, Charles
  See War
Green Day 16
Green, Grant 14
Green, Karl Anthony
  See Herman's Hermits
Green, Peter
  See Fleetwood Mac
Green, Susaye
  See Supremes, The
Green, Willie
  See Neville Brothers, The
Greenhalgh, Tom
  See Mekons, The
Greenspoon, Jimmy
  See Three Dog Night
Greenwood, Gail
  See Belly
Greenwood, Lee 12
Greer, Jim
  See Guided By Voices

Gregg, Paul
  See Restless Heart
Gregory, Bryan
  See Cramps, The
Gregory, Dave
  See XTC
Griffin, Bob
  See BoDeans, The
Griffin, Mark
  See MC 900 Ft. Jesus
Griffith, Nanci 3
Grisman, David 17
Grohl, Dave
  See Nirvana
Grotberg, Karen
  See Jayhawks, The
Groucutt, Kelly
  See Electric Light Orchestra
Grove, George
  See Kingston Trio, The
Grover, Charlie
  See Sponge
Grusin, Dave 7
Guaraldi, Vince 3
Guard, Dave
  See Kingston Trio, The
Gudmundsdottir, Björk
  See Björk
    Also see Sugarcubes, The
Guerin, John
  See Byrds, The
Guest, Christopher
  See Spinal Tap
Guided By Voices 18
Gunn, Trey
  See King Crimson
Guns n' Roses 2
Gunther, Cornell
  See Coasters, The
Guru
  See Gang Starr
Guss, Randy
  See Toad the Wet Sprocket
Gustafson, Steve
  See 10,000 Maniacs
Gut, Grudrun
  See Einstürzende Neubauten
Guthrie, Arlo 6
Guthrie, Robin
  See Cocteau Twins, The
Guthrie, Woody 2
Guy, Billy
  See Coasters, The
Guy, Buddy 4
Gwar 13
Hacke, Alexander
  See Einstürzende Neubauten
Hackett, Steve
  See Genesis
Haden, Charlie 12
Hagar, Sammy
  See Van Halen
Haggard, Merle 2
Hakmoun, Hassan 15
Hale, Simon
  See Incognito
Haley, Bill 6

Haley, Mark
  See Kinks, The
Halford, Rob
  See Judas Priest
Hall, Daryl
  See Hall & Oates
Hall, Lance
  See Inner Circle
Hall, Randall
  See Lynyrd Skynyrd
Hall, Tom T. 4
Hall, Tony
  See Neville Brothers, The
Hall & Oates 6
Halliday, Toni
  See Curve
Hamilton, Frank
  See Weavers, The
Hamilton, Milton
  See Third World
Hamilton, Page
  See Helmet
Hamilton, Tom
  See Aerosmith
Hamlisch, Marvin 1
Hammer, M.C. 5
Hammerstein, Oscar
  See Rodgers, Richard
Hammett, Kirk
  See Metallica
Hammon, Ron
  See War
Hammond, John 6
Hammond-Hammond, Jeffrey
  See Jethro Tull
Hampson, Sharon
  See Sharon, Lois & Bram
Hampson, Thomas 12
Hampton, Lionel 6
Hancock, Herbie 8
Handy, W. C. 7
Hanley, Steve
  See Fall, The
Hanna, Jeff
  See Nitty Gritty Dirt Band, The
Hanneman, Jeff
  See Slayer
Hannon, Frank
  See Tesla
Hansen, Mary
  See Stereolab
Hardin, Tim 18
Harding, John Wesley 6
Hardson, Tre "Slimkid"
  See Pharcyde, The
Hargrove, Kornell
  See Poi Dog Pondering
Hargrove, Roy 15
Harley, Bill 7
Harper, Ben 17
Harper, Raymond
  See Skatalites, The
Harrell, Andre 16
Harrell, Lynn 3
Harrington, Carrie
  See Sounds of Blackness
Harrington, David

See Kronos Quartet
Harris, Addie "Micki"
  See Shirelles, The
Harris, Damon Otis
  See Temptations, The
Harris, Eddie 15
Harris, Emmylou 4
Harris, Evelyn
  See Sweet Honey in the Rock
Harris, Gerard
  See Kool & the Gang
Harris, R. H.
  See Soul Stirrers, The
Harris, Steve
  See Iron Maiden
Harrison, George 2
  Also see Beatles, The
Harrison, Jerry
  See Talking Heads
Harrison, Nigel
  See Blondie
Harrison, Richard
  See Stereolab
Harry, Deborah 4
  Also see Blondie
Hart, Lorenz
  See Rodgers, Richard
Hart, Mark
  See Crowded House
Hart, Mickey
  See Grateful Dead, The
Hartford, John 1
Hartke, Stephen 5
Hartman, Bob
  See Petra
Hartman, John
  See Doobie Brothers, The
Harvey, Bernard "Touter"
  See Inner Circle
Harvey, Philip "Daddae"
  See Soul II Soul
Harvey, Polly Jean 11
Harvie, Iain
  See Del Amitri
Harwood, Justin
  See Luna
Hashian
  See Boston
Haskell, Gordon
  See King Crimson
Haskins, Kevin
  See Love and Rockets
Haslinger, Paul
  See Tangerine Dream
Hassan, Norman
  See UB40
Hatfield, Juliana 12
  Also see Lemonheads, The
Hauser, Tim
  See Manhattan Transfer, The
Havens, Richie 11
Hawes, Dave
  See Catherine Wheel
Hawkins, Coleman 11
Hawkins, Nick
  See Big Audio Dynamite

Hawkins, Screamin' Jay **8**
Hawkins, Tramaine **17**
Hay, George D. **3**
Hayes, Isaac **10**
Hayes, Roland **13**
Haynes, Gibby
　See Butthole Surfers
Haynes, Warren
　See Allman Brothers, The
Hays, Lee
　See Weavers, The
Hayward, David Justin
　See Moody Blues, The
Hayward, Richard
　See Little Feat
Headliner
　See Arrested Development
Headon, Topper
　See Clash, The
Healey, Jeff **4**
Heard, Paul
　See M People
Hearn, Kevin
　See Barenaked Ladies
Heart **1**
Heavy D **10**
Hedges, Michael **3**
Heggie, Will
　See Cocteau Twins, The
Hell, Richard
　See Television
Hellerman, Fred
　See Weavers, The
Helm, Levon
　See Band, The
　Also see Nitty Gritty Dirt Band, The
Helmet **15**
Henderson, Fletcher **16**
Henderson, Joe **14**
Hendricks, Barbara **10**
Hendrix, Jimi **2**
Henley, Don **3**
　Also see Eagles, The
Henrit, Bob
　See Kinks, The
Henry, Joe **18**
Henry, Nicholas "Drummie"
　See Mystic Revealers
Herman, Maureen
　See Babes in Toyland
Herman, Tom
　See Pere Ubu
Herman, Woody **12**
Herman's Hermits **5**
Herndon, Mark
　See Alabama
Herrera, R. J.
　See Suicidal Tendencies
Herrmann, Bernard **14**
Herron, Cindy
　See En Vogue
Hersh, Kristin
　See Throwing Muses
Hester, Paul
　See Crowded House
Hetfield, James
　See Metallica

Hetson, Greg
　See Circle Jerks, The
Hewson, Paul
　See U2
Hiatt, John **8**
Hickman, Johnny
　See Cracker
Hicks, Chris
　See Restless Heart
Hicks, Sheree
　See C + C Music Factory
Hidalgo, David
　See Los Lobos
Higgins, Jimmy
　See Altan
Highway 101 **4**
Hijbert, Fritz
　See Kraftwerk
Hill, Brendan
　See Blues Traveler
Hill, Dusty
　See ZZ Top
Hill, Faith **18**
Hill, Ian
　See Judas Priest
Hill, Lauryn "L"
　See Fugees, The
Hillage, Steve
　See Orb, The
Hillman, Bones
　See Midnight Oil
Hillman, Chris
　See Byrds, The
　Also see Desert Rose Band, The
Hinderas, Natalie **12**
Hinds, David
　See Steel Pulse
Hines, Earl "Fatha" **12**
Hines, Gary
　See Sounds of Blackness
Hinojosa, Tish **13**
Hirst, Rob
　See Midnight Oil
Hirt, Al **5**
Hitchcock, Robyn **9**
Hodo, David
　See Village People, The
Hoenig, Michael
　See Tangerine Dream
Hoffman, Guy
　See BoDeans, The
　Also see Violent Femmes
Hogan, Mike
　See Cranberries, The
Hogan, Noel
　See Cranberries, The
Hoke, Jim
　See NRBQ
Hole **14**
Holiday, Billie **6**
Holland, Brian
　See Holland-Dozier-Holland
Holland, Dave
　See Judas Priest
Holland, Eddie
　See Holland-Dozier-Holland
Holland, Julian "Jools"

　See Squeeze
Holland-Dozier-Holland **5**
Holly, Buddy **1**
Holt, David Lee
　See Mavericks, The
Honeyman, Susie
　See Mekons, The
Honeyman-Scott, James
　See Pretenders, The
Hook, Peter
　See New Order
Hooker, John Lee **1**
Hooper, Nellee
　See Soul II Soul
　Also see Massive Attack
Hootie and the Blowfish **18**
Hope, Gavin
　See Nylons, The
Hopkins, Doug
　See Gin Blossoms
Hopkins, Lightnin' **13**
Hopwood, Keith
　See Herman's Hermits
Horn, Shirley **7**
Horn, Trevor
　See Yes
Horne, Lena **11**
Horne, Marilyn **9**
Hornsby, Bruce **3**
Horovitz, Adam
　See Beastie Boys, The
Horowitz, Vladimir **1**
Hossack, Michael
　See Doobie Brothers, The
House, Son **11**
House of Pain **14**
Houston, Cissy **6**
Houston, Whitney **8**
Howard, Harlan **15**
Howe, Steve
　See Yes
Howell, Porter
　See Little Texas
Howlin' Wolf **6**
H.R.
　See Bad Brains
Hubbard, Greg "Hobie"
　See Sawyer Brown
Hubbard, Preston
　See Fabulous Thunderbirds, The
　Also see Roomful of Blues
Huber, Connie
　See Chenille Sisters, The
Hudson, Earl
　See Bad Brains
Hudson, Garth
　See Band, The
Huffman, Doug
　See Boston
Hughes, Bruce
　See Cracker
Hughes, Glenn
　See Black Sabbath
Hughes, Glenn
　See Village People, The
Hughes, Leon
　See Coasters, The

Johnson, Daryl
  See Neville Brothers, The
Johnson, Gene
  See Diamond Rio
Johnson, Gerry
  See Steel Pulse
Johnson, James P. 16
Johnson, Lonnie 17
Johnson, Matt
  See The The
Johnson, Mike
  See Dinosaur Jr.
Johnson, Ralph
  See Earth, Wind and Fire
Johnson, Robert 6
Johnson, Scott
  See Gin Blossoms
Johnson, Shirley Childres
  See Sweet Honey in the Rock
Johnson, Tamara "Taj"
  See SWV
Johnston, Bruce
  See Beach Boys, The
Johnston, Tom
  See Doobie Brothers, The
JoJo
  See Jodeci
Jolly, Bill
  See Butthole Surfers
Jolson, Al 10
Jones, Booker T. 8
Jones, Brian
  See Rolling Stones, The
Jones, Busta
  See Gang of Four
Jones, Claude
  See McKinney's Cotton Pickers
Jones, Davy
  See Monkees, The
Jones, Elvin 9
Jones, Geoffrey
  See Sounds of Blackness
Jones, George 4
Jones, Grace 9
Jones, Hank 15
Jones, Jamie
  See All-4-One
Jones, Jim
  See Pere Ubu
Jones, John Paul
  See Led Zeppelin
Jones, Kendall
  See Fishbone
Jones, Kenny
  See Who, The
Jones, Marshall
  See Ohio Players
Jones, Maxine
  See En Vogue
Jones, Michael
  See Kronos Quartet
Jones, Mic
  See Big Audio Dynamite
    Also see Clash, The

Jones, Philly Joe 16
Jones, Quincy 2
Jones, Rickie Lee 4
Jones, Robert "Kuumba"
  See Ohio Players
Jones, Sandra "Puma"
  See Black Uhuru
Jones, Simon
  See Verve, The
Jones, Spike 5
Jones, Steve
  See Sex Pistols, The
Jones, Tom 11
Jones, Will "Dub"
  See Coasters, The
Jon Spencer Blues Explosion 18
Joplin, Janis 3
Joplin, Scott 10
Jordan, Lonnie
  See War
Jordan, Louis 11
Jordan, Stanley 1
Jorgensor, John
  See Desert Rose Band, The
Joseph-I, Israel
  See Bad Brains
Jourgensen, Al
  See Ministry
Joyce, Mike
  See Buzzcocks, The
    Also see Smiths, The
Judas Priest 10
Judd, Naomi
  See Judds, The
Judd, Wynonna
  See Judds, The
    Also see Wynonna
Judds, The 2
Juhlin, Dag
  See Poi Dog Pondering
Jukebox
  See Geto Boys, The
Jungle DJ "Towa" Towa
  See Deee-lite
Jurado, Jeanette
  See Exposé
Kabongo, Sabine
  See Zap Mama
Kahlil, Aisha
  See Sweet Honey in the Rock
Kakoulli, Harry
  See Squeeze
Kalligan, Dick
  See Blood, Sweat and Tears
Kaminski, Mik
  See Electric Light Orchestra
Kamomiya, Ryo
  See Pizzicato Five
Kanawa, Kiri Te
  See Te Kanawa, Kiri
Kane, Big Daddy 7
Kane, Nick
  See Mavericks, The
Kannberg, Scott
  See Pavement
Kanter, Paul

  See Jefferson Airplane
Karajan, Herbert von
  See von Karajan, Herbert
Kath, Terry
  See Chicago
Kato, Nash
  See Urge Overkill
Katz, Steve
  See Blood, Sweat and Tears
Kaukonen, Jorma
  See Jefferson Airplane
Kavanagh, Chris
  See Big Audio Dynamite
Kaye, Tony
  See Yes
Kay Gee
  See Naughty by Nature
K-Ci
  See Jodeci
Kean, Martin
  See Stereolab
Keane, Sean
  See Chieftains, The
Kee, John P. 15
Keelor, Greg
  See Blue Rodeo
Keifer, Tom
  See Cinderella
Keitaro
  See Pizzicato Five
Keith, Jeff
  See Tesla
Keith, Toby 17
Kelly, Charlotte
  See Soul II Soul
Kelly, Kevin
  See Byrds, The
Kelly, Rashaan
  See US3
Kendrick, David
  See Devo
Kendricks, Eddie
  See Temptations, The
Kennedy, Delious
  See All-4-One
Kennedy, Frankie
  See Altan
Kennedy, Nigel 8
Kenner, Doris
  See Shirelles, The
Kenny G 14
Kentucky Headhunters, The 5
Kern, Jerome 13
Kershaw, Sammy 15
Ketchum, Hal 14
Key, Cevin
  See Skinny Puppy
Khan, Chaka 9
Khan, Nusrat Fateh Ali 13
Kibble, Mark
  See Take 6
Kibby, Walter
  See Fishbone
Kick, Johnny
  See Madder Rose

Layzie Bone
  See Bone Thugs-N-Harmony
Leadbelly **6**
Leadon, Bernie
  See Eagles, The
    Also see Nitty Gritty Dirt Band, The
Leary, Paul
  See Butthole Surfers
Leavell, Chuck
  See Allman Brothers, The
LeBon, Simon
  See Duran Duran
Leckenby, Derek "Lek"
  See Herman's Hermits
Ledbetter, Huddie
  See Leadbelly
LeDoux, Chris **12**
Led Zeppelin **1**
Lee, Beverly
  See Shirelles, The
Lee, Brenda **5**
Lee, Geddy
  See Rush
Lee, Peggy **8**
Lee, Pete
  See Gwar
Lee, Sara
  See Gang of Four
Lee, Tommy
  See Mötley Crüe
Leen, Bill
  See Gin Blossoms
Leese, Howard
  See Heart
Legg, Adrian **17**
Lehrer, Tom **7**
Leiber, Jerry
  See Leiber and Stoller
Leiber and Stoller **14**
Lemmy
  See Motörhead
Lemonheads, The **12**
Le Mystère des Voix Bulgares
  See Bulgarian State Female Vocal
    Choir, The
Lemper, Ute **14**
Lenners, Rudy
  See Scorpions, The
Lennon, John **9**
  Also see Beatles, The
Lennon, Julian **2**
Lennox, Annie **18**
  Also see Eurythmics
Leonard, Glenn
  See Temptations, The
Lerner, Alan Jay
  See Lerner and Loewe
Lerner and Loewe **13**
Lesh, Phil
  See Grateful Dead, The
Lessard, Stefan
  See Dave Matthews Band
Levene, Keith
  See Clash, The
Levert, Eddie

See O'Jays, The
Levin, Tony
  See King Crimson
Levine, James **8**
Levy, Andrew
  See Brand New Heavies, The
Levy, Ron
  See Roomful of Blues
Lewis, Huey **9**
Lewis, Ian
  See Inner Circle
Lewis, Jerry Lee **2**
Lewis, Marcia
  See Soul II Soul
Lewis, Otis
  See Fabulous Thunderbirds, The
Lewis, Peter
  See Moby Grape
Lewis, Ramsey **14**
Lewis, Roger
  See Inner Circle
Lewis, Roy
  See Kronos Quartet
Lewis, Samuel K.
  See Five Blind Boys of Alabama
Lewis, Terry
  See Jam, Jimmy, and Terry Lewis
Lhote, Morgan
  See Stereolab
Libbea, Gene
  See Nashville Bluegrass Band
Liberace **9**
Licht, David
  See Klezmatics, The
Lifeson, Alex
  See Rush
Lightfoot, Gordon **3**
Ligon, Willie Joe
  See Mighty Clouds of Joy, The
Lilienstein, Lois
  See Sharon, Lois & Bram
Lilker, Dan
  See Anthrax
Lillywhite, Steve **13**
Lincoln, Abbey **9**
Lindley, David **2**
Linna, Miriam
  See Cramps, The
Linnell, John
  See They Might Be Giants
Lipsius, Fred
  See Blood, Sweat and Tears
Little, Keith
  See Country Gentlemen, The
Little Feat **4**
Little Richard **1**
Little Texas **14**
Little Walter **14**
LiPuma, Tommy **18**
Live **14**
Living Colour **7**
Llanas, Sammy
  See BoDeans, The
L.L. Cool J. **5**
Lloyd, Richard

See Television
Lloyd Webber, Andrew **6**
Lockwood, Robert, Jr. **10**
Lodge, John
  See Moody Blues, The
Loewe, Frederick
  See Lerner and Loewe
Loggins, Kenny **3**
Lombardo, Dave
  See Slayer
London, Frank
  See Klezmatics, The
Lopes, Lisa "Left Eye"
  See TLC
Lopez, Israel "Cachao" **14**
Lord, Jon
  See Deep Purple
Lorson, Mary
  See Madder Rose
Los Lobos **2**
Los Reyes
  See Gipsy Kings, The
Loughnane, Lee
  See Chicago
Louison, Steve
  See Massive Attack
Louris, Gary
  See Jayhawks, The
Louvin, Charlie
  See Louvin Brothers, The
Louvin, Ira
  See Louvin Brothers, The
Louvin Brothers, The **12**
Lovano, Joe **13**
Love, Courtney
  See Hole
Love, Gerry
  See Teenage Fanclub
Love, Mike
  See Beach Boys, The
Love and Rockets **15**
Loveless, Patty **5**
Lovering, David
  See Cracker
Lovett, Lyle **5**
Lowe, Chris
  See Pet Shop Boys
Lowe, Nick **6**
Lowery, David
  See Cracker
Lozano, Conrad
  See Los Lobos
L7 **12**
Luccketta, Troy
  See Tesla
Lucia, Paco de
  See de Lucia, Paco
Luke
  See Campbell, Luther
Lukin, Matt
  See Mudhoney
Luna **18**
Lupo, Pat
  See Beaver Brown Band, The
LuPone, Patti **8**
Lush **13**

See Afghan Whigs
McConnell, Page
  See Phish
McCook, Tommy
  See Skatalites, The
McCoury, Del **15**
McCowin, Michael
  See Mighty Clouds of Joy, The
McCoy, Neal **15**
McCracken, Chet
  See Doobie Brothers, The
McCready, Mike
  See Pearl Jam
McCulloch, Andrew
  See King Crimson
McDaniels, Darryl "D"
  See Run-D.M.C.
McDermott, Brian
  See Del Amitri
McDonald, Barbara Kooyman
  See Timbuk 3
McDonald, Ian
  See King Crimson
McDonald, Michael
  See Doobie Brothers, The
McDonald, Pat
  See Timbuk 3
McDorman, Joe
  See Statler Brothers, The
McDowell, Hugh
  See Electric Light Orchestra
McDowell, Mississippi Fred **16**
McEntire, Reba **11**
MC Eric
  See Technotronic
McEuen, John
  See Nitty Gritty Dirt Band, The
McFee, John
  See Doobie Brothers, The
McFerrin, Bobby **3**
MC5, The **9**
McGeoch, John
  See Siouxsie and the Banshees
McGinley, Raymond
  See Teenage Fanclub
McGraw, Tim **17**
McGuigan, Paul
  See Oasis
McGuinn, Jim
  See McGuinn, Roger
McGuinn, Roger
  See Byrds, The
M.C. Hammer
  See Hammer, M.C.
McGuire, Mike
  See Shenandoah
McIntosh, Robbie
  See Pretenders, The
McIntyre, Joe
  See New Kids on the Block
McKagan, Duff
  See Guns n' Roses
McKay, Al
  See Earth, Wind and Fire
McKay, John

See Siouxsie and the Banshees
McKean, Michael
  See Spinal Tap
McKee, Maria **11**
McKeehan, Toby
  See dc Talk
McKernarn, Ron "Pigpen"
  See Grateful Dead, The
McKinney, William
  See McKinney's Cotton Pickers
McKinney's Cotton Pickers **16**
McKnight, Claude V. III
  See Take 6
McLachlan, Sarah **12**
McLaughlin, John **12**
McLean, Don **7**
McLeod, Rory
  See Roomful of Blues
MC Lyte **8**
McLoughlin, Jon
  See Del Amitri
McMeel, Mickey
  See Three Dog Night
McMurtry, James **10**
McNair, Sylvia **15**
MC 900 Ft. Jesus **16**
McPartland, Marian **15**
McQuillar, Shawn
  See Kool & the Gang
McRae, Carmen **9**
M.C. Ren
  See N.W.A.
McReynolds, Jesse
  See McReynolds, Jim and Jesse
McReynolds, Jim
  See McReynolds, Jim and Jesse
McReynolds, Jim and Jesse **12**
MC Serch **10**
McShane, Ronnie
  See Chieftains, The
McShee, Jacqui
  See Pentangle
McTell, Blind Willie **17**
McVie, Christine
  See Fleetwood Mac
McVie, John
  See Fleetwood Mac
Mdletshe, Geophrey
  See Ladysmith Black Mambazo
Meat Loaf **12**
Meat Puppets, The **13**
Medley, Bill **3**
Medlock, James
  See Soul Stirrers, The
Megadeth **9**
Mehta, Zubin **11**
Meine, Klaus
  See Scorpions, The
Meisner, Randy
  See Eagles, The
Mekons, The **15**
Melanie **12**
Melax, Einar
  See Sugarcubes, The
Mellencamp, John "Cougar" **2**

Mengede, Peter
  See Helmet
Menken, Alan **10**
Menuhin, Yehudi **11**
Menza, Nick
  See Megadeth
Mercer, Johnny **13**
Merchant, Natalie
  See 10,000 Maniacs
Mercier, Peadar
  See Chieftains, The
Mercury, Freddie
  See Queen
Mertens, Paul
  See Poi Dog Pondering
Mesaros, Michael
  See Smithereens, The
Metallica **7**
Meters, The **14**
Methembu, Russel
  See Ladysmith Black Mambazo
Metheny, Pat **2**
Meyers, Augie
  See Texas Tornados, The
Mhaonaigh, Mairead Ni
  See Altan
Michael, George **9**
Michaels, Bret
  See Poison
Michel, Prakazrel "Pras"
  See Fugees, The
Middlebrook, Ralph "Pee Wee"
  See Ohio Players
Midler, Bette **8**
Midnight Oil **11**
Midori
Mighty Clouds of Joy, The **17**
Mike & the Mechanics **17**
Mike D
  See Beastie Boys, The
Mikens, Dennis
  See Smithereens, The
Mikens, Robert
  See Kool & the Gang
Milchem, Glenn
  See Blue Rodeo
Miles, Richard
  See Soul Stirrers, The
Millar, Deborah
  See Massive Attack
Miller, Charles
  See War
Miller, Glenn **6**
Miller, Jacob "Killer" Miller
  See Inner Circle
Miller, Jerry
  See Moby Grape
Miller, Mark
  See Sawyer Brown
Miller, Mitch **11**
Miller, Rice
  See Williamson, Sonny Boy
Miller, Roger **4**
Miller, Steve **2**
Milli Vanilli **4**

Mills, Donald
  See Mills Brothers, The
Mills, Fred
  See Canadian Brass, The
Mills, Harry
  See Mills Brothers, The
Mills, Herbert
  See Mills Brothers, The
Mills, John, Jr.
  See Mills Brothers, The
Mills, John, Sr.
  See Mills Brothers, The
Mills, Sidney
  See Steel Pulse
Mills Brothers, The 14
Milsap, Ronnie 2
Mingus, Charles 9
Ministry 10
Miss Kier Kirby
  See Lady Miss Kier
Mitchell, Alex
  See Curve
Mitchell, John
  See Asleep at the Wheel
Mitchell, Joni 17
  Earlier sketch in CM 2
Mitchell, Keith
  See Mazzy Star
Mitchell, Mitch
  See Guided By Voices
Mittoo, Jackie
  See Skatalites, The
Mize, Ben
  See Counting Crows
Mizell, Jay
  See Run-D.M.C.
Moby 17
Moby Grape 12
Modeliste, Joseph "Zigaboo"
  See Meters, The
Moffatt, Katy 18
Moginie, Jim
  See Midnight Oil
Molloy, Matt
  See Chieftains, The
Moloney, Paddy
  See Chieftains, The
Money B
  See Digital Underground
Money, Eddie 16
Monk, Meredith 1
Monk, Thelonious 6
Monkees, The 7
Monroe, Bill 1
Montand, Yves 12
Montenegro, Hugo 18
Montgomery, John Michael 14
Montgomery, Wes 3
Monti, Steve
  See Curve
Montoya, Craig
  See Everclear
Moody Blues, The 18
Moon, Keith
  See Who, The
Mooney, Tim

  See American Music Club
Moore, Alan
  See Judas Priest
Moore, Angelo
  See Fishbone
Moore, Johnny "Dizzy"
  See Skatalites, The
Moore, LeRoi
  See Dave Matthews Band
Moore, Melba 7
Moore, Sam
  See Sam and Dave
Moore, Thurston
  See Sonic Youth
Morand, Grace
  See Chenille Sisters, The
Moraz, Patrick
  See Moody Blues, The
  Also see Yes
Morello, Tom
  See Rage Against the Machine
Morgan, Frank 9
Morgan, Lorrie 10
Morley, Pat
  See Soul Asylum
Morphine 16
Morricone, Ennio 15
Morris, Keith
  See Circle Jerks, The
Morris, Kenny
  See Siouxsie and the Banshees
Morris, Nate
  See Boyz II Men
Morris, Stephen
  See New Order
Morris, Wanya
  See Boyz II Men
Morrison, Bram
  See Sharon, Lois & Bram
Morrison, Claude
  See Nylons, The
Morrison, Jim 3
  Also see Doors, The
Morrison, Sterling
  See Velvet Underground, The
Morrison, Van 3
Morrissett, Paul
  See Klezmatics, The
Morrissey 10
  Also see Smiths, The
Morrissey, Bill 12
Morrissey, Steven Patrick
  See Morrissey
Morton, Everett
  See English Beat, The
Morton, Jelly Roll 7
Morvan, Fab
  See Milli Vanilli
Mosbaugh, Garth
  See Nylons, The
Mosely, Chuck
  See Faith No More
Moser, Scott "Cactus"
  See Highway 101
Mosley, Bob

  See Moby Grape
Mothersbaugh, Bob
  See Devo
Mothersbaugh, Mark
  See Devo
Mötley Crüe 1
Motörhead 10
Motta, Danny
  See Roomful of Blues
Mould, Bob 10
Moulding, Colin
  See XTC
Mounfield, Gary
  See Stone Roses, The
Mouquet, Eric
  See Deep Forest
Mouskouri, Nana 12
Moyet, Alison 12
M People 15
Mr. Dalvin
  See Jodeci
Mudhoney 16
Mueller, Karl
  See Soul Asylum
Muir, Jamie
  See King Crimson
Muir, Mike
  See Suicidal Tendencies
Muldaur, Maria 18
Mullen, Larry, Jr.
  See U2
Mulligan, Gerry 16
Murph
  See Dinosaur Jr.
Murphy, Brigid
  See Poi Dog Pondering
Murphey, Michael Martin 9
Murphy, Dan
  See Soul Asylum
Murray, Anne 4
Murray, Dave
  See Iron Maiden
Mushroom
  See Massive Attack
Musselwhite, Charlie 13
Mustaine, Dave
  See Megadeth
  Also see Metallica
Mwelase, Jabulane
  See Ladysmith Black Mambazo
Mydland, Brent
  See Grateful Dead, The
Myers, Alan
  See Devo
Myles, Alannah 4
Mystic Revealers 16
Nadirah
  See Arrested Development
Nagler, Eric 8
Nakamura, Tetsuya "Tex"
  See War
Nakatami, Michie
  See Shonen Knife
Narcizo, David
  See Throwing Muses

Nascimento, Milton **6**
Nashville Bluegrass Band **14**
Nastanovich, Bob
  See Pavement
Naughty by Nature **11**
Navarro, David
  See Jane's Addiction
Nawasadio, Sylvie
  See Zap Mama
Ndegéocello, Me'Shell **18**
N'Dour, Youssou **6**
Near, Holly **1**
Neel, Johnny
  See Allman Brothers, The
Negron, Chuck
  See Three Dog Night
Neil, Vince
  See Mötley Crüe
Nelson, Errol
  See Black Uhuru
Nelson, Rick **2**
Nelson, Shara
  See Massive Attack
Nelson, Willie **11**
  Earlier sketch in CM **1**
Nesbitt, John
  See McKinney's Cotton Pickers
Nesmith, Mike
  See Monkees, The
Nevarez, Alfred
  See All-4-One
Neville, Aaron **5**
  Also see Neville Brothers, The
Neville, Art
  See Meters, The
  Also see Neville Brothers, The
Neville, Charles
  See Neville Brothers, The
Neville, Cyril
  See Meters, The
    Also see Neville Brothers, The
Neville Brothers, The **4**
New Grass Revival, The **4**
New Kids on the Block **3**
Newman, Randy **4**
Newmann, Kurt
  See BoDeans, The
New Order **11**
New Rhythm and Blues Quartet
  See NRBQ
Newson, Arlene
  See Poi Dog Pondering
Newton, Wayne **2**
Newton-Davis, Billy
  See Nylons, The
Newton-John, Olivia **8**
Nibbs, Lloyd
  See Skatalites, The
Nicholls, Geoff
  See Black Sabbath
Nichols, Todd
  See Toad the Wet Sprocket
Nicks, Stevie **2**
  Also see Fleetwood Mac
Nico

See Velvet Underground, The
Nicolette
  See Massive Attack
Nielsen, Rick
  See Cheap Trick
Nilsson **10**
Nilsson, Harry
  See Nilsson
Nirvana **8**
Nisbett, Steve "Grizzly"
  See Steel Pulse
Nitty Gritty Dirt Band, The **6**
Nocentelli, Leo
  See Meters, The
Nomiya, Maki
  See Pizzicato Five
Noone, Peter
  See Herman's Hermits
Norica, Sugar Ray
  See Roomful of Blues
Norman, Jessye **7**
Norman, Jimmy
  See Coasters, The
Norum, John
  See Dokken
Norvo, Red **12**
Novoselic, Chris
  See Nirvana
NRBQ **12**
Nugent, Ted **2**
Nunn, Bobby
  See Coasters, The
N.W.A. **6**
Nylons, The **6**
Nyman, Michael **15**
Nyolo, Sally
  See Zap Mama
Nyro, Laura **12**
Oakley, Berry
  See Allman Brothers, The
Oakey, Philip
  See Human League, The
Oak Ridge Boys, The **7**
Oasis **16**
Oates, John
  See Hall & Oates
O'Brien, Dwayne
  See Little Texas
O'Bryant, Alan
  See Nashville Bluegrass Band
Ocasek, Ric **5**
Ocean, Billy **4**
Oceans, Lucky
  See Asleep at the Wheel
Ochs, Phil **7**
O'Connell, Chris
  See Asleep at the Wheel
O'Connor, Billy
  See Blondie
O'Connor, Daniel
  See House of Pain
O'Connor, Mark **1**
O'Connor, Sinead **3**
Odetta **7**
O'Donnell, Roger

See Cure, The
Ogre, Nivek
  See Skinny Puppy
O'Hagan, Sean
  See Stereolab
Ohanian, David
  See Canadian Brass, The
O'Hare, Brendan
  See Teenage Fanclub
Ohio Players **16**
O'Jays, The **13**
Oje, Baba
  See Arrested Development
Olafsson, Bragi
  See Sugarcubes, The
Olander, Jimmy
  See Diamond Rio
Oldfield, Mike **18**
Olds, Brent
  See Poi Dog Pondering
Oliver, Joe
  See Oliver, King
Oliver, King **15**
Olson, Jeff
  See Village People, The
Olson, Mark
  See Jayhawks, The
Onassis, Blackie
  See Urge Overkill
Ono, Yoko **11**
Orb, The **18**
Orbison, Roy **2**
O'Reagan, Tim
  See Jayhawks, The
O'Riordan, Cait
  See Pogues, The
O'Riordan, Dolores
  See Cranberries, The
Orlando, Tony **15**
Örn, Einar
  See Sugarcubes, The
Örnolfsdottir, Margret
  See Sugarcubes, The
Orr, Casey
  See Gwar
Orrall, Frank
  See Poi Dog Pondering
Orzabal, Roland
  See Tears for Fears
Osborne, Bob
  See Osborne Brothers, The
Osborne, Sonny
  See Osborne Brothers, The
Osborne Brothers, The **8**
Osbourne, Ozzy **3**
  Also see Black Sabbath
Oskar, Lee
  See War
Oslin, K. T. **3**
Osmond, Donny **3**
Ostin, Mo **17**
Otis, Johnny **16**
Ott, David **2**
Outler, Jimmy
  See Soul Stirrers, The

Plakas, Dee
  See L7
Plant, Robert 2
  Also see Led Zeppelin
Ploog, Richard
  See Church, The
P.M. Dawn 11
Pogues, The 6
Poi Dog Pondering 17
Poindexter, Buster
  See Johansen, David
Pointer, Anita
  See Pointer Sisters, The
Pointer, Bonnie
  See Pointer Sisters, The
Pointer, June
  See Pointer Sisters, The
Pointer, Ruth
  See Pointer Sisters, The
Pointer Sisters, The 9
Poison 11
Poison Ivy
  See Rorschach, Poison Ivy
Poland, Chris
  See Megadeth
Pollard, Jim
  See Guided By Voices
Pollard, Robert, Jr.
  See Guided By Voices
Polygon Window
  See Aphex Twin
Pomus, Doc
  See Doc Pomus
Ponty, Jean-Luc 8
Pop, Iggy 1
Popper, John
  See Blues Traveler
Porter, Cole 10
Porter, George, Jr.
  See Meters, The
Porter, Tiran
  See Doobie Brothers, The
Portman-Smith, Nigel
  See Pentangle
Posdnuos
  See De La Soul
Potts, Sean
  See Chieftains, The
Powell, Billy
  See Lynyrd Skynyrd
Powell, Bud 15
Powell, Cozy
  See Emerson, Lake & Palmer/Powell
Powell, Kobie
  See US3
Powell, William
  See O'Jays, The
Powers, Congo
  See Cramps, The
Prater, Dave
  See Sam and Dave
Prefab Sprout 15
Presley, Elvis 1
Pretenders, The 8
Previn, André 15
Price, Leontyne 6

Price, Louis
  See Temptations, The
Price, Ray 11
Price, Rick
  See Electric Light Orchestra
Pride, Charley 4
Prima, Louis 18
Primal Scream 14
Primettes, The
  See Supremes, The
Primus 11
Prince 14
  Earlier sketch in CM 1
Prince Be
  See P.M. Dawn
Prine, John 7
Proclaimers, The 13
Professor Longhair 6
Propes, Duane
  See Little Texas
Prout, Brian
  See Diamond Rio
Public Enemy 4
Puente, Tito 14
Pullen, Don 16
Pulp 18
Pulsford, Nigel
  See Bush
Pusey, Clifford "Moonie"
  See Steel Pulse
Pyle, Andy
  See Kinks, The
Pyle, Artemis
  See Lynyrd Skynyrd
Q-Tip
  See Tribe Called Quest, A
Quaife, Peter
  See Kinks, The
Queen 6
Queen Ida 9
Queen Latifah 6
Queensryche 8
Querfurth, Carl
  See Roomful of Blues
Rabbitt, Eddie 5
Rabin, Trevor
  See Yes
Raffi 8
Rage Against the Machine 18
Raheem
  See Geto Boys, The
Raitt, Bonnie 3
Rakim
  See Eric B. and Rakim
Ramone, C. J.
  See Ramones, The
Ramone, Dee Dee
  See Ramones, The
Ramone, Joey
  See Ramones, The
Ramone, Johnny
  See Ramones, The
Ramone, Marky
  See Ramones, The
Ramone, Ritchie

  See Ramones, The
Ramone, Tommy
  See Ramones, The
Ramones, The 9
Rampal, Jean-Pierre 6
Ramsay, Andy
  See Stereolab
Ranaldo, Lee
  See Sonic Youth
Randall, Bobby
  See Sawyer Brown
Ranglin, Ernest
  See Skatalites, The
Ranken, Andrew
  See Pogues, The
Ranking Roger
  See English Beat, The
Rarebell, Herman
  See Scorpions, The
Ray, Amy
  See Indigo Girls
Raybon, Marty
  See Shenandoah
Raye, Collin 16
Raymonde, Simon
  See Cocteau Twins, The
Rea, Chris 12
Reagon, Bernice Johnson
  See Sweet Honey in the Rock
Redding, Otis 5
Reddy, Helen 9
Red Hot Chili Peppers, The 7
Redman, Don
  See McKinney's Cotton Pickers
Redman, Joshua 12
Redpath, Jean 1
Reed, Jimmy 15
Reed, Lou 16
  Earlier sketch in CM 1
  Also see Velvet Underground, The
Reese, Della 13
Reeves, Dianne 16
Reeves, Jim 10
Reeves, Martha 4
Reich, Steve 8
Reid, Charlie
  See Proclaimers, The
Reid, Christopher
  See Kid 'n Play
Reid, Craig
  See Proclaimers, The
Reid, Delroy "Junior"
  See Black Uhuru
Reid, Don
  See Statler Brothers, The
Reid, Ellen Lorraine
  See Crash Test Dummies
Reid, Harold
  See Statler Brothers, The
Reid, Janet
  See Black Uhuru
Reid, Jim
  See Jesus and Mary Chain, The
Reid, Vernon 2
  Also see Living Colour

Reid, William
  See Jesus and Mary Chain, The
Reifman, William
  See KMFDM
Reinhardt, Django 7
Relf, Keith
  See Yardbirds, The
R.E.M. 5
Renbourn, John
  See Pentangle
Reno, Ronnie
  See Osborne Brothers, The
Replacements, The 7
Residents, The 14
Restless Heart 12
Rex
  See Pantera
Reyes, Andre
  See Gipsy Kings, The
Reyes, Canut
  See Gipsy Kings, The
Reyes, Nicolas
  See Gipsy Kings, The
Reynolds, Nick
  See Kingston Trio, The
Reynolds, Robert
  See Mavericks, The
Reynolds, Sheldon
  See Earth, Wind and Fire
Reznor, Trent 13
Rhodes, Nick
  See Duran Duran
Rhodes, Philip
  See Gin Blossoms
Rhodes, Todd
  See McKinney's Cotton Pickers
Rhone, Sylvia 13
Rich, Buddy 13
Rich, Charlie 3
Richard, Cliff 14
Richard, Zachary 9
Richards, Keith 11
  Also see Rolling Stones, The
Richie, Lionel 2
Richman, Jonathan 12
Rieckermann, Ralph
  See Scorpions, The
Rieflin, William
  See Ministry
Riley, Teddy 14
Riley, Timothy Christian
  See Tony! Toni! Toné!
Rippon, Steve
  See Lush
Ritchie, Brian
  See Violent Femmes
Ritchie, Jean 4
Ritenour, Lee 7
Roach, Max 12
Roback, David
  See Mazzy Star
Robbins, Marty 9
Roberts, Brad
  See Crash Test Dummies
Roberts, Brad

See Gwar
Roberts, Dan
  See Crash Test Dummies
Roberts, Marcus 6
Robertson, Brian
  See Motörhead
  Also see Thin Lizzy
Robertson, Ed
  See Barenaked Ladies
Robertson, Robbie 2
  Also see Band, The
Robeson, Paul 8
Robillard, Duke 2
  Also see Roomful of Blues
Robinson, Arnold
  See Nylons, The
Robinson, Chris
  See Black Crowes, The
Robinson, Dawn
  See En Vogue
Robinson, R. B.
  See Soul Stirrers, The
Robinson, Rich
  See Black Crowes, The
Robinson, Romye "Booty Brown"
  See Pharcyde, The
Robinson, Smokey 1
Roche, Maggie
  See Roches, The
Roche, Suzzy
  See Roches, The
Roche, Terre
  See Roches, The
Roches, The 18
Rockenfield, Scott
  See Queensryche
Rocker, Lee
  See Stray Cats, The
Rockett, Rikki
  See Poison
Rockin' Dopsie 10
Rodford, Jim
  See Kinks, The
Rodgers, Jimmie 3
Rodgers, Nile 8
Rodgers, Richard 9
Rodney, Red 14
Rodriguez, Rico
  See Skatalites, The
Rodriguez, Sal
  See War
Roe, Marty
  See Diamond Rio
Roeder, Klaus
  See Kraftwerk
Roeser, Donald
  See Blue Oyster Cult
Roeser, Eddie "King"
  See Urge Overkill
Rogers, Kenny 1
Rogers, Norm
  See Jayhawks, The
Rogers, Roy 9
Rogers, Willie
  See Soul Stirrers, The

Roland, Dean
  See Collective Soul
Roland, Ed
  See Collective Soul
Rolling Stones, The 3
Rollins, Henry 11
Rollins, Sonny 7
Romm, Ronald
  See Canadian Brass, The
Ronstadt, Linda 2
Roomful of Blues 7
Roper, De De
  See Salt-N-Pepa
Rorschach, Poison Ivy
  See Cramps, The
Rosas, Cesar
  See Los Lobos
Rose, Axl
  See Guns n' Roses
Rose, Michael
  See Black Uhuru
Rosen, Gary
  See Rosenshontz
Rosen, Peter
  See War
Rosenshontz 9
Rosenthal, Jurgen
  See Scorpions, The
Rosenthal, Phil
  See Seldom Scene, The
Ross, Diana 1
  Also see Supremes, The
Rossdale, Gavin
  See Bush
Rossi, John
  See Roomful of Blues
Rossington, Gary
  See Lynyrd Skynyrd
Rostropovich, Mstislav 17
Rota, Nino 13
Roth, David Lee 1
  Also see Van Halen
Roth, Ulrich
  See Scorpions, The
Rotsey, Martin
  See Midnight Oil
Rotten, Johnny
  See Lydon, John
  Also see Sex Pistols, The
Rourke, Andy
  See Smiths, The
Rowe, Dwain
  See Restless Heart
Rowntree, Dave
  See Blur
Rubin, Rick 9
Rubinstein, Arthur 11
Rucker, Darius
  See Hootie and the Blowfish
Rudd, Phillip
  See AC/DC
Rue, Caroline
  See Hole
Ruffin, David 6
  Also see Temptations, The

Rundgren, Todd **11**
Run-D.M.C. **4**
Rush **8**
Rush, Otis **12**
Rushlow, Tim
  See Little Texas
Russell, Alecia
  See Sounds of Blackness
Russell, Mark **6**
Rutherford, Mike
  See Genesis
    Also see Mike & the Mechanics
Rutsey, John
  See Rush
Ryan, David
  See Lemonheads, The
Ryan, Mick
  See Dave Clark Five, The
Ryder, Mitch **11**
Ryland, Jack
  See Three Dog Night
Rzeznik, Johnny
  See Goo Goo Dolls, The
Sabo, Dave
  See Bon Jovi
Sade **2**
Sadier, Laetitia
  See Stereolab
Sager, Carole Bayer **5**
Sahm, Doug
  See Texas Tornados, The
St. Hubbins, David
  See Spinal Tap
St. John, Mark
  See Kiss
St. Marie, Buffy
  See Sainte-Marie, Buffy
Sainte-Marie, Buffy **11**
Sakamoto, Ryuichi **18**
Salerno-Sonnenberg, Nadja **3**
Saliers, Emily
  See Indigo Girls
Salisbury, Peter
  See Verve, The
Salmon, Michael
  See Prefab Sprout
Salonen, Esa-Pekka **16**
Salt-N-Pepa **6**
Sam and Dave **8**
Sambora, Richie
  See Bon Jovi
Sampson, Doug
  See Iron Maiden
Samuelson, Gar
  See Megadeth
Samwell-Smith, Paul
  See Yardbirds, The
Sanborn, David **1**
Sanchez, Michel
  See Deep Forest
Sanders, Steve
  See Oak Ridge Boys, The
Sandman, Mark
  See Morphine
Sandoval, Arturo **15**
Sandoval, Hope

  See Mazzy Star
Sanger, David
  See Asleep at the Wheel
Santana, Carlos **1**
Saraceno, Blues
  See Poison
Sasaki, Mamiko
  See PulpSanders, Pharoah **16**
Satchell, Clarence "Satch"
  See Ohio Players
Satriani, Joe **4**
Savage, Rick
  See Def Leppard
Sawyer Brown **13**
Saxa
  See English Beat, The
Saxon, Stan
  See Dave Clark Five, The
Scaccia, Mike
  See Ministry
Scaggs, Boz **12**
Scanlon, Craig
  See Fall, The
Scarface
  See Geto Boys, The
Schemel, Patty
  See Hole
Schenker, Michael
  See Scorpions, The
Schenker, Rudolf
  See Scorpions, The
Schenkman, Eric
  See Spin Doctors
Schermie, Joe
  See Three Dog Night
Schickele, Peter **5**
Schlitt, John
  See Petra
Schloss, Zander
  See Circle Jerks, The
Schmelling, Johannes
  See Tangerine Dream
Schmit, Timothy B.
  See Eagles, The
Schmoovy Schmoove
  See Digital Underground
Schneider, Florian
  See Kraftwerk
Schneider, Fred III
  See B-52's, The
Schnitzler, Conrad
  See Tangerine Dream
Scholten, Jim
  See Sawyer Brown
Scholz, Tom
  See Boston
Schrody, Erik
  See House of Pain
Schroyder, Steve
  See Tangerine Dream
Schulz, Guenter
  See KMFDM
Schulze, Klaus
  See Tangerine Dream
Schuman, William **10**

Schuur, Diane **6**
Scofield, John **7**
Scorpions, The **12**
Scott, Ronald Belford "Bon"
  See AC/DC
Scott, George
  See Five Blind Boys of Alabama
Scott, Howard
  See War
Scott, Jimmy **14**
Scott, Sherry
  See Earth, Wind and Fire
Scott-Heron, Gil **13**
Scruggs, Earl **3**
Seal **14**
Seales, Jim
  See Shenandoah
Seals, Brady
  See Little Texas
Seals, Dan **9**
Seals, Jim
  See Seals & Crofts
Seals & Crofts **3**
Sears, Pete
  See Jefferson Starship
Secada, Jon **13**
Sedaka, Neil **4**
Seeger, Pete **4**
  Also see Weavers, The
Seger, Bob **15**
Segovia, Andres **6**
Seldom Scene, The **4**
Selena **16**
Sen Dog
  See Cypress Hill
Senior, Milton
  See McKinney's Cotton Pickers
Senior, Russell
  See Pulp
Sensi
  See Soul II Soul
Sepultura **12**
Seraphine, Daniel
  See Chicago
Sermon, Erick
  See EPMD
Setzer, Brian
  See Stray Cats, The
Severin, Steven
  See Siouxsie and the Banshees
Severinsen, Doc **1**
Sex Pistols, The **5**
Seymour, Neil
  See Crowded House
Shabalala, Ben
  See Ladysmith Black Mambazo
Shabalala, Headman
  See Ladysmith Black Mambazo
Shabalala, Jockey
  See Ladysmith Black Mambazo
Shabalala, Joseph
  See Ladysmith Black Mambazo
Shaffer, Paul **13**
Shakespeare, Robbie
  See Sly and Robbie

Sonnier, Jo-El **10**
Sorum, Matt
  See Cult, The
Sosa, Mercedes **3**
Soul Asylum **10**
Soul Stirrers, The **11**
Soul II Soul **17**
Soundgarden **6**
Sounds of Blackness **13**
Sousa, John Philip **10**
Spampinato, Joey
  See NRBQ
Spampinato, Johnny
  See NRBQ
Spann, Otis **18**
Sparks **18**
Sparks, Donita
  See L7
Special Ed **16**
Spector, Phil **4**
Speech
  See Arrested Development
Spence, Alexander "Skip"
  See Jefferson Airplane
  Also see Moby Grape
Spence, Skip
  See Spence, Alexander "Skip"
Spencer, Jeremy
  See Fleetwood Mac
Spencer, Jim
  See Dave Clark Five, The
Spencer, Jon
  See Jon Spencer Blues Explosion
Spencer, Thad
  See Jayhawks, The
Spencer Blues Explosion, Jon
  See Jon Spencer Blues Explosion
Spinal Tap **8**
Spin Doctors **14**
Spitz, Dan
  See Anthrax
Spitz, Dave
  See Black Sabbath
Sponge **18**
Spring, Keith
  See NRBQ
Springfield, Rick **9**
Springsteen, Bruce **6**
Sproule, Daithi
  See Altan
Sprout, Tobin
  See Guided By Voices
Squeeze **5**
Squire, Chris
  See Yes
Squire, John
  See Stone Roses, The
Stacey, Peter "Spider"
  See Pogues, The
Staley, Layne
  See Alice in Chains
Staley, Tom
  See NRBQ
Stanier, John
  See Helmet
Stanley, Ian

See Tears for Fears
Stanley, Paul
  See Kiss
Stanley, Ralph **5**
Stansfield, Lisa **9**
Staples, Mavis **13**
Staples, Pops **11**
Starling, John
  See Seldom Scene, The
Starr, Mike
  See Alice in Chains
Starr, Ringo **10**
  Also see Beatles, The
Starship
  See Jefferson Airplane
Statler Brothers, The **8**
Steele, Billy
  See Sounds of Blackness
Steele, David
  See English Beat, The
Steel Pulse **14**
Steely Dan **5**
Steier, Rick
  See Warrant
Stein, Chris
  See Blondie
Sterban, Richard
  See Oak Ridge Boys, The
Stereolab **18**
Sterling, Lester
  See Skatalites, The
Stern, Isaac **7**
Stevens, Cat **3**
Stevens, Ray **7**
Stevenson, Don
  See Moby Grape
Stewart, Dave
  See Eurythmics
Stewart, Derrick "Fatlip"
  See Pharcyde, The
Stewart, Ian
  See Rolling Stones, The
Stewart, Jamie
  See Cult, The
Stewart, John
  See Kingston Trio, The
Stewart, Larry
  See Restless Heart
Stewart, Rod **2**
Stewart, Tyler
  See Barenaked Ladies
Stewart, William
  See Third World
Stewart, Winston "Metal"
  See Mystic Revealers
Stills, Stephen **5**
Sting **2**
Stinson, Bob
  See Replacements, The
Stinson, Tommy
  See Replacements, The
Stipe, Michael
  See R.E.M.
Stockman, Shawn
  See Boyz II Men
Stoller, Mike

See Leiber and Stoller
Stoltz, Brian
  See Neville Brothers, The
Stonadge, Gary
  See Big Audio Dynamite
Stone, Curtis
  See Highway 101
Stone, Doug **10**
Stone Roses, The **16**
Stone, Sly **8**
Stone Temple Pilots **14**
Stookey, Paul
  See Peter, Paul & Mary
Story, Liz **2**
Story, The **13**
Stradlin, Izzy
  See Guns n' Roses
Strain, Sammy
  See O'Jays, The
Strait, George **5**
Stratton, Dennis
  See Iron Maiden
Straw, Syd **18**
Stray Cats, The **11**
Strayhorn, Billy **13**
Street, Richard
  See Temptations, The
Streisand, Barbra **2**
Strickland, Keith
  See B-52's, The
Strummer, Joe
  See Clash, The
Stryper **2**
Stuart, Marty **9**
Stubbs, Levi
  See Four Tops, The
Subdudes, The **18**
Such, Alec Jon
  See Bon Jovi
Sugarcubes, The **10**
Suicidal Tendencies **15**
Sulley, Suzanne
  See Human League, The
Summer, Donna **12**
Summer, Mark
  See Turtle Island String Quartet
Summers, Andy **3**
Sumner, Bernard
  See New Order
Sunnyland Slim **16**
Sun Ra **5**
Super DJ Dmitry
  See Deee-lite
Supremes, The **6**
Sure!, Al B. **13**
Sutcliffe, Stu
  See Beatles, The
Sutherland, Joan **13**
Svigals, Alicia
  See Klezmatics, The
Sweat, Keith **13**
Sweet, Matthew **9**
Sweet, Michael
  See Stryper
Sweet, Robert
  See Stryper

Travis, Merle **14**
Travis, Randy **9**
Treach
    See Naughty by Nature
T. Rex **11**
Tribe Called Quest, A **8**
Tricky **18**
    Also see Massive Attack
Tritt, Travis **7**
Trotter, Kera
    See C + C Music Factory
Trucks, Butch
    See Allman Brothers, The
Trugoy the Dove
    See De La Soul
Trujillo, Robert
    See Suicidal Tendencies
Truman, Dan
    See Diamond Rio
Tubb, Ernest **4**
Tubridy, Michael
    See Chieftans, The
Tucker, Moe
    See Velvet Underground, The
Tucker, Sophie **12**
Tucker, Tanya **3**
Tufnel, Nigel
    See Spinal Tap
Turbin, Neil
    See Anthrax
Turner, Big Joe **13**
Turner, Erik
    See Warrant
Turner, Joe Lynn
    See Deep Purple
Turner, Steve
    See Mudhoney
Turner, Tina **1**
Turpin, Will
    See Collective Soul
Turtle Island String Quartet **9**
Tutuska, George
    See Goo Goo Dolls, The
Twain, Shania **17**
Twitty, Conway **6**
2 Unlimited **18**
2Pac **17**
    Also see Digital Underground
Tyagi, Paul
    See Del Amitri
Tyler, Steve
    See Aerosmith
Tyner, McCoy **7**
Tyner, Rob
    See MC5, The
Tyson, Ian
    See Ian and Sylvia
Tyson, Ron
    See Temptations, The
UB40 **4**
Ulmer, James Blood **13**
Ulrich, Lars
    See Metallica
Ulvaeus, Björn
    See Abba
Unruh, N. U.

See Einstürzende Neubauten
Upshaw, Dawn **9**
Urge Overkill **17**
US3 **18**
U2 **12**
    Earlier sketch in CM **2**
Vachon, Chris
    See Roomful of Blues
Vai, Steve **5**
    Also see Whitesnake
Valentine, Gary
    See Blondie
Valentine, Rae
    See War
Valenzuela, Jesse
    See Gin Blossoms
Valli, Frankie **10**
Vandenburg, Adrian
    See Whitesnake
van Dijk, Carol
    See Bettie Serveert
Vandross, Luther **2**
Van Halen **8**
Van Halen, Alex
    See Van Halen
Van Halen, Edward
    See Van Halen
Van Hook, Peter
    See Mike & the Mechanics
Vanilla Ice **6**
Van Ronk, Dave **12**
Van Shelton, Ricky **5**
Van Vliet, Don
    See Captain Beefheart
Van Zandt, Townes **13**
Van Zant, Johnny
    See Lynyrd Skynyrd
Van Zant, Ronnie
    See Lynyrd Skynyrd
Vasquez, Junior **16**
Vaughan, Jimmie
    See Fabulous Thunderbirds, The
Vaughan, Sarah **2**
Vaughan, Stevie Ray **1**
Vedder, Eddie
    See Pearl Jam
Vega, Suzanne **3**
Velvet Underground, The **7**
Verlaine, Tom
    See Television
Verta-Ray, Matt
    See Madder Rose
Verve, The **18**
Vettese, Peter-John
    See Jethro Tull
Vicious, Sid
    See Sex Pistols, The
    Also see Siouxsie and the Banshees
Vickrey, Dan
    See Counting Crows
Vig, Butch **17**
Village People, The **7**
Vincent, Vinnie
    See Kiss

Vinnie
    See Naughty by Nature
Vinton, Bobby **12**
Violent Femmes **12**
Virtue, Michael
    See UB40
Visser, Peter
    See Bettie Serveert
Vito, Rick
    See Fleetwood Mac
Voelz, Susan
    See Poi Dog Pondering
Volz, Greg
    See Petra
Von, Eerie
    See Danzig
von Karajan, Herbert **1**
Vox, Bono
    See U2
Vudi
    See American Music Club
Wadenius, George
    See Blood, Sweat and Tears
Wadephal, Ralf
    See Tangerine Dream
Wagoner, Faidest
    See Soul Stirrers, The
Wagoner, Porter **13**
Wahlberg, Donnie
    See New Kids on the Block
Wailer, Bunny **11**
Wainwright III, Loudon **11**
Waits, Tom **12**
    Earlier sketch in CM **1**
Wakeling, David
    See English Beat, The
Wakeman, Rick
    See Yes
Walden, Narada Michael **14**
Walker, Colin
    See Electric Light Orchestra
Walker, Ebo
    See New Grass Revival, The
Walker, Jerry Jeff **13**
Walker, T-Bone **5**
Wallace, Ian
    See King Crimson
Wallace, Richard
    See Mighty Clouds of Joy, The
Wallace, Sippie **6**
Waller, Charlie
    See Country Gentlemen, The
Waller, Fats **7**
Wallinger, Karl **11**
Wallis, Larry
    See Motörhead
Walls, Chris
    See Dave Clark Five, The
Walls, Greg
    See Anthrax
Walsh, Joe **5**
    Also see Eagles, The
Walters, Robert "Patch"
    See Mystic Revealers

Willis, Larry
    See Blood, Sweat and Tears
Willis, Pete
    See Def Leppard
Willis, Victor
    See Village People, The
Willner, Hal 10
Wills, Bob 6
Willson-Piper, Marty
    See Church, The
Wilmot, Billy "Mystic"
    See Mystic Revealers
Wilson, Anne
    See Heart
Wilson, Brian
    See Beach Boys, The
Wilson, Carl
    See Beach Boys, The
Wilson, Carnie
    See Wilson Phillips
Wilson, Cassandra 12
Wilson, Cindy
    See B-52's, The
Wilson, Dennis
    See Beach Boys, The
Wilson, Jackie 3
Wilson, Kim
    See Fabulous Thunderbirds, The
Wilson, Mary
    See Supremes, The
Wilson, Nancy 14
    See Heart
Wilson, Ransom 5
Wilson, Ricky
    See B-52's, The
Wilson, Robin
    See Gin Blossoms
Wilson, Shanice
    See Shanice
Wilson, Wendy
    See Wilson Phillips
Wilson Phillips 5
Wilton, Michael
    See Queensryche
Wimpfheimer, Jimmy
    See Roomful of Blues
Winans, Carvin
    See Winans, The
Winans, Marvin
    See Winans, The
Winans, Michael
    See Winans, The
Winans, Ronald
    See Winans, The
Winans, The 12
Winbush, Angela 15
Winfield, Chuck
    See Blood, Sweat and Tears
Winston, George 9
Winter, Johnny 5
Winter, Paul 10
Winwood, Steve 2
Wiseman, Bobby
    See Blue Rodeo

Wish Bone
    See Bone Thugs-N-Harmony
Wolstencraft, Simon
    See Fall, The
Womack, Bobby 5
Wonder, Stevie 17
    Earlier sketch in CM 2
Wood, Danny
    See New Kids on the Block
Wood, Ron
    See Rolling Stones, The
Wood, Roy
    See Electric Light Orchestra
Woods, Terry
    See Pogues, The
Woodson, Ollie
    See Temptations, The
Woody, Allen
    See Allman Brothers, The
Woolfolk, Andrew
    See Earth, Wind and Fire
Worrell, Bernie 11
Wray, Link 17
Wreede, Katrina
    See Turtle Island String Quartet
Wren, Alan
    See Stone Roses, The
Wretzky, D'Arcy
    See Smashing Pumpkins
Wright, Adrian
    See Human League, The
Wright, David "Blockhead"
    See English Beat, The
Wright, Jimmy
    See Sounds of Blackness
Wright, Norman
    See Country Gentlemen, The
Wright, Rick
    See Pink Floyd
Wright, Simon
    See AC/DC
Wright, Tim
    See Pere Ubu
Wurzel
    See Motörhead
Wyman, Bill
    See Rolling Stones, The
Wynette, Tammy 2
Wynonna 11
    Also see Judds, The
X 11
XTC 10
Ya Kid K
    See Technotronic
Yamamoto, Hiro
    See Soundgarden
Yamano, Atsuko
    See Shonen Knife
Yamano, Naoko
    See Shonen Knife
Yamashita, Kazuhito 4
Yankovic, "Weird Al" 7
Yanni 11
Yardbirds, The 10

Yarrow, Peter
    See Peter, Paul & Mary
Yates, Bill
    See Country Gentlemen, The
Yauch, Adam
    See Beastie Boys, The
Yearwood, Trisha 10
Yella
    See N.W.A.
Yes 8
Yoakam, Dwight 1
Yoot, Tukka
    See US3
York, Andrew 15
York, John
    See Byrds, The
Young, Angus
    See AC/DC
Young, Faron 7
Young, Fred
    See Kentucky Headhunters, The
Young, Gary
    See Pavement
Young, Grant
    See Soul Asylum
Young, Jeff
    See Megadeth
Young, La Monte 16
Young, Lester 14
Young, Malcolm
    See AC/DC
Young, Neil 15
    Earlier sketch in CM 2
Young, Paul
    See Mike & the Mechanics
Young, Richard
    See Kentucky Headhunters, The
Young, Robert "Throbert"
    See Primal Scream
Young M.C. 4
Yo Yo 9
Yseult, Sean
    See White Zombie
Yule, Doug
    See Velvet Underground, The
Zander, Robin
    See Cheap Trick
Zap Mama 14
Zappa, Frank 17
    Earlier sketch in CM 1
Zevon, Warren 9
Zimmerman, Udo 5
Zombie, Rob
    See White Zombie
Zoom, Billy
    See X
Zorn, John 15
Zukerman, Pinchas 4
ZZ Top 2